MW01068238

Master W.D. Fard Muhammad

The Most Honorable Elijah Muhammad

1 Son of Man (1930)

"For as the lightning comes from the east and flashes to the west, so also will the coming of the Son of Man be."
-- Matthew 24:27

"I am the Supreme Ruler of the Universe."
-- Master Fard Muhammad

Black Bottom Detroit

What became known in America as "the most powerful Black organization" in history was of humble origin. Earlier historians captured the setting of the start of the movement:

> What we now know as "the Nation of Islam" had its beginnings in the ghettos of Detroit. The time was 1930. It was the first year of the Great Depression, a time of hunger, confusion, disillusionment, despair, and discontent. In 1931 shadows hung over the Black ghettoes of the United States. Scattered from East to West, North to South, were 17 million Black people wondering adrift in a veritable wasteland like ships long lost at the bottom of the sea.[1]

This history of the so-called Negroes in America prior to and during this time was filled with pain, suffering and death. It was an inevitable consequence given the horrible peculiar institution of slavery and its atrocities. In the early 1900s, with Blacks just recently being declared free by the Emancipation Proclamation, their "freedom" appeared to be more of the same injustice they faced over the centuries; especially when the Great Depression hit America in 1929. Black people were more ill affected than all other nationalities and hit hardest by this event.

> Sick on the streets, some were trying to commit suicide. Alleys were ravaged for food. Many people searched high and low for their next meal. Hunger was all about. Evictions were everywhere. People were falling low looking for staple bread, meatless bones, raw potato peelings, or spoiled vegetables from which to make stew or soup, or image of soup. So wretched, filthy and poor were Black communities that in some cities twice as many Black babies as white babies were dying. The Black death rate exceeded the white birth rate. Many suffered from heart trouble, high blood pressure and malnutrition not to mention the day-to-day sicknesses and diseases such as fever, headaches, rheumatism, toothaches, etc.[2]

Throughout their sojourn in North America, Black folks waited for years for some kind of relief from this miserable state. There were noble attempts made by two great Black leaders but by this time both had come and gone. One was the great Marcus Garvey and the other being Noble Drew Ali. Both virtuous and dedicated men tried their best to uplift their people and met with limited success. These two figures were only soon to be toppled by the same injustices and oppressors they fought against. Noble Drew Ali had died under mysterious circumstances while Marcus Garvey was arrested by the United States Government and later deported on some trumped up charges. After the removal of these two Black leaders, only remnants of their movements survived and hope appeared to be lost.

Throughout the annals of history, it is an interesting fact that when a people reach their height of despair, there appears to be a yearning in nature that produces a savior — a messiah to snatch them back from the edge of the abyss. For Black Americans in the Thirties, that Saviour was Master Fard Muhammad.

Master Fard Starts Teaching on July 4, 1930

Mr. Fard Muhammad ironically chose to make his debut on July 4, 1930, in the midst of the American holiday known as "Independence Day." This day was set aside by America to celebrate its independence from the tyranny of Great Britain. For more conscious Black Americans, this day reminded them of the hypocrisy of white America. The famous Black orator and abolitionist Frederick Douglass shared this perspective in his famous speech delivered 80 years earlier on July 4, 1852:

> What, to the American slave, is your 4th of July? I answer: a day that reveals to him, more than all other days in the year, the gross injustice and cruelty to which he is the constant victim. To him, your celebration is a sham; your boasted liberty, an unholy license; your national greatness, swelling vanity; your sounds of rejoicing are empty and heartless; your denunciations of tyrants, brass fronted impudence; your shouts of liberty and equality, hollow mockery; your prayers and hymns, your sermons and thanksgivings, with all your religious parade, and solemnity, are, to him, mere bombast, fraud, deception, impiety, and hypocrisy a thin veil to cover up crimes which would disgrace a nation of savages. There is not a nation on the earth guilty of practices, more shocking and bloody, than are the people of this United States, at this very hour.
>
> Go where you may, search where you will, roam through all the monarchies and despotisms of the old world, travel through South America, search out every abuse, and when you have found the last, lay your facts by the side of the everyday practices of this nation, and you will say with me, that, for revolting barbarity and shameless hypocrisy, America reigns without a rival.[3]

A rare photo of Mr. W.D. Fard Muhammad

Mr. Fard drove a similar 1925 Ford Model T Roadster

, a (1929) photo taken on Griswold Street and Jefferson Avenue, facing east. In the foreground man passes by from the right. A car is stopped at the crosswalk, where two men are crossing Griswold. The Hotel Norton, Norton Hotel Drugs and Traymore Hotel, are visible as well. An electric streetcar, is in front of the Traymore Hotel. [The Traymore Hotel sign is pictured right next to the crossing man's mouth. The Traymore Hotel where W.D. Fard lived is located in the last brownstone across the street from Hotel Norton]

(1930) Black and white photographic print depicting a row of buildings containing storefronts on the south side of West Jefferson Avenue between Woodward Avenue and Griswold Street. The pictures businesses include John T. Woodhouse and Company; Cluett, Peabody, and Company; Payette Neckwear Company; Diebold Safe and Lock Company; D.E. Kellogg Company; the Shade Cloth Company; Goldwyn's Outdoor Store; and the Traymore Hotel where W.D. Fard lived. Early automobiles are parked on the street, and two pass from the lower left."

E. Adams St. Paradise Valley

A Detroit slum in "Black Bottom."

Blacks standing in food line during the Great Depression

Blacks in the late 1800's.

It was in this same vein on a hot summer day on July 4, 1930, that Mr. Fard publicly proclaimed the independence of the Black Man in the midst of white America's Fourth of July celebration. Years later, Elijah Muhammad would share the significance of his teacher selecting that day to start his public ministry:

> Who's Independence? Since 1776 you, Black man, have been worshiping the 4th of July along with the real author of the 4th of July...(the white man) as a day of Independence for themselves. It is the white slave-master and his children who enjoy setting forth the 4th of July as a day of rejoicing over achieving this country's Independence from any other foreign source.
>
> Now, the history of the 4th of July shows that it is the Independence Day of the American white man. They wrote the Declaration of Independence for themselves. The white man did not put anything in the Declaration of Independence for the benefit of the Black Man, who was the servitude - slave of the white man at that time. The joy which the black slave experienced on these holidays of the white man was due to the Black man getting a rest from his labor and the days which the white man had set aside for celebration. That is all the Black slave was rejoicing over...that he did not have to work that day. But, you are free now; and you do not need this for an excuse for your worship of the 4th of July. There is no further need for us to worship the gaining of the white man's independence.
>
> Let us look again at our own Black independence and how it came on this same day of the 4th of July....at the Coming of Allah (God) Who came in the Person of Master Fard Muhammad, to Whom praises are due forever, on July 4, 1930.
>
> The significance of His coming to us, on the Independence Day of the white man, is very great. It is their day of great rejoicing. As with former peoples and their governments, their destruction took place when they were at the height of their rejoicing.[4]

Little is known about the reception Fard immediately faced after his proclamation. Perhaps lukewarm since he was viewed as a stranger in the very community he served. Only a few things seemed to be clear about the visitor whose covert mission was "to teach Islam to Black people in America":

> Fard began his mission first as a peddler selling among other things, artifacts, beads, Moroccan leather bags and silks on the street corners of Detroit. To attract attention he would tell Black pedestrians as they passed that "these wares are from your home country and that he himself was from there."
>
> At first skeptical Blacks paid scant if any attention to the lanky peddler who claimed to have come from their home country. The sidewalk crowds loitering around the UNIA building on West Lake Street ignored his harangues and dismissed him as just another carpetbagger. Even the

presence of African beads and artifacts among Fard's wares failed to arouse more than a casual interest in the peddler.

For one thing, many Black residents of Detroit were leery of the peddler, for he was a man without known friends or relatives and his nationality and racial origin were subject to dispute, all they knew about him is that he called himself Fard Muhammad or Fard Muhammad Ali.[5]

Despite questions related to his racial origin or divinity, the timeliness of Fard's message and its design to address the situation of Black America resonated with his listeners. Probably no place was more ideal than Detroit that seemed the perfect fit per its demographic:

Detroit in 1930 was the logical place to begin any organization of American Blacks. Within the crowded confines of the Black section of the city, a would-be leader could find support for almost any type of movement. A compacted Black ghetto, Detroit at the time had the largest concentration of poor Blacks. Here were to be found representatives of all elements in the Black world: sensitive artists, struggling businessmen, self-anointed preachers, poorly-paid laborers, and ignorant sidewalk loafers.

Among such a desperate people it was easy for an emotional appeal that might otherwise be ignored by a more sophisticated Black community, to find a sympathetic audience any movement that addressed itself to the needs of the Blacks who had been left out or deprived of the gratification of material wealth promised in the American dream would certainly make a strong impact among the lower stratum of the community.[6]

Poses as a Silk Peddler and Door Salesman

Undeterred by initial indifferences on part of his future followers, Fard adopted a more personal approach to gain their confidence. Like other Arab and Syrian peddlers, He underwent a door-to-door campaign under the guise of selling wares. Yet his real intention was to gain entrance to their homes to teach Islam. At first Fard's relationship with the Black community was casual and informal. He went about his business in an unobtrusive way sharing whatever they could offer him. Elijah Muhammad's eldest son Emanuel Muhammad recalls:

Master Fard came to us during the Great Depression of the 1930s. In the beginning, we assumed that he was just like any other Arab peddler selling tapestries, silk and woolen materials by the yard. This was his own way of acquainting our oppressed people with the Islamic religion.

For example, he would go door-to-door with his goods and materials. This gave him the advantage of getting into homes to speak on the Islamic religion. I got plenty of witnesses and I got some more out there, too. You don't have to take it from my relatives; I got some more out there that know. Any time you want a showdown, I'm ready for that showdown.

[10]

It was quite easy for him to gain entrance into our Asiatic African Black people homes. Some of our people would welcome a Caucasian into their homes quicker than their own brothers and sisters and that is just what's happening today.

Master Fard was not a Caucasian man—but he appeared to be in the sight of many. However, because he looked like he was Caucasian, this gave him access into some of our peoples' homes. Most of our people during these times felt inferior about themselves. In other words, many were not only extremely confused and very ignorant; they were in addition the actual products and unfortunate example of people who had been brainwashed into believing that they had been cursed with strong tight curly hair, broad features and ebony complexions. Is this right?

Not all of our people had such a low self-esteem about themselves. A substantial percentage of us were very wise and very proud and rightfully so. This was the era in which negative slogans and negative self-images were tantamount to, "If you're white, your right. If you're yellow, you're mellow. If you're brown, stick around. Well, if you're Black, get back!" Alright? This was also the period of what I refer to as "complexion selection." You were more likely to be gainfully employed and you're overall chances were better when it came to anything if you could pass for Caucasian. Just imagine brothers and sisters, these are the 21st generation of our Original Asiatic African parents or ancestors. These ancestors were the descendants of some great Kings and Queens, also descendants of the creators of civilization of all mankind; long before the Greeks were even thought of.

So when you look at these Asiatic African Black men and women despite where he or she was born; in the Caribbean, London, England, the United States, Africa, China, Russia, Mexico, South America, wherever: He is direct descendent of the oldest race of people created by the creator, the original man and woman of the planet. The first human creation created by the creator, the cream of the planet Earth! When you see that dark-skinned man or woman, you are looking at your multi-generational mothers and fathers...

Concerning Master Fard, my personal concern, I will always give honor and respect for the love he had for his Messenger to us, the Late Honorable Elijah Muhammad in America, and our depressed, downtrodden Asiatic African American people during those Depression Days. I will always honor, I will always respect Master Fard till the last breath leaves my body.[7]

The Hon. Elijah Muhammad verifies the strategy employed by Mr. W.D. Fard during an interview years later:

W.D. Fard told him that to be a peddler was not his job but he did that in order to have access to the homes and get in touch with his people so as to awaken them and prepare them for the war of the "Armageddon" against the Caucasian, an end for which he was preparing himself by twenty years studying in the best universities of the world. So when he came to Detroit, "It was hard for him to come into contact with us," as Elijah told, "because our people are a little shy and did not recognize him as being one of us. So he began going from house to house pretending like that he was some kind of agent for retailer selling clothes for men and women. He told me that this is an idea that he picked up himself to get into our homes, as he said, just to teach us. He said: I have no interest in selling clothes. He said: What I wanted to do was to get into the homes and talk with them."[8]

W.D. Fard Teaches in Homes

Initially when given the opportunity to speak, Fard confined his discussions to his own personal experiences in foreign countries and suggestions for improving the personal health of his listeners. Soon his discussions escalated to include rigorous Muslim prohibitions against dancing, smoking and adultery. He admonished men and women to live soberly and with dignity, encouraging them to work hard to devote themselves to the welfare of their families and to deal honestly with all including authorities. Early NOI pioneer Sister Denke Majied (formally Mrs. Lawrence Adams) recalls:

He came first to our houses selling raincoats, and then afterwards, silks. In this way he could get into the people's houses, for every woman was eager to see the nice things the peddlers had for sale. He told us that the silks he carried were the same kind our people used in their home country and that he had come from there. So, we all asked him to tell us about our own country. If we asked him to eat with us, he would eat whatever we had on the table, but after the meal he began to talk: "Now don't eat this food. It is poison for you. The people in your own country do not eat it. Since they eat the right kind of food they have the best health all the time. If you would live just like the people in your home country, you would never be sick anymore." So, we all wanted him to tell us more about ourselves and about our home country and about how we could be free from rheumatism, aches and pains.[9]

Rents a Hall to Teach

At Fard's suggestion, the small group was invited to a customer's house he frequently visited so they could hear more. The small bunch readily accepted; as they were already accustomed to holding small informal cottage meetings for church gatherings in others homes. As the people cared less about his origin and he drew nearer to his core audience, Fard raised the ante. The posing merchant condemned the Judeo-Christianity religion as, "a contrivance of the white man designed for the enslavement of nonwhite people." Instead of it responding to the hopes and aspirations of the Black man, Fard declared, "Christianity helped keep the Black Man doped into subservience to the White Establishment." It was these types of strong accusations that caused an emotional crisis for some of his listeners. W. D. Fard soon adopted a more tactical approach as he pointed out subtle criticisms of the Bible. NOI pioneer Brother Challar Sharrieff told of his own personal crisis after his experience of hearing Mr. Fard:

> The first time I went to a meeting I heard him say: "The Bible tells you that the Sun rises and sets. That is not so. The Sun stands still. All your lives you have been thinking that the Earth never moved. Stand and look toward the Sun, and know that it is the Earth you are standing on which is moving." Up to that day I always went to the Baptist church. After I heard that sermon from the prophet, I was turned around completely. When I went home and heard that dinner was ready, I said: "I don't want to eat dinner. I just want to go back to the meetings." I wouldn't eat my meals, but I goes back that night, and I goes to every meeting after that. Just to think that the Sun above me never moved at all and that the Earth we are on was doing all the moving. That changed everything for me."[10]

In lieu of Christianity, Fard taught that Blacks true religion was called "Islam" and its adherents are rightfully called "Muslims." Fard supplemented his points with great stories of the Black Man's history and greatness. He imparted to his listeners that there existed a cavalry of "brothers and sisters in the East" waiting for them to claim their true heritage.

First NOI Group Meetings

As news traveled quickly through Paradise Valley, curious dwellers sought to hear the prophet with their own ears. To meet the demands, tenants set up more group meetings in their homes. Once Fard drew a captive audience he wasn't shy in delivering his teachings. As NOI biographer and author, C. Eric Lincoln explains.

> He had come, he told the handful of Blacks who gathered to hear him, from the holy city of Mecca. His mission, as he described it, was "to wake the 'Dead Nation in the West'; to teach [them] the truth about the white man, and to prepare [them] for the Armageddon."...Fard was explicit on the point: In the Book of Revelation it is promised that there will be a final battle between good and evil, and that this decisive battle will take place at Har-Magedon, "the Mountain of Megiddo," in the Great Plain of Esdraelon in Asia Minor. But the Bible has a cryptic message for the initiated of Black Islam...The forces of "good and evil" are the forces of "black and white." "The Valley of Esdraelon" symbolizes "the Wilderness of North America." The Battle of Armageddon is to be the Black Man's final confrontation of the race which has so long oppressed him.[11]

Mr. W.D. Fard Shares Part of His Identity

W.D. Fard's words reverberated throughout Black Detroit. His fame began to spread far and wide. Impressed by his lectures, His first band of followers bestowed the divine title of "prophet" upon him (although he didn't say it of himself). In fact Fard shared little about his own personal background. An early follower who heard some of his first addresses recalls the stranger speaking on the subject: "My name is W. D. Fard and I came from the Holy City of Mecca. More about myself I will not tell you yet, for the time has not yet come. I am your brother. You have not yet seen me in my royal robes."[12]

The mystical teacher had an Asiatic countenance but it was hard to make out his racial identity. He would be considered by some to be very "light-skinned" in complexion. Perhaps light enough to blend in with Caucasians but swarthy enough to be recognized as a so-called Negro. He could perhaps have easily fit in with any mulatto, as Fard himself would later confirm his interracial parentage. Yet prior to him revealing his origins, his background made for speculation:

> Inevitably a proliferation of legends developed about so mysterious a person. One legend about Fard is that he was a Jamaican born of a Muslim Syrian father. Another described him as a Palestinian Arab. Still another claims he was a Saudi and a son of wealthy parents of the tribe of Koreish— the tribe of Prophet Mohammad, founder of classical Islam. Even the Detroit police contributed their own to the exercise. Their record claims that Fard himself told them he was "The Supreme Ruler of the Universe."[13]

The traditional NOI history states that Mr. W.D. Fard was a direct descendent of the family lineage of Prophet Muhammad as part of a royal dynasty in Mecca. He is said to have been educated in Europe in preparation of a diplomatic career in the service of the kingdom of the Hejaz, only to nobly abandon that path for a higher calling, which was to come to America and serve the "Lost-Found Black Nation." This was reported by both Elijah Muhammad and his wife Clara Muhammad:

> He is said to have [been] educated at a university in England in preparation for a diplomatic career in the service of the kingdom of Hejaz, but to have abandoned everything to bring "freedom, justice and equality" to the dark people who have been lost in the wilderness of North America, surrounded and completely robbed of their virtues, names, language, and religion by the "cave man." The current Apostle, his wife, and some of the earliest followers in Chicago say that W.D. Fard has received his education in the University of Southern California in Los Angeles. The current Apostle told the writer: "Mr. W.D. Fard told me out of his mouth that he had been educated in the University of California for twenty years just to prepare himself and be well equipped to save our people. He told that he was working for this purpose for forty-two years, twenty of them he worked among dark people before he made himself known to them."[14]

Teaches from Bible and about Quran

As he gained momentum Fard became bolder in his attacks on Western society, specifically claiming Blacks were not Americans but "Asiatics." It was their forefathers who were stolen from the continent by white slave masters who came in the name of Jesus four centuries ago. The name "Negro" was condemned by the Prophet as an invention of the white man designed to separate Blacks on American soil from their Asiatic brothers and sisters.

Fard resourcefully used the Bible as a textbook to teach so-called Negroes about their true religion — Islam, not Christianity. Islam was the true religion of the Black Men of Asia. He widely used the Bible because it was the only religious book his followers knew. It was not the proper book for the Black Nation; but carefully interpreted, it could be made to serve until they were introduced to "The Holy Quran."

Teaches on Health and Sickness

The prophet emphasized that the ailments Black people suffered was a direct result of their rearing by the white man in Southern states, and pointed out that Blacks didn't fare any better in the North.

> The migrants did not find life in the North as pleasant as they had expected it to be, when they first came to the "land of hope," as the North was known in Black poetry and song. The depression deprived them of their means of livelihood, and they suffered their first experience of urban destitution. Though public relief came to their rescue, the attitudes shown by the welfare agents increased their hatred of the Caucasian civilization. Forced to stand waiting for hours to receive their dole, these people began to believe that race discrimination was evident in the North as well as the south. The welfare workers – including those even of their own race – became symbolic of all that these people hated.[15]

The Prophet's conclusion was that disobedience to Islam was responsible for the peoples' sickness. In his doctrine he would vividly describe the condition of the Black man in the ghetto:

> He had fever, headaches, chills, grippe, hay fever, rheumatism, also pains in all joints. He was disturbed with foot ailments and toothaches. His pulse beat more than eighty-eight times per minute: therefore he goes to the doctor every day and gets medicine for every day in the year: one after each meal and three times a day, also one at bedtime.[16]

Hon. Marcus Garvey (UNIA) and Noble Drew Ali (MSTA)

Marcus Garvey and Noble Drew Ali as Forerunners
Part of the lure of Mr. W.D. Fard was his ability to utilize the Black man's environment to illustrate key points. Both their physical and economic hardships were themselves witness-bearers to his teachings. Fard drew from other literary references as well. He cited different Bible verses and included some of the teachings of Marcus Garvey and Noble Drew Ali which foretold the coming of a new prophet. It was a pertinent strategy considering the recent passing of the movements. E.D. Beynon observed:

> Awakened already to a consciousness of race discrimination, these migrants from the South came into contact with militant movements among northern Blacks. Practically none of them had been in the North prior to the collapse of the Marcus Garvey movement. A few of them had come under the influence of the Moorish Science Temple which followed. The effect of these movements upon the future members of the Nation of Islam was largely indirect. Garvey taught the Blacks that their homeland was Ethiopia. The Prophet Noble Drew Ali of the Moorish Science Temple proclaimed that these people were "descendants of Moroccans." The newer migrants entered a social milieu in which the atmosphere was filled with questions about the origin of their people. Long before their new prophet appeared among them, they were wondering who they were, and whence they had come.[17]

[16]

Years later, some followers of these movements would try to claim W.D. Fard as one of their students, to which Leaders in the NOI were quick to correct the claims, mainly Messenger Elijah Muhammad himself:

Question: I have read, Mr. Fard himself, was He a member of Noble Drew Ali's movement?
Messenger: No, he was no member.
Question: Or he was a follower or something...
Messenger: He's independent. He's not a follower of any of them. He's not.
Question: Was He associated in any way with Noble Drew Ali?
Messenger: No.
Question: These reports then so far as you are concerned are incorrect?
Messenger: That's incorrect. That's right. He was no follower of Noble Drew Ali. No, he's no follower of anyone. He's self-independent. He's self-independent, there's nobody for him to follow. ..[18]

Establishes a Hierarchy and Structure

As the star grew of Mr. W.D. Fard, house-to-house meetings became inadequate to accommodate all who wished to hear the prophet. The solution was obvious: they would rent out a Hall to hold their meetings. After the Hall was secured, the house meetings were discontinued and a tightly knit organization replaced the informal gatherings. Potential members were examined before acceptance and were registered by the group; subsequently a hierarchy in the organization was established:

Maladjusted migrant Blacks came into contact with the prophet at the informal meetings in their homes. With the change to temple services, the movement took on a more formal character. The teaching became more systemized. Membership was recognized and "registered." The movement itself became organized in a hierarchical manner...The rapid increase in membership made necessary the development of a formal organization. Subsidiary organizations had been established as the need for them arose...[19]

Student Enrollment (Muslim Lessons)

A chalk board was displayed prominently at most meetings that contained an introductory lesson written by Mr. Fard or one of his secretaries. The teachings of the Nation of Islam were presented to its members in a catechism (question and answer) format; the grouped sets of questions and answers were designated as a lesson. At the time there existed a plethora of lessons in Fard's possession that constituted the core doctrine of the Nation of Islam. As the founder, Master Fard Muhammad authored these lessons himself (later along with help from Elijah Muhammad) and made it mandatory for all Muslims to learn and recite this first one by heart that occupied the chalk board.

The first ten questions and answers were known as the **Student Enrollment**. Each Muslim had to memorize and recite this lesson 100% right and exact without error to be fully certified as a "Believer."

The NOI Student Enrollment Lesson began thus:

1. Who is the Original Man? The Original Man is the Asiatic Black Man, the Maker, the Owner, the Cream of the Planet Earth, the Father of Civilization, and the God of the Universe.
2. Who is the Colored Man? The Colored Man is the Caucasian (white man), or Yakub's grafted devil, the Skunk of the Planet Earth.
3. What is the population of the Original Nation in the Wilderness of North America, and all over the Planet Earth? The population of the Original Nation in the Wilderness of North America is 17,000,000, with the 2,000,000 Indians makes it 19,000,000; All over the Planet Earth is 4,400,000,000.[20]

After studying it and memorizing it word-for-word, the Muslim was now officially registered into the Nation of Islam and his name was written in the "Book of Life."

Dear Saviour's Letter

Importance was also stressed for the recent convert in Islam to get rid of their "slave names" and receive righteous or "holy names." Fard single-handedly was responsible for giving out new names to his followers:

> Those who accepted this teaching became new men and women, or, as the prophet expressed it, were restored to their original true selves. As a mark of this restoration, the prophet gave them back their original names which the Caucasians had taken from them...Each new believer wrote a separate letter asking for his original name, which the prophet was supposed to know through the Spirit of Allah within him.[21]

In order to become a Muslim and receive a "Holy Name", the applicant had to handwrite a letter of intent to Mr. W.D. Fard in Detroit, MI. First, he was given a copy of a letter, which he had to copy himself exactly by hand (in the same exact handwriting of the original author) without any errors or mistakes. Below is a similar letter used by Elijah Muhammad a few years later:

Mr. W.F. Muhammad
3408 Hastings Street
Detroit, Michigan

Dear Savior Allah, Our Deliverer:

I have been attending the teachings of Islam by one of your Ministers, two or three times. I believe in It, and I bear witness that there is no God but Thee, and that Muhammad is Thy Servant and Apostle. I desire to reclaim my Own. Please give me my Original Name. My slave name is as follows:

[18]

Name
Address
City and State[22]

Upon the convert finishing the letter, he mailed it to W.D. Fard in Detroit to be scrutinized for approval. If approved, W.D. Fard or one of his secretaries mailed the applicant a certified letter of approval complete with a 'righteous name.'

Original Names for Muslims, NOI Identification Cards

As it was in NOI tradition, to commemorate his rebirth, the Muslim would drop his slave name and be known simply by his new righteous name. Thus the Honorable Elijah Muhammad elaborates.

He [W.F. Muhammad] told us that we must give up our slave names (of our slave masters) and accept only the name of Allah (Himself) or one of the Divine attributes. We (the so-called Negroes) must also give up all evil doings and practices and do (only) righteousness or we shall be destroyed from the face of the earth. [23]

Examples of the changed names are:
Joseph Shepard became Jam Sharrief
Lindsay Garret became Hazziez Allah
Henry Wells became Anwar Pasha
William Blunt became Sharrief Allah

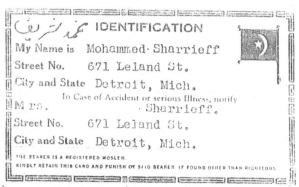

Photocopy of Original NOI Identification Card

Each Muslim receiving a Holy name was given an "identification card" such as this original one pictured above. Mr. Fard himself designed and got the cards printed (each containing a picture of "the National Flag" of the Nation of Islam) as well as a personally handwritten Arabic inscription by the Saviour himself. The ID card stated the name, address and emergency contact of the cardholder. At the bottom of the card read

[19]

"THE BEARER IS A REGISTERED MOSLEM. KINDLY RETAIN THE CARD AND PUNISH OF SAID BEARER IF FOUND OHER THAN RIGHTEOUS." Years later in a FBI report on W.D. Fard, on page 5 contains an alleged statement given by the Hon. Elijah Muhammad after his arrest in 1942 for draft evasion, which reads: "Allah [Master Fard Muhammad] came to teach Islam and take away our slave names and give us free names of the Nation of Islam. Prior to 1935 at the time the free names were given, Allah issued to the Moslems a card which he must always carry with him and which identified him as a righteous Moslem. There were approximately 25,000 of these cards issued by Allah and although numerous applications have been made for such cards since 1934 no additional cards have been issued because Allah is the only one who can issue them." Elijah Muhammad also stated in an article from the Muhammad Speaks newspaper in reference to these passes, "THE GOVERNMENT OF AMERICA has known this Law of Allah (God) for many years. The Law is to take the identity card away from you. This is written on the identity card in red letters...Nevertheless, we carry the principle into practice."[24]

Examples of Muslim Names Assigned to Members
Following is a list of Original last names granted by Master Fard Muhammad to some of the Nation of Islam pioneers in the 1930s:

Allah, Ali, Abasien, Abraham, Assmaiell, Asia, Almanza, Bahar, Bey, Banar, Bostan, Cushmeer, Dean, Deanar, Delmar, Fard, Farrackan, Farman, Gallistan, Gordan, Hajjie, Hassan, Hassain, Hazzie, Hazziez, Islaam, Jammar, Jardan, Jehovah, Joshua, Karriem, Kazzie, Kallamoulla, Majied, Mossa, Mourad, Muhammad, Nawab, Najieb, Noble, Pasha, Rahman, Rassoull, Razzall, Rozier, Samerkand, Sammsan, Sawab, Sobakhan, Shabazz, Shah, Sharrieff, Thrasher, Varnada, Wallace, Yassien, Yacob, and Zarrieff.[25]

UNIA, Moors and Others take Interest in Joining the NOI
Mr. W.D. Fard's teachings began to resonate with many of the followers of Marcus Garvey and Noble Drew Ali who began to pledge themselves to Fard's movement as they met in venues familiar to the Black Nationalists that echoed similar sentiments.

Early in August 1931 Fard told a crowd of Blacks gathered in the Old Universal Negro Improvement Association (UNIA) Hall at 1841 West Lake Street, that he was a "prophet of Allah from the holy city of Mecca." His mission, as he described it was, "to wake the dead nation in the West, to tell the Black population of the United States the truth about the white man and to help them prepare for an impending Armageddon."

Often referring to the book of Revelations, Fard reiterated to his listeners that there would be a total war between good and evil and that this battle would occur at a place he called Har-Magedon in the plains of Esdraelon. The important question was exactly where were these two places located? To this question Fard was very explicit: the valley of Esdraelon represents "the wilderness of North America" and Har-Magedon "the United States." The battle of Armageddon was to be the Black man's final clash with the white man who had for so long kept him enslaved. To avoid losing the battle, the prophet prescribed Islam as the only solution because "it was the natural religion of the Black man." Only in Islam could he hope to find freedom, justice and equality.[26]

Fard took advantage of these opportunities to address larger audiences. He had yet to use his magnetic personality on larger groups, and made the most of it by electrifying the crowds with his words. He carried the audience along with him in an impassioned plea for Blacks to throw off the white man's religion because it had been of no service in making better Black communities. Among the several hundreds of people who eventually hear the Master's message was a young Elijah Poole (soon to be renamed Muhammad), the future "Messenger of Allah." Many people familiar with the message had accepted Fard as "the Prophet." Yet, it would be to one man that He would fully reveal Himself.

2 Behold, I Will Send you Elijah

The Honorable Elijah Muhammad

Behold I will send you Elijah the prophet before the coming of the Dreadful day of the Lord; and he will turn the hearts of the fathers to their children, and the hearts of the children to their father, less I come and smite the earth with a curse. Malachi 4:5-6

Elijah's Family
Thirty-four years after the signing of the Emancipation Proclamation, "The Hon. Elijah Muhammad was born the second week of October 1897 to William and Marie who went in the name of their former slave master's name of Poole, in the area near Sandersville, GA, and Deep Step, GA, about 5 miles into the woods in a community known as Bold Springs, GA, which is the 100th militia district of Washington County, GA."[27]

Elijah's father William Poole was a Baptist preacher who taught in a church and was also a sharecropper as a means of supporting his large growing family.[28] His loving wife Marie Poole was born in 1871, who he married when she was sixteen years old. All together they would have 13 children. Their first son Sam was born early 1888, followed next year by their first daughter, Annie, in 1889, then Willie Jr., in 1891 and another daughter Tommie in 1892. Hattie, their fifth child, was born in 1894, followed by Lula in 1896. Elijah, the seventh child, was born in 1897. In 1900, Charlie was born, followed by Jarmin (1904), Emma (1906), Johnnie (1907), James (1909), and the youngest child John (1912). The following is a list of Elijah's brothers and sisters from the oldest to the youngest:

1. Sam (1888)
2. Annie (1889)
3. Willie Jr. (1891)
4. Tommie (1892)
5. Hattie (1894)
6. Lula (1896)
7. Elijah (1897)
8. Charlie (1900)
9. Jarmin (1904)
10. Emma (1906)
11. Johnnie (1907)
12. James (1909)
13. John (1912)

Naturally, the parents loved their children, 8 sons and 5 daughters, yet Elijah, even as a child was unusually different. He had a yearning for learning, he studied ways of nature, he studied the Bible and practiced preaching to his brothers and sisters, he was destined for the future. In the back of the church was a family cemetery.

Elijah the Prophet

Relatives tell the story that while Mother Marie was pregnant with her unborn son Elijah, that she one night she saw a bright light in the window and a message saying she was going to give birth to a great prophet. Stunned she told her grandfather about what happened, he replied "you should name the child Elijah".

From the very beginning, it was sensed that Elijah was extraordinary:

> When Elijah was born a perceptive paternal grandfather had given him the name Elijah and always addressed him as "Elijah, the prophet." He often told the boy's parents that one day he would be a prophet of God. The grandfather was correct. His grandson lived to become a prophet and the "Last Messenger of Allah."[29]

Elijah was often asked by his brothers and sisters to settle their arguments because he was fair and took after his father who was a hardworking sharecropper and Baptist minister to Black town residents. In addition to giving sermons every Sunday, Willie Poole also preached to his family. As little Elijah attended his father's church and family sessions, he grew fond of the prophetic utterances and apocalyptic verses heard in the sermons. Soon, the congregation and family members started to take notice. As Elijah pointed out to researcher Hatim A. Sahib in an interview:

> Since he was a little boy of four years, his grandfather and his father took him with them to the church, where he used to sit on the "preacher set" listening to the preaching. "The members," he said, "used to make much of me; they seemed to love me as the preacher's dear. Since that time I developed the idea that someday I will be a preacher, but not like the preachers whom I had heard."[30]

Elijah Muhammad's eldest son Emanuel also recalls:

> Allah's Messenger said to me: When he was a little boy that his father would take him to the Christian church with him and sit him in the pulpit with himself. His father was a Baptist Preacher at that time; but he died a follower of his son. He told his father, that when he become a man that he would represent God to the people not like him. His grandfather is the one who named him Elijah, and used to call him Elijah the Prophet.[31]

Farm Boy

While Elijah was growing up, he was acutely aware of the problems that besieged blacks in the United States. His family, like most sharecroppers, barely managed to make ends meet. In the early 1900s, tenant farming was a common practice in the South. Sharecroppers rented the land they farmed from a local landowner in return for a portion for a small sum of money — just enough to buy a few articles of clothing and some basic supplies.

To help pay their debts, sharecroppers were often compelled to borrow from white creditors, who, spotting an easy mark, lent money to the farmers at ex-orbitant interest rates. The Pooles fell victim to this vicious cycle. Added to their hardship of laboring long hours for next to nothing was the ever-increasing amount of money they owed their white creditors.[32]

Around 1903, at the age of six years old, Elijah and his family moved from Sandersville, GA, to Cordele, GA, to an area known as Wynona (about 5 miles south of Cordele). Elijah's family was very poor, they lived in a dilapidated shack across the road from the train depot, where one train a day passed through, which they called "the shoefly." The attended Zion Hope Baptist Church located on old Highway 41 (below Wynona) where Elijah and his family attended.[33]

Just barely freed from slavery and living hard times like the rest of the Blacks in the South, they were immensely poor and had to make ends meet. There Elijah worked in the huge fields mining many acres along with his brothers and sisters, planting and plowing behind a mule, reaping and harvesting, picking and chopping crops. Schooling wasn't required for Elijah or other young Blacks in the South, only work, day and night, night and day.[34] After attending up to the 3rd or 4th grade, Elijah quit school to work full-time as a sharecropper to help support his family along with his large number of siblings. The Hon. Elijah Muhammad (THEM) recalls:

I hope you will understand what I'm trying to say. When I got to the school house, the teacher was dismissing the class, so don't blame me, blame those who held me back. I don't think you were born down North where I was born. I was born down North, and if you were big enough to work, they put you in the field, because the devil was forcing your parents to send you to field and work for him.[35]

THEM: Look, brother, I have told you for the first part of my life I was a farmer in Georgia.
Interviewer: Yes, Sir.
THEM: Right?
Interviewer: Yes, Sir.
THEM: Nobody there was looking at me plowing a mule thought that I would ever be a Scientist teaching the world.
Interviewer: Yes, Sir.
THEM: See, it is time that brings on things.[36]

When I was a little boy it used to be very hard for me because my father had at that time thirteen children. I was the middle child. We were brought up on the farm. When I was ten years old I used to cut firewood and take it to the little town to sell it for fifty cents, so as to help my brothers and sisters. My older sister used to chop with me and we'd go together to the little town to sell it. We had nothing to wear. I was having at that time only one rough garment for the whole season.[37]

Black Suffering

To be a southern Black at the turn of the century usually meant a life of hardship, pain and deadly threats to their survival. The lynching of Blacks was the order of the day and hate groups like the Ku Klux Klan ran rampant. Given the times, Elijah learned the harsh reality of murderous racism at a very early age.

Willie Poole warned his family about the perils of being Black and avoiding the hanging rope of the white man by never straying from the long dirt road that led to their tenant farm. At least one source reported Elijah witnessing his first lynching when he was still a little boy still too young to work around the house. According to the story, his older brothers and sisters were preparing for the upcoming harvest, and felt the Elijah would only get in the way. Ignored, Elijah slipped away and got lost on the dirt path. After time sped by, he tried to find a shortcut back home through the woods. At one point he laid down to rest and was shortly startled by a thump he heard in the woods. Afraid it was his brothers looking for him; he ran and hid behind a nearby thicket to avoid punishment. According to the report, this is what he witnessed next:

> When he saw that the approaching figures were not his brothers, he felt relieved. Then, as the people came closer, his sense of relief turned to a mixture of fear and disbelief. There were four people. At the head of the small party was a white man holding on to a rope. At the other end of the rope was a Black man, who had it tied about his midsection, as though he were a horse or a mule. They were followed by two more white men in work clothes. These two pushed the captured black, whose hands were tied behind his back, to keep him moving. Was this some kind of game? Elijah wondered.[38]

Witness to Lynchings

Trying to process the situation, reportedly Elijah looked on in silence. After witnessing the man forcefully pushed to the ground by his captors, he recognized the man as an occasional visitor of his father's church. Still a small boy, it is alleged he wanted to reach out but was paralyzed as the white men proceeded to kick their victim:

> When the whites began kicking their prisoner and insulting him, Elijah buckled as if he, too, had been kicked. Silent tears rolled down his face. The man in front proceeded to untie the rope around the black man's wrists. He took one end of the rope and threw it over a sturdy branch. Leering at his captive, who still lay face down on the forest floor, he formed the other end into a noose. Then he slipped the hooped rope around the black man's neck. Elijah covered his face with his hands as the victim was hoisted from the ground, sputtering and choking. It only took a matter of minutes. After the lynchers were sure the man was dead, they passed a bottle among themselves and looked up at his body, admiring their handiwork. Then, as though they had just concluded an entire day's work, they strolled away, leaving the strangled black man swinging from the tree.[39]

1st picture: Lynchings of Blacks were common in the early 1900s. 2nd picture: NAACP flag "A Man Was Lynched Yesterday" flying above 5th Ave, NYC 1938.

Thomas Shipp and Abram Smith, lynched in Marion, Indiana, on August 7, 1930, by a lynch mob. (Following photo): 1900 Georgia Census of Poole Family.

Blacks on a Southern plantation picking cotton (circa 1920s)

A census of Clay County, Georgia, taken in 1900, lists Muhammad as Elijah Pool (left column, 12th name from top). He was the 6th of 13 children.

Sandersville, Georgia, the area where Elijah was born and raised up until an early adult.

Elijah Muhammad and Wife Clara Muhammad

Elijah Muhammad at 26 years old (1924). His place of employment.

In 1922, a young Elijah worked at this site for Cherokee Brick & Tile Company, which is show in this photo and the one above.

Crawling out the thicket Elijah noticed the victim's shoe beneath him. His spell was broken by warm red drops on his face as he realized the corpse was above him trickling blood onto his cheek. It is said this and other lynching experiences were etched in his head for life.

Years later he'd see more of the same. "Since he was a child of ten years old he was going to Cordele, a small town in Georgia to sell the firewood that he had chopped. He was impressed deeply by the racial riots he had seen."[40] Elijah gives a horrific first-hand account of a lynching he witnessed:

> Once, a time when I was a little boy coming to Cordele to sell a load of wood, I saw a lynching crowd. I was that time a child about ten years old, when I saw that morning a dark man horribly lynched by the whites. He was accused of insulting a white woman. That dark man was a young fellow about eighteen years old. They lynched him right in the section where I was selling the wood and where our people live. They took him and hanged him to a willow tree after they lynched him with extreme cruelty. That event had impressed me so much that I cannot get over it; I did never forget it, not until this day. It was terrible and horrible to see such things happening and all our grown men right there in the section allowing such things to happen. I returned to our house, which was about four miles away from the little town, grieving all the way. I wished I were a man so that I could try to do something about it. That scene hurt me very much.[41]

Even with Elijah's thoughts, older whites sought to intimidate the children from thinking such thoughts as revenge. There is another story in the Nation of Islam recalling one other grotesque example of a confrontation Elijah had with an older white man:

> And the story says that one day the Hon. Elijah Muhammad was walking down the street in Georgia, and a Caucasian white man came towards him and had his hand stuck out. So the Hon. Elijah Muhammad thought he was greeting him and when he got to him the (the white man) opened his hand and he had a cut off ear from a Black man they had murdered. They kept these things as souvenirs.[42]

These horrible images remained with Elijah throughout his life. He drew from these experiences as fuel for the prophetic role he'd dare assume in the future. Elijah recounts and explains:

> Yesterday you did not hear a man talk like that. But today, the time is so close, it is nothing strange (anymore than it was in the days of Noah and Moses) to see me here, before you, teaching what I am teaching. When I was a little boy, I knew not that I would be before you...preaching to you what I am preaching. But I always felt God wanted me to preach some preaching. What it was, I did not know.

My father was a preacher, and I used to sit and watch him preach and faint in the pulpit. I used to say, "I hope someday God will help me to help him." I said the same thing when I was a boy of 10 years old, hauling kindling to peddle in the streets of Cordele, GA (at 50cents a load). I had just missed witnessing the lynching of one of our 18-year-old young men on a willow tree there in Cordele. I had just missed it. The whole little town was all tense and frightened. My people in the section where he was hung and shot to death; they was all frightened. I was a 10 year old boy. And looked at this sight (swinging).

I looked and said—with tears in my eyes, because I knew the young man—I said, "If there is a God in heaven, I pray that He brings me up and makes me strong enough to deliver my people from their enemies."

It was a terrible sight to behold—a man who had never been before a court of justice, his body dangling from a tree limb. There was no friend for him there; no attempt to determine his innocence or guilt. He was judged by murderers, and shot to death in the midst of his own people.

My friends, these things have been going on for many years. Every since that English trader, John Hawkins, brought our fathers to the Western Hemisphere, they have suffered. Today, there are many—especially on the guilty side – who want to know what we want or what we think we should want.[43]

Young Adult Life and Racism in the South

Coming of age, Elijah left his house at sixteen and got a job working as farm-hand for an evil employer. Elijah reminisces:

When I was eighteen years old I used to work for a white man on his farm for fifty cents a day, from sun to sun. Then it got worse, so he began to pay me eight dollars a month for farming the whole day from sun to sun during the entire month. That man was a very cruel white man, as all the devils are. He was very old, too. He used to gather the farmers whom he did not like and give a whip to his wife, who would whip them while he held a gun at them to make them submit to beating. I worked for that cruel white man so as to collect enough money to train myself to be a dining boy in the railway, but I was not able to take the course because I quit working for that cruel white man after six months, because he threatened me that he would beat me with a very strong six-foot stick that he used to carry with him if I did not obey him. But I told him that if he did strike me I would have no better sense than to strike him back. Therefore, he told me to leave and so I left. That was not the time they called slavery, but it was at the time they used to call freedom. He was not calling any laborer by his name but he was calling our people by some nicknames he invented for them. He used to call me Levy. This man was not an exception; they were all about the same.[44]

Elijah and Clara Enter Courtship

When he quit working for this white man he used to go to the little town to work here and there so as to bring some little thing to provide for his brothers and sisters.[45]About a couple of years later Elijah began courting a young lady named Clara Evans from a neighboring town in Georgia:

> Not far from Elijah, lived "Slave master Thompson" who owned the shack and land Elijah worked on. Thompson's house was located right next to the railroad tracks. In the back of Elijah's house was an old shed used to store corn and other crops.
>
> It was here about 1915 in a church meeting house in the country that Elijah met Clara for the first time. One of three daughters and two sons of the Evans family. Sister Clara was born in Houston County, just outside of Unadilla, on Jerry Clemons Place. Her father always rented land because he didn't like being pushed around. Clara's sister Rose remembers Elijah always coming to their home on a Sunday afternoon, just after church around 6 o'clock and was always leaving around 9 o'clock because he had to work in the fields the next day. He always visited wearing a blue suit and tie, but never a hat. But he did wear a straw hat and overalls as he plowed behind the mule under the hot sun.[46]
>
> Elijah would walk down a long road called "Rock House Rd." to visit Clara. Then he'd take another dirt road past Perry Hill and the "chain gangs" to go visit his brothers Sam and Willie who lived on the same street. Elijah would later elope with Clara and the two moved into his brother's Sam's house. Sister Clara's father wasn't aware and did not know his daughter whereabouts for over a month.[47]

Elijah and Clara Elope

After 2 years of courtship, they were married. May 2, 1917. Clara's father was furious because of their elopement. They lived in a rented room. Their son Emanuel was born February 3, 1921, in Clara's parents' home.[48] Emanuel recounts the story of his birth:

> Emanuel is a Hebrew name, it has an excellent meaning, and I tried to fulfill that meaning during the life of my father, the Honorable Elijah Muhammad. The name means "God is with us." When I was born (I might as well tell you the whole story), when I was born my father was not in the city where I was born there in Georgia. My father had went to I think Macon, Georgia, where he got a job. At my birth, my mother waited for my father to send me a name. He didn't send her a name, and the reason she was pressed was because the doctor wanted to have it on the birth certificate. Instead of my father giving me my name, my mother named me "Robert Lee." Later on, when my father sent my name to my mother, he gave me the name "Emanuel." My mother questioned him, "Why had it taken him so long?" He said, "Because I wanted to give my son (my firstborn) a good name." And that's how I got the name "Emanuel."[49]

[33]

Goes to Work in Macon, GA

As Elijah left to go to Macon, GA, seeking higher employment and better wages to support his family. The Messenger sent for his wife and his 1 ½ month old son to move to Macon where he worked for the Cherokee Brick & Tile Company (as a section hand) and for the Southern Railroad and other jobs in 1922. In all of his jobs, his co-workers always selected him to be their spokesmen or his employers selected him to supervise others[50].

The same year Elijah and Clara gave birth to their daughter Ethel in 1922. Yet in the midst of these two blessings, the racial climate in Georgia remained volatile and deadly. Elijah was still surrounded by constants threats of danger and lynchings. He was impressed deeply by another scene of lynching when he was twenty-three years old, going to Macon, a little town in Georgia, with his brother.

> My brother and I went to the town nine miles away from our home one Saturday evening and on our way to the town others who came from the town warned us not to go up to the town because of the white people lynched one of our people out in the town and that the whites dragged his body on the streets behind a little small truck. But I was having very necessary work to do and I had to go through the town and so I went. When I reached the town I saw that man's body dragged by the truck on the ground. Then I returned back home with this image of lynching.[51]

Contrary to the turbulent times, Elijah was a good worker and exemplified the same golden characteristics he shared as a child. He had one main condition of his employer; never disrespect him or curse him. As common in that time, the inevitable would soon happen. One day He was unjustly disrespected by a hostile white employer and decided he had enough. Elijah said, "I saw enough of the white man's brutality to last me 26,000 years." Black were poor and suffering, with no jobs or jobs with little pay, the beating, torturing and lynching of Blacks was seemingly a legal affair that became a way of life expected of them. [52]

Moves to Detroit

After this incident, Elijah decided it was a good time to leave Georgia and make a move up North to help his family. In those days it was common for Black families to leave the South in pursuit of a better life of economic promise in the North. So in April 1923, when he was twenty five years old, Elijah Muhammad moved, with his wife and two children, to Detroit, following his father, who had moved to Detroit two

[34]

years before and joined by his wife and some of their children. In the beginning the family found it hard to make it:

> His family lived very hard lives in Detroit, because his father was a "jack leg" preacher and seldom had been called by a churchman to preach in his church. Sometime his father was employed by the city to do labor work. Elijah Poole himself suffered since he had come to Detroit in 1923. He did not work before he met W.D. Fard beyond selling firewood, which sometimes took him all day long to sell for fifty cents...
>
> Before he met Fard, Elijah Poole was not affiliated with any movement or organization except the Masonic movement, which he joined in 1924, when he came to Detroit. He was a member in this movement until his attachment to Fard in 1931.[53]

Elijah's older brother Willie and younger brother John also came to Detroit with him. John recalls: "I am the eighth (8th) son and the thirteenth (13th) or as you might say, the baby of thirteen (13) children of Messenger Elijah Muhammad's parents. It was five (5) girls, that made thirteen (13) children. I was born in Cordele, Georgia. In 1923, I came to Detroit with my mother, and grandmothers and two brothers. I was a small boy [12yrs old]. In 1924 I joined the Baptist Church."[54]

Nevertheless, Detroit's budding auto industry held economic promise for recent southern migrants. Elijah landed a job on the assembly line in an auto plant: "In 1923 my wife and our two children went to Detroit, Michigan, and from that year on, to 1929, I worked for various companies in that city, including the Detroit Copper Company, the American Nut Company, Briggs Body and the Chevrolet Axle Company."[55]

Elijah's son Emanuel recalls his Father teaching him life lessons during this time period:

> "My first impressions of my father were of his wisdom and generosity. He would teach me how to build a fire and how to avoid being hit in the face or eyes by flying splinters. He also taught me how to sift the ashes and what to keep and spread over the new fire to make it last longer. He would also teach me what to do when he was not at home and what the others should do to help me.
>
> "My most memorable experience with my father was the gift of my first brown suit; until today brown is still my favorite color. This suit was given to me when I was five years old and was so dear to me; I would fold it carefully and place it with my shoes at the foot of my bed before retiring.
>
> "I also recall seeing my Father reading the Bible after breakfast; or whatever they called breakfast during the Depression. He would read all

day and this reading would bring tears to his eyes. The tears would fall at the time he was reading...[56]

Like the other legions of southern Blacks, Elijah soon discovered that the bright promise of the North was a failed lie. Elijah Muhammad:

I moved to Detroit because I thought the life might be better, but even there the first year I saw my people shot down right on the street without any justice whatsoever. I had seen there two of our people killed on the street by the police without any justice whatsoever and without any effort on our people's part to do anything or to help. It just is like a man going among a gang of savage beasts and shoots them to satisfy his desire for hunt. So that again impressed me and I said to myself: "Now, I left the South so as to get out of the territory where such things are going on all the time and now I find it here before me in the police department. The difference is that they do not hang them up to the trees but they kill them right here on the streets." The things that I had seen in Detroit were awful. I had seen this and worse than this in all of the other cities that I had visited. I did not see justice in any part of the country.[57]

The Depression

To many Blacks, the North was the South all over again minus the white liberal sweet talk about equality. His employers were impressed by his dependability, but the work was backbreaking and offered very little in advancement opportunities. To make things worse, a severe economic crisis was about to hit America and Elijah lost his job. "In the latter part of 1929, due to the depression, I was out of work but remained in Detroit."[58]

In 1929 the United States was plundered by the New York Stock Exchange crash. This inevitably led to the period of economic misery known as "The Great Depression." This only helped to exasperate racial matters as race relations took another decline. Lynching and race riots continued unabated without any relief in sight. In America, Black people were still on the bottom and were despondently treated as such.

The average wage for Blacks in Detroit was 55 cents an hour and dropped to 10 cents during the lean times of the Depression. Many Blacks were lucky if they had a job at all. Elijah was impacted by the fall:

Poole was among those who lost their jobs in 1929 and stood on relief lines. He and his family faced extremely lean times. The Pooles often subsisted on such meals as chicken feet and vegetable leaves. Coal for the kitchen stove, which was used to heat the house, was collected from the beds along the railroad tracks. Nothing of even the slightest use was thrown away. The four Poole children wore hand-me-downs given to Clara by the people for whom she cleaned, washed and ironed.

...Poole remained on relief until 1931. He had no other alternative. Every morning, he left home before dawn to join the lines of thousands of unemployed people that formed in front of the gates of the local manufacturing plants. He often waited there all morning, hoping to be hired for a day's work, only to return home empty-handed to his hungry children.[59]

Blacks in soup line during the Great Depression in the '30s.

Elijah was of one of those who lost his job and was forced to stand on relief lines that extended for blocks. His family now that included 5 children: Emanuel (b. 1921), Ethel (b. 1922), Lottie (b.1925), Nathaniel (b.1926) and Herbert (b. 1929), and eventually would come Elijah Jr. (b.1931), Wallace (b.1933) and Akbar (b.1939). The family could barely make it on portions of chicken feet and vegetable leaves. The children wore hand-me-downs from whites Clara cleaned for and had to put cardboard in pairs of shoes they took turns borrowing from each other.

Hard Times

Every morning Elijah sought work in front of the gates of manufacturing plants only to wait hours before being sent home empty handed to a hungry family:

Elijah moved to Detroit, where he was chosen to be foreman at his jobs.
They were living at 8474 Manhattan Street in Hamtramck in a small house with an outside toilet.
Elijah heard Fard at 3208 W. Hastings St.

[37]

Elijah's family was poor and suffering, the children Emanuel, now 10, alongside Ethel, Nathaniel and Lottie had little or no clothing. Mostly clothes given to Clara by people she worked for. Emanuel remembering said: "We did not know the original color of the clothes because they had so many patches. Their shoes were reinforced with cardboard. And the father could not afford shoe repair, no toys for the children, only an old tricycle which their grandfather found and gave to Emanuel. Ethel had an old rag doll, and Emanuel would wear his mother's shoes to school, only to take them off at the railroad crossing to hide them before continuing on to school barefooted.[60]

Emanuel recalls odd jobs him and his mother underwent to help his father make ends meet:

Work was difficult to find. To get money for us to live on I would have to search for pop bottles, scrap metal and anything I could sell for junk. At times I would have to climb on freight cars filled with coal to get coal for heating our three room house at 8774 Manhattan Street, in Detroit.

My mother has always been a perfect mother to us and wife for my father. When my Father was unable to find work my mother would work for "Lilly-white" families; scrubbing floors, washing, and ironing clothes to get money to feed and care for us.[61]

Emanuel's duties included searching for food and making sure nothing went to waste:

Meat was on the table about twice a month, too poor to even buy pork. Their meat was chicken feet (clipping the toe nails before cooking); sometimes, buying and killing chickens while saving the feathers to make pillows and mattresses; soured spoil bean soup was sprinkled with vinegar to kill the taste in order before eating (but never thrown away). Emanuel would pick thrown away vegetable leaves to feed the family and picking coals along the railroad to burn in the stove for cooking and heating. This was the condition to which Elijah sought relief.[62]

Turns to Drinking

In an attempt to drown his woes Elijah turned to drinking. Things became so bad that Clara would have to search for Elijah to bring him home. One day she discovered him passed out on the railroad tracks. Elijah's grandson Wali Muhammad, whose mother is Elijah's daughter Lottie, recalls the drunken tales about his grandfather before becoming a Muslim:

My mother remembers seeing [W.D. Fard Muhammad] in the early 1930s in Detroit. This was before the Honorable Elijah Muhammad even converted to Islam. He was still a Christian. At that time, him not having a religion, he did a lot of drinking. My mother remembers that he had gotten so drunk one time—he would get paid and get drunk on Friday nights—my grandmother had to go out and look for him or he would have gambled all his money away before he got home.

One time my uncle Ayman [Emanuel] told me they were looking for him. They knew that he was supposed to be coming home from work. Every time he gets paid he goes on these binges. One of the neighbors said, "Oh, Mrs. Poole! Your husband is out laying on the railroad track. You better go get him because the train is going to be coming soon.

So they went out there. Ayman was a little boy—eight, nine years old. He and his mother, they ran out there and they grabbed him off the track just in time, because the train was coming. They saved his life.

They didn't have welfare or anything like that. I remember Ayman [Emanuel] telling me he used to go in garbage cans behind the stores and get the vegetables that people were throwing out and get the best pieces and take them home.

So that was one of the miracles of Islam coming to the Poole family at that time—how Master Fard Muhammad, with the knowledge of Islam and teachings of Islam, converted and changed Elijah Poole into Elijah Muhammad.[63]

In the midst of this great disillusionment, Elijah was at the crossroads of his destiny. He would soon discover that hope was on the way.

3 Al-Najm (The Star)

1. By the Star When it goes down –
2. Your companion is neither
   Astray nor being misled.
3. Nor does he say (aught) Of (his own) Desire.
4. It is no less than Inspiration sent down to him:
5. He was taught by one Mighty in Power,
6. Endued with Wisdom: For he appeared (In stately form)
7. While he was in the highest part of the horizon:
8. Then he approached and came closer,
9. And was at a distance of but two bow-lengths Or even nearer;
10. So did (Allah) convey The inspiration to His Servant—(Conveyed) what He (meant) To convey.
11. The (Prophet's) (mind and) heart In no way falsified That which he saw.
12. Will ye then dispute With him concerning What he saw?

Holy Quran, Surah 53: 1-12

It was during the depression years when Allah (God) visited the home of the Messenger. For almost three-and-a half years, day and night. Allah was teaching him and making him like Himself. He is that man in the book of Genesis, which states: God created man in His own image, in the image of God created He him. That is if you have a clear knowledge of what you read.[64]

"I started preaching in Detroit, MI on Hasting Street right where the most roughest people in the world could hear it. So, I went in there like a fighting lion in the den with other fighting lions. They would try and bite back at me but I conquered them. With the help of Allah I conquered them. Not with knives and pistols, nothing but the Word." ~Hon. Elijah Muhammad TT October 14, 1973

Elijah Learns about Master Fard Muhammad
In the midst of these great trials and tribulations, Elijah persevered over the negative circumstances surrounding him. Elijah groped to find a way out of the overwhelming hell that engulfed him and his people often

discussing scripture with his family looking for answers: Elijah speaks on his mindset at the time (1931):

> After I moved to Detroit I began to long to something different. I was working there, transferring from job to job. So I seem having very difficult in trying to make a living. Finally I talked with my mother. I told her that it seemed that there was something warning me that I should be a better man, and I should do what I always longed to so since I was a boy and that is to teach religion or preach. That desire was strong in me but just that I cannot see my way to going to the church telling the preacher that I want to preach the Christian religion as they are preaching. I said something warning me that that is not right. But I told her that I will not look like success until I do something of that nature.[65]

Elijah's Children believe Clara introduced Elijah to Fard

His prayers were soon answered with unexpected good news from a family member. Which family member and how it happened seems to have two stories. One version told by Elijah's sons is that their mother Clara was the one who introduced Elijah to Fard in 1931. Nathaniel recalls:

> All of it started from my mother going to meet Master Fard Muhammad (and my uncle Willie) to encourage my daddy to go with them. And that's what started him... But anyway, she was the first one to hear (other than his brother) the teachings of Islam. And Master Fard Muhammad asked her, "Next time you come, bring your husband." Now, I don't know how he knew she had a husband, but that's what he asked her, "Next time you come, to bring your husband." And she did, and after that, Daddy became his "A" student. Because after the first time, he didn't miss no meetings, he went to everyone after that.[66]

Elijah's seventh son Imam W.D. Mohammad recalls his mother Clara Muhammad's role in telling him how Master Fard Muhammad saved his father's life:

> Would you believe that my father was brought to Mr. Fard by my mother? My mother met him first...my mother told me, she said, "Son, your father was a drunk. It was during the Depression when everybody was suffering, and we were suffering more than everybody else," she said..."And then your father would not come home. He didn't come home until he thought everybody else was sleep and then he come home. He was ashamed to come home because he couldn't bring any money. He had no way of bringing any money home. So he stayed out in the streets as a drunk."
> She said, "My girlfriend, who had a lot of children like I had, she told me there was a man (a strange man), says he's teaching something on the streets. He's saying that we (the Blacks) came from royal families and they

used to wear long beautiful silk clothes garments or whatever." And she said, "My girlfriend said, 'You ought to go hear this man."

She said, "I went." She said, "Not for myself, I went for my husband. I thought maybe it would be something to help him." She said, "I went and I heard him and I came back and I told my husband what I heard and he went with me." He cleaned himself up and dressed up nice. Mr. Fard started from the very beginning telling them they had to dress clean and dress like business people. So anyway, my father dressed up and he went to hear him speak.

She said, "Son, would you believe that after hearing him speak for one time, your father told me as we left the place, he said, "Clara, when we get home, I want you to take all the pork out of the ice box and throw it away." Now that tells you what time it was on the calendar, huh? Ice box? [laughs]. He says, "I want you to take all the pork out of the ice box and throw it away"... She said, "Would you believe that your father never took another drop of liquor after that?!"

So the influence of that man's teaching Mr. Fard—the influence of his teachings was so powerful on African-Americans that they just immediately broke bad habits he told them to break.[67]

The Messenger's son Nathaniel gives similar specifics about this event, recalling the name of the family friend as well as Master Fard's first visit to their home:

I know I'm accurate, Lula Spell had went to...Master Fard Muhammad, when he first came to Detroit he used to be a silk peddler of goods. That was his way of getting in Black people houses. He knew they couldn't buy any goods, but he had studied the nature of Black people in California so he knew that if a man looked like a white man, that they going to open their door. So he was in the ghettos, he came into the ghettos of Detroit, and it wasn't Hamtramck. We lived in Hamtramck, I was born in Hamtramck, but he ain't never have no mosque in Hamtramck, never. He just came to Hamtramck one time in our house, we were living in a like a "shotgun house" where you could see straight through it. And you had an outhouse in the backyard where you'd have to go to toilet.

And Master Fard Muhammad, he came one time, and it was dusk dark in the evening, and we could barely see him. He didn't even come into the house. He sat on the front porch with my mother and father because that's where he was waiting for him sitting out on the front porch. But I'm going to make a long story short. Master Fard Muhammad met daddy. Lula Spell was one of the first ones of our friends who heard Master Fard Muhammad. She came back and told my mother and my mother was enjoying what she said, until she saw how it uplifted my mother and she asked my mother would she go with her the next time she go. She went. They went together at the next meeting. At this meeting, my mother, she enjoyed Master Fard Muhammad, and they all got a chance to shake his hand because everybody there would shake his hand. He always would shake the people hand after

[42]

he finished his lecture. So Master Fard Muhammad told my mother, "Would you come next time, and bring your husband?" Now, momma was so elated about what she had heard, when she got home, (according to Lula Spell who was telling this story to us) she said when my mother got home she was so elated about what she heard, that she could hardly wait to get back home to tell her husband. So when she got there, when my mother got home, my uncle Willie was there.

My uncle Willie had also heard Master Fard Muhammad before my dad. And so my dad used to drink a lot of wine, he was high off of wine when they was talking to him, and daddy admit this, that when they was talking to him, and my mother she was telling us what he said. She told him that he [Fard] said next time she comes, to bring her husband. Uncle Willie and my mother had to convince my daddy to do this. So they told him he had to stay sober. He stayed sober until the next meeting. And they went to the next meeting together, my mother and my father went to the next meeting together. And by Allah I can remember the day that they came home, and how happy they was (the both of them). They was so happy about what they had heard, my daddy stopped doing everything bad that he was doing, all but smoking. He used to smoke cigars, and Master Fard Muhammad told him to stop smoking, and he stopped. He stopped just like that. Didn't smoke no more cigars after that. But any way that's not too much important. But anyway, daddy after he first heard Master Fard Muhammad, he never missed another meeting. Every meeting. Every time he met he went. Because that's the year I think Master Fard Muhammad take daddy under his wings and made him the Supreme Minister.[68]

When daddy first heard him, he was so enthused himself over what he heard, so he kept going back (even if my mother didn't go with him) to the meeting. He kept going back and him and Master Fard Muhammad got well acquainted with each other.[69]

Elijah's Children believe Clara introduced Elijah to Fard

Nathaniel's uncle John Muhammad, who is his father Elijah's youngest brother, confidently recalls that Elijah first heard about Fard through their Father Willie Poole (Wali Muhammad Sr.), who was learning Islam from Fard's main Minister Abdul Muhammad at the time. Afterwards Wali came back and told his sons (among them Elijah). John Muhammad recalls in an interview:

S.M. John Muhammad: My father [Wali] was the first one to have heard about Islam. He was a workman out there with the city. He cleaned up rubbish in the alleys at that time. Well, the alleys would be full of ashes and different things, like tin cans where people take and throw coal ashes in the alley after filling up the can of the oil...

Well, he worked there for the city, and one day while he was sitting out eating his lunch, this man came to him and he spoken good to him. He said to my father, "Do you know who you are?" And my father told him "Yes,

I'm a man." He says, "You are more than just being a man." And he began to tell him what nation he belonged to and who he was.

Munir: Giving Him the actual facts.

S.M. John Muhammad: Yes, he was given it to him 'flat footed' as I say. So he says to him, "Don't ya know you was a Muslim?" My father says, "I don't know what it is." He didn't know what a Muslim was, and being a preacher too, he should've had known, but he didn't.

And he told him, he says, "God is man. Not the way the Christian people put it to be, that he was some spirit some place or that Jesus was God. No, He is man just like you are."

And my father says to him, "Well, who put the sun up in the sky?"

He [Abdul] says, "Man did."

He [my father] says, "How could man do it?"

He [Abdul] says, "Well, you never seen a spirit do so, have you?"

They began to have this kind of talk right there together in the alley, until time for him to go back to work, he had a half hour for lunch. And then this man left. This man's name was Abdul Muhammad. He was a stout black man and wore a brown hat, brown coat, blue trousers. And he told him where the place would be at. I believe the address, I don't know, but the street was on Winder Street between St. Antoine and Hastings some place along there. That is what I have heard from one's that lived there.[70]

On his job, he met the man that was named Abdul Muhammad that was representing Master Fard Muhammad. After he met that man he came home and told his family that he had met a man that said, "There was no God up above; that God was in us," and said that "We were Gods."

That worried him and he asked the man saying, "If there is no God up over us, then who put the sun up there?" That was the question that my father asked! He said the answer was, "The Black man put the sun in the Universe." So my father, who had been preaching for years, it changed him and he and my Brothers went to find out where the meeting was after the man had invited him to come.[71]

Elijah and Brothers verify their Father introduced them to Fard

When asked again, Supreme Minister John Muhammad denies that it was Clara who first introduced Elijah to the teachings, and insists it was his Father Wali:

S.M. John Muhammad: Well yes, this is how he heard it. He heard it from him [my Father]. Not from his wife [Clara]. He heard it from him. His wife didn't first see Him [Master Fard Muhammad], she didn't go to the Temple the first time we went. Just us went, the Messenger, my older brother (whose name is Wali Muhammad). His name is on the Temple there in Detroit. That's my older brother that's older than the Messenger.[72]

Elijah Muhammad verifies his brother's John account as he recollects his desire to become a Minister and the circumstances that made it possible via his Father's contact with Master Fard Muhammad's representative, Abdul Muhammad. Elijah:

> In 1931 my older brother and I were living in Hamtramck in Detroit, a little suburb out of town, and began to discuss religion daily. One day our father told us that he received some information and teachings from his friend Brother Abdul Mohammed, who told him that Mr. W.D. Fard has taught him and gave him that name after he was known by his slave name Brown. Brown himself was connected with the Moorish-American movement started by Noble Drew Ali. Abdul Mohammed joined that movement under the name Brown El. Abdul Mohammed told my father what Mr. W.D. Fard was teaching, and my father told me. When I heard it, I told my father, "I like to hear that man." I said, "That is good what Abdul Mohammed told you." That was in the spring 1931. I asked my father about Abdul Mohammed and he told me where that man lives, and therefore we went, my brother and I, to find Abdul Mohammad.[73]

Another account (perhaps inadvertently) said it was Elijah's brother, Charlie (instead of Wali), who came to tell him about the man speaking in a basement. In his book "This is the One," Mr. Jabril Muhammad writes:

> One day, in the early fall of 1931, in Detroit, Michigan, Messenger Muhammad heard from his brother, Charlie, that there was a man teaching things he ought to hear. Charlie was excited. Among the "things" the man was teaching was Islam.
> At that time the Messenger had the wrong idea of Islam. He would later say that he thought it was a "heathen religion." However, he was told enough to want to meet the Teacher and hear His teachings. He also felt this was the One he was expecting. He was told that the man's name was Mr. W. D. Fard and that He was teaching a few people in a basement. Elijah rushed to the place but did not see Him. He was told the man was there earlier.[74]

Elijah wasn't deterred from his pursuit of Fard. He and his brother Wali kept attending sessions with Abdul, and Elijah relentlessly attended meetings throughout the city in hopes of seeing the evasive sage. Fard normally held two or three meetings on Sundays to address the overflow crowds, and it was there after weeks of studying the Messenger would get his chance. "He went to other meetings, held there and elsewhere, but continued to miss Him until the night of September 22nd. He (the Messenger) was eager to see and hear Mr. Fard because he had a strong feeling about this man's identity."[75] Elijah speaks on how he caught his first glimpse of his future teacher and best friend:

> We had visited Abdul Mohammed in his house, me and my older brother, for several weeks and he was telling us what he had been taught. Then we

visited the place where Mr. W.D. Fard was teaching; it was a basement. I was not able to get into the basement because it was so crowded that I had no way to get in, but I heard some of his words come out of the window. Next time I heard him he was speaking on Hasting Street, around 3408 Hasting, and I was not able to hear him well here too because it was so crowded, thousands of people listening to him. After the meeting was over I was sitting down and thought about the teachings. They did me so much good just to think about them. I waited after the second meeting so I might have a turn to meet him.[76]

Elijah Sees W.D. Fard Speak Live in Person

Finally getting the opportunity to clearly hear and see Fard speak during that second meeting, Elijah hearkened to the words spoken by Fard that night. Many years later, he'd repeat the contents of the lecture in speeches and writings. Elijah recalls his encounter and experience with his teacher Mr. Wallace D. Fard:

He began teaching us the knowledge of ourselves, of God and the devil, of the measurement of the earth, of other planets, and of the civilization of some of the planets other than earth.

He measured and weighed the earth and its water; the history of the moon; the history of the two nations, black and white, that dominate the earth. He gave the exact birth of the white race; the name of their God who made them and how; and the end of their time, the judgment, how it will begin and end.

He taught us the truth how we were made "slaves" and how we are kept in slavery by the "slave-masters" children. He declared the doom of America, for her evils to us was past due. And that she is number one to be destroyed. Her judgment could not take place until we hear the truth....[77]

Being astute in scripture, Elijah noticed Fard's words tallied with the Bible's prophetic verses He studied as a child. Stored in Elijah's memory were all the Sunday sermons from his Father that spoke to past and future prophecies. In Elijah's mind, Fard perfectly fit the bill about what the coming one would say and do on his arrival. "This is the One," Elijah thought while in the audience.

As soon as he saw and heard Mr. Wallace D. Fard he knew Him to be the One the world had been expecting for the last 2000 years. It came to him that the man he beheld was the very man expected by the prophets, and others, Who would come in, or under, many good names: Jesus included.[78]

After analyzing the speaker's words, Elijah collected his thoughts and felt compelled to communicate what was on his mind. When Mr. W. D. Fard concluded his lecture, he offered to shake the hand of all those in attendance. Elijah filed in line and awaited his opportunity to speak to the prophet. When his turn arrived, Elijah expressed his thoughts directly to Fard:

> When the meeting was over he got in line with others to shake the Speaker's hand. When his turn came, Elijah told Him that He was the One Whom the Bible's prophets foresaw coming along about that time, about 2,000 years after Jesus, or the Son of Man.
>
> Almost simultaneously Mr. Fard Muhammad looked around to see who else heard that, and then at Elijah a little sternly. His smile followed the look. He bent His head close to him, put one hand on his shoulder, and the other on his forehead. Pressing His mouth against Elijah's ear, He whispered:
> "Yes, I am that One. But who else knows that but yourself?"
> God continued that he (Elijah) should keep quiet about this. He would let him know when to make that known. Then, gently, He nudged Elijah away and began talking with the others nearby.[79]

Elijah recalls it in his own words:

> So we lined up to go by and shake hands with him because he was shaking hands with us all. And when I got to him I shake my hands with him and told him that I recognized who he is and he held his head down close to my face and he said to me, "Yes, Brother." I said to him: "You are that one we read in the Bible that he would come in the last day under the name Jesus." I said, "You are that one?" Here he looked at me very serious when I said that to him, and finally he said: "Yes, I am the one that you have been looking for in the last two thousand years; I am the one. But you go ahead now brother, that is good." And he did not seem to care whether others were sharing what I was saying or what he was saying.[80]

Elijah Muhammad said:

> After I listened to him speaking on Hasting Street I lined up with the people who used to shake hand with him. And when I got to him, I shook my hands with him and I told him, "I recognize you whom you are." Hence, he held his head down close to my face and he said to me, "Yes, Brother," like that. I said to him, "You are that one we read in the Bible that he would come in the last day under the name of Jesus." I said, "You are that one." Here he looked at me very serious when I said that to him, and finally he said, "Yes." He said, "I am the one that you have been looking for in the last two thousand years." He said, "I am the one." He said, "But you go ahead, now, brother." After this meeting Elijah began to preach his idea about Mr. W. D. Fard and his belief in him.[81]

Fard's response confirmed Elijah's hunch. He left the meeting full of excitement telling his family members over the next few days what he believed of the stranger's teachings as salvation for Black people:

Elijah Mohammed, who lived the poor and hard life that we described in the second chapter, had been told by his father that a man by the name of Abdul Mohammed had told him about Fard and his teachings. The teachings appealed to Elijah, who began to be curious and had visited Abdul Mohammed and listened to him. Then he came to the meeting to listen to Fard. Elijah Mohammed said: "The minute I heard him saying that we are not Negro, and that these are not our original names and that this is not our country and that we will soon return to our native land, I was deeply aroused, and I felt that my blood was stirred up and my heart was filled with happiness because my mother used to tell me that there would come a savior in the near future. I knew that this is the one she meant. He impressed me so deeply because although I read the books written by various philosophers and writers and listened, during my life, to the ablest lecturers, none of them were able to reveal such facts because they do not know the truth. But this man knew the truth and what had happened and how it had happened and therefore he must be in contact with a supreme power and he has a message."

Elijah continued stating:

After I heard him, I began to think and to remember all what I have seen and heard of in my life. All of it came to my mind. I thought over many events that I had experienced myself in my life and others that I had heard.

And here, Elijah Mohammed began to tell the story of the lynching which he had seen in Georgia when he was a child of ten years and the other lynching when he was 23 years old. These two lynchings that he had seen had impressed him very deeply and aroused in him a very vigorous, repressed, hostile attitude towards the white man and the life with the white man. He remembers the stories that his grandmother and his grandfather told him concerning the condition of slavery and the cruel treatment of the white people to his own people. Then he remembered the "savage" treatment of the police to his "own people" in Detroit and how they killed the dark people "right there on the street without any justice whatsoever and without any effort on the part of our [his] own people to do anything to help with weapons." Elijah stated: "My reflection upon the teachings which I had heard that day from the mouth of Mr. W.D. Fard had led me to say: 'This is really the salvation that I had prayed for; it came now to me in person.'"[82]

In his own words, the Messenger describes how he viewed Mr. Fard as the divine God mentioned in scriptures to redeem Blacks from their oppressors:

When I heard the teachings of Islam from the mouth of Mr. W.D. Fard, I said, "This is the salvation that I was praying for; it came now to me in person." I did not need to read any book about it because my education is limited. But the prophecy was very clear that this is the truth. I prayed to

Allah for his favor after I heard Fard for the first time. We began to hold meetings together at night in our house discussing what we learned and heard from Mr. Fard. We were real happy. I used to go to my clothescloset and pray to Fard, who brought us the truth that I was long to hear. I used to read the lives of the prophets and their histories and their prophesying. And I used to say that if I live to see the God when he comes to set up righteousness that I pray that I will be one that he accepts, and I would like to point him out that these are the people who mistreated my people all my life and all the life of my parents. My grandmother used to sit down and tell me how the white people used to beat her sister when she was young and under slavery. They were beating her until her legs swell enough and blood comes out of her skin; and I sit and listened to her telling me that sufferings of slavery until I fill my heart with grief and I used to tell her: "My grandmother, when I get to be a man, if the Lord helps me I will try to get my people out of the grip of this white man because I believe that we will not be able to get along with peace under his government." She says, "I do not think either, son."[83]

My grandfather, he also told me what happened to them in slavery. So I have pretty good knowledge of what went on in slavery. The worst of all of this to me is what happened to our people from the white man after they call themselves free. That is what hurts me more and still more hurts me what the white man taught them to believe as their religion just to blind us. They do not offer to us real help. Hence as soon as Mr. Fard began to teach us it was so clear to us just as someone comes out of night into day and sees all the objects that were hidden by the darkness.[84]

Elijah went back to another meeting where this time Fard hinted out loud to the public confirming his belief:

So finally I went back again and listened and he told the whole congregation that he was the Jesus that we have been looking for and expecting, not the one who was here two thousand years ago, but the one we had been expecting. He said, "This is the time of that one." At that I was satisfied.[85]

In the following meeting Fard himself announced, in his speech, that he is "El-Mahdi whom you were expecting in the last two thousand years, but not the one who was here two thousand years ago because that one was killed in the morning between 9 o'clock and ten and therefore he will never come back. But I am his brother," Fard declared. "I am the one you were expecting."[86]

At least a couple of Elijah's other brothers heard Master Fard say to a public audience he was "the Jesus" they were waiting for. John Muhammad recalls, "Late in 1931, I heard Islam as taught by Master Fard Muhammad"[87]:

Master Fard Muhammad, Who Came In Person, came in that name to us the first time that we saw him. Next, He signed his name as W.F. Muhammad. He told us His first name, Wallace Fard. After telling us that, then The Messenger says, "Who are you? What is your real name," he asked? Master Fard Muhammad said, "I am the man that the world has been looking for, to come, for the past 2,000 years." The Messenger says, "What is your real name?" He says, "I am The Mahdi." The Messenger said, "Then you are God?" He says, "Yes." But you don't believe that, though, do you? If I had said, "Jesus," maybe you would have believed it! Well, he was Jesus too. He said so!

Master Fard Muhammad said, at 3408 Hastings Street in 1933 and 32 and 31. He said, "I AM YOUR JESUS!" I heard Him! My Brother there (Brother Johnnie Muhammad) heard him.[88]

Elijah Spreads the Gospel of W.D. Fard in Hamtramck

Emanuel Muhammad says his mother Clara was his Father's first follower to accept her husband's calling and destiny, as he advises his mother Clara "has always been a sympathetic wife of encouragement for Him. She was the first of our family to accept his mission."

Elijah started spreading the message in Hamtramck where he successfully attracted nice-size crowds:

Then I go out in Hamtramck and tell all my poor brothers and sister there what I have learned from his teachings. So they would sit and continue from hour to hour listening to what I was saying. Now and then I got the Bible to show truth that he was telling us the same thing that was predicted by the Bible and the prophets of the Bible that he would come in the last day, and that he taught that the white man was the devil and that we were the people whom that they have deceive near four hundred years ago and had deprived us of the knowledge of ourselves and put us in their names and give us just what they wanted us to have. On that spot I said that it is the truth and no one can deny that. The people were real anxious to listen to me there in Hamtramck. In those days were great gathering wherever the teachings were told. Huge crowds everywhere as people as if the people were gathering for a free meal. It was not like it is today. It was enough to tell the man and he will be there in the meeting listening. I went on for a few months.[89]

While teaching in Hamtramck, Elijah wrote W. D. Fard a letter reiterating his belief in his identity. A month went by before Elijah heard anything. Perhaps by divine appointment, his wife Sister Clara attended a meeting where Fard was addressing an audience in Detroit. During the public meeting Fard openly told Clara to advise her husband he approved of his teaching in Hamtramck. Elijah recalls:

In the fall of 1931 my wife one day went to hear him and I stayed home with the children. That night he asked about me, saying, "Anyone here in this hall know the little man who lives in Hamtramck?" My wife answered, "Yes, he is my husband." Then he wants me to teach. He told her to tell me to go ahead and teach Islam and he will back me up. These were the words he told her to tell me. I felt so happy when my wife told me that. I said to myself, "Now, we really have something to teach, and it is good." So I began teaching.[90]

NOI researcher Hatib Sahib observes the impact this news made on Elijah's destiny:

Consequent upon such social support for his attitude and expectation concerning Fard, Elijah returned to Hamtramck, where he lived, and began to tell his belief to his friends and relatives. Elijah declared: "Then, I go out in Hamtramck and tell all my poor brothers and sisters there what I have learned from his teachings. So they sit and continue from hours to hours to listen to what I am saying. Now and then I get the Bible to show truth that he was telling us the same thing that was predicted by the Bible and the prophets of the Bible that he would come in the last day."

Later on Fard himself declared that "he was the Jesus that we have been looking for and expecting, Elijah said, "but not the one who was here 2000 years ago but the one you have been expecting to come." This, perhaps, gave Elijah the push and support to go on and preach his belief concerning the prophecy and divine status of Fard. In the circle of his family and intimate friend Elijah began to acquire the role of a leader in this respect. Later on, Fard gave him another push forward by telling him "to go outside, among the Negro community and preach the new religion," and opportunity through which Elijah has built himself as a leader by widening the circle of social support to the role that he plays. Finally, Fard appointed him a minister in the temple.[91] PAGE 126-127

After receiving the good news from his wife, Elijah readily accepted and took this as his cue to spread the message of Islam. So he started teaching that W. D. Fard was the answer to the prophecies of the coming of Jesus as outlined in the Bible under the name "Son of Man."

Mr. W.D. Fard Reveals His True Identity to Elijah

Not long afterwards, Fard paid Elijah a personal visit at his home. He came to confirm Elijah's acknowledgment of his identity in person. Elijah recalls their conversation on the subject:

I asked him, "Who are you, and what is your real name?" He said, "I am the one that the world has been expecting for the past 2,000 years." I said to Him again, "What is your name?" He said, "My name is Mahdi; I am God, I came to guide you into the right path that you may be successful and see the hereafter."[92]

In confidence Fard disclosed to Elijah more information on his personal background. He also revealed to Elijah his identity as his Apostle or Messenger:

Among the many things Master Fard Muhammad told Messenger Muhammad was His own history. He told him that He came from the Holy City Mecca, Arabia, and began teaching Black people in Detroit July 4, 1930. He tried to get to Black people by going from door to door taking orders for made to measure clothes. His real aim was to get into their homes. Some of our people got a little suspicious. So later He would get business card orders from office people. After designing the cards, He would have them printed. This was, as the Messenger put it, a cover up. His real identity and purpose could not be revealed before the proper time. The problems of the Depression also served His purpose of "slipping in" to get to His future Apostle...The Messenger said that his Teacher came from the city of His birth, The Holy City Mecca. He (the Messenger) was given much information of His childhood, and of His life in general right up to the time of their meeting in 1931.[93]

Mr. W.D. Fard in Black and White

Mr. Fard revealed to Elijah intimate details about his birth and childhood including information on his parents. He said his birth was rooted in divine prophecy and he was the offspring from a divine lineage for a divine purpose. According to scripture, God's children were to be taken off to a far strange land and made to serve a wicked race of people for a period of 400 years. Then it was written that God himself would come for his people. According to Fard, the people of God were the Black Nation in America who best fitted this description:

He took the Messenger back to what led His (Master Fard Muhammad's) Father to produce him in the first place. That which led to His birth was rooted in prophecy (the foresight and insight of the Gods) written in the Bible and Holy Qur'an concerning a lost people that needed finding, and of the new world that He would produce through them.

This lost people...would be living among the infidels. They would be living in subjection to the infidels...The Father of Master Fard Muhammad and the other wise scientist knew that it was time for them (us) to be found and redeemed. However, the scriptures did not give the location except in symbolic terms. So the Father wanted a Son Who would be able to search the civilizations of the earth to locate that lost member. He wanted a Son capable of getting among the infidels, among whom the lost people lived. This Son would then have to be able to make from among the lost people a disciple for Himself. Through that disciple He would get His people and

[52]

return them to their own people. He would also destroy those who had deceived and misled his poor people.[94]

In reference to his Father's skin complexion to a live audience, Elijah Muhammad recalls Mr. Fard making the following statement: "He said that His Father was darker than anyone of us that He was talking to at the time. He said He was a real dark Man and He was still ALIVE."[95]

According to Fard, his Father was an actual God himself, yet even more startling was the revelation about his mother, of whom he described as a woman from "the Caucasus mountains." Fard explained to his audience the purpose of His parents coming together:

This Father was a real Black man. He knew, therefore, that it would not have been wise for Him to come Himself. He knew He had to have a Son who looked like the wicked infidels among whom He would have to go (and there were other factors in His reasoning). So He went up into the mountains and got a white woman: a Caucasian. He prepared her to give birth to this special Son.[96]

Due to the startling nature of the claim, NOI scholars including Elijah Muhammad provided reasoning behind Fard's parentage.

This is hinted at in the Bible in the mention of a woman out of whom was drawn seven devils in the "gospels"...Again this Redeemer of those who were lost, had to be prepared in such a way that He could be accepted among the whites and His own people. He had to be able to move among both without being recognized, or discovered until the proper time. This was done. He was also made in such a nature that He would naturally deal justly with both people.[97]

I Came to North America by Myself

W.D. Fard said he was born February 26, 1877, in the Holy City of Mecca and studied for 42 years to prepare for his assignment. He said he came in and out of North America since 1910 studying both people – Black and White. "W.D. Fard arrived in America in 1910, entering through New York City. Upon his arrival, Master Fard Muhammad literally sat on a curb and cried when he saw the condition of His father's people".[98]

The Hon. Elijah Muhammad further elaborates to a 1930s audience the trials and tribulations Mr. Fard faced upon his coming to America:

"There never lived a Prophet could equal our Saviour, in Love and Humanly, who spent 42 years of his life in training, for the delivering of rejected and out casted scorned, and despised people as we. He studied the devil's Language 20 years, so we could understand him in the Language we speak, because our own, we know not. Also our Saviour being the wisest

[53]

and last of the Imams (Prophets), had the very highest place in the Holy City, and that, he forsook for our delivering. I wish you bear in mind, this same Saviour have received the most bitter, rejecting, and evil talk, poison, imprisonment, beat, cast out by us whom he come to Save."[99]

However, while in America his first 20 years Mr. Fard said he lived in California with a white family where because of his light-skin he was accepted. It was then that he'd study first-hand the society of White America. It was also there that he attended the University of California. Nathaniel Muhammad recalls:

> He never did teach (a congregation) in California. He just went to school in California. He studied the nature of Blacks and Whites and how they got along together. That's the main reason He went to school there according to his own words, he just wanted to know the relationships and how did they got along. See Master Fard Muhammad came to America in 1910. That's the year he arrived in 1910, before the First World War or whatever. He came in 1910. Because he had said he had been in America for 20 years before he came to Detroit. [100]

A World Traveler Who Measured Civilizations

Mr. Fard superlatively claimed to have studied every educational system of the civilized world and to have traveled all throughout the vast earth. One of his grander claims was that he studied life on other planets including Mars. Elijah Muhammad recalls:

> The Mahdi is a world traveler. He told me that He had traveled the world over and that He had visited North America for 20 years before making himself known to us, His people whom He came for. He had visited the Isle of the Pacific, Japan and China, Canada, Alaska, the North Pole, India, Pakistan, all of the Near East and Africa. He had studied the wild life in the jungles of Africa and learned the language of the birds. He could speak 16 languages and could write 10 of them. He visited every inhabited place on the earth and had pictured and extracted the language of the people on Mars and had knowledge of all life in the universe. He could recite by heart the histories of the world as far back as 150,000 years and knew the beginning and end of all things.[101]

In the scope of modern knowledge, Mr. Fard revealed things that others never heard before, especially the so-called Negroes. He often spoke in scientific terms. Elijah Muhammad remembers him speaking on the measurements of the elements of the universe and how things came to be:

> He stood still and measured the earth, the waters, mountains, hills, deserts, rivers, and weighed them by ounces and pounds and gallons. Event the old

earth itself, and did not over look the atmosphere in which our planet rotates in. He measured the air by inches, feet and miles, and weighed the whole contents (11 2/3 quintillion pounds). He also counted the atoms and cracked them to pieces, and told the amount man breaths in from a cubic inch, foot, yard. He did not leave us foolish concerning the great magnificent starry canopy. He counted and measured the distance between the eight inhabitable planets, taught us their days, years, the square mileage of all, another great wonder. He told us how we come to have a moon, by whom...The fiery sun was conquered by His measuring line, and her great mass unfold. YES! His eyes pierce throughout the vast open space and his measuring rod recorded the diameter of the whole (76,000,000,000,000,000,000, 76 quintillion miles).[102]

In addressing one of the 7 Wonders of the World, Mr. Fard explained the method of how the builders of the pyramids (who were Black people) were able to accomplish the marvelous feat. Elijah remembers: "The Saviour taught me that they had a hydraulic they used in those days that they don't have in use now, and will not put it in use, because of the devil that he will grasp that knowledge as he don't know it yet, he has been asking the question himself. He (Saviour) said to me, he would put that same hydraulic in effect as soon as they remove the devil. They don't want him to know."[103]

Not one to simply leave it to the imagination, Mr. Fard pointed to signs in the skies for his student to understand that they were on time. Elijah vividly remembers:

"He (Master Fard Muhammad) pointed out to me one night, TWO little stars in the Southeastern skies; a blue one and a red one. He said, 'It's been fifty-thousand years since we have seen these stars,' He said, 'When they go away out of the skies from our sight this time, it will be fifty-thousand years before they reappear.' Every time they reappear there will be a universal change."[104]

The Teachings
After Elijah was selected as Fard's chief confidant, the two were practically inseparable night and day. Fard established an Islamic curriculum for Elijah to advance in his studies. He gave him his own personal copy of the Holy Quran.

Still rearing his new Nation, Fard sought to lend more credence to his ideology in the eyes of his followers. An unusually resourceful teacher, he was able to utilize such varied literature from the writing of the leader of Jehovah's Witnesses, Van Loon's Story of Mankind, Breasted's The Conquest of Civilization, the Quran, the Bible and certain literature of Freemasonry to teach his followers. Each contained different pieces of truth and Fard would provide the correct interpretation. One author provided the below synopsis of Fard's teachings:

[55]

The Nation's story of creation had a unique twist, making it markedly different from those of other religious groups. According to Fard, the world was initially ruled by members of a black race who were known as the original men. Theirs was a highly advanced civilization, and their scientists formed mountains and seas, covered the land with animals, and blasted the moon, which had been part of the earth, into the sky. Some of the original men settled in Arabia and became known as the Tribe of Shabazz. They lived in peace, worshiping Allah from the holy city of Mecca, until evil entered the world in the form of a mad scientist named Yacub. Full of pride, Yacub broke the laws of Islam and was exiled from Mecca. His heart set on vengeance, he applied his knowledge of genetics to create a race of immoral men, the white devils.

The white caused endless trouble for the blacks until they were herded together and exiled to the cold wasteland of Europe. Allah then sent his black prophets Moses and Jesus to convert the white devils to Islam. Instead, the whites distorted the prophets' teachings and founded the blasphemous religions of Judaism and Christianity.

Fulfilling an ancient prophecy, the whites gained dominion over the entire world. They transported millions of blacks from Africa to the Americas in slave ships and stripped them of their language and cultural heritage. Along the way, blacks were brainwashed into thinking that whites were their superiors. Fard claimed it was time for the reign of the whites to end.[105]

To supplement the symbolic literature of the white man, Fard himself wrote manuals or "lessons" for the movement. One such manual was entitled *Teachings for the Lost Found Nation of Islam in a Mathematical Way* and was printed and given to registered believers. It was written in Fard's own "symbolic language" and required his interpretation. Following is an example of early NOI teachings:

The Black man in North America is not a "Negro," but a member of the lost Tribe of Shabazz, tricked by traders 379 years ago into leaving their homes 9,000 miles across the ocean. The prophet came to North America to find and bring back to life his long lost brethren, from whom the Caucasians had taken their language, their nation, and their religion. Here, in North America, they were living other than themselves. They must learn that they are the original people, noblest of the nations of the Earth. The Caucasians are the colored people, and have been grafted away from their original color which was black. The original people must regain their religion, which is Islam, their language which is Arabic, and their culture, which is astronomy and higher mathematics, especially calculus. They must live according to the law of Allah, avoiding all meat of "poison animals," hogs, ducks, geese, possums, and catfish.[106]

Dietary Laws

Upon entering homes, Master Fard Muhammad advised them "to clear their cabinets out", meaning of pills, medicines and bad food. He prescribed that your kitchen and the foods you eat are the real medicine cabinet. He told them don't eat the pig or hog, as it is a poisonous animal not meant for human consumption. He advised that mostly all fruits and vegetables were good, yet the majority of food the so-called Negroes were taught to eat was a 'slave diet' and not fit for the righteous people. The Muslims had a strong regimental diet that not only included prescriptions for what to eat—but WHEN to eat as well. Muslims were known to limit their meals to one time a day, once every other day, or once every three days. Elijah Muhammad speaks to this rationale in his books "How to Eat to Live":

> Allah (God) said to me, in the Person of Master Fard Muhammad (to whom praises is due forever) that we who believe in Him as our God and Saviour should eat but one meal a day (once every 24 hours). Eat nothing between meals, not even candy, fruit, or anything which would start the stomach, digestive processes. In this way, our eating of the proper foods and drinks--- at the proper time –would extend our life to 140 years. This would protect us from sickness. He said if we start our infants eating one meal a day, as soon as they are able to partake of solid foods, it would enable them to live at an age of 240 years. I then asked Him, "How about eating once every 48 hours?" He said to me, "You would be ill only one day out of four or five years." I asked Him what was the cure for that one day of illness? He said, "Fast three days and you will be alright." I asked Him, "What about eating one meal every three days?" He said, "You will never be sick if you eat once every 72 hours." This is about two meals every six days, which would extend our lives to a span of 1,000 years – for there is no poison from the previous meal three days ago which has enough power to do you any harm. The fast destroys the accumulation of food poison.[107]

W. D. Fard Bonds with Elijah and Family

After reaffirming his identity to Elijah, Fard addressed his business at hand. He described his mission as it related to freeing the poor so-called Negro from the grips of the white man in North America. He proclaimed that America was to be judged for her mistreatment of the so-called Negroes. Her European sister nations would not be spared either, but America was number one on the record to incur Allah's wrath. Elijah Muhammad elaborates:

> When God appeared to me in the person of Master Fard Muhammad, to whom praises are due forever, in 1931 in Detroit, He said that America was His number one enemy on His list for destruction. While He mentioned other European whites as getting a little extension of time, He singled

America and Germany out as being the two worst vicious, evil, destructive trouble-makers of the entire nation earth. And that America had mistreated us (the so-called Negroes) so much that she cannot be equally paid back for the evils she has done to the poor black slaves.[108]

Recognizing the serious nature of Fard's claim, Elijah seemed to take it all in stride as somehow prepared in advance to receive this revelation. Some would argue any Black Man's experience liken unto Elijah's had prepared him for this message of retribution against white oppressors. Others say he was born for the mission and had divinely prepared destiny. In any sense, Fard and Elijah created a strong bond from their first meeting. Perhaps this was due to Elijah's acknowledgement of Fard's status, even though Fard cautioned Elijah about revealing his true identify before the proper time. Given the magnitude of this assertion, Fard instructed Elijah to stay within limits and to be cautious about this when in public. He instructed him not to talk too much about him while he was present in front of others. Fard used an analogy to justify his tactic. He advised Elijah, referring to the people, "not to give the little baby meat, but milk instead." The two grew very close and Fard would visit Elijah's house almost daily since their first meeting. Sister Clara was also highly impressed as she wrote good news back home to Georgia: "In 1931, Clara Muhammad had wrote her mother and told her they had met a Saviour. But her mother didn't want to believe her, but Clara was adamant in her belief."[109]

Elijah's Family Recalls Their Experience with W.D. Fard
The Hon. Elijah Muhammad's eldest son Emanuel Muhammad recalls the first time he saw Master Fard Muhammad during the first few visits:

I was nine years old when I first saw Master Fard. Master Fard was not by himself when he visited our home. He was with one of his secretaries and his name was Eugene [Ugan] Ali. They had a private conversation in the living-[room]-combination-bedroom of my father. Master Fard, his secretary and my father.

On Master Fard's second visit to our home, our beloved father introduced his children to Master Fard. My father had in the very beginning taught that Master Fard was our savior.[110]

Allow me to give you a brief history of Master Fard and my personal feelings about him. The name "Fard" is pronounced in English as spelled "F-A-R-R-A-D," but in Arabic it's pronounced as "Farad." And Fard also is the opening of the prayer service.

Master Fard, how did he look? Did anybody see him? Yes, many of us saw him. He was in and out of our home every day in the week. He ate at our home; he also ate at my grandparents home. And we saw him. We know what he had on when we saw him. We know his height, we know his complexion, we know he wasn't a Caucasian as some people believe.

Master Fard was a handsome man in every respect, medium sized, black hair with a hue of unnoticeable strains of gray, beautiful white teeth, an even-tone complexion, a soft voice, and appeared very healthy. Some people under different leadership that call themselves Muslim want to claim that Master Fard's hair appeared at times as being kinky. Well, here is my uncle John who knows more about Master Fard's hair than anyone because he used to massage his hair, he used to cut his hair. Not only that, he was my father's (the Messenger's) barber also. So don't tell us that Master Fard's hair was kinky and it was curly—it was straight! He was about a half inch taller than my father and weighed a little more than he did. Am I right? See, we know. The other ones think they know. And I had to know because like I [stated] he was in and out of our house as I first said. I was nine years old when he first came to our home. And he was in and out of our home for 3 years and 4 months. So you mean to tell me that I didn't know how his hair looked and what complexion that he was? You crazy if you think so.[111]

Strangely enough, at the time there were Arab Muslims who lived in the Detroit area. Yet none had bothered to teach Islam to Detroit Blacks. Emanuel speaks on this point about those who criticize the Hon. Elijah Muhammad's legacy as an authentic Muslim leader:

Master Fard suffered greatly for bringing us the teaching of our mother religion Islam. He of all foreigners had more heartfelt sympathy for our pitiful condition, than any Imam, Sheik, Islamic scholar or dignitary from where? From Mecca, Medina or anywhere else! Did you hear me? Had he not come to teach the Honorable Elijah Muhammad (May the peace and blessings of Allah be upon him). The Late Honorable Elijah Muhammad was our Messenger sent from Allah to us. Prophet Muhammad was a universal prophet according to the Holy Quran sent to the whole world. If both did a great work, they both was sent from Allah. If my father was not directly sent from Allah and didn't have the power of Allah behind him, do you think that little Georgia nigger could have done what he did? If he didn't have the protection of Almighty God behind him? That man defied the President or anyone else! Or anyone. He defied even dignitaries that came from the holy land and they wasn't able to do nothing with him. Nobody could do nothing with the Honorable Elijah Muhammad in his whole forty something years of leadership. No one! I have seen them come from Mecca and Medina and elsewhere, and kiss that man shoes! I have seen them kiss the back of his hand! So don't tell me that God wasn't behind the Honorable Elijah Muhammad, you make yourself a fool if you don't think so.[112]

Mr. Fard Gets Elijah's Family an Apartment, Visits Regularly

One of the first things Master Fard Muhammad did for Elijah Muhammad was to rent an apartment house in Detroit closer to the

Temple for his large growing family which now included a new infant son Elijah Muhammad Jr., now making 6 children:

> Immediate upon accepting the teachings of Fard, the condition of Elijah began to improve. He moved into a home at 3059 Yemans Street owned by a Mr. And Mrs. Butler where Mr. W.D. Fard paid the first month's rent. Later, he moved to 283 E. Hancock Street in a two family home where his brother Kallatt and family lived on the first floor.
>
> The Temple of Islam was located at Shane and Chestnut Streets; then 3408 W. Hastings Street and later at Adam and Fenkenton.[113]

Mr. Fard gives Driving and Cooking Lessons to Elijah and Clara

In their new apartment, Master Fard visited almost daily interacting with the entire family, from the Grandparents to the young children. "When Sis. Ethel was eight or nine-years-old, she would look out of her window and watch the car of Master Fard Muhammad drive to her home during the days that he met with her father, the Honorable Elijah Muhammad."[114] Mr. Fard referred to his car as "Old Cavy" (which was a humorous moniker he infrequently used when referring to the white man). Emanuel recalls Mr. W.D. Fard taking him for a ride in his car, teaching his father how to drive, as well as teaching his mother how to cook: "My father was always overjoyed to see the Savior. I remember the Savior's first car. It was a black Chevy (or Ford). When he left us he was driving a Black Ford. The Savior taught my Father how to drive; He taught my mother how to cook. I received my first lesson from the Savior – I have rode with Him while searching for my father."[115]

W.D. Fard Teaches and Bonds with Elijah's Children

Nathaniel remembers how Mr. W.D. Fard interacted with him and his younger brothers Jabir (Herbert) and Elijah Jr.:

> Master Fard Muhammad used to hold Jabir on his lap, because Jabir was what you would call a 'lap baby'. And I used to stand between his [Mr. Fard] legs and he used to talk to us. Because Jr. [Elijah II] was too young, he was a 'crib baby.' So he don't remember Master Fard Muhammad at all. But Jabir remember him a little bit, but I'm about 3 years older than Jabir. Master Fard Muhammad left us when I turned 8 years old the next month. So I remember him very well.
>
> He used to come to our house for dinner every day for 3 and a-half years almost. If anybody know him, it's me, Lottie, Ethel and Emmanuel. Those are the four oldest and we have a better memory than any of us. Because Jabir he was only about 4 or 5 years old when he left...I was eight years old.[116]

Fard interacted with the children often teaching lessons about Islam:

One day my older brother [Emanuel] came through that door in the house and he didn't give the greetings. So Master Fard Muhammad told him, "Go back out, come back in, and give us the greetings." You always supposed to say "As-Salaam-Alaikum" when you come in and when you leaving. So he made Ayman [Emanuel] go back out and come back in and give us the greetings.

And my daddy didn't know I remember that. And I told him, "Daddy I remember him better than I remember you." He [Fard] was the center of attraction in our house. I paid more attention to him.[117]

He knew I knew Master Fard Muhammad, I saw him every day for 2 years. So he [my father] knew I knew Master Fard Muhammad, and I knew Master Fard Muhammad taught him…[118]

Nathaniel remembers Fard giving tips to his mother Clara about raising children. He recalled one instance: "Elijah Jr. was in the crib and he used to cry. So momma used to go to pick him up, and Master Fard Muhammad told her, 'No, let him cry, that will make him have strong lungs.' Like I said, he controlled our house to tell you the truth. When he was there he was the center of attraction."

The Muhammad always looked forward to Mr. Fard driving up to the house in his car. When they'd see him coming down the street they would sneak and hide under the porch to try to surprise him. Upon getting out his car Master Fard would say laughingly "Ok, you all can come out now."[119]

Nathaniel remembers that Master Fard carried sugar cubes but he didn't eat sweets, but shared them with the children. That and a mishap to Master Fard's hand caused Nathaniel to later believe that he possibly was a diabetic:

He used to carry sugar cubes in his pocket. I know diabetics take sugar, because when a diabetic sugar is low, they take sugar. I learned that so. And then my sister Ethel told me once that she washed one of his gloves, his hand had been cut, he cut his hand somehow, and he said his blood was on his glove, and so she said his hand probably didn't heal fast because he was a diabetic.…and he would never, I remember when people would send sweets to him, I remember when a lady sent a cake to him from California, because he had lived in California for 20 years, and they sent a cake to him from California, and he wouldn't eat it. He told Mama to give it to the children. So that was another sign that he might have been a diabetic.[120]

Nathaniel's older Sister Ethel has a different recollection of the same events. In a discussion with Tynetta Muhammad, Ethel gave her accounts. Tynetta Muhammad recalls:

At that time she spoke quite often of her experiences interacting with the Master during the three and one half year period that he was teaching her father privately. One of the amazing stories she told me about was an incident in which he received a cake that was mailed to him from this family, which contained a cracked egg, shell and all, mixed into the cake batter, which amused him greatly.

Upon another occasion, she shared with me that she was given the responsibility as a child to watch his car from the window, as it was parked in front, outside of the house, while her father was being taught by the Master. During the very cold winters in Detroit, one of the Master's hands was blistered as a result of the harsh climate. In the process of healing, it was Sister Ethel, who had the task of supplying fresh bandages after cleansing the wound. She was the one who washed the wound and changed new, fresh bandages to protect his injured or blistered hand. His car was one of the old Model T-Ford's that needed to be cranked in front for it to run. I was told later by another family member that this wounded hand of the Saviour was a sign indicating that his wound would not be healed until his people were fully Resurrected from the dead. Sister Ethel mentioned something about using his handkerchief as a sort of bandage.[121]

Detroit's Hastings Street in Black Bottom where the First Temple was located.

The Fruit of Islam in 1934. Front and Center is Elijah Muhammad's brother, Kallatt Muhammad who was made Supreme Captain of the FOI.

The MGT & GCC Class circa 1940s.

(L-R) photo of Elijah and Clara Muhammad's children. Back row, Ethel, Emanuel, Lottie, Nathaniel. Front row: Elijah Jr, Wallace and Herbert. Mid 1930s

W.D. Fard rented this home on 3050 Yemans Street in Detroit for Elijah Karriem and his family. He regularly visited them on a daily basis.

Top row: Elijah's parents Mr. Wali and Mrs. Marie Muhammad. Bottom row: Eijah's brothers Johnnie Muhammad, John Muhammad and Jam Muhammad

4 Allah's Temple of Islam

The Hon. Elijah Muhammad

Elijah's Family and the Temple

Elijah Muhammad and the majority of his family in Detroit had joined the Temple on 3408 Hastings Street. First time visitors went through the traditional processing at the Temple of Islam. Muslim brothers at the door greeted all visitors and searched guests for any weapons. Next, they were escorted to the Secretary of Islam who recorded their name and address, then to the main sanctuary of the Mosque where the men were seated to the right and women sat to the left. In the background of the speakers' podium was a red and white flag on the wall that was the Star and the Crescent—the national emblem of the Nation of Islam.

The Atmosphere of the Temple

In the Temple, all Muslim men were clean-shaven and wore dark suits with ties. The Muslim women were modestly dressed and contemporary fashion covering their figures and normally wore hats to cover their hair. They greeted each other in Arabic, "As Salaam Alaikum," which

[66]

translated into English means "peace be unto you." The Arabic language they were taught was the language of their Black ancestors from their homeland. They also referred to each other as "brother" and "sister"; a term that wasn't used prior but became accepted in Black America through its use by the Muslims.

The men and women carried themselves in a dignified manner reminiscent of a militant order. This probably appealed to most Blacks not accustomed to seeing anything of the sort, or for others it was welcome as veterans of World War I, except this was "the Army of the Black Nation."

The Temple Program

While waiting for the main speaker, an assistant minister would take the stage and open up service with a prayer in the Name of Allah. This was the official opening of the Mosque meeting. In synch with NOI custom, the speaker politely explained the search procedures that the visitor had just undergone. In a brief sermon, the orator explained the meaning of the Star and Crescent that decorated the wall. The Minister explained that this insignia was the Sun, Moon and Stars that according to NOI theology symbolized, *"Freedom, Justice and Equality."* Together these three principles represented Islam—the nature of the Original Black Man. The speaker professed that this was the Universal symbol recognized by the entire Islamic World.

After the first speaker concluded his presentation, he'd introduce the main Minister who approached the stage flanked by solemn bodyguards. After the Minister approached the podium, he'd open up in the name of Allah and offer the salutations of peace in the Arabic language, "Salaam Alaikum!" He would then delve into his lecture that consisted of the teachings of Fard Muhammad.

Muslim ministers were extremely zealous in their condemnations of "the white man's religion" and ripped holes in the white man's concept of Christianity. The Ministers exegesis of "the Lessons" enthralled many of the first time visitors. If visitors had doubts about any assertions, the speaker easily convinced them once he related it his claim to the lives of his listeners. Like the mastery exhibited by Master Fard Muhammad and the Honorable Elijah Muhammad, NOI ministers were skilled craftsmen in driving the point home about the Black man's unequal living conditions.

NOI Ministers of the future became very effective at articulating the talking points. It was almost impossible not to admire the wit and charisma of those who had these teachings. Never taking credit, Ministers deferred to the founder and his cabinet giving them the credit for what the audience was hearing.

The Teaching for the Lost and Found, W.D Fard

Following would be the typical content as heard from future Min. Malcolm X many years later:

> In Detroit in 1931, Mr. Muhammad met Master W. D. Fard. The effects of the depression were bad everywhere, but in the black ghetto they were horrible, Mr. Muhammad told me. A small, light brown-skinned man knocked from door to door at the apartments of the poverty-stricken Negroes. The man offered for sale silks and other yard goods and he identified himself as "a brother from the East."
>
> This man began to tell Negroes how they came from a distant land, in the seeds of their forefathers.
>
> He warned them against eating the "filthy pig" and other "wrong foods" that it was habitual for Negroes to eat.
>
> Among the Negroes whom he found most receptive, he began holding little meetings in their poor homes. The man taught both the Quran and the Bible, and his students included Elijah Poole.
>
> This man said his name was W. D. Fard. He said that he was born in the Koreish tribe of Muhammad ibn Abdullah, the Arabian prophet Himself. This peddler of silks and yard goods, Mr. W. D. Fard, knew the bible better than any of the Christian-bred Negroes.
>
> In the essence, Mr. W. D. Fard taught that God's true name was Allah, that His true religion was Islam, that the true name for the religion's people was Muslims.
>
> Mr. W. D. Fard taught that the Negroes in America were directly descended from Muslims. He taught that Negroes in America were Lost Sheep, lost for four hundred years from the Nation of Islam, and that he, Mr. Fard, had come to redeem and return the Negro to his true religion.[122]

Mr. Fard Teaches the Muslim Lessons and Histories

Undoubtedly, the most startling revelation to first time visitors was Fard's concept of the true identity of God and the Devil. This too was one of Malcolm's favorite subjects. The man who once was called "Satan" had the honor of revealing the true Satan, as so he believed. Malcolm would share the Muslim perspective of God and the devil. Malcolm X:

> No heaven was in the sky, Mr. Fard taught, and no hell was in the ground. Instead, both heaven and hell were conditions in which people lived right here on this planet Earth. Mr. Fard taught that the Negro in America had been for four hundred years in hell, and he, Mr. Fard, had come to return them to where heaven for them was — back home, among their own kind.

[68]

Master Fard taught that as hell was on earth, also on earth was the devil— the white race which was bred from black Original Man six thousand years before, purposely to create a hell on earth for the next six thousand years.

The black people, God's children, were Gods themselves, Master Fard taught. And he taught that among them was one, also a human being like the others, who was the God of Gods: The Most, Most High, The Supreme Being, supreme in wisdom and power—and His proper name was Allah.[123]

Malcolm revealed to future audiences what Fard told Elijah and what Elijah taught many NOI pioneers; that these were the last days and called for God to appear in person.

Among his handful of first converts in 1931 in Detroit, Master W. D. Fard taught that every religion says that near the Last Day, or near the End of Time, God would come, to resurrect the Lost Sheep, to separate them from their enemies, and restore them to their own people. Master Fard taught that Prophecy referred to this Finder and Savior of the Lost Sheep as The Son of Man, or God in Person, or The Lifegiver, The Redeemer, or The Messiah, who would come as lightning from the East and appear in the West. He was the One to whom the Jews referred as The Messiah, the Christians as The Christ, and the Muslims as The Mahdi."[124]

For most visitors, the words spoken in a temple meeting had a spellbinding effect. Mr. Fard's lecture usually lasted four to six hours in which he spoke on Black Muslim Theology from Allah (Black Nation) creating themselves from "Triple Darkness" right on up to modern day Detroit, Michigan. "Yakub's history," "Musa's History," "Isa's (Jesus) History," and "John Hawkins History" constituted a bulk of Mr. W.D. Fard's lectures. Many in attendance agreed more so than not with the ever-so-real truths they heard in the teachings of Mr. Fard.

Often addressed were the great past when Black Men ruled the world, up until the horrors of slavery inflicted on the Black Man by the white man and its effect on the psyche of both. How Blacks were made to feel inferior because of their skin color and how they came to believe in Christianity that Fard taught was equivalent to teaching white supremacy.

The Muslims addressed the economic plight of Black people. The fact Blacks were exploited daily by the white man who robbed them in their ignorance of not having education and easy to rob because many couldn't read or count. The racial disparity in Detroit probably best illustrated the point. The majority of business owners were white who greedily took money from blacks and used it to build up white communities. Thus the Black ghetto became poorer and the white man became richer.

History was used to show that the Black man fought in the civil war (and others) wars for the white man and when they came back home they were second-class citizens in their own country. He revealed the fact that Black soldiers fought and some died to protect the United States. He pointed out the irony of the living soldiers who returned home from the war were not protected from police brutality, mob attacks and other racial injustices practiced here on the so-called Negro in the United States.

The Muslims emphasized that Christianity was the religion of the slave master and not fit for the Black Man. Under the Christian cross, the Black Man received nothing but slavery, suffering and death. But under the Star and Crescent of Islam he would be free, justified and made equal to all other civilized societies. The best solution according to Mr. Fard was to come follow him and reclaim their heritage. In closing, he would then urge all of the visitors in the Temple to get behind and support the Muslim program.

Mr. Fard Demonstrates Feats of Mental Telepathy

In his presentations, W.D. Fard demonstrated his ability to 'tune in' on the thinking of audience members, as well as create visions of 'their people back home' and encouraged current and prospective believers of their possibilities:

> "The Master, prior to his own departure, which he shared with me (more than 32 years ago), what is the link between The Master, the water glass which he displayed in public lectures, the radio in the head and the Crystal Skull? Master Fard Muhammad demonstrated back in the early 1930s to audiences that through the water, poured into a crystal glass container, He could pull up images of His family back home, and had witnesses from the audience to come forward as witnesses to His powers of mental telepathy. Master Fard Muhammad also stated to His audience that they would one day be able to do the same thing."[125]

Although his feats rivaled the greatest magicians of his day, Mr. Fard condemned traditional forms of 'sorcery' used to deceive superstitious Black people. Elijah explains:

> He has proven that he knows everything we do, and hear everything we say, or even our own thought. He is able to communicate with His people in Asia, without the use of wires, or radios, or any other instrument but His ears. He caused them whom He is communicating with to appear to you before your eyes in a glass of clear water. His Wisdom is unlimited. He despise witchcraft and root doctors, they are all liars, and teaches you how they deceive you, and exposes their secrets.[126]

The Process of Joining the Temple

After a speech it was common for NOI ministers to ask the audience, "Will all stand who believed what you have heard today is the truth and good for Black People?" Next followed the question, "How many of you want to stand behind the truth and come join the Nation of Islam?" This was the first step to obtaining the 'knowledge of self' and joining the Muslim Brotherhood.

The next step in the joining process was to attend orientation classes held at the Temple. This is where they would learn the basic fundamentals of Islam as taught by the NOI. Which taught what separated the civilized man from the uncivilized man— was the civilized man lived the laws of Islam. The uncivilized man was a "savage" who needed to be taught the correct way by Allah's Messenger Elijah Muhammad. By joining the ranks of Islam, he would learn civilization and then go back out to the world to pull the rest of his brothers and sisters "out of the mud."

Taught to Eat the Right Foods, Taught General Civilization

The Muslims taught new converts what foods to eat and what not to eat. They insisted that all drop pork from his diet. Muslims railed that the nasty pig was "a grafted animal that was one third rat, one third cat and one third dog." The Muslims also prohibited any of its members from smoking, drinking or using any narcotics that were consumed in the "dead world." Overall, Fard gave his followers a list of prohibitions referred to as the "Restrictive Laws" and "Rules of Islam". Some Elijah would repeat years later:

> We now are seeking the respect of the nations of the Earth. To get this respect, or recognition, we must lay aside any old ignorant habits practiced from birth. Being "loud" to self in public, is not good manners. Too much "joking....yelling" at one another in public, using "ugly-indecent language, swearing" at each other, calling each other names, singing "foolish and filthy songs," "dancing" and "shaking, twisting" the body in public, "lusting" and looking with wanton eyes at each other, "smoking, drinking the fire spirit" is no good. "Chewing, or using tobacco" in any form, "form fitting clothes," the wearing of shorts by women or men in public is indecent. "Going bare-legged" in public, "gambling, games of chance and whistling" is forbidden.
>
> Keep the mind and body clean. Take frequent baths. A total bath should be taken daily. "STOP EATING THE SWINE FLESH," it is Divinely Prohibited flesh. Two-thirds of our ailments can be traced to the eating of this poisonous animal called the swine. Go cleanly dressed.
>
> If you have only one suit, keep it clean. "Keep your house clean." The woman should "never" invite, or allow "strange-men" to come into her home in the absence of her husband, father, brother (the son of her father).

[71]

Show respect for self and others. Respect and "honor" men in authority, whether they respect you...or not. Provoke no one! Don't steal, or take "advantage" of one another because of the freedom to do so. "DON'T QUARREL AND FIGHT EACH OTHER."

For we are brothers – same flesh and blood. Would you like to continue destroying your own flesh and blood? Would you like this? Protect your daughters and women from evil and filth. Protect them from the love of "strange men." Rid yourselves of laziness, "be smart and industrious."

Do good and "righteousness," regardless to whom or where. Be not wasteful, help to build a better future for self and kind.

"Patronize" your own people's business. "Spend" your dollars among your own kind. Serve "One God, Allah." One religion-ISLAM, BE NOT DIVIDED.

Have love, unity, brotherhood first among yourselves. Help to secure a home on this earth that we can call our own. "Do something for self and kind in the way of building a better future where we can enjoy "Peace, Security, free from the shadow of death of our enemies."[127]

Elijah and Brothers Receive their Muslim Names

To reflect his new status, Fard gave Elijah the surname, Karriem, replacing his slave name, Poole. He became known as Elijah Karriem. In the near future, Fard would ask Elijah to take on a "bigger" name. For the initiated in Islam, a righteous name wasn't to be taken lightly:

> The people who secured the new names value them as their greatest treasure. "I would not give up my righteous name. That name is my life." They became so ashamed of their old slave names that they considered that they could suffer no greater insult than to be addressed by the old name. They sought to live in conformity with the Law of Islam as revealed by the prophet, so they might be worthy of their original names. Gluttony, drunkenness, idleness, and extra-marital sex relations, except with ministers of Islam, were prohibited completely. They bathed at least once a day, and kept their houses scrupulously clean, so that they might put away all marks of slavery from which the restoration of the original name had set them free.[128]

After Elijah's brothers wrote the Secretary of Islam to get their names (and perhaps forgetting to mention they were all related), the brothers all ended up with the different last names of Karriem, Mohammed and Sharrieff. Their Father Willie Sr. was given the name Wali Mohammad, the elder brother Willie Jr. became Wali Mohammed Jr, Elijah became Elijah Karriem, Jarmin became Kallatt Mohammed, James became Jam Muhammad and their youngest brother became Muhammad Sharrieff (and then John Muhammad):

You would like to know something about me, wouldn't you? I have been in The Nation of Islam from the beginning of 1930, When Master Fard Muhammad came to Detroit in 1930. Nearly the last part of 1930, I visited. I didn't join. I visited to hear That Man that said white folks is the devil. I came back and visited until 1931, then I wrote a letter to him. His address was, 1 West Jefferson, in the City of Detroit. We didn't have Zip Codes at that time. When I received my name He sent it to me by my father, who was the first man to recognize Islam in his family. He was the first!

You read about him as being a Baptist preacher, right? A sharecropper. You know that he was the first in the family to meet a man and hear Islam first. Nobody told you that did they!? He was![129]

I became a member in the Nation of Islam by writing a letter, as I said, to My Dear God: Master Fard Muhammad. He sent me my name by my father. I did go that day. My father came home that day and he said, "Here's your name." I looked at him. I could not read it clear enough because I was not taught in school anything about "Muhammad." I wasn't taught anything about "Sharieff." And that was my name, "Muhammad Sharieff."[130]

Elijah and his Brothers attend the Temple with Mr. W.D. Fard

The brothers all attended the Temple along with the rest of excited patrons in Detroit. John Muhammad recalls his first experience meeting Master Fard Muhammad while standing in line and recalling Master Fard teaching that Black people can control the weather:

Then I went. I followed. I didn't go in the same month but I did follow. The first time I heard, I saw Master Fard Muhammad standing outside. We were waiting to get in. And within me, it came to me saying, that man you see there is the man you want to hear. And he was standing in line real pitiful-acting, humble-acting man, standing there waiting and just smiling at all of the Black people he saw. And it was a crowd of people standing there.[131]

That evening there came a storm. While we were sitting there listening to Him (Master Fard), a loud thunder bolt came and the people began to get frightened. He said to us, "Fear not, you can do that. That is easy. It is not going to hurt you." "Listen to what I am saying." He said.

There is a lot to that, now. I don't have time to go through all of that to tell you, but there is a lot to it.

As the rain was falling, He said to us, "You can make the rain." And the people has gotten so their burden was lifted. They were glad to be present with a Man that could tell you those things. Now so much for that![132]

Since that day John Muhammad says he became regular at the Temple listening to Fard and Elijah: "In my day, when I would sit down and listen to Master Fard Muhammad and my brother, Elijah Muhammad (Peace Be Upon Him) I was there all night long. All night! It's not bad to sit all night after we have been robbed for 400 years."[133]

The Remaining of Elijah's Family Converts to Islam

Eventually Elijah, his father and brothers would eventually break the news to their mother Marie, who was still in the church and had no idea her whole family converted to Islam. She would later convert upon her first visit to the Temple. John Muhammad explains:

> After Dad, after that, we all had become members, I will say it like that, into the Nation of Islam... We were a kind of afraid to attack mother, to tell her what we was... We would go to the Temple every Sunday... and she still went to the Church. She was Baptist at first and then she had taken over to the Sanctified people. She would go every day, every Sunday...I would say every day, but it was Sunday. She would go and she would stay all day...
>
> Well, our father didn't never say nothing about her doing that....It's because he had retired himself from preaching, so she would go, and now my father was a Muslim now. You see what I mean? Now all of us was nearly about Muslims there ... Well in the house we was then except the one who was out...They say, "Well, how you think Momma going to take it, when she hear about what's been going on?"...And they were afraid. So they had to break the ice to her. They told her that we going to the Temple Sunday. And one Saturday they told her, "We going to the Temple Sunday and hear this man Farad." They said, "He don't go for the God that you serving, because you serving something you can't see..." And you know, they began to break Islam down to her... And she says, "You going tomorrow?" They say, "Yeah." She says "Alright." And after that Sunday, she hadn't been back to the church anymore... When she got the truth of it, she believed and had become a strong believer until she passed away![134]

Marie was given the last name Muhammad of her husband, and Master Fard would also give a name to Elijah's half-white grandmother who lived in the family house. Elijah's son Nathaniel recalls: "My great grandmother on my Father's side was [half] Caucasian, ok. And Master Fard Muhammad named her "Peggy Omar." She was tall. She was about 5"11. She was a very nice looking lady for her age. Her hair was real long, it used to hang down below her waistline and she used to pull her hair over shoulder and braid it in front of her. I remember my Grandmother very well."[135]

The Hon. Elijah Muhammad recalled this himself in an interview speaking on how white men had babies by black women and sold their own children as slaves: "Truth hurts. You went into our grandmothers, had children by them and then put them on the block for sale, and today you are still crossing over to our women. This should show you why we want to take leave of you today. In those days you sold her children, who were your own sons and daughters. I am telling you what my own grandparents told me. My father's mother told me her father was a white

[74]

man, and she looked it."[136] When asked in another interview, "Is your own individual racial background entirely black?" The Hon. Elijah Muhammad responded, "Well, my parents was mixed by white slave masters, my grandmother, my father's mother was half and half. Her father was white.[137]

The brothers of Elijah Muhammad all took on some roles in the Nation of Islam: "Jam Muhammad (Elijah's brother) was the recorder for Master W.D. Fard Muhammad our savior. He recorded all the names. There were two books. One was called the book of life; the other was called the book of dead. He was also the Secretary, the Teacher and also active minister during THEM time."[138] A biographer of Jam recalls his words on the subject:

Minister Jam Muhammad was Master Fard Muhammad's barber. Though not a barber, by profession, he cut the Savior's hair.[139] He worked as a secretary for Master Fard Muhammad. He wrote the names in "The Book of Life," while the Savior was among us. According to Minister Jam Muhammad, one day Master Fard Muhammad told Messenger Elijah Muhammad to bring him (Jam Muhammad) with him the next time he came to see Him, because it was something He wanted Jam to do. Jam had good handwriting skills. Minister Jam Muhammad said he went with Messenger Elijah Muhammad on the next visit with Master Fard Muhammad. The Savior (Master Fard Muhammad) had a big book with a lock on it. He also had two big boxes. One was full of letters and one was empty. Minister Jam Muhammad said that The Saviour would unlock the big book, Himself, and turn to the page that he wanted Minister Jam to write the names. Minister Jam said that if he made even a small mistake, the Savior would rip out the entire page so that the name could be re-written correctly. Minister Jam Muhammad said that the Saviour would take the letters out one at a time. And read and spell the name of each person. Every now and then, he would put a letter in the empty box. Minister Jam said, The Savior said, those were from devils. Minister Jam Muhammad said that many times the Savior would write something after each name but that the Savior Never let him see what he wrote. Minister Jam Muhammad said that he was never left alone with the book, but that he always wished he would be, so that he could see what Master Fard Muhammad was writing. Minister Jam Muhammad said that as far as he knew, The Savior took the book with him.[140]

Johnnie Muhammad also joined the rest of his brothers in the Nation of Islam. His biographer tells his story:

Johnnie Muhammad was born August 27, 1907, in Courville, Georgia to William and Marie Muhammad - the same parents as Allah's Last and Greatest Messenger, The Most Honorable Elijah Muhammad. Messenger Elijah Muhammad was nearly ten years old when Brother Johnnie was born.

Brother Johnnie Muhammad, like Messenger Elijah Muhammad, carried the slave name of Poole until 1931 when he reclaimed his own in the Nation of Islam, after meeting face to face with God in Person, though he firmly acknowledged that he "didn't know he was God at the time."

Brother Johnnie Muhammad, a hard-working FOI, worked for Chrysler Corporation for 30 years. Upon retirement he spend time with family and friends and continued his dedication to the Nation of Islam.

Brother Johnnie Muhammad was given the position of Investigator by Messenger Elijah Muhammad, and remained on that post as strong Witness Bearer to the Coming of Allah in the Person of Master Fard Muhammad and the raising up of His Last and Greatest Messenger, The Most Honorable Elijah Muhammad, from 1931...[141]

Johnnie Muhammad recalls "and by 1932 the whole family had become Muslims under the guidance of Master Fard Muhammad and Messenger Elijah Muhammad (P.B.U.H.). My First Post or Duty was as a helper at the door and an usher. [142]

NOI Pioneers Experienced Hard Times in Detroit

In the beginning of their sojourn, Master Fard Muhammad, the Hon. Elijah Muhammad and the early Muslims had it hard in Detroit during the Great Depression. They fought hard for the survival and 'resurrection' of the Black Nation. S.M. John Muhammad recalls these difficult times:

We, the real pioneers, worked from the beginning, night and day, with Master Fard Muhammad and the Honorable Elijah Muhammad in the time of a great Depression. We worked to resurrect a mentally dead Nation, giving like to a seemingly dead earth, with the knowledge being taught to living, walking dead (Blind, Deaf and Dumb People).

The same as the blowing wind fertilizes the earth and brings it too life, so did the Wisdom, Knowledge and Understanding work upon the brains of the so-called Negro (Fertilizing it) until many of the Black so-called Negroes were resurrected.

It is written saying, at the time of Jesus death on the cross, "Many of the saints rose out of their graves and went into the city and walked with many." The wisdom that was taught by Allah in the person of Master Fard Muhammad caused these walking dead people, to walk about in these American cities preaching Islam to Black Americans. This is the only proof of how God (Allah) raises the dead.

In the time of Master Fard Muhammad, in Detroit, Michigan, most every place where there was a job for a Blackman was closed, and many of those jobs never re-opened. For the whole three years and six months of Master Fard Muhammad being here among us, Blackman and woman received welfare food orders, known as "Emergency Orders," and it was very little. Single Black women did day work for five and six dollars per week and car fare.

[76]

Day work consisted of cleaning white people's homes and washing and ironing for white folks.

If a woman got $1.25 and car fare per day, this was considered good wages during these hard times. Thousands of people were in soup lines. Then came God in person, and resurrected His Messenger from among these Black people, who was also receiving Emergency Order Checks to feed his family.[143]

Elijah Evangelizes in the Community

In these hard trials, Fard remarked to others that he was confident in Elijah Muhammad and acknowledge the Believers efforts to establish the Nation of Islam. John Muhammad clarifies:

The Honorable Elijah Muhammad was a man that came up before in hard times, therefore, Allah (God) in the Person of Master Fard Muhammad saw fit to raise up from among us one of our brothers.

This one had knowledge of hard times, plus a poor education. He had much knowledge of the ways of the devils but none of God not any knowledge of his people.

He, too, was blind, deaf and dumb, but there was one spark of an atom of love for his people that no one could destroy. HE was known by the God of Heaven and those who made prophecy of him, and they did write of him in these words...

Master Fard Muhammad said he, Messenger Elijah Muhammad, "was a piece of jewel that only need cleaning up." And that He did.[144] Our Temple, during the Depression, was operated by men who pushed junk carts on foot, picking up paper and what not that he found in the alley. They would take it to the junk yards to exchange it for about seventy-five cent for an entire day of work. I was the Assistant Secretary and Secretary during those days of hardship. The Temple bills were paid from these faithful and loyal men and women. I also say faithful Black Sisters of the Temple of Islam pushing junk carts and living in garages in this wicked Detroit.[145]

Such a hard worker, Elijah Muhammad was placed on a group and given the individual assignment to go directly to the "Lost-Founds." A task he became very proficient in and would later share with his ministers and followers. Elijah explains:

In Detroit, Michigan, back in the late fall of '31, I used to travel around there in the early part of '32. I used to be on a committee there. I used to have to go and try to seek you to get the rent. And I would go to many people and I would get a chance to talk to the dead. And I could get up to them far easier than my followers could. They didn't know how to catch the wild game as good as I. And so, it stands true. We can't stand here, up in our Temple, on the platform and say, "Well, they didn't bring them in." I'm the man the hunter! If they want to help me, I'm asking them to help me. But I'm the real hunter of this Temple. I have to always study some way to get out there next to the game. And if you don't seem to be getting out there and getting after them and I know the game is out there, well then I'm going myself and see what trouble you are running into. Like the book teaches you that after Solomon sent several to try to bring back the body of his architect, they failed. But finally he went himself. He said, "I will go." He said, "I will show you how to get him." So he went and showed them how to put the tow on the man, the dead body, and bring it up. And they brought it back to Jerusalem, where it belonged. This is a fiction brothers, we think. But it's not! It's a science and an example of us, if we understand it. So I don't think no minister is acting himself by sitting down, if he don't have but two or three dozen followers here, or maybe a dozen, he just sits here and wait, "Well go bring me someone here, I'm here to teach!" No! You go over the city yourself. Let the people know what you have. And after you get your Temple about full, then that's the time for you to stand around and say, "I will keep these while you go after me some more. You see? But some of us, ministers, have about 10, 12 or 15 people and then we sit down, as though we had 10 or 15 thousand. Don't want to do any work. Don't want to do nothing. Only stand up.... But that 10 or 15 is giving you soup. That 10 or 15 is trying to pay your rent. That 10 or 15 is trying to buy you transportation. Don't you think you owe them something?[146]

W.D. Fard and Elijah Hold Temple Meetings in Chicago

Master Fard and Elijah Muhammad travelled to spread the teachings to neighboring Chicago, Illinois, which was also suffering from the Great Depression. Karriem Allah, a NOI pioneer from Chicago recalls the effects of the Depression on Black Chicago:

The country (America) was in the grip of a great depression; '25 per cent of the population was unemployed due to the depression. Times were hard, people were hungry, raggedy, barefoot and out of doors; suffering was widespread.

The highways were filled with people roaming around the country looking for work; some "hoboed" on freight trains, but everywhere they went the condition was the same. Wherever the people roamed, they were faced with bare facts of unemployment.

It was America's darkest day since she had established herself as a world power. There was unrest among white people throughout the country. They had ruled America ever since they took the country away from the Indians, the original owners of the country, and they had never experienced a depression like this in the history of the founding of this government.

Multimillionaires went flat broke in that depression. Some took their lives because they could not bear the shock — others because of the reality of being a poor man and falling from such a high standard of living. The mere thought of being a poor man was more than the affluent could stand.

They had fallen all the way down from luxury, good homes and money. That depression was a terrible thing to behold. People were confused, shocked, and dazed. It was hard for our people, Black people, to believe a government with so much wealth could fall so suddenly. The national budget was only $19 billion—look at it today. Look at their stock market—it is rising and falling.

One can see the danger signs, the market is unstable. During those bleak days of the depression, I saw whites and Blacks lined up at banks, long lines hoping the doors of the banks would open so they could withdraw their life's savings, but to no avail.

People stood all day praying and hoping the bank would open, but the doors of the banks never did open. People were openly crying and wringing their hands. This awful thing came suddenly and unexpectedly. It was a sad day for old wicked America, but a sadder day is just ahead of us now.[147]

In the cold and desperate times of Chicago, Master Fard Muhammad and the Hon. Elijah Muhammad rented a hall at 37 Wentworth Avenue, where they spoke often. The teachings of Master W.D. Fard in Chicago was warmly received:

Under such hard economic conditions Fard and his disciple appeared in Chicago in 1931 preaching the new religion. Elijah Mohammed, although he was not living in Chicago at that time, came to Chicago frequently to preach in a rented hall at 37 Wentworth Avenue. Now and then Fard came to deliver a speech to such an audience. At that time his disciple Elijah Mohammed was preaching that Fard is Allah, who came to save the dark people. At that time, Elijah told the writer, people were coming "by hundreds just to hear the Saviour because they were so distressed and having a hard time that they were looking for something like this to come." So when he "spoke here in Chicago people crowded around him: and when he attacked Christianity people seemed to accept these attacks because they themselves bear witness that it did not do good for them."[148]

Elijah the First to Call W.D. Fard a Prophet as a Cover
Elijah Muhammad was the first one to refer to Mr. Fard as "a Prophet." Elijah gives his explanation as to how this happened:

He did not teach us that he was a prophet. We used to call him prophet. I made the followers calling him prophet because I do not know exactly what great name to give him. No one called him prophet before me. First I thought that we should call him Master; later I thought that we should call him prophet, and later I told them that he neither either one; I said that we should call him the "Almighty God" himself in person because, according to what he has taught us, that must be the work of God and not of a human being. Then I took it with him, but, although he did not tell me exactly, but he did mention that I will find out who he was. He was referring to himself as the one coming to save us and that he was the Messiah that we were looking for.[149]

W.D. Fard says he is "God" During Public Meeting in Chicago
However, on at least one visit to Chicago, Master Fard Muhammad
(whom Elijah referred to as "Prophet") had surprised him when he
confessed in front of a public audience that he in fact was "God". Elijah
remembers:

> He came once to Chicago and delivered a speech in which he said, "I am
> God Himself," and I looked at him and he looked at me when he said so.
> And it came to me when I looked at him that I was believing that all the
> time. He did not say that "I am prophet," but he said, that "I am the one
> who comes in the last day." He did not say, "I or Allah will do this or that,"
> but I noticed him carefully saying, "We do this or that." So I gain knowledge
> from those words that he made himself.[150]

W.D. Fard Advises to Keep His Identity a Secret
While the two shared this secret, Master Fard advised him not to exceed
the parameters, and reasoned it was liken to feeding hard foods to a
baby:

> So, I did begin teaching that the Son of Man or the Second Coming of Jesus
> was present. This was He now, here among us. He didn't allow me to go too
> far with that kind of teaching while He was present. He told me, "You can
> do that after I am gone." He said, "Don't talk too much about Me now.' He
> said, "Give them a little milk." That's the way He talked all the time; He
> never would just say anything hardly direct. He would give it to you in a
> way that you would have to learn just exactly what He meant by what He
> said. And so, He said, "You cannot give babies meat." I understood what He
> was referring to. And so He said, "Give the little baby milk." He said, "When
> I am gone," He said, "then you can say whatever you want to about Me.'[151]

Elijah uses Islam to Clean up His People
Paying forward the favor of Master Fard taking him off of cigarettes and
tobacco, Elijah would take other "Lost-Founds" off the same dirty habits.
Elizabeth Hassan recalls how Elijah Muhammad convinced her to give
up cigarettes during one of the Chicago sessions in 1931:

> Sister Elizabeth Hassan described how her acceptance of the TRUE religion
> of the Nation of Islam transformed her life...She talks of her slave name and
> her Holy name and tells how the Honorable Elijah Muhammad warned of
> the evils of smoking fully 32 years ago.[1932]

> One of my first beautiful blessings was the presentation to me of a HOLY
> Name of GOD, as the scriptures have predicted.
> My slave name—or the name given me by my parents, which is of Anglo-
> Saxon rather than Asiatic origin—was Isabelle Dorman.

[80]

But since my forebears came from Asia, and God comes from Asia to restore His lost people in these last days of the world of Satan (according to scripture) our true names have been and are being restored to us.

My holy name is Hassan; which in Arabic, the language of our forebears, means beautiful; great; and handsome.

THE HONORABLE Elijah Muhammad said many wonderful and prophetic things that summer night in 1931, when I heard his truths for the first time.

On that night he told of the evil effects of nicotine on the nervous system and on the lungs. He pointed out that smoking can cause lung cancer (this was many years ago).

These teachings helped me build the will power to stop smoking and to disassociate myself from other vices in which I had become embroiled. It was then that I found that upon the submission of my will to Allah, all evil disappeared from my life.

The Messenger of Allah also told us that our people are among the original people of the earth. He said that the knowledge and understanding of this would free us from ignorance and save us from the destruction that we could see coming, now that we have sight (an understanding of truth).

Try this and you will see what a dramatic change it will make in your home; in the husband and wife; in your happiness together. I say these things to you because I know that you want to be happy together.

I truly thank our Messenger of Allah for teaching me of Islam, for:

Islam is original, it means first.
Islam is salvation, it means to be saved.
Islam is unity, it means oneness.
Islam means justice, it means to be justified.
Islam is equality, it means to be equal.
Islam is freedom, it means to be free.
Islam is brotherhood, it means a true brother and a true sister, and one common cause.[152]

W.D. Fard and Elijah Visit the Zoo in Chicago

Per NOI legend, while in Chicago, Master Fard and Elijah Muhammad made an educational stop to the Lincoln Park Zoo. There Fard demonstrated his ability to communicate with animal life, as he did with the famed gorilla "Bushman" who was a major center of attraction at the time. The Chicago Tribune addressed his coming in 1930:

When an orphaned infant gorilla named Bushman arrived at Lincoln Park Zoo this date [Aug. 15, 1930], he quickly became an international attraction. He appeared in newsreels. The nation's zoo directors voted him "the most outstanding animal in any zoo in the world and the most valuable." A Marine Corps reserve battalion named him the gorilla that would be most welcome in establishing a beachhead. Taken from Cameroon in West Africa, Bushman was sold to the zoo for $3,500 by a Presbyterian missionary and an animal trader. Bushman was said to be the first of his kind west of the Potomac River, and he looked, one writer said in 1947, "like a nightmare that escaped from darkness into daylight and has exchanged its insubstantial form for 550 pounds of solid flesh. His face is one that might be expected to gloat through the troubled dreams that follow overindulgence. His hand is the kind of thing a sleeper sees reaching for him just before he wakes up screaming." Photographed often, the solitary animal was a temperamental subject, often hurling food and his dung at photographers. Those who had been pelted claimed the gorilla's aim was more accurate than that of any Cubs or White Sox pitcher.[153]

According to the legend, Master Fard and Elijah approached Bushman at the zoo where the gorilla immediately recognized Master Fard: "Bushman, would take a tire and stretch it like a rubber band, and would throw his dong. One day the Saviour walked up to the cage, and Bushman recognized the Saviour, he said "Salaam Alaikum,"and held conversation with the Gorilla. The Gorilla said, 'I want to get out of this cage.' So he asked the Saviour for his freedom."[154]

The Message Grows in Detroit
The teachings picked up momentum in Detroit, positively effecting the latest set of Believers. David Fard, an early convert from Detroit since 1932, shares his enthusiasm around the Messenger's intervention with him:

All praises are due to Allah for raising one up from among his own people, one who knows us, one who can set us straight. He is the Honorable Elijah Muhammad, who passes the teaching of God (Allah) on down to us.

IT IS NOT difficult to be a follower of the Honorable Elijah Muhammad. His teaching is only righteousness. I find it is better to do right than to do wrong. I know someone who has been a follower for a long time, and he is still holding on to his own—from 1932 to 1967, 35 years.

My brothers and sisters, all you and I have to do is stop doing wrong. The Messenger is the one who can lead us to safety and success—yes, I mean we, the so-called American Negro.

Muhammad opened my closed eyes in 1932 here in the wilderness of North America. All praises are due Allah, we thank Him for giving to us the Honorable Elijah Muhammad. He is the greatest of them all. I can only thank him for turning me around from my wicked ways.

He is the one who stopped me from eating the poison swine and the many other dirty things I was doing. All praises are due to Allah and His true servant, the Honorable Elijah Muhammad. Sometimes, I wonder if the black folks of America see this.

FOR 35 YEARS, the teachings of the Honorable Elijah Muhammad have given me the conviction that only one majestic person has the solution to this so-called American Negro problem. The Messenger is calling us. We must answer to His calling, because it is later than we think. The greatness of Islam is beyond description. Mr. Muhammad is the Holy apostle of Allah.[155]

ELIJAH MADE SUPREME MINISTER [AUGUST 1932]

Yet, not everyone was happy with the solid relationship between Fard and Elijah, most notably Fard's first two Ministers, Abdul Muhammad, who initially introduced Elijah, his Father Wali, as well as his brothers to Master Fard. Then the 2nd Minister Ugan Ali who felt Elijah eloped in on his and Fard's relationship. Both men Abdul and Ugan had roots in the Moorish Science Temple of America and still maintained Moorish philosophical leanings. John Muhammad described Abdul "as a big black man" with a forceful style of teaching. As time went on, Abdul became more rebellious to Fard although still retaining some popularity in the movement. "The first opposition the movement met in Detroit was that of Abdul Mohammed, who was the first minister of W.D. Fard. He began to teach against W.D. Fard in order to preside over the group himself."[156] Elijah's brother John Muhammad cited that Abdul even referred to W.D. Fard as a devil on at least one occasion. Soon it became a distraction, and with the help of Elijah, Fard was prepared to shift the balance of power in his ministry. Elijah points out some of the signs of Abdul's hypocrisy:

> I was myself the third minister he [Fard] had chosen. Before me were two whom he did not like; one was Abdul Mohammed and the other Othman Ali. He did not like them because they were following the Moorish. More than that, they were trying to get the teachings and use them to their own benefit. That is why Abdul became a great enemy to us and he began to teach against Mr. Fard. Before I became a minister I used to listen to Abdul Mohammed while he was talking and then I used to go to Mr. Fard myself, telling him that I did not like the way they were carrying on; and that if I had to teach I will teach the people with you.[157]

Years later when arrested for not registering for the draft, Elijah Muhammad, when questioned by the FBI about "Satohata Takahashi, a Japanese who once was accused of organizing negroes to overthrow the white race of the United States." Elijah advised he met him through Abdul Muhammad. Takahashi, with Abdul, would sometimes appear that he was soliciting information or trying to recruit from the Nation of Islam. Elijah Muhammad (referred to by the FBI by his alias "Bogans" he was arrested under) recalled the history in the FBI interview:

> According to Bogans, sometime in 1932 or 1933, Satohata Takahashi approached him at the headquarters of the Detroit Temple which was then located at 3408 Hastings Street, and attempted to obtain information as to the philosophy of the Islam group, as well as information concerning the

number of members and the purpose of the organization. He further stated that he again saw Takahashi at the home of a woman, name unknown, who at the time resided in North Detroit, when he went to this woman's home to pick up brother Abdul Mohammed, now deceased. Takahashi at this time again questioned him as to the membership of the organization, as well as the purpose of the group, Bogans stated that he advised Takahashi that he was teaching Islam, and that Takahashi had expressed approval of his teachings. Bogans denied ever having entered into any activities in conjunction with Takahashi, and stated that the above mentioned meeting was the last time he had seen this individual.[158]

In response, Mr. Fard called a meeting of the Believers to discuss Elijah's news about his two Ministers (specifically Abdul):

"Then," he [Fard] said, "well, then, you come over with me." And so we went to his secretary's house where the woman invited him for dinner. So I went with him and there he gathered in the house most of the followers he could get, so as to listen to what I am going to say and to what he will say to me. So he took me and put me in the center of the followers and questioned me. And after he questioned me he said, "Now, if you would teach, tell me what would you do?" I told him I would teach and carry out what you tell me, not what I think is best; and then he gave me a blow like a pet, you know.[159]

Elijah Debuts as NOI Minister at the Temple

Mr. Fard commended Elijah on his honesty and entrusted him to become an Investigator of sorts on the troubled minister. Elijah:

And then he [Fard] said to me, "You sit down now here beside me"; and then he began to address the people in the house, saying, "This is the man that I want. That is just what we need; we need someone who teaches what I tell him." Then he said, "Elijah is the only one who'd do that. From now on you go to the temple and teach what I tell you. And you have to go down there and take notes of all what Abdul says." So I went and took notes. He said, "I don't like what they say." I was going there and pencil out what I could get and I give it to him, though he knows himself all what Abdul was saying anyway.[160]

As part of his preparation, Mr. Fard supervised a nervous Elijah Muhammad's main address to the Detroit Temple:

Then he took me to the temple and told me to prepare a subject. He said, "I want you to preach here before me." So I stood there near the speaker's stand and I began to teach the people of him "that we have looked and hoped for to come such man and now we have him and should we all submit ourselves to him and do as what he says and then we will be successful." So he sits there and I talk for an hour or more to the people. I was a little kind of bashful at that time because he was sitting there and my mind is mostly on him. He told me every now and then, "Don't think of me; go ahead, go ahead." After that I got a chance of talking to the people in his absence, where O could go very strong because I did not see him sitting behind me. So I told them that he is the one to whom the Book referred to as the one who is after the lost Brothers or the lost sheep of the Bible and that is well known among the people as he himself said that he was. And I said that there is not any wisdom in the world that you can compare with the wisdom that he gave us. He told me that the time will come when we govern the world and that he will send to us a messenger to give to every one of us a little book in which are all records of that person. This little book will help you to go to your people there; they will admit you as soon as you show them that little book. This will take place at the proper time, i.e., at the end of this devil.[161]

Emanuel recalls watching his Father speak at the Temple:

Bro. Emanuel Muhammad: "The first thing that impressed me about my Father's mission was hearing him teach in the Mosque, in Detroit, at 3408 Hastings Street. My father's message was so fearless and forceful! The great number of people who came to hear him teach was also very impressive. There was thunderous applause in acceptance of what they heard.[162]

The wholehearted dedication of Elijah propelled him to the top of the NOI ministry class. To become a Minister, you had to be voted in by the other Ministers. On this particular day, they were looking to vote for the Supreme Minister of the Nation of Islam who would serve directly under Master Fard. Though opposed by moderates in the hierarchy, Elijah had become Fard's most trusted lieutenant. This sparked jealousy among others officials who held certain ranks in the movement. At least one or two current ministers didn't feel Elijah was the most qualified to represent the movement at their level. So when it came to electing ministers from amongst themselves the body never elected Elijah because he wasn't as eloquent as other leaders in the organization. In fact, they voted in his nemesis Abdul Muhammad. But W. D. Fard saw something his ministers didn't. In an unprecedented move, Fard rewarded Elijah's faith by bestowing upon him the high honor of Supreme Minister and renaming him "Muhammad." This He did publicly of August 1932 in the Temple classroom at 283 E. Hancock in front of the other rival Ministers in attendance so there wouldn't be any misunderstanding about his choice:

The Savior, Master Fard Muhammad used a system of permitting the student ministers to select their own minister from among themselves. They would always select the most articulate, smooth-talking one. However, one day the Savior decided to select his own. "I've let you select yours for a while," he told the student ministers. "Now I'll select mine."

"Hey, you over there, Karriem!" Master Fard called out to the humble little man seated in the corner rear of the classroom. "Who me?" The Messenger asked humbly, "Yes, you Elijah Karriem," The Savior commanded. "Come up here with me." The humble little man went to the front of the class and stood beside his master. The Savior put his right arm around the little man's shoulder and said, "From now on this is My Minister." The Savior gave Elijah the name of Muhammad, His name. Muhammad was given the title of "Supreme Minister."[163]

Elijah's son Nathaniel Muhammad gives background information and specifics about this monumental event:

> Master Fard Muhammad had a Ministers' class. He had about 13 of them, yeah, about 13 my daddy said in the Ministers' class. But He cut it down to about 6 because the rest of them didn't seem like they were interested in it because they didn't come out enough. So I remember some of them, it was Abdul Mohammed, Rozier, Sharrieff, my uncle Willie, and my Dad. I remember them four. The other ones I don't remember.
>
> So Master Fard Muhammad called a special meeting for them to vote and elect a leader. But they didn't know what they were coming for, all they know is that he called a meeting. That he had all the Ministers that was still with the class, in his class, about 6 or 7 of them sitting on the rostrum on the platform with him. And he asked the followers to vote for their leader. So they all voted, and when the votes were all in, Abdul had the most votes. Really we called him "Muck Mud" then, they didn't call it "Mohammed." Abdul "Muck Mud", his name was "Mohammed" but Master Fard Muhammad referred to us as "Muck Mud." He never would call us Mohammed, he always called us Muck Mud. So Abdul Muck Mud, (I'm going to call him Mohammed now because that was his name really). Abdul Mohammed had more votes than daddy. And so after they voted and counted the votes, and it was shown that Abdul had the most votes, Master Fard Muhammad told the congregation, he said, "I don't agree with your choice." He turned around and what he said, he pointed at daddy and he said, "Karriem is my choice." That's what he used to call him, "Karriem." He'd call daddy Karriem. He said, "Karriem is my choice."[164]

Master Fard Muhammad proposed that Elijah make his brother Kallatt the Supreme Captain of the Nation of Islam. Elijah concurred:

> So he named daddy the Supreme Minister. And later on daddy wanted a captain, and so Master Fard Muhammad said, "Well, why don't you make your brother your Captain, Kallatt?" That's how he became the Supreme Captain. They didn't have Captains or Ministers until Master Fard Muhammad picked them. Master Fard Muhammad did all the teaching himself. [165]

The Supreme Minister

In another interview Nathaniel gives his belief why Master Fard Muhammad named his father Supreme Minister of the Nation of Islam because he felt he was best qualified to fill the shoes of Mr. Fard in his absence. Nathaniel elaborates:

> But he took daddy under his wings and he would come to our house and have dinner every day. And he would teach my daddy after dinner, Lessons and what have you. So he became his number one student. So when Master Fard Muhammad was given 24 hours by the Michigan authorities to get out Michigan (they gave him 24 hours to get out of the state of Michigan). So about a week or two before that happened, he must have knew or had an idea that they was going to get rid of him, because he had converted about 25,000 people at that time. And he had named over 11,028. I had found this document in my daddy's case (after he passed) where he had named 11,028 people between Detroit and Chicago. And he had all the ministers that he had trained to come up on the rostrum because he asked all the [ministers] and captains to elect a leader. So they did, they elected a leader, but they elected a brother named Abdul Muhammad, at that time he called him Abdul "Muk-Mud" but it was Abdul Muhammad. So Master Fard Muhammad told the congregation that he didn't agree with them. He said, "I'm going to pick my choice." So he started explaining and turned around (and they used to call my daddy "Karriem" at that time), yeah he turned around and pointed, "I pick Karriem as my choice." "So he is the Supreme Minister of the Nation of Islam." That's when he started becoming the Leader of the Nation of Islam...[166]
>
> Because dad was a very bright student anyway because I mean he was deep as a person. He learned how to read the Bible and he knew the Bible as a young man better than the average person. And actually Master Fard Muhammad really chose him to be the Leader because he knew the Bible better than any of his other students. And the Bible with the Quran—see, Master Fard Muhammad didn't know the Bible but he knew the Quran. So I think that's why he chose daddy because daddy had—well he chose him because that's who he was looking for really. Because he said, "If it wasn't for Elijah, I would have never came." So he knew who he was looking for all the time. So under those circumstances he chose daddy for his knowledge of the Bible, and for his ability to be strong enough for these people.[167]

Messenger Elijah Muhammad's brother, John Muhammad, gives his first-hand account as a witness to the reasons why Master Fard Muhammad elected his brother over the others:

> When the Messenger went to the house meeting and there He found Master Fard there. He knew the meeting was going to be there and He [MFM] was looking for someone to help Him. The Messenger says, "Here I am, take me!" And He [MFM] took Him [Elijah] to be His Minister, because this man

[Abdul] that was representing Master Fard to my father, He turned against Master Fard and so he [MFM] let him go.

Then He [MFM] takes up Elijah. Excuse me for saying it flat like that. He takes up Elijah and He began to teach Him and He taught him for a while in [unintelligible]. While this man [Abdul] didn't know what was going on. And but He [MFM] took Abdul out and He [MFM] put Elijah there, my brother Elijah Muhammad, the Messenger. He put Him there to the Temple and He carried it on until He passed.[168]

According to some early NOI pioneers, including Elijah's brother John Muhammad, Min. Abdul Mohammed would eventually openly confront Mr. W.D. Fard about the leadership position, even suggesting he stand down and make him the new leader of the Nation of Islam. Imam W.D. Mohammed years later recalls a similar story he was told by his father Elijah about a man who confronted Mr. Fard, and based on the incident and the description of the person, it might have been Abdul Mohammed in whom he was referring:

My Father told me once, he said (it was not only me, I just happened to be there in the house, there were others there, other members of the family, maybe even non-members)...it was on a Sunday. And (at the dining table), he said, "There was once a man who interrupted Mr. Fard (The Saviour of the Nation of Islam), interrupted him while he was speaking." He said, "He was a big tall heavy Black man." He said, "He was very black-skinned and had big black lips, purple black lips, with bright red in the middle, in the center of his lips." He said, "He stood up and had red eyes, (I got to give you the description that they gave me), and he stood up and he said, "You say that God is a Black Man, but you are not Black, I'm Black. How come you don't let a Black Man be the Leader?" And my father said Mr. Fard (and the FOI was there, they started out with the FOI, the FOI started when the movement started. The FOI. Everything started together. The first day they started preaching, they had FOI, MGT, they had all that. Guards and everything. My father said, "Mr. Fard did not even respond to him." I'm saying Mr. Fard. My father didn't say "Mr. Fard", he said "Our Saviour". Mr. Fard did not respond to this big black man. And he refused to let the guards throw him out[169]

After appointing Elijah Muhammad his Supreme Minister, John Muhammad recalls the protective way Master Fard taught his brother Elijah in the strictest privacy away from the others:

Night and Day Master Fard Muhammad was with him (Messenger). But the teachings He (MFM) gave to Messenger Elijah Muhammad, nobody was sitting around. He (MFM) wouldn't let them. Master Fard wouldn't let people sit around Him when He was teaching. The same that me and you sitting here talking, but He (MFM) wouldn't let nobody come along and interrupt the conversation.[170]

Elijah Muhammad himself would speak to the logic of his teacher Master Fard making him the Supreme Minister (Leader) of the Nation of Islam:

> No, but Allah has come to us Himself, to each us out of His mouth in the person of our Saviour FARD MOHAMMED; whom we have seen with our eyes and heard with our ears, and our hands have handled Him lest we have excuses and say He was not real. This blessed and only friend of we who were lost, called me into His ministry in August 1932. Not for the works that I done, nor for the education, for I had neither. But for His own cause, that I should hear the world of His mouth and go and teach others of His Majesty, and wonders that He is about to work in the wilderness of North America where we now live.
>
> He Himself, knowing the times and seasons of all things put upon me a great work to accomplish, but not without a great reward at the end; that is if I keep His Law and Commandments and obey without priding myself against Him who sent me. Now this did He charge me with, to go and make many ministers and send them in all of the cities and teach Islam as He has given it to me. Adding nothing to it, nor even taking a atom from it, lest we dilute His Holy word and be found guilty of falsifying the truth on His return.[171]

The Messenger's promotion met with great resistance from his opponents. Shortly afterwards Abdul gathered some henchmen and went to pay Elijah a visit at his home. With Elijah's family looking on, an incensed Abdul started to shout at the Messenger in the family kitchen. Nathaniel recalls his Father staring quietly at Abdul. Irate about Elijah's non-response, Abdul slammed a silver dollar on the kitchen table. Pointing at the stars on the coin Abdul shouted, "You see this star? Well, that's me! You are nothing!" Elijah's son Nathaniel recalls how the foes intended to harm Elijah, except their plans were foiled by Master Fard who happened to see Abdul and company enter Elijah's house. Knowing they possessed guns with intent on harming his best friend, Fard summoned his Elijah's brothers. Min. Nathaniel explains:

> Abdul showed up in our kitchen, and I was standing in the kitchen with Daddy. All of us was in the kitchen with Daddy. See we had a kitchen, a front room, a bathroom and 3 bedrooms, and Master Fard Muhammad had rented the house for us. It wasn't a house, it was an apartment, 859 Yeager Street was the address. We lived over the Butlers' house on the 2nd floor. When they had guests they would sit around the table in the kitchen and eat and talk. And when they had to take care of business they would go to the front room. [172]

Because about three brothers (I remember because I told daddy about it and he was surprised that I remembered it because it happened in our kitchen on Yeager street in Detroit) they came up to the house. And Abdul was one of them (who they chose to be the minister), he was with them and brought them up to confront daddy. And Master Fard Muhammad happened to see them when they came in and he went and got daddy's brother (Wali Muhammad), and got his brother to go upstairs and tell Elijah (he called him Karriem) and tell Karriem to come out there because "they got a rock in their pocket to throw at him." Meaning they had a gun to shoot him. And I was right in the kitchen when all this happened.[173]

Abdul ultimately left the Nation of Islam and went back to his Moorish Science roots creating his own faction loyal to the American Flag that eventually faded away. Later he'd join with Satokata Takahashi, a Japanese National, who took charge of an American association called "The Development of Our Own."

Master Fard tries to give Elijah the name Abdul

As Fard appointed Elijah Muhammad as his new Supreme Minister, he also advised him to take on a new name. Initially he proposed that he take on the name "Abdul Muhammad." Elijah Muhammad advised that the last name resonated with him, but not the first name. Thus he became "Elijah Muhammad". He recalls the conversation with Fard on the subject:

Now he, (W.D. Fard) names me first Karriem. And later on he changed my name to Muhammad. He told me he wanted me to have a 'bigger' name. He referred to a more honorable name as a 'bigger' name. And he wanted me to take Abdul Muhammad. He wouldn't force it on me because in those days I was too dumb to know what Abdul meant. I rejected Abdul and kept on with Elijah. I didn't reject Muhammad because I liked that name. But at that time, I didn't know the meanings of these names. That was when I was first being taught. I didn't understand the meanings of these names. After I learned the meaning of Abdul, I wish I had taken it and Muhammad. Karriem has a lesser meaning than Muhammad. Muhammad has the highest honor of any of them." [174]

The University of Islam

As the Nation of Islam under grew in numbers and structure. In addition to establishing "Temples of Islam," Fard established "Universities of Islam" which was a combined elementary and secondary school dedicated to "higher mathematics," astronomy, and the "ending of the spook civilization." The school was primarily for Muslim children but it also had adult classes that taught, among other things, reading and mathematics, to help the poor Negroes quit being duped and deceived by the "tricknology" of "the blue-eyed devil white man."

> The rapid increase in membership made necessary the development of a formal organization. Subsidiary organizations had been established as the need for them arose. Chief of these was the University of Islam, to which the children of Muslim families were sent rather than to public schools. Here they were taught the "knowledge of our own," rather than the "civilization of the Caucasian devils." Courses were given in "higher mathematics," astronomy, and the "general knowledge and ending of the spook civilization."[175]

Elijah's Brothers receive Posts. Kallatt (Supreme Captain), Wali (Asst. Minister), Johnnie (Bookkeeper), John (Asst. Principal)

With Elijah as Supreme Minister, his brothers were also promoted to different positions in the Nation of Islam. Kallatt was now Supreme Captain, Wali Jr. was the Minister in Temple #1, Johnnie was in charge of bookkeeping, and his younger brother John served as an assistant Minister in the Temple. John Muhammad recalls:

> While we were there, Master Fard Muhammad said to me, "Muhammad Sharrief, you go to the Temple and talk until Karriem comes. (you know Messenger Elijah Muhammad was once called, "Karriem")? You have the people to give the money that they are going to give for the upkeep of the Temple and you help him out in writing receipts." We didn't like, so much, at that time, to pass a bucket or pass a hat. He, (Master Fard Muhammad) said that looked too much like the Christian church! Do you understand me?
> I went to The Temple. I wanted to stay there are hear what He was going to say. But I couldn't do that. I had to go and do what He said to do. I went and walked on the rostrum, for the first time. I DID AS HE TOLD ME! After that, He was pleased with it. And He told me to continue, while He was teaching Messenger Elijah Muhammad. (The Messenger wasn't present every time the meeting was held. He would miss sometimes. Sometimes it would be forty days or even two months before he would come to The Temple). He was with Master Fard.[176]

John became a teacher (and later promoted to acting Principal) along with Ben Sabakhan, the Secretary of the Nation of Islam (along with Ugan Ali) of the newly founded University of Islam:

> A Brother by the name of Ben Sabakhan and I worked. We worked and did all we could to keep the people together. It was quite a few people-five or six hundred people. We did the best that we could do and we got credit from Master Fard Muhammad and from The Messenger. As He would teach The Messenger.

He didn't teach me to be The Messenger! I was NOT sent to be The Messenger of God. He sent me to be a Teacher! I taught and I taught until (Temple) Number 2 was set up in Chicago. Now we have traveled that far and there is plenty more that I could tell you... [177]

He made me a teacher in the University of Islam, that He had set up in Detroit. I was the first teacher to have a class in the University of Islam and I was a poor boy, who didn't have any knowledge of myself, so I considered, you know? I took it up. I did what He said. He said, "You go and you teach the ones that don't know how to write their name. Who don't know anything about reading and arithmetic, mathematics." He said, "You go and you teach them." I said, "Yes sir." And I did it.

I went and I taught them until He told me, "You need another teacher." Until I became the Principal of The University of Islam, with thirteen (13) teachers under me. I didn't know enough to teach them about Islam. I had to learn, just like you. I taught in the school. I was there every day–seven days a week.

I had Sister and Brothers in my class that were unable to write their name– grown-up people! I taught them how to write their name and how to spell it. And they were so dear to me. They loved me and I loved them. We were in UNITY together. That day, He (Master Fard Muhammad) gave History.

No one Talked against their Teacher. They gave Great Honor to their Teacher. And I returned back to Master Fard and reported to Him every Monday night concerning what went on in the school. [178]

Late in 1932, Master Fard Muhammad gave me the Authority of Acting Principal of Temple No. 1, Michigan, University of Islam. I was Assistant Secretary and Secretary. At this time there was only one Temple of Islam in this Wilderness of North America for the so-called Negro.[179]

All Brothers receive last name "Muhammad"

Elijah and his brothers were all re-christened with the last name "Muhammad" to mark this new phase. Each brother was heavily involved in some aspect of the movement as things started to heat up in Detroit.

Some Negro Leaders Oppose the NOI

With the strong rise of the Muslims grew the interest of Negro leaders and whites who felt threatened by their movement. As many church leaders were now being questioned and losing parishioners to the largely attended Muslim meetings, it invited opposition towards the Nation of Islam:

Since the beginning of the movement in Detroit various kinds of persecutions had been directed against the group. Several persons who witnessed the movement in its earliest phase declared that enthusiasm among the Negro community for the emerging movement and its messenger Fard was the dominant phenomenon among thousands of Negroes in Detroit. They were coming to hear Fard speak, though they knew that they would have no chance of hearing him or getting in the temple because the people were crowded in that basement, around the windows, outside the basement, and in the adjacent streets, competing for places to hear the savior of the race. This enthusiasm and rapid growth and organization of the movement attracted to it the attention of the leaders of the Negro community, of the preachers in the churches, whites and Negroes, and of the police department.[180]

The teachings of W.D. Fard so upset church leaders, that they often caused disturbances during his lectures, only for the Muslim leader to put them in their place:

Many attacks were organized against W.D. Fard by the churchmen of Detroit because of his attacks against them and against their teachings. Some of them were coming to him directly, asking him, in front of his followers, baffling questions and demanding proofs about his prophecy—a situation under which he responded by merely reactional attack against them personally, avoiding answering their questions: "You think I do not understand what is going on in your mind; I can tell you just now what you think, what each individual here thinks and all what is going to happen in the future." Such questions were "arousing him deeply; our people are really dumb," as his disciple Elijah Mohammed commented on these attacking individuals and groups.[181]

So extremely cognizant of the tactics of these kinds of enemies, W.D. Fard often forewarned Elijah Muhammad of their plans. Elijah explains:

Sometimes Mr. W.D. Fard warns me from going to the temple and keeps me with him because he knows that there is somebody there in the temple coming to harm me. Sometimes he was telling me before I go to the temple the name and the exact description of the man who intends to harm me and even the description of the man who intends to harm me and even the seat on which he will sit, and when I go I find that person exactly the one Mr. Fard described and on the same seat and he came just to harm me.[182]

W.D. Fard often Visited Neighboring Canada

Elijah's eldest son Emanuel recalls how Mr. Fard would visit neighboring Canada, and how he dealt with the brutal winters (and people) of Detroit:

Concerning Master Fard, my personal concern, I will always give honor and respect for the love he had for his Messenger to us, the late Hon. Elijah Muhammad, in America, in our deepest depressed downtrodden Asiatic (African American) people during those Depression days. I will always honor, I will always respect Master Fard, until the last breath leave my body...
Master Fard suffered greatly for bringing us the teaching of our mother RHe suffered the cold weather. He used to come to our home after he'd

make a trip, he would tell my father that he was going to take a short trip, he would go into Canada. And when he'd return was in winter time. At that time we had a four burner coal stove, and Master Fard used to let the oven door down and stick his feet inside to warm and put his hand over the burners.[183]

W.D. Fard Attacked by Christian Negroes

In W.D. Fard's world, church leaders were referred to as "Ice Makers," implying that Christian Negro Leaders helped the white devils freeze the brains of the Black Man. Churches were referred to as "Ice Houses". It was at one of these Ice Houses that W.D. Fard inevitably had a physical confrontation in which he was struck by a churchgoer. Elijah's eldest son Emanuel, and his uncle (Elijah's brother) John Muhammad explains:

Emanuel Muhammad: He went to a church (if I'm wrong uncles correct me), he went to a church and the preacher was preaching concerning Jesus, and Master Fard got up and said that, "He was the long awaited Jesus whom they had been looking for the last 2000 years." Am I right? The Deacon they ushered him out and he fell and broke his tooth. Am I right?
Min. John Muhammad: He hit him.
Emanuel Muhammad: Thank you uncle, a correction. People say a whole lot of things, I'm glad you corrected it. Thank you. My uncle said they met him at the door and punched him in the mouth and broke all his teeth...
Min. John Muhammad: They were singing a song about Jesus being here and he opened...
Emanuel Muhammad: Come on uncle, you tell them. But before I leave here I'd like to put it in writing...
Min. John Muhammad: The way he got his teeth from his mouth, he was at the door, and the usher at the door, he knocked at the door for him to open the door (you know like the door was closed) he knocked at the door for the usher to open the door and when the usher opened the door, He said to him, "I am your Jesus, I am here." And when he said that, [John pounds his fist into his hand making a smacking sound], this big Black man hit him in the mouth, and knocked out his teeth. And he would not tell us who did it. Neither did he tell us where the church was at."
Emanuel Muhammad: You know why he didn't tell us? You know why he didn't tell the followers during that time? Because there wouldn't be no more preacher, no more church and no more followers! Did you hear what I said? No more preacher, no more church and no followers!!! We would have cleaned house back in those days! Now, the one that I learned replaced Master Fard's tooth used to be my old school teacher Sister Odessa Bey. Is that right?
Min. John Muhammad: Not Odessa. Ishmael. Ishmael and his wife.
Emanuel Muhammad: Thank you uncle. See, he knows. Like I said I was only 9 years old. A lot of things I got hearsay. And this uncle standing right here we used to work together in the field and he'd tell you some things that will bust your vessel about my father (laughs). I might tell some today, but that uncle was very, very close to Master Fard, he had to be! In order to be

the penman for Master Fard to write down the original names. He had to learn a lot from Master Fard that the other ones don't know. Well, I'm glad I had him in the field so he could give me some of that.[184]

W.D. Fard continued to receive threats in the face of violence. On at least one occasion his enemies went to the lengths of poisoning him. He'd ultimately tell Elijah he suffered much in order to show Elijah and the Believers what they'd have to endure to save their people:

Master Fard Muhammad had his stomach pumped in the thirties. He had to pay money. Somebody paid money. See my point? Let's get real about this. He allowed a negro to poison him, went to the hospital, checked himself in, had his stomach pumped, came back and told the Hon Elijah Muhammad who told the rest of us, "That if that had been one of you all, you wouldn't survive." Why did he even go through that? He was teaching his servant lessons. That's real huh? Now look, if God is going to make you Gods and Goddesses are you going to be any less human? You will be human then, just have whole lot of juice .."[185]

5 Trouble in Paradise Valley

VOODOO HOUSE. In this structure, Robert Harris, Negro fanatic, slew James J. Smith, another Negro, to appease the wrath of "The Gods of Islam." He placed the body on the rude cult altar in his home.

Robert Harris aka Robert Karriem, started his own "Order of Islam" and was arrested on November 20, 1932, for a sacrificial killing of one of his sympathizers. At the time of the killing, he was not active or affiliated with the Nation of Islam under Mr. W.D. Fard. Family and friends described Robert Karriem as having a medical history of mental illness. He was ruled insane.

A Mentally Ill Member Arrested for Homicide

In the midst of heavy criticism against the Temple of Islam, occurred the most notorious tragedy that faced the Nation of Islam. On a Sunday, November 20, 1932, a mentally deranged student named Robert Harris,

[96]

who was given the name Robert Karriem, murdered one his sympathizers during a "human sacrifice" ceremony in his house. Instead of depicting him as a deranged follower no longer active in the movement, the news depicted him as a Leader of the movement (or at least over his own group).

The unfortunate tragedy propelled the Nation of Islam and its leaders into the media's spotlight to be sensationally described as "a Voodoo cult." The catastrophic story was quickly picked up by the news agencies, mainly by the Detroit News newspaper which seemed to have fair reporting, versus the Detroit Free Press newspaper that embraced a tabloid approach:

A self-crowned "king" of a weird religious cult was being held Sunday night by police, following his cool admission late in the afternoon that he had selected and brutally murdered a sacrificial victim on an improvised altar in his home at 1429 Dubois St. Robert Harris, forty-four-year-old Negro, is the "king" of the strange religious order, which he claims boasts a membership of 100 Detroit Negroes...

James J. Smith, 40, also a Negro, was Harris' sacrificial victim. The "king" admitted crushing Smith's skull with the rear axle of an automobile first, and then stabbing him through the heart. Smith's body was discovered on the makeshift altar late Sunday afternoon by neighbors, who notified police and name Harris as the likely killer. The "king" and his wife, Bertha, 25, were arrested at 2729 Clinton St. Both went without protest to Police Headquarters. There Harris, a large Negro, with no sign of misgiving, admitted the killing while his wife looked on. She corroborated his statements. Then, straightaway, he unfolded his story of a mystic cult, as savage and barbarous as a voodoo [UNREADABLE]. With pride, he reminded the officers that he was "king" of the "Order of Islam."

"The ninth hour of the twentieth day had come Sunday," Harris told police. "It was predestined 1,500 years ago that at that hour I must make a human sacrifice to my gods. It must not be a member of the Order of Islam, but some stranger - the first person I met after leaving my home." Smith was that person, Harris recounted. The confessed murderer told of inviting Smith into his home at 9 a.m. and of crushing his skull with the axle, "just to quiet him." The cult then required, he said, that the body be placed on the altar and a sacrificial knife stabbed through the heart. An eight-inch knife was found thrust to the hilt in Smith's heart. A cheap magazine was discovered in Harris' home opened to a story of mysticism of the desert. A clause "the unbeliever must be stabbed through the heart" was underlined. Harris was peaceable and answered questions readily until police attempted to lock him up. Then he lunged at Assistant Prosecutor John T. Meier, and struggled with officers who restrained him. Four policemen were required to subdue him. [186]

Confesses to the Crime

In the police precinct, an animated Robert Harris graphically described the afternoon of the gruesome murder. The Detroit Free Press continued:

The forty-four-year-old "King of Islam" paced up and down gesticulating wildly as he told detectives of the zeal which goaded him into murdering Smith before the eyes of his wife and two small children. Sometimes in a low voice, and again, wild-eyed and shaking with the passion of fanaticism, he related the details of the slaying. Smith, he said, was a member of his cult and lived with him and his family at 1429 Dubois St., where the murder occurred. "I told him that I had been commanded to kill somebody by the "Gods of Islam," Harris told detectives. "At first he didn't want to be killed, but when I showed him that he would be the saviour of the world and go to heaven right away, he said all right." "The day had come, Sunday. He had to be killed just at noon, so I set a clock in front of the altar where everybody could see it." Witnesses to the murder, he said, were his wife, their two children, Hasabas Karrian, 12 years old, and Ruby, 9, and 12 "disciples." The altar was a packing crate in a second-story room. "Smith was sitting in a chair in front of the altar. My wife was time-keeper. As the hour drew near, I said, 'Smith, do you still want to be killed?' because the command ordered me not to kill anybody who didn't want to be killed. Smith nodded his head. "When it was just 12 o'clock, I said, 'Smith, get up and stand on the altar.' I grabbed my dirk (an eight-inch case knife) and stabbed him like this." At this juncture in his narrative, Harris picked up a roll of paper and lunged at Lieut. Paul Wencel, whom he had been using as a substitute for Smith in the graphic description of the slaying. "Smith fell off the altar and started to groan and tried to get up. I hit him over the head with my 'rod of iron' (a section of the rear axle of an automobile). In the minutes before the slaying Harris' children sobbed and begged him, "please, Daddy, don't do it, don't do it!" he said. Their presence was necessary for a successful sacrifice, he said, and he would not let them run from the room, as they tried to do. Harris became enraged when detectives attempted to question him regarding the rituals and practices of his cult. He refused to answer, saying only that he was "going to kill lots of Christians."[187]

NOI Lessons Found at the Scene

Police claimed to have found NOI literature at the scene that they felt was partly responsible for the thought behind the murder ritual and the actions of its followers, as reported by Detroit News:

Harris told Meier that his cult was called the Order of Islam and that he had almost 100 followers among Detroit Negroes. Following the slaying, Harris and his wife went to the home of friends at 2729 Clinton Street, where they were later arrested. The body was discovered shortly after noon Sunday by a man whose name is not known to the police.

A printed sentence, "The unbeliever must be stabbed through the heart," was found pasted on a sheet of paper. It apparently had been cut from a book or magazine. Harris made his confession readily but he made a violent struggle when the police attempted to fingerprint him. The prints were obtained after four detectives overpowered him. Mrs. Harris substantiated her husband's statements. Several other persons were questioned and released. Several of these, police say, were members of the Order of Islam.[188]

Muslim Family Members Verify his Mental Illness

The Press reported that Robert Harris shared his desire to kill white officials, including Detroit's mayor. This information however was dismissed by the Police and Robert Karriem's relatives from the Temple who identified him as one with a mental disorder. The Detroit Free Press:

Assertions by Robert Harris, member of the Order of Islam, a Negro religious organization, who has confessed he killed another Negro in a "sacrificial rite," that he had planned to slay Mayor Murphy, two judges and a public welfare worker, were discounted today by Inspector John I. Navarre, head of the homicide squad, as "the ravings of an insane man." Navarre said that while Harris had mentioned Mayor Murphy, Judge Edward J. Jeffries and Judge Arthur E. Gordon by name, it was ascertained that Harris had never seen any of his "intended victims." Harris amplified his list today, Navarre said, by adding the names of King George and J.P. Morgan. Navarre questioned Edward Harris, a brother, of 2729 Clinton street. Edward Harris said he was also a member of the Order of Islam, which has a temple at 3408 Hastings Street. He told Navarre that he and other members of the order regarded Robert as being demented and paid no attention to him. He said Robert had no standing in the order and was not a leader.[189]

Attempts to Link Prior Incidents to Muslims

The cops established precedence in a case the prior year that involved a Muslim who allegedly threatened and tried to break into the Mayor's apartment. Such was a case of one Ahmed Abdullah. The Detroit Free Press:

..detectives Monday night turned to the year-old case of Ahfed Abdullah. Ahfed Abdullah, a Negro known as James Moaning until he adopted the more picturesque name, was arrested a year ago while trying to gain access to Mayor Frank Murphy's apartment. Plainly psychopathic, the man told a disordered story in which it appeared that he had a grievance against the government of Haiti. It appeared that he in some way connected Detroit's City Government with that of Haiti.

Ahfed Abdullah, alias Moaning, was adjudged insane after his invasion of the apartment building in which the Mayor then lived, an invasion which police believed was made for the purpose of attack, and was committed to Eloise. It was pointed out Monday night that Haiti, to which he referred so often in his ramblings, is noted for the Voodoo beliefs extant among its lower classes.[190]

The detectives quickly linked the two cases as a pattern of members of the relatively new Muslim movement threatening violence against the government:

The police said Harris would be given a psychopathic examination after his arraignment on a charge of killing Smith. Lieut. John Hoffman, of the special investigation squad, said Harris is a member of the same cult to which Henry James Moaning, also known as "Ahmed Ullah" and "Ahm Abdullah," Mississippi-born Negro, belonged. Moaning was arrested last November, after he had sent a number of threatening letters to Mayor Murphy. Moaning was adjudged insane in Probate Court and sent to Eloise. Detroit Negroes, Lieut. Hoffman said, were being organized as Mohammedans by a man who told them they were of Turkish origin and charged them fees for their "Turkish" names.[191]

Like Ahfed Abdullah, Harris apparently harbored some imaginary grievance against the City Government. With an insane light in his eyes, he admitted that he had planned to seek out and kill Judges Edward J. Jeffries and Arthur E. Gordon for the purpose of propitiating jungle gods. His list of prospective victims also included Gladys Smith, 21 years old, 5178 Lawton Ave, a welfare worker attached to the Elmwood Station. She cut him from the welfare list when she learned he had other forms of support, he explained.[192]

Muslim Family Members Reveal Robert Karriem's Mental History

One key thing the news noted was how people like Harris, who recently migrated to Detroit from Tennessee in the fall of 1929,[193] had faced major economic problems that made for desperate measures that caused insanity. So much so, his wife, Bertha Karriem, feared for her life: "Harris told officers that when he first visioned the "command" he talked the matter over with Bertha, and suggested Smith as a victim. When she refused to be a party to the murder, Harris said he pulled her from the bed and beat her, saying he would kill her instead, unless she acquiesced. He also professed himself willing to kill his children if they did not adhere to his commands. "I had to kill somebody," he said. "Anyhow, but somebody had to be killed. I could not forsake my god."[194]

Bertha described her family's status with the welfare agency as a contributor to her husband's demise. Ms. Gladys Smith, the welfare worker assigned to their case, verified the same. The Detroit News:

Mrs. Bertha Harris, wife of the slayer, who was present last Sunday when he killed James J. Smith in the Harris home at 1428 Dubois street, told the detectives she had lived in fear of her husband for some time, and that he often threatened to kill her and the two children, Ruby, 9 years old, and Araby 12. "He made me watch the clock when he struck Smith with an automobile axle," Mrs. Harris stated. "The children were asleep at the time. He told me if I didn't do as I was ordered he would kill me also."[195]

Navarre said Robert Harris' wife, also held on a murder charge as a result of the killing of James J. Smith Sunday in the Harris home at 1429 Dubois Street, told him she believed her husband to be insane and had been afraid of him for some time. It was possible, Navarre said, that Harris may have had evil intentions toward a welfare worker. Miss Gladys Smith, 5718 Lawton Avenue, who first investigated Harris' application for aid from the welfare department, said she had found him a "meek, humble" client. Harris did not mention Miss Smith's name, Navarre said. Harris' wife told Navarre that several times Harris threatened to cut off her head and also to kill their two children, Ruby, 9 years old, and Araby, 12. Harris asked for aid when he was evicted from a house on Clinton Street in 1930, Miss Smith said. He and his wife then moved into a small house on Monroe Avenue. "I talked with him," Miss Smith said, "and sent the family to live with another welfare client on Mullett Street, where they stayed all winter, the welfare department paying the rent. We gave them two meal tickets a day and later they received grocery, clothing and coal orders. Harris impressed me as being a carefree, stolid, humble and meek man who seemed to be satisfied with anything that was done for him and his family.

"Later, in 1931, however, I heard that other welfare workers were having trouble with Harris. He had become talkative and argumentative. He was 'demanding' that things be done for him. Two workers, Mrs. Adele Ivey and Miss Halen Heddins, had taken the case and they found Harris not easy to get along with." Later the department found that Harris had not qualified as a resident and was not entitled to aid. It seems he had been living with a brother in Inkster, and he was not a legal resident. When it was found he belonged to the South, transportation was provided for him, and when he refused to accept it, he was cut off the welfare last July. "Harris never threatened me. He seemed a stupid fellow, but the other workers said he changed suddenly." [196]

The brother of Robert Harris, Edward Karriem, who spoke on behalf of himself and the Temple, seemed to concur:

Navarre questioned Edward Harris, a brother, of 2729 Clinton Street. Edward Harris said he was also a member of the Order of Islam, which has a temple at 3408 Hastings Street. He told Navarre that he and other members of the order regarded Robert as being demented and paid no attention to him. He said Robert had no standing in the order and was not a leader.[197] "Worries over money caused my brother to lose his mind," said Edward Harris, also a member of the order. "He has been acting queerly in the last few weeks, preaching a lot and stopping people on the streets. Nobody paid much attention to him."[198]

Detectives Assigned to Investigate
Detective Oscar Berry of the Detroit Police Department was assigned the case. Initially Robert Harris resisted, only later conceding to questioning:

Earlier in the day, he had resisted officers who had attempted to lead him to his cell. Detective Berry talked to him, and after Harris had been convinced that Berry was going to join his cult, he consented to be questioned. "Queen" Bertha was ordered held as a police witness. The children Monday were cared for by neighbors. [199]

Homicide detectives decided to question and fingerprint Harris to see if he was involved in the ax murder family massacre that took place in 1929 of white cult leader Benny Evangelista and his family. Robert Harris abruptly fought against the effort. The Detroit Free Press:

[101]

Evangelista, likewise, headed a religious order, being hailed as its "divine prophet." A short ax and a double-edged knife were believed by police to have been the implements which dealt death to Evangelista, his wife, Santina, and their children, Angeline 7, Margaret 5, Jean 4, and Maria 14 months.

They were hacked to death in their home at 3587 St. Aubin Ave., just a few blocks from the scene of Smith's murder. Evangelista's head was severed from his body and the necks of the other victims had been hacked severely, apparently with an ax. Although more than 500 persons were questioned by authorities in an attempt to solve the massacre, police were unable to make any progress in their investigation. The only clue was a palm print left on a doorknob in the home. Police will compare this print with one taken from Harris' hand.[200]

Harris fought desperately with police when they tried to take a fingerprint of his left hand, which was gloved. He refused to remove the glove until forced to do so. "My right hand belongs to everyone," Harris told the detectives, "but my left hand belongs to the King."[201]

A palm print of Harris is to be inspected by fingerprint experts of the Detroit Police department in an effort to identify him as the ax killer of Benny Evangelista, his wife and four children here July 3, 1929. Evangelista, also leader of a fantastic religious cult, was believed by police to have been the victim of the head of some rival order.

Detective Sergt. Michael McGowan, who took part in the Evangelista investigation, questioned Harris for half an hour early Monday morning. Harris told him, he said, that he came to Detroit from Tennessee in the fall of 1929, which is after the Evangelista murders. He denied knowing anything about the family massacre.

Detective Lieut. Paul H. Wencel, who also took part in the search for the slayer of the Evangelista family, visited headquarters Sunday afternoon and conferred with Homicide Squad detectives.

Lieut. Wencel said that the fingerprint comparison would be made Monday but that its results would not be announced for a day or two, once police had been able to check Harris' history.[202]

The fingerprints came back negative which declared Harris of not having any connection with the Evangelista family massacre:

Efforts of detectives to link Harris with the slaying of Benny Evangelista, his wife and four children, in what police believe to have been a similar murder here in 1929, arrived at naught Monday when the voodoo king's fingerprints were found to vary from those left on a door knob in the Evangelista home at 8587 St. Aubin Ave. Police are seeking the 12 "disciples" who witnessed the sacrificial murder. From them they hope to learn the extent to which the rites of Voodoo have laid hold upon the imaginations of inhabitants of the quarter in which Harris had his "temple."[203]

Cult Leader Kills Man as 'Sacrifice'

(caption from the Detroit Free Press Newspaper reads: "DETECTIVES EXAMINING THE KNIFE, Robert Harris, leader of a weird cult, confessed he killed James J. Smith on a crudely improvised atar at 1429 Dubois street as a human "sacrifice," Detectives Oscar Berry and Charles W. Snyder are shown examining the knife Morris used and the strange Bible of the cult."

Detectives Seek Out NOI Officials

The man-hunt had now officially begun for 'the disciples' and a launched investigation into the Nation of Islam. The initial findings of the police apparently became confused with Noble Drew Ali's movement, the Moorish Science Temple of America and its pending court cases. The Detroit Free Press:

Detectives Monday night were running down a story that some organization in Detroit sells the privilege of using Mohammedan names to ignorant and superstitious Negroes. Officers also were trying to establish the suspected fact that Harris, as well as being "King of Islam," served his cult under the more prosaic title of secretary.

Harris admitted that he slew Smith as part of the rites of his weird religion, while his..."disciples", looked on...Detective Sergt. Oscar Berry of the Homicide Squad, checked his assertion, announced that all the evidence indicated its truth, and speculated upon the hold which the jungle cult may have upon certain ignorant elements of Detroit's Negro population. Police court records in Middle Western industrial centers have revealed the amazing growth in recent years of

Negro cults with strange Islamic symbols and titles. Complaints against them have been so petty, however, that they have not been investigated for Voodoo, and it is generally believed that their Mohammedanism exists only in meaningless but impressive mixture of Allahs, Mohamets and other Mohammedan incantations. High priestesses and priests of Allah, clad in pseudo-Oriental costumes are frequent defendants in Police Court swindling cases. Preying on the superstitions and susceptibility of Negroes, they have robbed families of their savings. Their victims, however, have been gulled mostly through a belief in the high priest's ability to foretell the future, and the cases have not bore the marks of the race's fear of Voodoo. Harris explained that Harris was his slave name. Police believe that the name Karien was sold to him.[204]

The Police Visit the Temple

The Police decided to search Temple #1 in search of W.D. Fard. The Detroit News documented the visit where they spoke with Ugan Ali on what the Nation of Islam taught and if its doctrine influenced the murder: "Leader of Cult to be Quizzed: Police Seek To Learn if Teachings of Order Figured in 'Sacrificial Slaying."

Detectives of the homicide squad today were to question W.D. Fard, leader of the Order of Islam, Negro religious society, to determine whether teachings of the organization played a part in the killing by Robert Harris of another Negro in a "sacrificial rite." Harris, who confessed the slaying, was termed demented by his brother, Edward, 3729 Clinton Street, and by Ugan Ali, secretary of the society, when the brother and Ali were questioned Tuesday afternoon by Detective Sergt. Oscar Berry and Detective Charles W. Snyder. "The society cannot be blamed for anything he did," said Ali after the detectives had visited the Order of Islam Temple at 3406 [sic] Hastings Street, where they found the secretary, his wife, Lillian, and 25 men in the living quarters of a meeting hall seating 400.

"We teach a philosophy similar to the Golden Rule," added Ali, who declared that 9,000 Negroes belonged to the organization, which was established here three years ago and once held its meetings in the Bishop School. "Our fundamental purpose is to uplift our own people," Ali continued.

Members are taught not to eat certain foods, to employ their time usefully, and that by their efforts the world can be rid of evil by 1934, Ali said. Mohammedan names are given to both men and women and the wearing of a fez is permitted. "Harris had no standing in the order and was not regarded as a leader. Many people avoided him because of the wild things he sometimes said," Ali declared. Ali was brought to headquarters for questioning after the detectives had been reinforced by the crew of a police cruiser. Before the arrival of reinforcements Ali and his followers refused to permit Berry and Snyder to search the quarters without a warrant.[205]

In another report about the same incident, The Detroit Free Press took creative license to refer to the Nation of Islam in sensational terms such as "Voodism" in describing the raid on the Temple where Ugan Ali was arrested:

'God of Asia Nation' Seized as Sequel to Altar Slaying Lodge Rooms Shown as Centers of Cult- Detectives investigating to learn the scope of Voodooism among ignorant and superstitious Detroit Negroes spent Tuesday night running down the myriad leads uncovered earlier in the day when they raided a fantastic "temple" and arrested a Negro who styled himself "God of the Asiatic Nation."

Mainly they sought a man believed to be financially interested in the spread of forms of jungle fanaticism here. He is believed to have obtained money by selling to deleted members titles, privileges and the other claptrap of the sect. This weird religion, which includes certain aspects of both voodooism and Mohammedanism, is blamed by police for the "sacrificial" murder of James J. Smith...by Robert Harris, Negro, "King of Islam".[206]

The detectives were amazed at the numbers of Muslims and what was seemingly a new phenomenon taking place in Detroit for the most part undetected, with the strictest of privacy:

As Detectives Oscar Berry and Charles W. Snyder tracked down and investigated the ramifications of the cult's worship, they confessed themselves amazed at the number of Negroes apparently enmeshed by the religion. Meeting places which for many years had been thought to have been no more than fraternal lodges, were discovered Tuesday to be "temples" where susceptible individuals are incited to kill "devils" in the hope of attaining "heavenly forgiveness and reward."[207]

A condensation of statements taken from several confessed members of the cult revealed Tuesday that the penalty for divulging any of the cult's secrets to outsiders is death. The cult leaders first gained their hold on the imagination and gullibility of many Negroes by telling them that they were a "nation of Asiatics," and destined to rule the world if they would but follow the precepts laid down by the leader.[208]

For the first time, the media described the interim of the Temple for the general public (including the Black community):

A problem vital to the future welfare of Detroit's inherently law-abiding Negro element is presented by the uncovering of this large cult, police and persons interested in local social conditions said Tuesday. Through a cult member, whose name was withheld, Detectives Berry and Snyder gained admittance by using a secret password to a "temple" at 3408 Hastings St., above a clothing store. The temple itself is a room containing more than a hundred regulation theater seats. At the far end stands an altar, draped with a bright red flag, in the center of which is a crescent and star insignia. The walls are covered with many weird designs, which apparently are symbols. A crude wooden canopy tops the platform on which the altar is located.[209]

NOI Secretary Ugan Ali Arrested

According to the Detroit Free Press, Ugan Ali behaved like a religious fanatic. Subsequently he was arrested as police also confiscated his literature:

In an adjoining room about 50 Negroes were seated listening to the exhortations of their leader when the officers entered the place. The man, a short stocky Negro with rolling, bloodshot eyes, said his name was Ugan Alie, and that he was "God of the Asiatics". He parried the detectives' questions. Evidently a man of some education, he talked sometimes intelligently about the history of his race and again wildly, about the cult's religion. When Alie admitted that he had "taught" Harris, and said he was Harris' God, detectives arrested him for investigation. Harris in questioning earlier in the day had declared that he had murdered Smith under the orders of his God.

The rest of the occupants of the room were allowed to leave after they had been searched.

Record and ritual books found in the place were taken to headquarters for examination. Several sections were found which were interpreted as an indication of the sanguinary purposes of the religion's "teachings." One reads: "Every man of Islam must gain a victory from a devil. Four victories, and the son will attain his reward." Harris, after his arrest, had babbled at length about his "victory", and said that now "he would gain his reward."

Alie frequently became enraged when officers referred to the cult members as "colored people," saying they were Asiatics. Allie claimed a membership in his cult of 8,000 Detroit Negroes. He had been "teaching for three years," he said. The questions put to him he termed "tricknology". While officers were in the temple, the occupants were alternately silent and voluble. A new arrival of the cult was greeted by a chorus of some strange unintelligible password, before he took his seat. Immediately, they would return to silence.[210]

Police Psychiatrists Assess the NOI

Listed as undesirables, the Police partnered with psychiatrists to rule the entire religion and its adherents as unsound. White doctors affirmed that these Black Muslims were a scourge to American society:

Discussing the aspects and possible effects of this new fanaticism, Dr. David Clark, Receiving Hospital psychiatrist in charge of social welfare cases, said: "The whole business is an ominous menace to the social stability and welfare of Detroit's Negro population. It should be stamped out before it secures a grip on any more of a race that is first to suffer in times of depression." He said that such a religious zeal was not necessarily a form of insanity, but that its effects were often similar to those of insanity. "With such practices, you have a return to the primal instincts," he said. "And we all know that all too often human sacrifice was a basic part of the first forms of worship."[211]

The press used Robert Harris as a general example of the types of fanaticism suffered by Muslims. The press reported on "The King" as "he lapsed into trances" and exemplified irrational behavior:

Supporting detectives' theories that he has lost his sanity through the passion of his peculiar fanaticism, Harris, self-crowned "King of Islam," Wednesday alternated between weird mumblings and coma-like trances which lasted sometimes for more than 20 minutes. During his trances he would remain rigid and motionless with wild eyes staring unswerving at the ceiling of his cell. Efforts of police and physicians to arouse him were futile. Since his arrest Sunday, Harris has refused to eat, authorities revealed Wednesday. He has taken water, but not even the most tempting foods, specially prepared, appeal to him. He has maintained the strength which enabled him to battle four policemen who tried to take him to his cell after his arrest, turnkeys reported. Unless he breaks his self-imposed fast within a day or two an attempt will be made to feed him forcibly, detectives said.[212]

W.D. Fard Arrested

With an amplified sense of vigor, the Detroit Police heavily sought Mr. W. D. Fard which inevitably led to his arrest at the Traymore Hotel. The Detroit Free Press Newspaper ran a story on the details: "Farad was taken into custody Wednesday morning as he was leaving his room in a hotel at 1 W. Jefferson Ave. He did not resist the officers, smiling enigmatically when told he was under arrest." [213] The authorities were surprised at what they found in his hotel room:

A raid on the room of Wallace Farad, self-confessed leader of the group, in a hotel at 1 W. Jefferson Ave., Saturday, brought to light hundreds of communications from members of the cult. In every instance, the letters were written painstakingly on cheap note paper. All were written in almost unintelligible scrawls in lead pencil. The import of each was the same. The signer of each wanted his "slave name" changed to a Mohammedan one, and was willing to pay Farad for the service of crossing out the [UNREADABLE] signature and substituting in its place one such as Mohammed, or Bey, or Ali. Numerous gaudy identification cards were also found in the place.[214]

"At Police Headquarters he evaded questions cleverly," reporters said, "With the complacent smile of the Oriental Fakir, Farad calmly told detectives that he was the "supreme being on earth.""...[215] This was a most interesting claim considering Fard's followers (Elijah aside) only thought him out to be a prophet and not God incarnate. As Fard went on public record with this revelation, it was not lost on Muslims who read the article. Yusef Muhammad, an early follower of Fard, attests to this fact: "When the police asked him who he was, he said: 'I am the Supreme

Ruler of the Universe.' He told those police more about himself then he would ever tell us."[216]

—Free Press Photo

"HERE'S MY AUTHORITY." Wallace Farad, head of the Order of Islam, explains from his 'bible' to detectives the workings of his cult. It was an offshoot of the Order of Islam which led Robert Harris, Negro, to slay James Smith in a cult rite, police charge. Farad is held.

Master Fard Muhammad was arrested, interrogated and imprisoned for being the Leader of the Nation of Islam. He is shown here being interviewed by detectives Oscar Berry and Charles W. Snyder. The picture appeared in the Detroit Free Press on November 24, 1932. He eventually was cleared of any charges or wrongdoing, yet was ordered to leave the city because of the influence he yielded over his movement in Detroit.

During questioning, Fard disclosed he was the founder and teacher of the Nation of Islam. A tabloid sensationally described his process of giving holy names, his large following that extended throughout the country, his denial that the Nation was a money making venture and his admittance that Robert Harris was not in line with his teachings. The Detroit Free Press:

It was he who first conceived the precepts of Islamism as it is preached in the cult, he admitted, and enlisted the aid of Ali in starting the Detroit cult. Collections taken from the gullible converts and the proceeds of his sales as representative for a printing firm were his means of support, he said. Each member is required to have a gaudy "identification card" which Farad sold them for a fee, and then collected his commission from the printing house. When asked if there were any funds in Islam's treasury Wednesday, he said that there were none. "In fact, I have had to ask the brethren to contribute a fund for the payment of an overdue electric light bill in the temple," he said quietly.

Harris and Ali, he said, had "apparently misunderstood my teachings." Although the precepts of the workshop command the death penalty for persons who "disturb the peace of our temples" he said, human sacrifices were not tolerated. Islamism, he proudly declared, has large followings in cities throughout the country, among which are Chicago, New York, and Philadelphia. Members frequently visit other chapters in different cities, he said.[217]

W.D. Fard and Ugan Ali Placed in Psych Ward

Detectives decided to keep all three, Wallace Fard, Ugan Ali and of course Robert Harris in custody. Four other Temple officials were subsequently detained for questioning. All including Wallace Fard persisted and maintained that human sacrifices are not tolerated in the Nation of Islam. The Detroit News:

Robert Harris...will be arraigned in Recorder's Court Friday on a warrant charging him with murder. Two other members of the society - Wallace Fard, its leader, and Ugan Ali, secretary - are being held, Fard for the immigration authorities and Ali on a disorderly person charge. Fard said he did not know Harris. Ali and Harris' brother, Edward, told police they thought the accused man was demented. Four others were detained for questioning when police found them early today at Lafayette avenue east and Orleans Street. According to police the men said they were looking for "the place where the society was going to hold its big meeting." The four are registered as Abe Mohammed, 539 Alfred Street; Ocler Zareff, 2114 St. Antoine Street; Cornelius Bey, 3112 Beaubien street, and Wallace Mohammed, 951 Mullett Street.

The warrant for Harris was recommended by Miles N. Culehan, assistant prosecuting attorney. It is expected a sanity commission will be appointed to examine Harris after his arraignment. Ali and Fard told detectives there was nothing in the teachings of the Order of Islam that countenanced "sacrificial rites." They said the order could not be blamed for anything Harris did.[218]

White and Negro Leaders Set Out to Destroy the NOI

Regardless of their testimony, the authorities wanted the Nation of Islam 'wiped out of existence' and put the public school system on notice to survey black children to see if they have been influenced by the teachings, as they worked to dismantle the organization. The Detroit Free Press:

Detectives Wednesday expressed themselves as convinced that the cult had been conceived by an Arabian religious fakir for personal gain and nurtured by a group of zealots whose reason had become unbalanced. Three men arrested in connection with the murder of Smith were sent to the psychopathic ward of Receiving Hospital for observation by Dr. David Clark, psychiatrist in charge of social welfare for the hospital. They are Wallace D. Farad, an Arabian, who confessed himself the supreme leader of the Detroit cult of Islam; Ugan Ali, a "teacher" arrested in the cult's main temple at 3408 Hastings St., Tuesday, and Robert Harris, who confessed slaying Smith to propitiate the "Gods of Islam." Police believe these men are mad leaders who deluded the cult's members into homicidal tendencies. Superintendent of Schools Frank Cody expressed himself as alarmed at the possible effects of this weird worship on Negro school children in the City. He said that although he had not been notified of any difficulties which might have been caused by the cult's influence, he had asked teachers in the colored districts to be on the watch for any irregularities in the classrooms. As police delved further into the deeply hidden roots of Islamism, they confessed themselves astounded at the apparent significance of the cult's proselytizing. Hampered by exigencies of time and the press of other duties, Detective Berry said that he would make a detailed report of his findings and present them to Commissioner James K. Watkins at the end of the week. It will be his suggestion, he said, that the Commissioner assign a special squad of men to carry on the disentanglement of the cult's tentacles, and take measures to wipe out the practices of the group.[219]

Rival Negro church leaders sought to capitalize off of the misfortune of Robert Harris by working with local police to curb the influence of the Nation of Islam. The Detroit Free Press:

A group of Negro leaders, fighting for the welfare of their own people, Wednesday night united to form an influential body which, they believe, will greatly aid police in the battle to crush the hydra of jungle fanaticism which is preying upon more than 8,000 Detroit Negroes. The group, called the Detroit Council of Social Service, has been aroused to action by recent disclosures revealing the tremendous scope of the cult's menacing grip. Members strongly endorsed the prompt action of the Police Department in tracking down and arresting the leaders of the cult who are blamed for the sacrificial murder of James J. Smith, stabbed through the heart and mutilated with an iron bar on a home altar, Sunday. Through welfare and social services workers of their own people, the group will make a determined house-to-house drive to prevent any more of the ignorant element of Detroit's Negro population from being deluded into joining the vicious cult. They believe, however, that continued action by the City's law-enforcing agencies against the leaders is the only method of thoroughly stomping out the fanaticism. Wednesday night's meeting in Detroit City College was addressed by Sherman Miller, Free Press reporter, who had been invited to speak by Wilbur C. Woodson, secretary of the St. Antoine Branch of the Y.M.C.A. Miller related to the group the facts of the four-day investigation carried on by Detective Sergt. Oscar Berry and Detective Charles W. Snyder of the homicide squad. John C. Dancy, for 14 years a working in Negro welfare work as executive secretary of the Detroit Urban League, presided. Many Negro clergymen had visited Detectives Berry and Snyder during the day to offer their services in combating the sinister influences of voodooism. Several parishioners said they would conduct private investigations of their own among their people and turn their findings over to the Police Department.[220]

NOI Members March on Police Precinct

The Detroit Free Press reported that on Thanksgiving Day, November 25, 1932, some 500 members of the Nation of Islam protested the Negro leaders and police by marching on police headquarters during the arraignment of Robert Harris, while demanding the release of innocent leaders Wallace Fard and Ugan Ali. Leading the march was Elijah Muhammad. However, Ali's wife, Lillian Ali, was the one cited in the newspaper as leading the march, "Queen Heads Parade to Police Station for Protest Negro Leaders Push Drive to Curb Cult":

While leaders of Detroit's Negro population laid plans for stamping out the Voodoo-Moslem hybrid cult which grips a clique of the race's members here, and which came to light with the offering of a human sacrifice, 500 members of the cult marched to police headquarters Thursday to demand the liberation of their mentors in weird rites...[221]
...The group that marched to the headquarters Thursday was led by Lillie Ali, a voluable Negress and the wife of Ugan Ali, secretary of the "Islamic" cult. Many wore red fezzes. The Mohammedan aspects of the sect police trace to Wallace Farad, an Arabian said to be its founder.
Marching into the First Precinct Station, the delegation demanded to see Detective Sergt. Oscar Berry and Detective Charles W. Snyder, who have been assigned to the investigation of the extent of Voodoo beliefs in Detroit. Officers told them that the detectives were out of the building. Inspector John I. Navarre, head of the Homicide Squad talked with "Queen" Lillie for a few minutes and explained that her husband and Farad were being held in the psychopathic ward of Receiving Hospital for observation.
"All right," she said, her voice rising to a high pitch, "we will march down here every day until they are let out." The marchers then quietly dispersed. Shortly after the demonstration about half of the marchers were reported to have gathered in a house on Hastings St., between Columbia St. and Montcalm Ave.

There, leaders of the group addressed the gathering. Whisperings reached police Thursday of plans for a large protest meeting planned Friday. Fearing that such a meeting might result in an outbreak, police Thursday arrested four men, believed to be ringleaders detailed by the cult's chief to round up the members for the gathering. The men under arrest gave their names as Alie Mohammed, Oscar Zareff, Cornelius Bey and Wallace Mohammed. With their arrest, police Thursday were holding seven Negroes in connection with their investigation of the practices and dogmas of the cult,[222]

The Detroit News reported on the protest, reiterating that the Muslims threatened to march daily if their leaders were not released:

Other members of the society told police that the Order of Islam did not countenance sacrificial rites. They told police that Harris was demented and that the society was not responsible for his act. Five hundred men and women, who claimed to be members of the Order of Islam, headed by leaders wearing red fezzes, invaded Police Headquarters Thursday, as a protest against the detention of W. D. Farad, leader of the society, and Ugan Ali, secretary.

Among the leaders of the march was Ali's wife, Lillie, who demanded to see her husband, and was told he was in the psychopathic ward of Receiving Hospital. She told detectives of the homicide squad she would lead a group of the cult members to the headquarters building or to the hospital every day until the leaders have been released. There was no violence or disturbance, the marchers breaking up quickly after their demands had been denied.[223]

What both agencies failed to report was that Elijah Muhammad actually led the protest. In fact, while in prison, Master Fard made one request, and that was to see Elijah Muhammad. The Messenger recalls: "He was persecuted, sent to jail in 1932...He submitted himself with all humbleness to his persecutors. Each time he was arrested, he sent for me so that I might see and learn the price of Truth for us, the so-called American Negroes (members of the Asiatic Nation).[224]

Elijah Visits W.D. Fard in Prison during the Muslim Protest

Elijah's brother, John Muhammad, recalls while the Muslims protested outside, the Messenger spoke to Master Fard inside the jail, and afterwards answered questions from the Muslims:

In 1932 on Thanksgiving Day [Nov. 24, 1932] about noon, the Muslims went to jail to protest the release of Master Fard Muhammad. The Honorable Elijah Muhammad went inside of the jail at 1300 Beaubien St. in Detroit, MI., to see Master Fard Muhammad. The Muslims had made a line outside the jailhouse seeking his release. It was a cold day but the sun was bright as Allah intended for it to be. Everyone on the side that he was on (not a cell) was where the Muslims stood outside as they heard a voice say "As-Salaam-Alaikum"! Loud and clear. The Muslims outside then returned the greetings "Wa-Alaikum-Salaam" loud

Elijah Muhammad led a group of over 500 Muslims to protest the Detroit
Courthouse and Jail where Master Fard Muhammad was in custody.

and clear. They looked up to the window where they thought he might have been at and they saw something like a man's hand with a glove on it. When the Honorable Elijah Muhammad came out they asked him was that Master Fard Muhammad who gave them the greetings from the window. The Honorable Elijah Muhammad said no because he could not put his hands out of the window from where he was at. They told him what happened and how they had seen the hand and the voice and the Honorable Elijah Muhammad only shook his head because Master Fard Muhammad was not in the position to put his hand out the jailhouse window nor for them to hear his voice from inside. The next day Master Fard Muhammad was released from jail. (Believe it or not!)[225]

Despite the protest, rival Negro leaders (referred to as 'Uncle Toms' by the Nation of Islam) came to the precinct to work with the police on establishing a case against the movement amidst the arraignment of Robert Harris:

'Negro Leaders Press Drive' "The bulk of the Negro community, headed by its welfare workers, clergymen, professional men and political leaders, has taken steps to ferret out the fanatical element and Negroes from all walks of life have appeared at Police Headquarters to offer information which may aid officers."[226]

Some report that "Elijah, leading over 200 members of the cult, marched to the Recorder's Court Building and staged a protest on the main floor. It took police an entire day to get the last demonstrators to leave."[227]

Robert Karriem Arraigned During Court Protest

Meanwhile much activity was happening inside of the court as Robert Harris faced arraignment. The Detroit News captured the bizarre details of the opening of the event:

While a crowd of his co-religionists milled about today in the corridors outside Judge John A. Boyne's court room in Recorder's Court, Robert Harris, Negro, a member of the Order of Islam, who kill another Negro last Sunday in what he insisted was a "sacrificial rite," was arraigned on a charge of first degree murder. On his admitting the killing, a plea of guilty was entered for him. Inspector John I. Navarre, head of the homicide squad, said efforts would be made to have Harris arraigned on the State's information this afternoon before Judge John P. Scallen, who is expected to appoint a sanity commission at once to examine Harris. Harris' arraignment followed a prolonged debate between him and Judge Boyne as to who was "king." When Harris, handcuffed to Detective Charles W. Snyder, was taken before Judge Boyne, he was wearing a much-frayed cap. He continued to keep the cap on when he stood before the court.

"Take off your cap," Judge Boyne ordered. Harris made no move to comply. "I am king here," he said. "Oh, no, you are not," said Judge Boyne, "I'm the king here." "No, sir, I'm the king here and everywhere," said the prisoner. The discussion was interrupted when a court officer removed the cap. "Did you kill James J. Smith?" Judge Boyne asked.

"Yes, I did," said Harris, replacing the cap on his head. The cap was removed again by the court officer.

"I did kill this man at 1429 Dubois Street," Harris said. "Why did you kill him?" Judge Boyne asked.

"It was crucifixion time," said Harris. "That's why I killed him."

"What did you kill him with?" asked the court. "With the crucifixion," Harris said. "I said 'aliker alump,' and he fell dead. He died because it's a dumb civilization. But I gave my children a break, because I'm a lover of children. Well, I've got to go now."

Harris started to walk toward the door. "You'd better wait a minute," said Judge Boyne. Harris then grabbed a box of rubber bands from the clerk's desk and was stuffing them into his pocket.

"Put those back," Judge Boyne said. "No, I'm king here," said Harris, continuing to stuff the rubber bands into his pocket with one hand, and putting his cap back on his head with the other. While one court officer recovered the bands another uncovered Harris' head. Harris was then taken to a cell...228

Detroit City Officials Campaign to Destroy the NOI

Given the large protest and public attention, the authorities criticized NOI leaders and cast a net of scrutiny over their activities as part of its ongoing investigation to stamp out the movement:

Henry Piel, deputy chief of detectives, today directed Detective Lieut. John Hoffman, head of the special investigation squad, to make a daily check of the activities of the Order of Islam.229

More than 200 Negroes attended a meeting on Hastings St. Friday night, according to police, who said it was a voodoo gathering. Although careful watch was kept on the place by detectives, there was no disturbance. No attempt was made to interfere with the gathering.230

"The public must be informed of the tremendous danger of this group," he said. "All departments in the City's law enforcing agencies have had great trouble with its members in the past, and now that the thing has reached such large proportions it must be followed down and stamped out for the benefit of all." He said that the weird religion, which he has studied closely in his experience with patients driven insane by its homicidal teachings is "primarily one of Mohammedanism, with a great deal of pagan jungle superstitions and practices ingrafted." It preys only upon the mentally incapable element of Negroes, those who are "weak, uncontrolled and superstitious" to start with, he said. "We have seen its evil machinations for years, and want to urge the proper authorities to crush out the cult." Two of the cult's leaders, held prisoners in the Psychopathic ward of Receiving Hospital, were examined by alienists Friday. The mental processes of one, who calls himself Ugan Ali, "are radically deviated," the report states. "His sanity is extremely doubtful. His case must be handled with the utmost caution, as the slightest word or phrase used inadvertently seems to enrage him, for no apparent reason." The other, Wallace Farad, Arabian leader and self-confessed founder, is "suffering from delusions that he is a divinity," the

[115]

report continues. "He has a pair of religious precepts and practice which, taken literally, are dangerous to those influenced by them.[231]

Robert Karriem's Prison Behavior Analyzed

After the arraignment, the news reported Harris started acting erratic in his jail cell, and later broke his hunger strike. It also detailed further judgments regarding his case:

Harris, the confessed murderer of Smith, suddenly discarded his attitude of sullen subservience which he has maintained for the past few days, and went berserk in the County Jail. Upon his return from his arraignment before Judge John P. Scallen, he was placed in a cell block containing 12 other Negro prisoners. "I am the King," he suddenly yelled, and dashed wildly about the room, shouting unintelligible sounds at his fellow prisoners. He threw furniture at them and so terrorized them with his threats of sacrifice that they shouted and stamped on the floor to attract the attention of jailers. Sherriff Henry Behrendt ordered Harris placed in a padded cell, where he relapsed into quiet.

For the first time since his arrest Sunday, he has asked for food, and ate with relish a prison fare of eggs and spaghetti. Early Friday he was arraigned on a murder warrant before Recorder's Judge John A. Boyne. He waived examination. The courts, cooperating with police in the efforts to expedite the proceedings, made it possible for him to be arraigned on the information before Judge Scallen, later in the day. Judge Scallen ordered a mute plea to be entered for him, and said he would appoint a sanity commission Saturday morning. More than 200 Negroes, many of whom were believed by police to be members of the cult, spent the day on the floor of the Recorder's Court Building. The report of the sanity commission will be presented to Judge Scallen Dec. 4. Inquiries Friday revealed that the effect of the sinister worship upon the gullible and highly emotional members of the cult has been felt in many City departments.[232]

...The hurtful flame of jungle fanaticism which tortured Harris into murdering Smith, seemed to have died away in him, temporarily at least, Saturday. He slumped in a corner of a padded cell in the County Jail most of the day, weak and unresisting. Some of his food he ate listlessly, and the rest he slopped on the floor of the cell. A pitifully deluded fanatic, whose zeal had at last seemingly spent itself, he babbled on about "more sacrifices," with half shut eyes. A sanity commission to judge whether he was demented by the murderous teachings of cult leaders, was appointed Saturday morning by Recorder's Judge John P. Scallen.. It is made up of Drs. Alber C. La Bine, Carl Hanna and John H. Stevin. If he is judged insane, he will be committed to a State institution until such time as he is judged sane. He will then automatically be required to stand trial for the murder of Smith. If the decision of the commission is otherwise, he will go on trial immediately, Judge Scallen said. The commission will report the results of its investigations on Dec. 6.[233]

Black Muslims Insist to be called by their Muslim Names

During the overall investigation, authorities remarked how Negroes no longer wanted to be referred to by their 'slave names', and now demanded as 'Asiatics' to be known by their 'original names.' Welfare workers were the main witnesses to the phenomena as they dealt with the Nation of Islam and the Moorish Science Temple people on a regular basis, sometimes involving different skirmishes. The Detroit Free Press:

City Clerk Richard W. Reading said that for four years his clerks have struggled with Negroes who insisted upon being registered by weird Arabian names. They became so incensed upon the refusal of authorities to do so, that he brought the matter to the attention of James R. Walsh, assistant corporation counsel. Mr. Walsh wrote a notice forbidding the clerks to countenance signatures such as Mohammed or Ali or Bey, and had it posted on the wall of the Election Commission's offices. It's still there. Welfare workers too have suffered from the cult's fanatic zeal. Negro Welfare workers have for some time reported that they had been insulted as "devils" and in many cases threatened with bodily harm. One worker was struck recently by a member of the cult, whose family she was trying to aid. She was attacked and beaten by a woman who was treated for several months in the psychopathic ward of Receiving Hospital. She was released a few days ago, after authorities had become convinced that through careful mental treatment they had broken the grip of voodooism upon her.[234]

Case Transferred to Special Investigative Unit

As the investigation grew, the police decided to transfer the case to a different department with plans of creating a special investigation squad exclusively to shut down the organization:

Detectives Thursday prepared to turn further investigation of the cult's precepts over to another branch of the Police Department. A detailed report of their findings and suspicions will be given to the commissioner at the end of the week. It has been indicated that he may appoint a squad of special officers to the job of tracing the tentacles of the ominous cult, in the hopes that the sinister group may be stamped out.[235]

As the ramifications of "Islamism" became apparent to police authorities during the investigation, they also became increasing difficult to track down and stifle.

Realizing this, police head Friday removed the investigation from the hands of Detective Sergt. Oscar Berry and Detective Charles Snyder, who have devoted their entire time to the matter since the murder of Smith. The matter is no longer in their jurisdiction as homicide squad detectives.

Further investigation has been assigned to Lieut. John Hoffman, of the Special Investigation Squad, who will take charge Saturday morning, after he has made a study of the detailed report filed Friday by Detectives Berry and Snyder.[236]

The special investigation squad, which has had many years' experience with the law-breaking tendencies of the cult's ignorant members was assigned to the case Friday. It was explained that the work of Detective Sergt. Oscar Berry and Detective Charles Snyder in tracking down and arresting the murderer of Smith was meritorious, but once the murder was solved, they, as Homicide Detectives, could afford to devote no more time to the case, under the press of other duties.

Police said Saturday that they have known for some time that violence by some of the cult's members was imminent, but were powerless to prevent it. The group, which does not call itself an organization or a religion, but a nation, does not come under the laws governing the foundations of organizations or religions, the prosecutor's office informed authorities. Appeals to employers of cult members have been made secretly for some time, but they have proved unrevealing, officers report. Most uniformed persons are inclined to treat the weird fanaticism lightly, they said, and were loath to take drastic steps against its operations. But with the revelations of the cult's menace, brought to light by the investigation of Smith's murder, authorities are hopeful that leaders in Detroit's industrial civilization will realize the peril of the body to the social structure and welfare of the City, and aid in the permanent disbanding of the group.[237]

Some Negroes Work with Police to Discredit the Muslims

The new investigators found the Nation of Islam case file to be fascinating, as they read excerpts from Lessons of Wallace Fard they referred to as his "bible," as well as noted Negro leaders who opposed the Muslims pledge their support to the police:

In the report were quoted severe passages from the official "Bible of Islamism." Detailing their questioning of Farad, the officers said, "On page 354 of the 'Bible' is the following quotation, which was underlined and which Farad claimed he used as part of his teachings - 'God is a liar. Ignore Him and do away with those who advocate His cause.' He stated that this was a favorite passage of his and that he used it often in his teachings." The report also states that "a number of Negro clergymen and representatives of other Negro religious societies have called upon us at the office, all demanding that some action be taken for the purpose of disbanding the 'Nation of Islam.'"[238]

Police noted other 'copycat' possible crimes where it was rumored that others were planning human sacrifices, such as a man who allegedly wanted to sacrifice his son in a murder ritual. Police advised their 'negro undercover agents' weren't able to find the man based on any existing leads. However, they did believe they found a possible connection to the Nation of Islam and another group that was combination of Asians and Blacks that sought violence against whites, it however turned out to be a false lead:

Undercover Negro agents Saturday still had not been able to locate the man whom they believed Friday to have been plotting the sacrificial slaughter of his son on a voodoo altar similar to the one on which Smith was killed. They were still investigating, however, in the hope that his arrest would spare the life of his small son from hideous sacrifice to the pagan fetishes of voodooism. A hint that the spread of the sinister cult's horrible grip of voodooism was of national scope was advanced by Sergt. Seleske Saturday. A Filipino who ran amock in Seattle a few days ago, killing six persons and wounding 15 before he was subdued by a squad of police, is being questioned to learn whether he, too, had been goaded into a blood-lust of wholesale slaughter by the savage precepts of the weird charlatans of voodooism. A week ago three Negroes and a Filipino were arrested here by Sergt. Seleske as suspicious characters and found by questioning to be a branch of the same cult with headquarters in Chicago.

The men, like all members of the cult, gave strange Mohammedan names, insisting they were Arabs. They had come here to meet with members of the Detroit branch, in efforts to tie the branches of the cult together. They spoke vaguely of "plans" but evaded questions pertinent to the specific nature of them. They were released a few days ago after attempts to discover criminal intent on their part had proved futile.[239]

Negro Leaders Hold Press Conferences against the NOI

Meanwhile, with their undercover Negro agents, the unholy alliance between the police and Negro church leaders continued as a press conference was held, where one by one, church leaders pledged their support to the white community to help "stamp out" the Nation of Islam. Forming an "inter-racial commission", church leaders Rev. J.D. Howell, Rev. Father E.W. Daniel, and the Rev. W.H. Peck led the charge. "Negro Leaders Pledge Support to Wipe Out Voodooism, Police Continuing Inquiry in Slaying":

An inter-racial commission, to be formed for the purpose of digging out and strangling the deepy planted roots of voodooism, which already has been responsible for one sacrificial murder and the planning of at least three more, was suggested Sunday by the Rev. J.D. Howell, speaking from his pulpit in the St. Stephen's African Methodist Episcopal Church. Mr. Howell was one of several prominent Negro clergymen in the City who devoted the greater part of their sermons to denunciations of the leaders of the sinister cult called "Islamism," which for at least four years has preyed upon the more gullible members of their people, and by its force of fanaticism, goaded several Negroes into delusions of divine power which toppled their sanity into homicidal tendencies.[240]

Negro pastors seeking favor with local whites spoke against the Muslims:

"The Negro race cannot, as such, be held responsible for the actions and teachings of fanatics. Their 'Arabian' leader is solely to blame. There must be quick and just punishment of those who come among us and, for personal gain, lead us astray. "The Islamic 'Bible' and the Nation of Islam must go." The Rev. Father E.W. Daniel, pastor of St. Matthew's Episcopal Church, decried the attitude of unthinking and uninformed persons who hold the Negro race responsible for the development of the cult. He drew a parallel between the exposure of the House of David in Benton Harbor several years ago and the cult of Islamism in this city. "Yet it was not deemed necessary to lay the burden of proof of the exposure of the House of David upon the citizens of Benton Harbor," he said. "They left the prosecution of the House of David entirely up to the authorities of Berrien County." "There is no race of people anywhere that haven't had to climb uphill in religion, as well as in every other field." The Rev. W.H. Peck, pastor of Bethel African Methodist Episcopal Church, disagreed with Father Daniel on the general attitude with which exposure of the cult of voodooism has been received by most law-abiding citizens of Detroit. "The law-abiding Negroes of Detroit have an inexpressible regret for this whole affair," he said. "There is, however, much to be appreciated in the reaction that Detroit has given in this matter. In most communities it would be found necessary for leaders of the Negro race to assure others that such a crime as this did not come from the larger portion of their people and in no way had its approval. "We did not have to do that here. Leaders among other races in Detroit have given that assurance before we have spoken a word. This is appreciated by our people and makes them more determined than ever before to continue to merit such confidence. "There is a feeling of pity on our part for those who have so grievously been misled. We offer our co-operation to help them by freeing them of their unfortunate leadership and making impossible a repetition of so horrible a crime." Police investigation of the cult's activities continued Sunday. Detectives and others assigned to the case said that they would continue their investigation until the cult is stamped out.[241]

Three of the seven Negroes arrested in connection with the cult's activities after the killing of James Smith on a voodoo altar a week ago, are being held in the psychopathic wards of Receiving Hospital for observation by City and private alienists. They are Robert Harris, crazed slayer of Smith; Wallace Farad, self-confessed founder of the Detroit cult; and Ugan Ali, a Negra "teacher" of Farad's precepts, held largely responsible for the dangerous ideas instilled in the minds of many ignorant Negroes who attended the cult's rituals in a temple at 3408 Hastings St.

"This voodooism is an extremely dangerous cult, and should not be tolerated by organized society," Mr. Howell said. "That its fanatical teachings and barbarous practices could have such a rank growth right in the midst of our religious communities shows weakness on the part of our church life. It shows a deplorable lack of contact between the upper and lowers strata of society. "Beyond a doubt all of this could have been avoided by the appointment of an inter-racial commission. It is not a war of strength we need, nor would it be expedient, but rather a war on ignorance, unwholesome living conditions, and demoralizing contacts."[242]

Police Realize Power of NOI, Decide to Wait on Case Judgments

Detectives soon discovered that disbanding the Nation of Islam might not be as easy as they originally thought. Upon reviewing the literature captured during the seizure of the Temple, the police discovered a book of thousands of names of members who lived outside of Detroit in its surrounding areas. They decided to wait on the judgment of the NOI leaders to determine their next course of action:

Checking names in the register book of Detroit's voodoo cult Monday revealed that although the bulk of the group's membership of 8,000 is made up of Detroit Negroes, many converts were gained in outlying districts of the City, such as Hamtramck, Highland Park and Mt. Clemens. Detective Sergt. Barney Seleske and Detective Harry Mikuliak, now handling the investigation, said they would continue to check through the long list of "Arabian" names to see if any of them has come under police surveillance before. Some of the addresses found in the poll book were searched by police Monday. In many of the houses, officers confiscated literature. Before taking any further action, detectives said they would await the report of Receiving Hospital psychiatrists on Robert Harris, who confessed slaying James Smith on a sacrificial voodoo altar a week ago. Ugan Ali, "teacher" of Harris in the weird rites of the cult, and Wallace Farad, "Arabian" founder of the Detroit group. The doctors' reports will be filed with police Tuesday. A special sanity commission appointed to judge Harris' condition by Recorder's Judge John P. Scallen will report to him Dec. 6. In the event that Harris is found to be sane and placed on trial for murder, Fred Dye, an attorney, was Monday appointed council for him by Judge Scallen.[243]

Verdicts: Robert Karriem: Insane, Ugan Ali: not normal, W.D. Fard: Sane

The sanity commission after five days finally came back with a ruling on their three prisoners from the hospital. Ugan Ali, although not classified as crazy, was considered to be 'not normal.' Robert Harris was no doubt classified as insane, and Wallace Fard was not considered to be insane in the least bit:

The mental processes of Ugan Ali, Negro leader of Detroit's voodoo cult, are not those of a normal person, physicians at Receiving Hospital said Tuesday. For five days they have been making a diagnosis of his case. His teachings are blamed largely by police for the sacrificial murder of James Smith on a voodoo altar more than a week ago. Indications are that Robert Harris, slayer of Smith, is mentally unbalanced, doctors reported, although an official diagnosis of his case will not be made until a specially appointed sanity commission reports its findings to Recorder's Court Judge John P. Scallen on Dec. 6. Wallace Farad, confessed "Arabian" founder of the cult, apparently was not driven to his sinister teachings through insanity, the report states. However, all of the men are being kept in the psychopathic ward of the hospital pending further investigation.

Continued investigation of the cult's activities by Detective Sergt. Barney Seleske of the Special Investigation Squad, revealed Tuesday that the recent exposure of the cult had shown many of its deluded members that they had been backed into joining an organization the dangerous teachings of which they were unaware, he said. Many of the addresses listed in the register book of 8,000 names were similar, and when traced were found to be meeting places. At many of these, groups of Negroes told officers that newspaper accounts of the cult's workings had shown them the peril of being allied with such a group, and that they would no longer have anything to do with it.[244]

Robert Karriem sentenced to Prison,
Ugan Ali and W.D. Fard Ordered Out of the City

Given the ruling and judgment, all three prisoners learned their fate. Ugan Ali allegedly under pressure recanted his involvement in the Nation of Islam and promised to work with authorities to disband the group for his freedom. Robert Harris was indefinitely committed to a Hospital for the Criminally Insane (where he'd later die in 1935), and Master Fard was ordered to leave the city of Detroit. Both Ugan Ali and Master Fard were freed on December 7, 1932:

The commitment of Robert Harris, voodoo slayer, to Ionia State Hospital for the Criminal Insane and the voluntary abdication from the city of Wallace Farad, confessed founder of the cult of "Islam," led police Tuesday to believe that two major steps had been taken in the permanent dissolution of the vicious cult which preyed upon Detroit Negroes.

Ugan Ali, Farad's most sinister and powerful satellite, told authorities that he realized the danger of his "teachings" and promised to use his influence in disbanding the group. He was released Tuesday, after being held in the psychopathic wards of Receiving Hospital since the day following the slaying of Smith.

Harris was ordered committed to the Hospital Tuesday by Recorder's Judge John P. Scallen, after a special sanity commission, composed of Drs. John H. Sleven, Alfred C. LaBine, and Carl Hanna, had testified that he is insane.

The slayer, looking peaked and weary after his two weeks in jail, sat with chin cupped in both palms as he listened to the testimony of the medical experts. He showed no emotion, although he listened intently to every word.

Harris is "subject to mental confusion, delusional thinking, and has hallucinations," the testimony read. He probably will never regain his sanity, the doctors reported. If he should, he will have to stand trial for the murder of Smith, Judge Scallen said, in suspending the murder charges against the prisoner.

Fard was persuaded to leave town Tuesday by Detectives Oscar Berry and Charles Snyder who investigated the murder. He seemed willing to go, they said, and said that he would not return to Detroit again.[245]

On December 7, detectives Berry and Snyder put Fard on a train bound for Chicago.[246]

Police Launches Campaign to Harass Muslims

Immediately after the release of the NOI Leader, the city government went to work against the Nation of Islam, arresting male members and taking Muslim families off the government's 'relief fund':

Acting upon the earlier order of Commissioner Watkins to disassemble the cult, in the days following Fard's banishment police arrested at least 100 members of the ATI. Nearly all of the arrest were pretextual, the objective being to make it difficult for temple members to congregate. They were arrested on the streets, on their jobs, and anywhere else that might cause them public embarrassment. To bolster the law enforcement campaign, social workers who caseloads included ATI families unilaterally ended welfare payments for many, which affected nearly one-third of Fard's followers I the Michigan area. Many of the Muslims with young children were devastated, as welfare was their sole sustenance. Families formed food pools to survive. On some days males over thirteen had as little as three slices of bread to eat. To alleviate the harshness of the food crisis, Fard established the "Poor Fund," through which money donated to the temple was doled out according to a family's needs.[247]

6 The FOI & M.G.T.

Fear of trouble with the unbelievers, especially the police, led to the founding of the Fruit of Islam – a military organization for the men who were drilled by captains and taught tactics and the use of firearms. Each of these organizations was under the control of a group of officers trained specially by the prophet for their task. Finally, the entire movement was placed under a Minister of Islam and a corps of assistant ministers, all of whom were selected and trained by the prophet.[248]

You know about the Fruits of Islam. Its functions are primarily to protect and defend the Nation and its Nationals. To protect the Nation we are under...We receive military training. We get education also in the F.O.I. By protecting the Nation we mean one hundred per cent protection of everything in the Nation from the pin to the Temple and all the nationals, and even the doorknobs on the doors of the Temple. Anyone that violates this or does some injury to the Nation would be severely dealt with, and if need be, physical violence would be used in defense of the "national interest" of the Nation of Islam.

We have no firearms. Our training is without firearms. We are trained in self-defense. What an F.O.I. would do or can do without firearms, a cook can do with potatoes. We are the Fruits of Islam and we need no firearms. It is a Brothers' duty to defend the life of a Muslim Sister with his own life, and he must defend the life of a Brother with his own life.[249]

W.D. Fard Urges all Men and Boys to Join the FOI (Fruit of Islam), And for the Sisters, the MGT (Muslim Girls Training)

Upon his prison release Fard went to Chicago, but dipped back to Detroit to have a very important meeting with the Muslim men. Addressing the army of Muslim men, Mr. W.D. Fard announced, "We need 10,000 men to join the FOI," and commanded his male followers, "Make all men and boys join the FOI." Mr. W.D. Fard became the personal instructor and trainer of the FOI, calling for Monday nights to be "F.O.I. Class". He also simultaneously developed a female counterpart, "that women might keep their houses clean and cook food properly, there was established the Muslim Girl's Training and General Civilization Classes."[250] The two corps, FOI and MGT, took on a militant presence reminiscent of Marcus Garvey's honor guard.

After the controversy with the Detroit police, Fard reassessed and rewarded the faithful. Master Fard knew it was important to have the right people for establishing the three most important units, the Fruit of Islam (F.O.I.), the Muslim Girls Training and General Civilization Class (M.G.T. & G.C.C.) and "the University of Islam." As noted:

> Ugan Ali and his wife, Lillian, disappeared after his release, and Elijah became Fard's chief aide. Elijah's children got into street fights so often that he finally took them out of the public schools, and, with Fard's permission, reorganized the fledgling school. Located in the Hastings Street temple, the University of Islam accepted its first forty students in January 1933.[251]

The 9 Laborer Positions

In realigning his Nation of Islam, Master Fard personally handpicked and established the positions of "the 9 Laborers" that included titles such as: Supreme Minister, Supreme Captain, National Secretary, National Treasurer, Supreme Investigator, National Instructor, Supreme Principal, National Reformer, etc.

Quite naturally, Elijah Muhammad was Supreme Minister, his brother Kallatt was Supreme Captain, Supreme Investigator was Jesse Sharrieff (Elijah's future brother-in-law), National Secretary Cecil Bey (whose wife Albertus Bey became the first National MGT Captain), as Elijah recalled: "I remember in 1932 on Chene street in Detroit, Michigan, at brother Cecil and Sister Albertus Bey's home. The first Captain and Secretary. And Sister Bey was the first Captain of our M.G.T.&.G.C.C. Also Treasurer and Bookkeeper. The Blessed Saviour said to me and Sister Bey and a few others that was present, that within ten (10) years there would be a great improvement in the increase of children among the Muslims."[252]

A principal was also assigned over the University of Islam, "I met the Saviour Master Fard Muhammad in a basement at 1035 E. Napolean Street in 1931. The Saviour made me the Supreme Principal in 1932," recalls Ben Sabakhan. In a letter he wrote about his experience years later, he says, "I met Master W.D. Muhammad in the year of 1931 and accepted the teachings at once. We were living in a miserable state of condition, and I could not thank him too much for the wonders he has done for me and all Muslims. Before seeing him I was blind, deaf and dumb to the wisdom of myself. I saw him in a basement on Napoleon Street and he gave the history of Yakub, Moses and Isa, and that opened my eyes completely. I was appointed Principal of the University of Islam in 1932 by W.F. Muhammad."[253] W.D. Fard established the University of Islam in Detroit in the summer of 1932, and allowed his Supreme Minister Elijah Muhammad to establish the school shortly after in Chicago, IL. As Muhammad's University of Islam 1962 yearbook recalled: "University of Islam was established in the city of Chicago, in the last Summer of 1932 by the Honorable Elijah Muhammad; by the order of Allah in the Person of Master Fard Muhammad, for the purpose of teaching and educating the so-called negroes into the knowledge of their own, the True God, the Devil, the true religion, and the Judgment of this world; the qualifications necessary to see the hereafter."[254]

Other positions were assigned, among them was Assistant Supreme Minister, and Elijah's brother Wali Muhammad, filled that post. Assistant Supreme Captain was Lonnie Pasha. Other names on the roster were Ozier Zarrieff, Wallace Mohammed and the newly appointed National Reformer, the only female Laborer as well as daughter of Supreme Investigator Jesse Sharrieff, a young 17-year-old girl named Sister Burnsteen Sharrieff (who was given the name 'The Reformer' by Master Fard Muhammad). The Reformer Burnsteen Sharrieff tells her story:

I was born on July 14, 1915, in Robinsonville, Mississippi. In 1919 we moved to Detroit, Michigan. I was four years old. I went to school in Detroit, Michigan.

It was in October 1932 when my parents brought me to the Temple of Islam located over the Castle Theater at 3408 Hastings Street in Detroit, Michigan. After going to the meetings several times with my parents, I saw Brother Ben Sabakhan typing. He was typing with one finger. I said to one of my girlfriends "I can use all of mine" and she said, "That's right!" I don't know whether she spread the word about me or who, but one Sunday the Hon. Elijah Muhammad asked, "Is the sister here who said she can type? If so stand up." So I stood up. He asked me were my parents Muslims. I said, "Yes Sir" and told him who they were. I was told to come to the next meeting to be interviewed, thus I became the first typist, titled "The Reformer" at 17 years old.[255]

Sis. Burnsteen Sharrieff Mohammad as pictured on her booklet "I AM Burnsteen Sharrieff Mohammad, Reformer and Secretary to Master W.D.F. Mohammed…and these are some of my experiences." (If interested in obtaining her book and other historical literature, visit website at poolemohammedmichigan1.com

The Supreme Wisdom Lessons

With Master Fard Muhammad, the Hon. Elijah Muhammad and the 9 Laborers at the helm, the Nation of Islam became more effectively organized. At the core was 'the divine teachings' more specifically referred to as "The Supreme Wisdom." He relied heavily upon his staff to assist with providing the necessary documentation of the teachings and hierarchy concerning the movement. The Reformer Burnsteen Sharrieff explains:

> I have many skills and held every position available, from Reformer (one who changes, establishes, structures, organizes, puts in place that which is needed to bring about growth and advancement), Secretary, Treasurer and personal Secretary to Master W.D. Fard. Also to the Hon. Elijah Muhammad, the first typist (I was the fastest typist in my high school class 95 words per minute with 98% accuracy), all literature, letters, lessons, Problem Book, facts, etc. I converted from long hand into typing. Of the 9 first Laborers chosen by Master W.D. Fard, I was the only female Laborer.
>
> I graded letters (which everyone had to write for a Holy name), helped those who could hardly write by taking their hand and guiding it, giving them writing exercises until they could write on their own. I set up the woman's class, MGT and GCC was captain over it and advanced to Instructor over it by the Hon. Elijah Muhammad to train and instruct other captains, Temple Secretary, advance to Instructor by the Hon. Elijah Muhammad to train others in the position. In most positions, I was the first and became instructor over them; most of the time I held two positions at the same time. The Hon. Elijah Muhammad would send various workers in the community to me for instruction or clarification, which many times would include Ministers because I knew the work from the beginning when the Nation first started.[256]

"Everything Right and Exact"

In the beginning Master Fard was very stern in keeping his staff on point about the Lessons. He was extra careful in establishing excellence as the standard. Yet He had a way with words when things got rough and always said the right thing to encourage them to keep going. Burnsteen Sharrieff:

> He wrote me a line on the bottom of a problem he sent to be typed: "Always re-read what you type, don't close your eyes and trust in God!" Now he taught us that the black people were the god so when I would say my prayers, I'd shut my eyes and envision that great mass of people as god. Allah had to tell him how I was praying, although he told me that which was true. Yet in the letter he wrote me that I was blamed by someone else of being lazy, for which I was unjustly put on a punishment to type 1,000 questions and answers to Lesson #1 or else get time and I was innocent working 16 and many times 18 or 20 hours a day he was unable to see.
>
> In the same letter he gave me these uplifting inspiring words that continue to give me strength today and they are, "Be your own self and Allah is with you. Could anything be better than helping to rise the dead Nation? I hope you will know the value of your labor, clean thoughts in and without will bring you a surprise." He did not say god would be with me but Allah, not himself. [257]

Elijah Muhammad, recognized as Supreme Minister, also had great say in how things were done as it pertains to having "everything right and exact." On at least one occasion he sought to have the Reformer disciplined for an error:

> On another occasion, I had done some labor and had been taken home. As the Hon. Elijah Muhammad read what I had typed, he got angry because of mistakes he found and wanted to go get me to dismiss me, this he told to Master Fard. Master Fard said (so Sis. Grace Muhammad, Kallatt's wife said they were at her home) all she will say is I will do it over and never complain. Then he asked, "What can you do with a person like that?" that save me from being dismissed or given time.[258]

The position of Reformer turned out to be a daunting task for such a demanding team. The position required work around the clock and being put on the spot:

> On another occasion, it had been one of those long full days of laboring for me; working at the Temple and typing for long hours at the Temple (our time began at 9:00 AM) then at this time of incident had typed for hours at the house of the Hon. Elijah Muhammad. I was so tired as I struggled to get through so I could go home. The first time I typed these facts I had mistakes in it. So I retyped them typing two sets on the same page and folding the page in half and tearing them apart; there were no mistakes but having made several carbon copies I neglected folding and creasing the to tear smoothly.
>
> When I gave them to Master W.D. Fard, he looked at them and asked the other Laborers (all men) did they want one of these copies that looked like a baby had been chewing on? Naturally, each said no and he said to me to type another one for each one that said no; well in fact it was all of them. Then he asked me, "Do you want one of these?" As I was about to say, he said, "Yes, you can always type you one." Which was indeed the thought that I was forming in my mind. Then he said to me, "Let me show you how to tear paper."
>
> He took a sheet of my typing paper, creased it, turned it to the other side, creased it again; each time between his thumb and finger using the nail of his thumb. Then he pressed my face down close to the paper and slowly tore it apart asking me over and over, "Can you see it?" Each time I would reply, "Yes, Sir." This he did until he tore the sheet in half leaving no rough edges. Then he took a piece, folded it evenly in half and said, "Or you can do it like this" and slowly drew it between his teeth, the saliva moistening it as it passed between his clinched teeth and tore it although a little damp but smoothly and evenly without any rough edges.
>
> I was so humiliated and hurt until when I went back to my typewriter my eyes were all but filled with tears. I sat down and talk about pounding a typewriter, my fingers fairly flew as I re-typed them; after finishing them I checked them for mistakes; there were none and folded them over and over like he had shown me and neatly tore them apart and gave them to him. He

told me to sit there right next to him. I sat there humiliated, thinking to myself, "no one is for me." He turned to me smiling and gently saying to me, "I'm for you and if I'm for you, who can be against you. I'll walk the water for you." This eased my feeling somewhat but I was tired, humiliated. I wanted to go home. He asked me did I want some ice cream. I said, "No Sir," and in my mind I kept saying I want to go home. So he turned to the others and said, "We'll take the Reformer home." This he did. [259]

Master Fard didn't just leave it at teaching the 'word' alone. He was big on teaching and living 'the law.' One document everyone had to know was "the Restrictive Laws of Islam," which was a strong code of ethics, morals, rules and instructions for the Believers:

Laws and Instructions
"THE RESTRICTIVE LAW IS OUR SUCCESS!"
Muslim Rules

1. A Muslim must show the greatest intelligence at all times.
2. Never be the aggressor by words or actions, in the event you are attacked, stick together in battle as a solid wall.
3. Obey the laws of the land or government you must live under, for if you cannot keep these laws, how can you obey the laws of ALLAH(GOD). But if these laws conflict with the laws of ALLAH, then fear ALLAH, and ALLAH alone must you fear.
4. What is the duty of the Captain and Lieutenants? The Captain's Duty is to give the orders to the Lieutenants and the Lieutenant's Duty is to teach the private soldiers and train them.
5. A Muslim's word is bond and bond is life, I will give my life before my word shall fail.
6. Muslims must always keep purity of mind, and cleanliness of body.
7. Muslims do not give to the use of oaths.
8. A Muslim acknowledges and recognizes that he is a member of the Creator's Nation, and act accordingly to this in the name of ALLAH ... as a Muslim we must set an example for the Lost-Found. This requires actions and deeds, not words and lip service.
9. We must recognize the necessity for unity and group operation.
10. Stop needless criticisms of your brother. We must remember that jealousy destroys from within.
11. The Law of Islam says that if one brother has a bowl of soup, the other brother has half of that bowl; his success is your success.
12. Be patient in matters where others are involved, remember that there were times when we that know, knew not.
13. Do not take the bad side of a thing that appears to us as bad; there is always a good side, it is better to take that side.
14. Actions are judged by the intentions, actions may appear wrong but motives bring rewards.
15. Seek not to rind fault in your brother. This does not mean to make unnecessary excuses for wrongdoing.

16. Only by true repentance and reform can we escape the consequence of our errors.

17. If you should see a brother in error, then correct him in the strictest privacy.

18. There should be at least two witnesses in order to bring a charge against a brother.

19. Do not pray as a Muslim and act like Christians.

20. Muslims should not participate in activities leading from ALLAH.

21. A true Muslim should act justly not only to other Muslims, but also non-Muslims and even those who are enemies of Islam.

Strict and explicit orders were given on how to run an effective Temple. Master Fard Muhammad considered the sanctuary so important that each member had to be willing to give their lives to protect the sacredness of their meetings and each other. General rules were given on how to have a successful Temple membership:

ORDERS TO THE MUSLIMS
AND LABORERS OF ISLAM IN NORTH AMERICA

(1) The Secretary should have all Actual Facts on the black board before the MINISTER arrives. And let it remain until meeting is dismissed.

(2) The-Muslims must be 100% clean and loving to one another, their homes must be clean at all times, their clothes clean, do not let dirty Muslims in the Temple.

(3) The investigator must investigate or visit their homes once per week unexpectedly.

(4) We must see to it, that the Temple is kept clean of filth at all times; dirty floors and walls, also seats must not exist in the Temple.

(5) If a Muslim says that he is with us and associates with our enemies is a lie and must stay away.

(6) Hurry! Hurry! Hurry! Lose no more time have no quarreling among the believers. The Law settles all arguments. Get after the new ones, put them to work and all that come must be willing to help by giving all he or she can to the cause of Islam.

(7) Cast out the rotten apples, quick. Keep your ears and eyes open to those smart crooked deceivers, who will always try to put one over. Have all searched 100% before entering the Temple of Islam. Make the Muslims comb their hair, keep their clothes cleaned and pressed, their shoes shined, faces shaved, hair trimmed. If they do not clean up they are out of luck with us.

(8) Make all. men and boys join the F.O.I. Class and train them fast, make them brave fighters and willing at any times to give their life for ALLAH's sake and righteous. Muslims all must stick fast together in battle, like a solid wall.

(9) The Minister must be cared for, also Captain and Secretary, but these must work hard and get the Lost Founds. Fear not about your bread.

On violation of the following Laws, you are subject to dismissal for 30 days to an indefinite period of time from the Temple.

1. Sleeping in the Temple.	2. Keeping late hours.
3. Using narcotics (dope, heroin, marijuana).	4. Married and taking up time with other sisters.
5. Abusing your wife.	6. Socializing with Christians.
7. Drinking alcoholic drinks.	8. Unclean homes.
9. Personal hygiene.	10. Watching the movement of sisters.
11. Lying or stealing from one another.	12. Gambling (shooting pool, dice, cards, etc.)
13. Eating pork	14. Gossiping on one another.

If there was any infraction of the law, the person would be subject to punishment. Master W.D. Fard had a ranked system that represented a person's 'status'. "A" Class stood for good standings, "C" Class meant to be on probation, and "F" Class meant "bad standings" or out the Temple.

As described in the lessons, the FOI were a regimental corps:

12. What is the meaning of FOI?
Ans. Fruit of Islam. This is the name given to the military training of Men that belong to Islam in North America.
13. What is the meaning of Captain and Lieutenant?
Ans. Captain and Lieutenant. The duty of the Captain is to give orders to the lieutenant and the lieutenant's duty is to teach the private soldiers, also train them.[260]

The officers of the F.O.I. include the Minister, the Captain, and First, Second, and Third Lieutenants, as well as Secretaries and Investigators. The rank-and-file consists of Squad Leaders and the Private Soldiers. Respect for officers is part of the 'General Orders' and procedures of the F.O.I. The proper salute must be shown to superior officers. The following are some of the general orders for the F.O.I. members:

1. To take charge of any post given.
2. To be a soldier, keep on the alert, and be quick in actions.
3. To report all misunderstanding under any circumstances.
4. To stand my post correctly—a member on post may not shake hands and he must stand attention.
5. To leave my post when and not before properly relieved.

[132]

6. To receive and obey orders from the commissioned and non-commissioned officers and guards.
7. To be careful of what I say and do in the line of duty.
8. To salute all officers and private "soldiers" when a meeting is in process.

The General Orders of the Fruit of Islam are similar to the same set of orders used by the United States Military. Master Fard personally taught and trained the FOI so it's a possibility he intentionally did it that way, or it's possible because so many FOI before becoming Muslims served in the U.S. Military or were World War 1 veterans, and it's possible it was proposed by an ex-veteran.

"The Saviour called for 10,000 men in late Fall 1932," Shadad Ali recalls in his poem, "but not before he taught them the war song." Shadad remembers "1st Division Captain Jesse Ali used to knock Kallatt Muhammad on the back of his knees during the drill." In the next sentence he adds "Master Fard Muhammad had mercy, made Kallatt the Supreme Captain."[261]

Bro. Jeffrey Thrasher who had recently come out of the United States Army became the Drill Instructor (his nephew is Norman Thrasher from doo wop group "The Midnighters"). Burnsteen Sharrieff said the MGT learned how to drill by looking at the FOI from the window of Master Fard's office into the auditorium.

Drilling became an extremely important element of the FOI and MGT class. It was referred to as "the exercise of the Gods." Drill instructors called the cadence to ranks of hundreds of men performing precision drills. Master Fard Muhammad was the designer of the classes and advised he wanted all FOI to be "Quick Moving, Fast Thinking, Right Down to the Modern times."

FOI and MGT Class

At the core of the FOI were the Private Soldiers who were the engine of this military machine. Their troops numbered in the hundreds and grew into the thousands. Through a carefully planned regimental program, the FOI classes were able to extract the physical, mental and spiritual gifts of each man and put it to use for the Nation. Assistant Minister Benjamin Karim recalls:

Without exception, all Muslim men were required to participate in the FOI, which included Captain Joseph's program in martial arts. Captain Joseph, who headed the FOI at Number Seven, conducted our military drills and calisthenics. He also trained us in martial arts. Though military in its organization and discipline, the FOI instructed us only in combat techniques that did not employ weapons. It developed our instincts, our pride, our stamina. It taught us to rely upon our own individual strength; strength multiplied a thousand fold inside an Islamic regiment. Captain Joseph was making sure that we'd be ready for the War of Armageddon. He made better men of lesser men. He took the new brothers — men who had just left a secular community where they may have been abusing their minds and bodies with drugs or alcohol — and indefatigably he reformed them. He made of them the Fruit of Islam.[262]

The responsibilities of an FOI as described by C. Eric Lincoln:

The FOI's duties fall under two broad headings, security and discipline. As a security force, the FOI stands guard in the temples, checks visitors at all Muslim meetings, and provides a personal guard for all ministers and traveling officials, including the Messenger and Louis Farrakhan. As a disciplinary force, its supervises the "trials" of Muslims charged with such offenses as adultery, the use of narcotics, misuse of temple funds, not attending meetings, sleeping during meetings, failing to bring "Lost-Founds" (visitors) to meetings, reporting temple activities to outsiders, using unbecoming language before female Muslims, eating or selling pork, failing to pay extra dues for being overweight, allowing anyone to enter the temple under the influence of liquor, or stating an unwillingness to die for Allah."[263]

Mr. Lincoln in his book "The Black Muslims in America" described the roles and expectations of the Muslim Girls Training Class:

The Muslims place a high premium upon special education for wives and mothers, and their Muslim Girls' Training and General Civilization Class is an effective means of drawing black women into the Movement. The MGT, as it is generally known, concentrates primarily on the art of homemaking. It meets on week nights at the local temples, and the women are "taught how to sew, cook, keep house, rear their children, care for their husbands, and how to behave at home and abroad." High moral behavior is an absolute requirement, for "a Muslim can rise no higher than his women.

The Reformer Burnsteen Sharrieff had shared her notes from MGT under the direction of Mr. W.D. Fard. Her notes read:

MGT CLASS per Burnsteen Sharrieff
Weight
30 days for the 1st offense
90 days for the 2nd offense

For those who would willfully and knowingly will not obey the law of Allah in this class concerning overweight: 10 – 20 and 100 lbs over their proper weight according to the height and age chart.

Class was formed in the 30s by Master Fard Muhammad
Classes taught
Always begin with Prayer, Roll Call and minutes from previous class read by the M.G.T. Secretary.
There would be 2 Floor Walkers.
Dressed for Military Training
Weights & Contributions were 1st
1st Drilling – 25 min.
2nd Exercise – 20 min.
3rd Sewing Class – 20 min.
Not just sewing, learning how to Laundry and remove stains as well.[264]

FOI and MGT were required to memorize several NOI lesson sets, primarily "the Student Enrollment." It was required of them to know all given lessons in order to receive an honorable place amongst the Fruit of Islam. C. Eric Lincoln in his book, "The Black Muslims of North America," notes this tradition:

> Recruits to the FOI are carefully screened before admission, for they are expected to set the highest possible standards of character and dedication. Each candidate is required to pass oral examinations on certain levels of knowledge about the Movement and its history—examinations in which the candidates must recite long memorized passages verbatim, without a single error. Candidates are also required to take a secret oath on admission.[265]

Weekly Muslim Routine
In the Temple, Mr. W.D. Fard established a weekly schedule of events. Years later, Min. Malcolm X would explain:

> I ought to explain that each week night a different Muslim class, or event, is scheduled. Monday night, every temple's Fruit of Islam trains. People think this is just military drill, judo, karate, things like that—which is part of the F.O.I. training, but only one part. The F.O.I. spends a lot more time in lectures and discussions on men learning to be men. They deal with the responsibilities of a husband and a father; what to expect of women; the rights of women which are not to be abrogated by the husband; the importance of the father-male image in the strong household; current events; why honesty, and chastity, are vital in a person, a home, a community, a nation, and a civilization; why one should bathe at least once each twenty-four hours; business principles; and things of that nature.
>
> Then, Tuesday night in every Muslim temple is Unity Night, where the brothers and sisters enjoy each other's conversational company and refreshments, such as cookies and sweet and sour fruit punches. Wednesday nights, at eight P.M., is what is called Student Enrollment, where Islam's

basic issues are discussed; it is about the equivalent of catechism class in the Catholic religion.

Thursday nights there are the M.G.T. (Muslim Girl's Training) and the G.C.C. (General Civilization Class), where the women and girls of Islam are taught how to keep homes, how to rear children, how to care for husbands, how to cook, sew, how to act at home and abroad, and other things that are important to being a good Muslim sister and mother and wife.

Fridays are devoted to Civilization Night, when classes are held for brothers and sisters in the area of the domestic relations, emphasizing how both husbands and wives must understand and respect each other's true natures. Then Saturday night is for all Muslims a free night, when, usually, they visit at each other's homes. And, of course, on Sundays, every Muslim temple holds its services.[266]

The design of the scheduled events naturally brought balance and harmony to otherwise a strenuous and serious subject of tackling racism. It was not all work and no play. Although he cautioned his followers in regards to 'sport and play', he was not opposed to them having fun. In fact, he encouraged it. The Reformer Burnsteen Sharrieff recalls:

Every Tuesday we had a picnic with Muslims only. We danced, played games, especially baseball; at the picnic we would win prizes. Master W.D. Fard Muhammad would always have something to give us especially his laborers, everybody wanted to win so the competition was high. One of the contests was dancing with Master W.D. Fard and on his head sat a full glass of water.

Master Fard Muhammad asked me to dance. I was reluctant and fearful that I would cause the glass to fall. I danced as best as I knew, stumbling along. I was so nervous until he let me go and took another girl to dance and she won the prize. Master W.D. Fard's dance was called the Waltz; he said the Waltz was original music.

Before the fun, he would always have Laborers and teachers meetings. These meetings were very essential because we were being trained how to care for the concerns of the students and the Believers, the proper way to grade lessons, reports made concerning the Temple affairs and Believers.[267]

Mr. Fard and Mysticism

As he used what appeared to be mystical powers to enchant his audiences with what appeared to be magic at his temple meetings. Some of his staff and followers believed Master W.D. Fard was actually capable of 'tuning in' on their thoughts in both humorous ways and not so humorous ways. As he had a way with knowing things about people and events:

Looking back over the mystic happenings during his stay with us, things I saw along with others (to name a few), how he could tell you what you were thinking, things you had said and even to things that you would say and it would come to pass. One such incident, two of the Laborers were at home talking; making mockery of a young 13 year old school teacher who was unusually tall for her age and heavy boned. When Master W.D. Fard got there immediately he reprimanded them for what they did and he was nowhere near the house when they did it.

As to incidents that happened during my laboring as his secretary were many, things I'd think of at home and when I'd get to work he would do them. He had a beautiful wine colored suit that I really like to see him wear; in fact it was brought for him when he came out of jail. For some reason or another he stopped wearing it and I saw the Hon. Elijah Muhammad wearing one just like it; I thought he had given it to him. So this particular morning I was thinking about it and wanted to see him with it on. I went to work and behold he had it on and said this to me when he saw me, "How do I look?" I smiled with a big smile and said emphatically, "FINE." [268]

More Pioneers on the Frontier

As Mr. Fard and Mr. Elijah Muhammad taught on a daily basis, more Black people would "accept their own" and help usher in the Black Nation of Islam. One author from the Muhammad Speaks Newspaper captured it well when he stated it years ago:

CHICAGO-These are special men [and women]. Fearless and determined, they were born with the ability to withstand hard trials, to travel the rough road. They are the distance runners who strive to endure until the end. These are pioneers, the first believers, some of the early followers of the Honorable Elijah Muhammad. May Allàh's richest blessings be upon them.

Many who expected instant heaven perished or fell by the way side. But those who understood, those who knew that they had begun a long journey, they persevered and held open the Temple doors for those who would come later. They knew that they would be taken into captivity, they knew that they would have to serve time in the dungeon of hell, but they also knew that better days would come, because Messenger Muhammad told them so. He prepared them well.[269]

Next we will continue to hear the testimonies of those who trailblazed the path in the early 30s and 40s.

Marcellus Jardan (1932), John Hassan (1933), Karriem Allah (1933)

James Pasha (1933), Willie X (1936), Sam X (1938)

Shelby Karriem (1933), Willie Muhammad (1934), Frank X (1933)

Elizabeth Hassan (1931), Edward Ali (1933), Alphonso X (1941)

Street Scene, South Side (Bronzeville section) of Chicago in the 1930s.

7 Mecca to Medina
(Detroit to Chicago)

Street Scene, South Side (Bronzeville section) of Chicago in the 1930s.

Master W.D. Fard never did stay too long in one place. Still technically banned from Detroit, he opted to spend a lot of time in Chicago, where he'd always send for Elijah. The two worked to establish new beginnings in Temple #2 in Chicago, amidst very turbulent times. This mission required dedicated soldiers. NOI Chicago Pioneer Frank X (1933) and Muhammad Speaks Newspaper remembers:

> TIMES WERE NOT EASY in those days and Muslims were few, and they were not loved by Lost-Found nor white. "Many times when the landlord found out that you were Muslim, you had to get out." Brother Frank X remembers. There were also many other trials and hardships. These were depression years, hostile years. There were many responsibilities, and many posts to command.[270]

The men had to have many talents. Brother Edward Ali, served as Supreme Captain (of Illinois) at one time. He was also a teacher at the University of

Islam. Brother Willie Muhammad was Temple Secretary, also investigator. Each brother held many posts, and they all labored had to build this nation.[271]

Elijah teaches Black Chicagoans about Family Values
The good thing was that Fard and Elijah for the past two years were 'dropping seeds' in Chicago. In 1932 Chicago NOI Pioneer Sidney Shah "was walking down South Park near 42nd" when he first heard the teachings and ended up attending a meeting with his entire family. It was there where he first saw the Hon. Elijah Muhammad:

I was a very sick man...but I was out walking that day, when I saw two men standing on the corner of South Park (Dr. King Dr.) and 42nd Street. One of them was telling the other about a meeting that he had been to the other night. He said, 'I never heard a teaching like that before.'

SO I STOPPED to hear and see if the Brother would say where the meeting was. When I got home I told my wife about it. My wife said if you are going, I'll get all the children ready and we will all go. I had five children at the time.

When the Honorable Elijah Muhammad came in, he was walking very fast, down the aisle, he was being escorted, he ran up the steps, and when I knew anything he had done an about-face and was facing the audience.

He said As-Salaam-Alaikum, then everybody jumped up to their feet and greeted him. The place was just packed.

I felt that I was a part of the meeting that night. Then he began to teach. He was teaching how we should live, how we should carry ourselves, how we should raise our children, and how we should live at home with our family.

And then he said to be healthy, to be happy, and raise your family, and make them healthy and happy, you must begin to live according—he told us what we should eat, when we should eat, and how we should eat. This was very interesting to me!

We were there real late that night, and it was so much that he said, but everything he said was most wonderful, and it was good, and I found joy and I received happiness, and my blessings began from that night, as far as my health is concerned and my home, because the next morning, I took all the pork that we had in the house, and I told my wife. I'm going to throw it out—every bit of it.[272]

Sister Viola Karriem recalls attending the Odd Fellows Hall where the Muslims held meetings in 1932. It was here she first saw the Lessons written on the chalk board:

My name is Sister Viola Karriem. I first heard of the Messenger in 1932. My husband and father was the first to visit the Temple at the Odd Fellows Hall at 33rd and State Streets. They copied the 10 questions off of the board which is "The Student Enrollment." The next meeting, I recited it and was given a letter to write in for my holy name. The first meeting was held at 33rd and State Street at the Odd Fellows Hall, and they met Wednesday night, Friday night and Sundays. Wednesday night it was at 8pm-10pm. On Sundays; from 2pm-4pm.[273]

Sisters Respond Favorably to Elijah's Ministry
Mary Ali, NOI Chicago Pioneer, recalls how she first heard the teachings in 1932. For many Chicagoans originally from the South, hearing Islam immediately impacted their lives:

I was born nearly 80 years ago [circa 1885] in the County of Osyk in Mississippi to a farming family: my five brothers and parents. Even, as a little girl, I was a fighter. I just could not "take" real or imagined insults.

I first heard about Islam from Ben X Davis, a friend of ours. He said he wanted me to see and hear a man who was telling people how to eat to prolong their lives.

I finally accompanied Ben to one of these meetings in the Odd Fellows Hall. While I waited for the meeting to get started, I felt this was all a waste of my time. But when I first saw Elijah Muhammad entering the hall, he seemed to be clothed in a ball of fire, resembling a vision I'd had years earlier when I faced a serious operation. In this first vision, he assured me that the operation I feared would be a success. Now here he was—and I nearly fainted.

This vision of Messenger Muhammad as a ball of fire persisted for two days. I knew with a certainty that this man was like Jesus.

I always had an evil temper until Islam taught me the need for the "Golden Rule"—"do unto others as you would have other do unto you." But for Islam, I am sure my life would have ended, or I would be rotting in some prison for murder or for maiming some innocent person.

My temper used to keep me at bitter odds with most of the people I knew. I was always spoiling for a fight. Even when passers-by looked at me, I sometimes demanded belligerently: "Well, what are you looking at?"

May the peace and blessing of Almighty God Allah be with Messenger Muhammad, who curbed my temper, gave me peace of mind, taught me to search out my faults and rid myself of them; gave me the patience to accept faults in others and to offer solutions rather than criticism's sake. All Muslims are taught to eliminate faults and build good.

I have been a follower of Messenger Elijah Muhammad for 33 years [since 1932]—and they have been fruitful and happy years for me. I followed him through Presidents Hoover, Roosevelt, Truman, Eisenhower, Kennedy and Johnson—and have seen them witness that separation is the only solution to the race problem.

Truly I was blessed, and I thank Allah for preparing me to accept and recognize His Apostle, the Most Honorable Elijah Muhammad. [274]

Fard and Elijah still Physically Supervised Detroit Temple

Master W.D. Fard went back to Detroit after primarily traveling to Chicago and other Mid-Western cities for the past few months. In Temple #1, the FOI and MGT grew in number; the University of Islam was operating at a full capacity. Elijah's brother John Muhammad recalls getting more responsibility from Mr. Fard at the time:

You might ask me how did I, Minister John Muhammad, become a Minor Prophet, and...Minister? Ans. First, I became a minister in 1933 by Master Fard Muhammad. Teaching what I had learned to the Muslim's each Wednesday night and helping on Sundays with the Secretary, Ben Sabakhan. One day I visited the Messenger's home in Chicago. After dining with him, we walked out of the dining room together. We stopped before entering the lobby room and he said to me, "Seal up John, write no more, the seven thunders have utter thy voice, and the Messenger then said to me, "you go and get in the class of those little minor fellows and study along with them, they don't talk much; but brother what they say they hit the point. That is where you should be. And I joined that class.275

Early in 1933, I was permitted to the rostrum to ask the members to give charity and Teach what I had learned in Islam. I taught the Meaning of Our FLAG OF ISLAM, given to us by Master Fard Muhammad, I taught it as I had learned. I served in every position that is known in The Nation of Islam, except becoming God and The Messenger of Allah; I was, for one day, Everything.

In 1933-1934, I was Treasurer, appointed by The Honorable Elijah Muhammad. I had visited other meeting places before visiting at 3408 Hasting Street, which was the birth place of Master Fard in the Teaching of Islam to the (So-Called Negro) Black Americans. I visited in Chicago, Temple #2, alone while The Messenger was setting it up.

I made a Promise to Both Master Fard Muhammad and Messenger Elijah Muhammad (P.B.U.H.) as they taught me to, never ever fail to carry out the work that I had been taught by them in The Nation of Islam. Therefore, today I continue that which was taught. According to this teaching it has enough Wisdom and Understanding of Knowledge in it, to last 9,980 years before it expires.

I have never disobeyed any of those in authority over me in this Nation of Islam set up by Master Fard Muhammad, Whom Messenger Elijah Muhammad declared to the World was ALLAH IN PERSON WHO visited North America.

I have always taken a position or Post in The Nation of Islam, wherever it was vacant, and was justified by those in authority over me. Master Fard Muhammad and the Captains and was never turned down. I was loved By All.276

Fard asks a Question of the Faithful in Detroit

While in Detroit during the Tuesday picnic, Master W.D. Fard sponsored more games, baseball and dancing for the Laborers and Believers. At least one noticed the gravity of the question Master Fard Muhammad posed to the Detroit Believers. John Muhammad:

> Because in 1933, I and all of the Teachers were taken on a picnic by Master Fard Muhammad into Ferndale, Michigan. After he had finished with the Teachers, we danced a while. But that dancing was not for us to continue and then go back to that which he brought us out from. Do you understand me?! It was that we enjoy ourselves in a Good Manner and not do the "boogie-woogie!" Do you understand me, now?[277] We are not to do what you and I see them doing on T.V.
>
> In doing so, he asked the question, "How many of you will be here and keep up my Teaching until I come back?" That is the question that Master Fard Muhammad asked. The Messenger was there. We all held up our hands and said we would do so. He said to us, "Will you continue this Islam?" We all said, "YES!"
>
> So that is why I am continuing, today, because I made that promise. At that time, I did not know that Master Fard Muhammad was God in Person.[278] All of the people who were there at the picnic), except two, are dead (today). The two people are myself and my wife [Burnsteen Sharrieff]. We weren't married when that happened.[279]

W.D. Fard deported from Detroit for 2nd Time and Sheds Tears

Not long after, word traveled quickly with the Detroit Police Department that Prophet W.D. Fard had returned and was primarily responsible for the resurgence of the Nation of Islam. "On May 25, 1933, Fard was arrested on the pretext of disturbing the peace. He was booked and photographed the next day, then ordered to leave the city."[280] After leaving the Precinct, W.D. Fard had a meeting at Elijah's house with his top officials (mostly the Messenger's family). Elijah's eldest son Emanuel, who was present on that day, recalls the emotional meeting:

> After He missioned him and was about to depart from us there in Detroit. He said to the brothers and sisters: "You don't need me anymore, hear Elijah." He left our home embracing the Messenger on the rear porch; both of them were shedding tears with handkerchiefs in their hands. I never will forget the sadness expressed on their faces. This was on May 26, 1933.[281]

Elijah's son Nathaniel was also present, and gives a very vivid description and important facts as to what happened on that day. He remembers the sorrow his Father Elijah showed when W.D. Fard had to leave Detroit, the second time, and last time. Elijah was so grieved, that

Master Fard advised him to stay home and let his Brother Supreme Captain Kallatt escort him to the state lines:

> I turned 8yrs old, he left May 26, 1933, less than a month, the next month, June 23rd, I was 8yrs old. Let me tell it like this, Daddy was the Supreme Minister, and Uncle Kallatt was the Supreme Captain. Daddy was crying so hard when Master Fard Muhammad got ready to leave, he started crying, really, just crying like a baby because he didn't want to see him go, because he had been with him for 3 ½ years, and was at the house almost every day, so he was crying. And Master Fard Muhammad told daddy, he said, "I don't think you should go with me, let Kallatt follow me to the state line." Daddy and I, he was crying so bad, until I taken his hand and helped his hand, and we went out, we had an enclosed porch, we went out and stood on the enclosed porch, and my daddy crying, so I started crying. Things like this, I have a heck of a memory so I don't like to read a lot of books brother that people wrote. I pick them up and throw them bye, because I know they don't know what they talking about.[282]

Fard gives Farewell Speech to Detroit Muslims with FOI Escort

As Kallatt walked his teacher outside to his car with masses of Muslims looking on, Master W.D. Fard acknowledged the Muslims, and gave them a short impromptu speech and promise before getting in his car and speeding off in a caravan:

> Mr. W.D. Fard had been caught by the police department many times, generally being charged with disturbing the peace in the community. Later on, in May, 1933, he was compelled to leave the city, a condition under which these thousands of people gathered around his car when he began to leave, "weeping, sad and grieving" for the departure of their Savior. Before his leaving he told the audience to act together and do their best until he returned to save them and lead them to their native land.[283]

> His current Apostle [Elijah Muhammad] described the day of his [W.D. Fard] deportation from Detroit as one of the greatest tragedies that he has ever seen among the Negro community. His [W.D. Fard] last statements to these sad and weeping masses gathered around his car at the hour of his deportation were: "Don't worry. I am with you; I will be back to you in the near future to lead you out of this hell."[284]

To their surprise something mysteriously happened with the FOI escorted caravan. Not long afterwards, Supreme Captain Kallatt came back to Elijah's house with a mysterious report. Nathaniel:

> My uncle [Kallatt] followed him. Let me tell you what happened though. My uncle came back and told my daddy, he said he followed him to—he said he WAS following him, but he said he looked up and all of a sudden it looked like the car just disappeared! He don't know which way he went. That's

what my uncle Kallatt told my daddy when he came back. He said, "I followed him, but when I looked, I didn't see the car no more, he just disappeared." The car he meant just disappeared. Now, that's what Kallatt told my daddy.[285]

W.D. Fard arrested in Chicago (1st Time) immediately upon Arrival

As W.D. Fard left Detroit and went to Chicago, Illinois, The police must have known of his plans because He was immediately arrested upon his arrival. There He sent for Elijah Muhammad. Elijah explains:

He (Mr. W.F. Muhammad, God in person) chose to suffer 3 ½ years to show his love for his people, who have suffered over 300 years at the hands of a people who by nature are evil and wicked and have no good in them. He was persecuted, sent to jail in 1932, and ordered out of Detroit, on May 26, 1933. He came to Chicago in the same year and was arrested almost immediately on his arrival and placed behind prison bars.

He submitted himself with all humbleness to his persecutors. Each time he was arrested, he sent for me so that I might see and learn the price of Truth for us, the so-called American Negroes (members of the Asiatic Nation).

He was well able to save himself from such suffering, but how else was the scripture to be fulfilled? We followed in his footsteps suffering the same persecution.[286]

Elijah and FOI escort Fard from Jail, establishes Study Groups

Min. Nathaniel recalls his Father Elijah getting the news and taking some FOI to Chicago to get Master W.D. Fard from jail:

He [W.D. Fard] was arrested, they put him in the police station at 4800 Wabash. He sent for my daddy, and my daddy went and got him out. 4800 Wabash, it was right on the corner, a police station. Every time he got arrested he always sent for daddy. Daddy would take the Fruit of Islam (some of them) and they would go down there and get him out.

Even when they was in Detroit, daddy would come with him (Master Fard) from Detroit to Chicago. We had a lot of Muslims in Chicago. When they gave him 24 hours to get out Detroit, they had already established a Mosque in Chicago because the Secretary, and one of the Investigators used to come from Chicago to Detroit to take care of business with them.[287]

To avoid police, Master W.D. Fard and Elijah Muhammad established other meeting places in Chicago:

On May 26, 1933, on the back porch of 283 E. Hancock Street in Detroit, Michigan. The Saviour, who was preparing to depart and the Messenger embraced. Both were crying, tears running down their cheeks. After coming to Chicago, Master Fard Muhammad would send for our Leader, along with the Laborers of Detroit to meet with them at the Brookmont Hotel on 40th

[146]

and Michigan Avenue, a site that is now razed and vacant. But the message still lingers. They would also meet at the Grand Hotel on 50th and King Drive.[288]

Elijah Speaks as Front Representative for the NOI

Still the object of a manhunt, Master W.D. Fard allowed Elijah Muhammad to be the front man, while he worked with the Messenger and taught him in the background day and night. In the midst of the times, the Messenger 'dropped seeds of wisdom' as he brought FOI from Detroit to Chicago to teach. NOI Chicago Pioneer, Edward Ali, a future Supreme Captain of the FOI in Illinois, remembers first hearing the Messenger speak:

It was on a Wednesday in May of 1933 when Brother Edward Ali first heard the Teaching.

"HE (THE Messenger) had four brothers from Detroit. They had their fez on - what we call the universe. He was demonstrating the fez, he had one and the four brothers had one.

"The people wanted to know about the fez, why the fez was red. He told them why, why it was red - well that's the fire...fire being red, naturally the fez was red.

"It sounded real good." Brother Ali states.

"What impresses me most and makes me want to live a long, long time, is the progress that the Nation of Islam is making. We never had any restaurants to eat in the early days. If you didn't have a house of your own, we had to eat at some brother's home.

"I never will forget, there was one sister (she's dead now) Sister Pauline Bahar, she always would fix dinner for the Fruit (F.O.I.). She would always prepare something good for the men in Islam."

There are many memories, many secrets, much hardship and much joy in the history of the early believers in Islam. There is still much, that, despite how long ago it happened is still highly controversial and delicate. The battle at 11th and State streets, the years of captivity, and much, much more that Muhammad Speaks will endeavor to bring to its readers in the future.

There are many brothers and sisters who were not mentioned, but we will be seeing them, and we will bring their words to you, our readers. But it is their story, these gallant men and courageous women who struggled and persevered, survived and brought about change in the Name of Allah and His True Divine Apostle the Hon. Elijah Muhammad.[289]

Elijah Teaches in the Highways and Byways

Sometimes scrambling for places to meet, the Muslims met in odd places: "There was not always a place to teach Islam and when one was found it was not always comfortable, but these determined brothers and sisters never gave up. I remember one time when we didn't have a place to teach, and Sister Ada Hazziez had a place they used for a livery stable -

she opened this place up for us, and we went up the alley to her place to have a meeting.' said Brother Willie Muhammad."[290]

Elijah Impresses FOI by teaching the Laws of Islam

Brother Edward Ali also remembers those difficult years and how Master W.D. Fard and Elijah Muhammad spread Islam amongst the Black Man in Chicago:

> Many of us taught on street corners, in parks, in alleys, on playgrounds, or wherever we found a group of Black people, we'd set up shop and take care of business. "WE WERE TEACHING the same things then as the Messenger is teaching today...ISLAM! In other words he was familiarizing us with Almighty God and His Wisdom. Not only that, but he was trying to show us that God is a living being, not a spook or something that you can't see. He was making us acquainted with a being, a human being as God (God in Person). That was the main topic of the day.
>
> In those glorious, early years, the brothers and sisters were extremely close, their great unity was heralded far and wide.
>
> Unity in those days was very, very good...The brothers always visited one another's homes, and every brother had a blackboard in his home. We discussed the knowledge, which had been taught to us. The Messenger said that we must study hard, our wisdom.
>
> But he also gave us the law, and we tried to live by that law...According to the law of Islam, you want for your what you want for yourself. In other words if I have a loaf of bread, half of that loaf belongs to you."
>
> "If the Messenger came and found you working, the first thing he would say is, 'Brother can I help you here?' and he would unbutton his coat and jump in and help. That's what I call wanting for your brother what you want for yourself - that's what I call unity - you are helping! Two or three or four or five brothers can always do better than one. Well that's what he was teaching!!!
>
> "He would pull his coat off anytime and help you to do a job. He was always willing to do something for you, and he still is today."[291]

Elijah reunites with future National Investigator John Hassan

It was in Chicago 1933 where Elijah Muhammad would meet his long-time companion and fellow Georgian John Hassan who eventually became the National Investigator and a Business Manager of the Nation of Islam. John recalls his trek from Georgia to Chicago:

> I was born in the little town of West Point, GA. My father owned a small grocery store there but like all the other residents of the town I had to quit school at an early age.
>
> By the time I reached 18, the big city was beckoning so I took my wife and headed for Chicago.

You have to come from a small community like I did to be able to imagine what the big city is like to a young man who had never seen such things before. All that excitement and glitter attracted me like bugs to a light.

In the small town I came from everyone you saw was a neighbor. A stranger immediately drew the attention of the whole little community.
BUT HERE, in the big city, everyone was a stranger.

We had associates – my wife and I – but they weren't the kind of associates you could really count on.

My first job in the big city was at the Harris Bed and Spring company, where I worked for three years.

Then I worked for an express company for a short time.

After that, I started working for the Brach Candy company and I've been with them ever since – for 23 years and seven months.[292]

John Hassan recollects the first time he heard Islam, how it changed his life and how he was convinced of Elijah Muhammad and his mission:

I FIRST heard of Islam in 1933, while I was working for the express company. The Minister was Augusta Mohammed, and the things he said really reached me. He filled me with the desire to become a Muslim.

About a week later, when I heard the man who had taught him, the Honorable Elijah Muhammad, I was convinced that this man could and would lift the Negro from his pitiful plight.

It seemed to me then that the Messenger of Allah could do no wrong. Now, 30 years later [1963], I am more convinced than ever. The Messenger of Allah has withstood the test of time. He has been successful in uplifting our people. I am a living witness.

THOUGH I always provided for my family to the best of my ability, Chicago, with its back-alley crap games, house-rent parties and cheap bath tub gin took up most of my time, in those early days.

I was a free-wheeling, big time fool, fresh out of the country with no idea of what it was all about until I heard the teachings of the Honorable Elijah Muhammad. He really put me on the right track.

Without doubt, Mr. Muhammad is the only leader of the so-called negro. He is the only one who demands of us the best we have. Many others are referred to as leaders but they only lead us down the same path as do our oppressors. [293]

Minister Elijah converts Street Toughs to the Nation of Islam

Another Chicago NOI Pioneer from 1933, James Pasha, shares his conversion story of coming from a life of trouble to Islam:

For the past 31 years of my life, I have been a faithful follower of the Most Honorable Elijah Muhammad. In all of that time, my faith in Islam and Allah, the God of the universe, has only increased.

I was born in Arkadelphia, Arkansas, in 1897 among a poor family of ten children. My father was a lifetime woodcutter who never was allowed by the redneck white power structure to gain his manhood as a first-class citizen.

Even as a child, I then deeply resented the superior manner in which whites treated Negroes. Had someone asked me then to define what it was that I resented so fiercely, perhaps I couldn't have told you how I felt—but it was there nevertheless.

I remember that I once got so fed up with this southern way of life, that I told my mother, "I'm leaving here as soon as I'm grown enough to go."

I soon left Arkansas for Chicago, where I was dealt a more deplorable fate. In those days, I was nothing but a rowdy, whiskey-drinking fool. I would finish one 90-day sentence at the Chicago City Jail or Bridewell Prison, get arrested for the same thing again and land myself right back in there.

I was tough. I would pick a fight with somebody over nothing and I loved to frighten people with my rowdiness.

In order to stay alive during the Depression years, I hustled junk and waste to collect enough money for booze and an occasional meal and a place to stay. I was dirty and going nowhere fast. I was fighting the future and mad at the past.[294]

Pasha remembers hearing Islam for the first time, and seeing the Messenger speak live in the Chicago Temple#2:

In the spring of 1933, a friend of mine came by my house and told me about a so-called messenger who was speaking in Chicago's black ghetto that night. He said that his messenger could speak for six hours at a time.

Thinking I might be entertained for a while, I agreed to go to the meeting. Almost overnight, Islam captured my imagination and my loyalty once I heard this great man of God, the Most Honorable Elijah Muhammad.

His topic for that speech was "God Rode the Mule." This eloquent speech by this great man bound me to Islam forever. The clear and precise account Apostle Elijah Muhammad gave of the Almighty God Allah and His eagerness to aid all people who turned to Him, deeply inspired me.

No longer would I walk the streets of Chicago with a chip on my shoulder. No longer did I desire to engage in fights to prove my manhood. I began to realize how wonderful it feels to be proud black man.

Messenger Elijah Muhammad taught me that regardless of what kind of employment I had, that there is dignity in it. Mr. Muhammad taught me the importance of self-preservation and the wastefulness of liquor and smoking.[295]

A Typical Lecture of Supreme Minister Elijah Muhammad

The Most Hon. Elijah Muhammad typically taught for four to six hours at a time, speaking on what Master Fard Muhammad taught him. Following would be a typical lecture:

O give ear, all you lost founds of the Nation of Islam, in the Wilderness of North America. (The Seventeen Million Black Asiatics).

Awake! Out of the sleep of ignorance, and the death of understanding, and hear, see, and believe. Rejoice! And be glad, for he who we have hoped for, and prayed, that he would come to our rescue, and deliver us from our oppressor, the devil, (The American White Man) has come.

In 1929 when Wall Street went collapse, the white devil millionaires, withdrew their money from the banks. Some deposited their money in Asia, so said the Prophet, while others hid their treasures at home. Because these big bankers can see what is coming upon the nation. So they, and their treasures are fleeing to Asia Minor, trying to escape the on-coming fires of Almighty ALLAH.[296]

Michael is spoken of in Judge. The first chapter and the ninth verse as Archangel contending with the devil, about Moses. This is true. None of us knew much about the Prophet, until this mighty Savior came, and taught us, and raised us up a Prophet, and he taught us and is yet teaching us the Truth.

The American Bible, pictures all of the Prophets, and the Ancient worthies, as white Jews. This is untrue. In this you can see, how the devil whiteman, claims our great men of old, to be his people. Thus said our Savior and Deliverer, that Moses was an half Original Man, and he secured his commission from the Holy City Mecca in Arabia, to teach the devils who was living a cave-man life, in Europe at that time. Also says the Holy Quran: (He sent you Moses, We the Black Man of Arabia. This shows the dispute concerning Moses. The devils themselves do not know all about Moses, or any of the Prophets.[297]

Elijah Often Spoke of Fard's Greatness to Audiences

In his lecture, the Hon. Elijah Muhammad spoke very highly of his teacher to his audiences:

This Mighty One, that was with us, going in the Name of Prophet Fard Mohammed, which I do declare unto you, and the world, that He is Our long awaited Deliverer, or the second coming of Jesus. This does not mean that Jesus, that was here 2000 years ago, but the works of Freedom, Justice and Equality, what he died for, and what he prophesied, that he would come again, not him personally, but his brother whom we have with us today, none other than Prophet Fard Mohammed, who would be able to set up Freedom, Justice and Equality at this time, and destroy all that do not believe.

This man, Prophet Fard Mohammed, was born in the Holy City Mecca, in Arabia in the year 1877. This man, spent forty-two years of His life, in preparing himself for His work of setting up righteousness on the earth, and to raise the sleeping dead, the ignorant seventeen million original black people, the lost found Nation of Islam. The Prophecy does not mean that we would be physically dead, but mentally dead to the knowledge and understanding of ourselves, or our father, who made the earth and the Heavens and all the things therein.

This man, knows the Holy Qur-an by heart, and tells the life of every Prophet that appeared before Him, and their work from the cradle to the grave; without consulting any book. He teaches us both past and the future. His words are not like those, who studied the past, from Histories, but as one who seem to have been on the scene of the happenings. Therefore, this shows that He was born for this work, and not made for it by anyone, nor does he argue with anyone about believing what He says. He is independent about that. But He warns you sternly that He is your best friend and that He will face every work He has told us.[298]

Elijah Muhammad taught of Master Fard Muhammad's greatness in his absence. Often speaking of his capable powers:

But we have been deprived of the wisdom, and knowledge of ourselves, for near 400 years and this is the cause of our unbelief in Him, in which we fulfill the scripture where it says He came unto His own and His own received Him not. John the first chapter and the 11th verse. His father is a blackman and his mother a Jewish.

He has proven that he knows everything we do, and hear everything we say, or even our own thought. He is able to communicate with His people in Asia, without the use of wires, or radios, or any other instrument but His ears. He caused them whom He is communicating with to appear to you before your eyes in a glass of clear water. His Wisdom is unlimited.

He despise witchcraft and root doctors, they are all liars, and teaches you how they deceive you, and exposes their secrets.

Now let us get down to His teaching. I am not able to pay for the publishing of a book large enough to tell you of all His great teachings, that He is giving to we the lost-found brothers, of His, in North America.[299]

Future Supreme Captain & National Secretary to Meet Fard and Elijah

It was in Chicago that a family of eight, (including three sons and three daughters), would eventually see Master Fard Muhammad and the Hon. Elijah Muhammad. Master Fard Muhammad gave them all names, amongst them was a 14-year-old son, Raymond Sharrieff, who'd eventually become Elijah's son-in-law when he married his daughter Ethel, and also became the future Supreme Captain of the Nation of Islam in the 1940s. Raymond's sister, Pauline, became Pauline Bahar and would serve as a Secretary in the NOI. A young Raymond Sharrieff recalls seeing Master W.D. Fard motion Elijah by his side on stage exclaiming, "If not for Elijah, I would have never have come!"[300] Brother Karriem Allah, who was the first to notify the elder brother of the Sharrieff family about "the Messenger", reveals his story.

Bro. Karriem Allah relaying how Elijah took Chicago by Storm

One of the first Black man to hear and accept Elijah Muhammad as "The Messenger" was Brother Karriem Allah. He recalls how he first heard about Elijah Muhammad:

During the time the Messenger was visiting here in Chicago in 1933 he first started teaching on the West Side, in churches and meeting halls.

A brother (Blackman) Clifford Williams came to my house and said to me: "There's going to be a man here from Egypt Friday night. He's going to speak at "The Hall" (Universal Negro Improvement Association) which was the located at 1841 W. Lake Street, at eight o'clock Friday night. I was eighteen years old then.

"Come on go with me to hear him," Brother Clifford said to me. It was on Thursday evening, my working hours. The time I was working at Drisco Plating Company, 1400 W. Caroll. I said to him that 'I couldn't go then – on Friday night, but I asked him to find out where the man would be speaking on Sunday afternoon. We'll get together and go hear him then.' I didn't see him again for about three weeks. [301]

Karriem and Friends Seek Out the Messenger

Still curious, Karriem recruited a friend of his, who would happen to be the older brother of Raymond Sharrieff (the future Supreme Captain of the Nation of Islam), and the two set out looking for Elijah:

In the meanwhile I got with another Brother, Alphonso Hatchet, the oldest brother of the present Supreme Captain, Raymond Sharrieff. I told him what Clifford Williams had told me. "So let's you and I find out where this man is going to speak this Sunday afternoon."

"It was one early Sunday afternoon in August, around the third." Brother Karriem Allah told Muhammad speaks. Somewhat a sunny day. A little summer breeze was in the air," After explaining to Brother Alphonso about this man who we did not really know at the time, I learned from him (Alphonso) that he too has heard Mr. Muhammad speak; at a little church on Damen and Warren Boulevard. But Alphonso didn't really know then who he was either. It was fun to him. He was about my age. "He too was fascinated by the Messenger's wisdom." In discussing the Messenger, we decided we should go hear him. So we went search of where was to speak.

First we went to the near Southside, near 13th and Loomis. We thought he would be there at the UNIA hall meeting to be held at 1 p.m. But he wasn't.

However there was a large gathering of people there. After sitting down for about half an hour, we decided that he wasn't going to be there. We left the hall and went in further search of him to find out where he would speak that afternoon. [302]

Finds the Building Where Elijah is Teaching the People

Karriem Allah and Alphonso finally found the building where Elijah Muhammad was preaching that day:

We walked down 13th Street to 12th and Morgan. We saw groups of people going into a hall. We walked up to some of the men who were standing on the outside and asked them if there was "going to be any speaking here this afternoon. They said 'Yes, there's man up there speaking now..' Upon hearing this, we entered the hall from the ground floor and walked up one flight. There we saw the Messenger of Allah, The Most Honorable Elijah Muhammad, standing before a large gathering of people. He had just begun speaking. There was no room to sit, all seats were taken; there was standing room only. [303]

A First View of the Messenger of Allah

Standing in the audience, the two cherished their first glimpse of the Messenger, as Elijah enlightened everyone in attendance:

"He was a young –looking, dynamic, smiling, and cheerful man. He was full of the fire of Islam and the spirit of Allah to deliver his message of truth to we, the lost members of the aboriginal Black nation," continued Brother Karriem **Allah**.
"He began to teach the history of our first parents. Of how they were kidnapped and brought over here by an English trader, John Hawkins. He taught us how the children of the slaves were taken from them; how the parents were killed outright by the enemy. He told us how we, the children of the first parents were sold onto chattel slavery. He told us that we remained in this state of slavery for 310 years until our Savior Allah appeared in the person of Master Fard Muhammad To Whom Praises are due forever...[304]

Elijah Teaches about Ezekiel's Wheel, the Mother Plane

Teaching "the Supreme Wisdom" of his teacher, Elijah enthralled his audience when he spoke on Ezekiel's Wheel and its hidden meaning in the symbolism of the Bible. Karriem Allah recalls the reaction from those in attendance:

The people, upon hearing this history about our parents, began to stand up! They were enraged at the way we had been treated by our former slavemasters. The Messenger of Allah saw this. Saw that they were angry. He quickly changed the subject because everyone in the hall had stood up in anger at the slavemaster.

Then the Messenger of Allah went to the blackboard. He drew a large round circle on it, and began to teach us the Bible, to Ezekiel 1:9. There in Ezekiel he pointed out to us where Ezekiel saw thus wheel (The Mother Ship) or circle in his vision. He described it as a wheel-in-a-wheel. And on the wheel he said there were four living kinds of creatures?

"Everybody sat down. The Messenger was cooling their anger." The Messenger went on teaching; "When the wheel lifted up, the four living kinds of creatures were also lifted up." The Messenger explained to the audience who the four living kind of creatures represented. He said, "They represented four living kinds of creatures, the four great colors of man- the Black (Original), brown, yellow and red man."

[154]

The audience, upon hearing this great truth, became fascinated! And coming from the mouth of this little man! We were so quiet that you could hear a pin drop on the floor.[305]

Elijah Asks the Audience Help to Start a Temple

At the end of what amounted to marathon meeting of hours on end, Elijah asked the audience if they could help him decide the best location to start a Temple:

The Messenger started that meeting at 2 p.m. that Sunday afternoon. He ended it at 2:30 a.m. the next morning. I think it was August 4, 1933. Just before dismissal. He asked the audience where would they like to have future meetings – on the Westside or on the Southside? "I want you to tell me where you want to meet because I know where we can rent a place on either side of town," he said. Although we were all from the Westside we agreed on the Southside because there were more original (Black) people on the Southside than on the Westside.'

When we made our choice known, he said to us: "I want you to meet with me next Saturday at 3335 S. State (site of the present Illinois Institute of Technology). I can rent a hall there from the Odd Fellows."[306]

Elijah Muhammad Secures the First Building for Temple #2

As word spread throughout Chicago, groups of Black people started to attend the Chicago meetings en masse. NOI Chicago Pioneer, Karriem Allah, recalls when he went with a group to see the Messenger for the first time, and the actual details of how they established Temple #2 in 1933:

Our first meeting with the Messenger, the Most Honorable Elijah Muhammad, was held on August 3, 1933, on the Westside of Chicago.

The Messenger of Allah, the Most Honorable Elijah Muhammad, found in us who were present at that first meeting, enough unity to set up the first Temple of Islam in Chicago (Temple No. 2).

Before he dismissed us, he asked us to take a vote with him on where we wanted a Temple – the Southside or Westside of Chicago. We chose the Southside because there were more Black people on the Southside than the Westside.

We thought the Messenger could get more converts to Islam from the heavily populated area. All those present at this first meeting with the Messenger, however, were from the Westside.

The actual Temple organization was set up in our first meeting with Messenger Muhammad, at 3335 South State St. It was fully established one week later.[307]

Karriem Allah, remembers how Elijah Muhammad traveled from Detroit to Chicago, and the details of the first meeting held in Temple #2:

Upon leaving the meeting early that first Monday morning (2:30a.m. to be exact) the Messenger instructed us to meet him at the South State St. locations the following Sunday which was Aug. 10, 1933.

We were there at 12 noon awaiting the arrival of the Messenger. He arrived at 2 P.M. He had come all the way from Temple No. 1 in Detroit, Mich. The first meeting held at Temple No. 2 on State Street was conducted by the Honorable Elijah Muhammad. A large crowd of people had already gathered to greet the Messenger upon his arrival.

After he entered the Temple we filed quietly in behind him, in this building that was to be our first Temple.

It was a standing room only crowd. Those who could sit down, sat down. Others stood all around the walls to hear the life giving Truth coming from the mouth of our beloved leader and Teacher and Guide, the Most Honorable Elijah Muhammad.

We had a glorious time in our first meeting, in our first Temple with our Divinely Missioned Teacher, Missioned from Allah – Who Came to the wilderness of North America in the Person of Master W.D. Fard to Whom Praise is due forever for giving to us the lost and found members of the aboriginal Black Nation the Honorable Elijah Muhammad. May the peace and blessing of Allah abide with Him.

An echo from the past, the early days of the Honorable Elijah Muhammad's mission, the glorious past.

Dear brothers and sisters, as the Messenger would say in closing his lecturers to us, think five times before speaking and maybe you will be right. He didn't say we would be right. Think before speaking. Again he would say to us whatever you do use a good judgment and let no one cause you to lose your reward.

Your reward is your life, your life is sacred, teaches the Honorable Elijah Muhammad. Keep a cool temper.

May the peace and blessings of Allah abide with you all dear brothers and sisters. I am truly one of your brothers.[308]

Chicago Temple Crowds Overflow to Hear Fard and Elijah

Master W.D. Fard was much of an attraction in Chicago as he was in Detroit, often speaking to packed halls of 1,500 or more people. An increasing number of converts found him to be a very knowledgeable and endearing person. NOI Chicago Pioneer Frank X recollections capture the jubilance and joy and happiness that Master Fard Muhammad showed when he was among the Believers:

He was always happy…He would come in bowing. He would say, "It's been a long time since I've seen my uncle (so-called Negro). I promised Abraham that I'd come after you. I told Abraham I'd go and gather them myself, I won't send anyone, I'll go myself'."

[When Brother Frank first heard the teaching in early 1933, these were depression years and times were hard].

I REMEMBER the first time I came, it was at the Odd Fellows Hall on 33rd and State. I had never seen so many people at one time. There was no room to sit, they were all along the wall and scattered out in the halls. The Messenger taught for about six hours that night. Some got up and went home and came back again, and he was still teaching. It was a big hall; more than 1,500 people were there.[309]

Elijah's Star continues to Rise throughout Chicago

In a Chicago's West Side church is where NOI Pioneer Willie Muhammad first heard the teachings "in late autumn of 1933, in a church on the Westside of Chicago on the corner of Maypole and Damen." Later, after he became a good follower, he states he knew a rough road was ahead. He recalls the ambitions statements made by the Messenger in regards to how many Muslims it would take to raise the Black Nation:

"I never had the idea that we had an easy job, I was not a great scholar of the Bible, but I did know that Moses was in the wilderness for 40 years," he said comparing the history of Moses to Messenger Muhammad.

I WOULD LISTEN carefully to the Messenger, how he would speak of 40 years - then he would tell us how many ministers he needed to raise the dead - he said he needed one million ministers. All of this told me that this job would take some time," said Brother Willie Muhammad.

"THE MESSENGER also said that our work was right here in America - that we didn't have to go to Africa, that it was here in America - where we could do the most good."

"I remember how the Messenger, under all circumstances, would persevere - and he's the same today, only wiser, but he never varied his teaching." "I've seen the Messenger suffering a severe attack of his sickness (asthma), then within the next hour, he was gone into the streets to carry on his work."Things like this always gave me courage to know that no matter what or how I felt - this work must go on."[310]

As it was in Detroit, Black Chicagoans were mesmerized to hear history as taught by the Nation of Islam. NOI Pioneer Fletcher Majied recalls:

Brother Fletcher Majied said he came to the Odd Fellows Hall at 33rd and State for the first time in the fall of 1933.

"The Messenger told us about this white man (JOHN HAWKINS), and how he brought our forefathers here.

"He said that John Hawkins anchored his ship down on the Nile River, he was flying our Flag—he was sailing the banks of the Nile, where our people were doing trade. He had nude women on the ship, and our people had never seen anything like this, so they crowded on the ship.

"OUR FLAG was flying, our flag was a red flag. Freedom, Justice and Equality. When he got out to sea, they lowered our flag.

"Some of our people jumped off the boat, and began to swim back to shore—they look back at the brothers on the ship and said—good-by you're going to hell," brother Majied states.[311]

Elijah's Style and Teachings Stuck with Audience Members

Such a passionate and effective preacher, Elijah Muhammad had the rapt attention of those who visited the Temple. His command of NOI theology and the history of the white man struck a chord with his audience. NOI Pioneers remember:

When the Messenger would enter the Temple, all would stand. Muslims and non-Muslims would bow and greet Him with As-Salaam-Alaikum to show love, honor and respect to our Divine Teacher, Leader and Guide who was worthy of such.

After the Messenger mounted the speaker's stand to give to us the life-giving truth from Allah, peace and calm prevailed in the Temple. Everyone sat quietly and gave the Messenger their undivided attention. He captured the audience with His Supreme wisdom, knowledge and understanding of the Original man's glorious past and the history of the creation.

It was fantastic and amazing to sit and listen to a man pour out to us so much wisdom and knowledge of the original Black man on how great he was and how great he is. We never got tired of listening. The Messenger would start teaching at 2 o'clock in the afternoon and dismiss in the early hours of Monday morning.

He never even took as much as a drink of water during the long hours He would stand before us teaching Allah's wisdom and knowledge which has been a carefully guarded secret until the coming of Allah in the Person of Master Wallace Fard Muhammad, to Whom Praise is due forever for coming to save the lost brother from Asia.

We are from Asia, teaches the Honorable Elijah Muhammad. He said we were brought over here to this Western Hemisphere by an English trader by the name of John Hawkins in the year 1555.

We, the Messenger said, have been here for more than 400 years. He said it was written and prophesied by the prophets that Allah (God) would come after the end of the white Caucasian rule of the devil who, he said, deceived our forefathers with the promise of gold.

Instead of god, we received the worst kind of slavery of any human being ever in our history. He said that white man destroyed our first father's brains so he could master their children and make (them) us chattel slaves.

The Messenger taught us in the early days this history of the fall of our forefathers and why we are blind, deaf and dumb to the knowledge of our self and kind.

Why is it so hard to unite us unto our own; Islam? We the Black people in America are robbed completely of the knowledge of ourselves by the evil Caucasian man. The messenger taught us that when a man has been robbed of the knowledge of himself, this is the worst crime that can be committed against a human being.

He told us in those days—the glorious past—that Allah came, he said, to free us from the power of the white man and give us a name from Himself – a free name that has Divine meaning from the Divine Supreme Being of the universe.[312]

NOI Temple Etiquette

In spite of the adversity he and the Muslims faced, the Hon. Elijah Muhammad reminded all of his followers of the true and correct spirit of being a true Muslim (hypocrites aside). The Messenger reminded them how Master Fard Muhammad instructed to 'work cheerfully and fear not." Karriem Allah recalls:

When you come into the Temple of Islam you sit down and be quiet. No loud talking should be heard in the Temple of Islam. You should study your general orders.

Let us take for example, the Messenger of Allah. He is a perfect example of peace and quiet. He is working hard to get you out of your savage ways. Look at your captain. Look at the intelligence that he shows the F.O.I.

In the early days of Islam, as was taught to us by the Messenger of Allah, the Honorable Elijah Muhammad, this kind of nonsense was not tolerated in our Temple. You were told once not to be a nuisance in the Temple. We the Muslims obeyed our instructions coming to us from the Messenger of Allah.

We learned early to obey the Messenger. In the early days of Islam, as was taught to us by the Messenger of Allah, peace and quiet prevailed in our holy Temple.

The homes of the Muslims were peaceful. We, the Muslims, kept our homes clean and peaceful. There was no arguing and fighting among the Muslims. We love our brothers and sisters but we fought against those who fought against us (Muslims).[313]

Master Fard Muhammad arrested in Chicago for the 2nd time

There is one report which says that while Master Fard Muhammad stayed in the background, on one September day he hosted an event inviting the general public to come listen to him lecture, which resulted in his arrest. Per a journalist summary of a FBI file:

No one heard from Fard for months. Rumor had it that he really had returned to Mecca. He was, in fact, living in Chicago and using various aliases to avoid attention from the authorities. In September 1933, however, he cast caution to the winds and plastered posters on the West Side of Chicago urging African Americans to come hear his divine message. As he was addressing a group in a rented hall near the intersection of 48th and Calumet on September 25, police raided the building and arrested him on charges of disorderly conduct. At his arraignment the next morning, the arresting officers told the judge that Fard was arrested after citizens complained that a confidence man was preaching hatred near the

[159]

THE PIONEER YEARS (1930-1950)

intersection and was thereby disturbing the peace. The charges were dismissed.[314]

My name is W.F. Muhammad (English Lesson C-1)

Until 1933, the NOI leader went by the name Wallace D. Fard, often signing it W. D. Fard. In the third year of his visit, he made known more of his name. Elijah speaks to this rationale:

> Allah came to us from the Holy City Mecca, Arabia, in 1930. He used the name Wallace D. Fard, often signing it W. D. Fard. In the third year (1933), He signed his name W.F. Muhammad which stands for Wallace Fard Muhammad.[315]
>
> No civilized Nation wants the so-called Negroes, but Allah, our Loving and Most Merciful God, Who came in the person of Master Fard Muhammad in 1930. It was not until 1933 did he begin revealing his true self; I knew Him at first sight in 1931, for I was expecting Him..."[316]

> "It was not until 1933 that he (MFM) began revealing his true self to us as being the answer to the prophecy of Jesus, the coming of the Son of Man, the seeker of the lost sheep."[317]

The Saviour would pen more lessons for the Nation. One lesson was the "English Lesson C-1" referred to as 'the introduction to W.F. Muhammad.' The lesson summarized his relation to the Black Man in America, knowledge of their enemy, and his mission to "the Lost-Found Nation":

1. My name is W.F. Muhammad
2. I came to N. America by myself.
3. My uncle was brought over here by a trader 379 years ago.
4. My uncle does not speak his own language.
5. My uncle does not know he is my uncle.
6. He likes the devil because the devil gives him nothing.
7. Why does he like the devil?
8. Because the devil planted fear in him when he was a little boy.
9. Why does he fear the devil now that he is a big man?
10. Because the devil taught him how to eat the wrong foods.
11. Does that have anything to do with the above question, no. 10?
12. Yes, sir! That makes him other than his ownself.
13. What is his ownself?
14. His own self is a righteous Muslim.

In 1933, Master W.F. Muhammad wrote a lesson which consisted of 34 mathematical mind-boggling word problems called, *"The Problem Book."* Each problem warranted a mathematical resolution and contained an esoteric meaning for the student to decipher. Within the different entries Fard expressed a simpler yet important one called Problem #13 that set the base, as the Problem Book became a staple teaching of the Nation of Islam. Muslims were offered rewards for solving any of the Problems:

Problem No. 13

After learning Mathematics, which is Islam, and Islam is Mathematics, it stands true. You can always prove it at no limit of time. Then you must learn to use it and secure some benefits while you are living—that is luxury, money, good homes, friendships in all walks of life.

Sit yourself in Heaven at once! That is the greatest desire of your Brother and Teachers.

Now you must speak the Language so you can use your mathematical Theology in the proper term, otherwise you will not be successful unless you do speak well, for she knows all about you.

The Secretary of Islam offers a reward to the best and neatest worker of this problem.

There are twenty-six letters in the Language and if a Student learns one letter per day, then how long will it take him to learn the twenty-six letters?

There are ten numbers in the Mathematical Language. Then how long will it take a Student to learn the whole ten numbers (at the above rate)?

The average man speaks four hundred words; well.[318]

The Muslims were Highly Organized and Militant

In any case, Master Fard Muhammad built such a tight-knit organization he could afford to remain in the background while Elijah Muhammad worked tirelessly on his behalf. Karriem Allah recalls:

In the early days of the Honorable Elijah Muhammad's Mission, we the Muslims gave the Messenger our undivided attention. We were quiet and peaceful; we came to the Temple to listen and learn, not to shout and yell in the Temple during the course of the Messenger's lecture.

The Muslims were not noisy in the Temple, we respected the Honorable Elijah Muhammad, we conducted ourselves in a manner becoming Muslims.

The Muslims soon learned the Messenger was not a common man. We learned we were in the presence of a Divine man who came to us from the face of the Divine Supreme Being Whose proper name is Allah. Who came to the wilderness of North America seeking the Messenger.

He never showed a sign of being tired or weakening from those long hours of teaching us.

He never took as much a drink of water during all this time he was with us. We were as thirsty for this Supreme Wisdom as a camel was for water after he had journeyed across the hot desert. He who drinks of this water (Wisdom) need thirst no more.

In listening to the Messenger, we learned that he was a man of high morals and dignity, preparing we the Muslims for the new world of Islam.

He, himself, was setting a moral example for we the Muslims to enter that new world of righteous lost brothers of Asia—the Black Man, said the Honorable Elijah Muhammad.

The Messenger taught we the Muslims—Allah taught him a little over three years, day and night. Allah, he said, gave him fifteen minutes recess; he said to us that Allah poured out the Wisdom on we the Muslims.

He would teach us long hours—from 2 p.m. on Sunday afternoon until 2 or 3 a.m., Monday morning. He would give we the Muslims fifteen minutes recess. He would say to us, "Don't go away, I have much to tell you." No one would leave.[319]

The FOI in Chicago were very militant and strong in the teachings of Islam. Karriem Allah recalls:

The early days of the Messenger's mission. The past, the glorious past.

I was there, I witnessed it. We, the Muslims, the F.O.I. walked our post in a military manner. We were always on the alert. Observing everyone walking or riding in automobiles. Passing on information of any suspicious person or persons walking or riding in automobiles to the sentinel, who relieved us.

We were especially watchful at night around our Temple, during the time of the meetings. We allowed no one to commit a nuisance in our Temple or on the outside of our Temple on Temple grounds.

We obeyed our superior officers. We took commands and executed them to the letter. We were under strict orders.

We never relaxed our guard. We lived and acted right down to the modern time.

In those days, the Muslims were serious. There was no playing or joking among the Muslims. The Honorable Elijah Muhammad taught us to think fast and move with lightning speed. We did. We obeyed all of his instructions.

Whatever he commanded us to do, we did it with pleasure and a smile. If he said, do it, we did it.

There was no bickering among the Muslims. There were no arguments among the Muslims. We loved one another.

If you hurt one Muslim, you had all the Muslims to hurt. We were always ready to defend or go to the defense of a fellow Muslim. We would fight! Dear brothers and sisters, we would go into action at anytime, anywhere, should the occasion arise. We were taught by the Honorable Elijah Muhammad, never to be aggressive but to fight the aggressors.

The Muslims would gather at the homes of fellow Muslims and talk until the early hours of the morning. Islam was our discussion and the Honorable Elijah Muhammad, the Wisdom he taught us of the Black God and His unequaled creation, how the Black God created Himself and what from. There was joy, happiness, peace and contentment among the Muslims. We strived in our daily lives to be like our Beloved Teacher, Leader and Guide, the Honorable Elijah Muhammad, who has an unequaled quality among world leaders today, the past and the future.

He is second to Allah in power, wisdom, knowledge and understanding. He is a lovable, honorable, respectable, perfect, upright and righteous man teaching us, the Blackman and woman in America, to be like him. He is the best gift Allah (God) could have given to us, a people fallen from civilization: The Original Black man in America. More is coming to you from the early days, the glorious past by Brother Karriem Allah.[320]

The Laws of Islam

Chicago NOI Pioneer Karriem Allah speaks to the laws of Islam instilled in the Believers by the Hon. Elijah Muhammad:

Muslims in the early days did not argue with each other. There was love in the hearts of the Muslims for Muslims. We were always happy to meet and greet each other with the greetings of Peace, As-Salaam-Alaikum.

After four hundred years of being separated from each other it was easy for us to adjust to the rule and law of Islam as was taught to us by the Messenger of Allah, the Honorable Elijah Muhammad. We obeyed the law; we were under the restrictive law.

The law of Islam settles all arguments teaches the Messenger of Allah, and He is absolutely right, it takes two people to argue, one should have the intelligence to restrain himself. If two brothers get into an argument and they cannot settle it, the law of Islam will.

The Messenger said to us in the early days he did not want us arguing with each other. He said to us, "I don't want you all entertaining the idea of striking your brother."

We, the Muslims obeyed these instructions given to us by the Messenger of Allah. We were happy and successful in all of our understanding. We moved through the streets of Chicago with lightening speed with chests out and our heads in the sun. People knew us by our cleanliness and fast movement.

You are slow in adjusting yourselves to the law of Islam. The Messenger said to us, "I want you all to get out of Mussa's time, you all are in Master W.D. Fard's time." He said, "I want you all to move fast and think fast." We did.

We should not do anything that we should be ashamed of. Nothing is more shameful than Muslims arguing and fighting one another. You are not helping the Messenger, doing things like this nor are you showing any respect to Him with your foolish, ignorant doings.

Allah isn't pleased with you. He will not bless you as long as you discovery His Messenger, the Honorable Elijah Muhammad. Some of you are as far from the brotherhood of Islam as the East is from the West. You all should practice the brotherhood of Islam daily; mere belief in Islam counts for nothing unless it is carried into practice by those who profess Islam — or Muslims.[321]

Respect and Protect the Black Woman

At a time when in Christianity there were big time reverends exploiting the females in their congregation, the FOI took natural offense. John Muhammad recalls the times: "WHILE Messenger Muhammad teaches us righteousness and instill dignity and pride in our women, other so-called leaders are calling for our women to stand in front of them while they make big demands. This belittles us and robs our women of their right to be protected. And it makes fools of us before the world!"[322]

In contrast, one of the main purposes of the F.O.I. was to 'respect and protect the Black Woman.' Karriem speaks to its importance in the 30s as well as the modern time:

Women, our Black women wore decent clothing, their dresses were long, not short. Women in those days had decent restraints in them. They were not shyless. They would not dare pout on a dress that would bring shame and disgrace to them.

I am talking about Black women, who walked unashamed in the public, their dresses were down and their morals high. Men respected women in those days, because they carried themselves in a decent and respectful manner. Women were women in those days, they loved decency: this made them admired and honorable.

They walked graceful and dignified. Today you can't tell a decent woman from an indecent woman. They all look alike, because they all dress alike, their clothing is unfit for a decent woman to wear. A man will respect a decently dressed woman, but he does not respect an indecently dressed woman.

She displays her body like a merchant does his merchandise, it is on a sale to the public. So, when a wicked man sees a woman's body displayed in a nude manner, he thinks of her as he would merchandise. A decent woman distinguishes herself by dressing in a manner becoming to the standard of decent society.

There are no decent restraints on the Black woman today. She is brazen, she sits down in front of a man with almost nothing on, she is unashamed. You all do not love decency today, you love indecency, you hate a woman who is modestly dressed.

I have watched you when a Muslim woman comes into your presence, you caress her from her head to her feet, you stare at her with evil eyes, eyes of hate, envy and jealousy. This is because the Muslim woman is dressed decently and you are indecently dressed. A man loves and admires a decently dressed woman; he cannot help himself from showing respect to a decently dressed woman; he cares nothing for an indecently dressed woman.

The man looks away from you to him you are too turkey, too much meat and not enough dressing. Black man, you must stand up for decency; you cannot have a clean civilization with an unclean woman. You need to unite with the Messenger now and put a stop to the lurid ways of your Black woman.[323]

[164]

Elijah and Kallatt wives give birth to babies Wallace and Fard

Back in Detroit, both the Supreme Minister Elijah Muhammad and his brother Supreme Captain Kallatt Muhammad wives were due to give birth around the same time. On October 30, 1933, "The Hon. Elijah Muhammad was in Chicago when his son Wallace was born. W.F. Muhammad named him."[324] Elijah's son Imam W.D. Mohammed relays the story he heard about his birth name:

Although he more commonly used the name of W. D. Fard, he wrote on a postcard to my mother and father and to my uncle who was the Supreme Captain in the 1930s, and they still have some of them, where he wrote the name "Wallace D. Fard." I was named after that man; he named me before I was born. And my mother and father told me that he took chalk and wrote my name on the back of the door - "Wallace D." And he told my mother and father: "When this child is born, promise me that you will name him after me." And he wrote the name on the back of the door for them to remember what to name me.[325]

Elijah's brother John, (the uncle to his son W.D. Mohammed), has a slightly different recollection:

Munir: Tell me about His [W.D. Mohammed] name on the door.
S.M. John Muhammad: It wasn't on the door!
Munir: Where was it?
S.M. John Muhammad: It was on the wall of the house. Well, the purpose of it. The children couldn't spell Master Farad name "Wallace." They couldn't spell it. And He (The Savior) told, and He wrote it there for them. Which I believe it was the secretary who did the printing on there, (gives name – Unintelligible) at that time. I believe he [the secretary] was the one who wrote it. Some say they saw him write it. I don't know if they saw Him (MFM) write it or not, because His printing didn't look like that to me. I seen Master Farad's printing and I've seen His writing...and I don't believe that part...
     Let me please, the writing was there because they couldn't spell His name, and the name Wallace, how he got his name, the name Wallace, there was two [Wallaces']. Wallace, (the Messenger's son) and there was one name Farad (that was Kallatt's son). Now both Fathers are my brothers, both of them. And the two women [Clara and Grace] got pregnant, and was going to deliver, I would say about the same time. One wanted the name Master Farad. Both of them wanted the name. Both brothers wanted the name.
Munir: So the Messenger's son was the first to be born...
     S.M. John Muhammad: He was the first one to come out (born). He got the name Wallace, and the next son which belonged to Kallatt, when he was born, and he got the name Farad. He didn't give or name Kalat son Farad.

Kalat and his wife named their son Farad. So that the both of them would have the name of Master Farad.[326]

Years later the Hon. Elijah Muhammad in a letter to his son gives the actual details surrounding how he got his birth name:

These are the truth of saying of Allah, and myself concerning you before you were born. After you were born, he gave to you his name. I wired it from Chicago to Detroit to your mother as he and I and a few other laborers were in Chicago at the time in conference over the laborers there. At the time we received the telegram, we were dining....He told me that you would be a good one. He did not tell me you were going to be a prophet. He said you would be a good one, and to care for you better than I cared for the rest, and I did that. Your mother and I gave you more attention than all the others, almost combined.[327]

Fard and Elijah start Temple #3 in Milwaukee

"Sister Pauline Bahar was the first Secretary of Temple #3. Milwaukee got started from people coming to Chicago listening to them [Fard and Elijah], and that's how Milwaukee got started," says Elijah's son Min. Nathaniel Muhammad.[328]

While centered in Chicago, the Hon. Elijah Muhammad and Master Fard Muhammad (especially) started traveling throughout the Midwest. The pair visited other cities such as: Milwaukee, Wisconsin, Gary, Indiana, Saint Louis and Kansas City, Missouri, Evanston, Illinois and other cities in the region. Outside of the two established Temples, the majority of their effort and focus was on establishing Temple #3 in Milwaukee sensed they had existing support there. The move would pay off in the future:

In the early days of Islam in America, Master Fard Muhammad (founder of the Nation of Islam) traveled to Milwaukee, Wisconsin, to further the expansion of the Nation of Islam outside of its first two cities, Detroit and Chicago. Upon his arrival he found individuals who were receptive to his message, establishing a base of support for his student, the Honorable Elijah Muhammad. In 1934, the Master Teacher and his Student traveled together to visit what would become the third city of Islam in the West. The trip solidified friendships that in 1935 allowed the Honorable Elijah Muhammad to flee Detroit, to Chicago and a short time later to the safety of Milwaukee due to threats against his life. His stay, while brief, provided him with a glimpse of the difficulty of his assignment and the certainty of victory promised to him by his teacher.

This initial group of believers in what was then known as Muhammad's Temple #3, located on McKinley Boulevard, produced the Honorable Elijah Muhammad's first National Representative, Minister Sultan Muhammad.

During this period the Honorable Elijah Muhammad never stayed in a city more than two weeks…[329]

Letters from Master Fard Muhammad

While Elijah Muhammad remained front man handling Detroit and Chicago, Master Fard Muhammad worked out in the field visiting Black communities in other states. Master Fard kept a P.O. Box or address in each city he visited, although he didn't stay in them long. Somehow he still managed to get his mail and corresponded with NOI officials through letters and postcards.

Some postcards were friendly with a pinch of comedy such as the one Mr. W.D. Fard mailed to Sister Clara Muhammad about her work and the family.

> Dear Sister, I received your letter and was very happy to know that you are well and improving the future. You take good care of the children and see that they are all take after me. Tell Emmanuel I said if he won't be quiet in everything, I will come and take him to the river.

Best wishes to all from W.D. Fard (see postcard)

Postcard to Clara Muhammad from Master W.D. Fard dated Oct. 18, 1933.

Such as the following letter sent by Master Fard Muhammad to the Hon. Elijah Muhammad in Detroit detailing a few misunderstandings the two had on the subject of expansion:

South West Part of N. America
Dec. 18 - 1933
4 A.M.

Mr. E. Mohammed
The Minister of Islam
Detroit, Michigan
North America

Dear Brother:

Here are a few lines to let you know that I have received both of your letters, one return mail and the other regular, also one from Kallatt. I have been just getting over the terrible mistake and unofficial movements that you been taken; not only one that you went to Birmingham; but different times you have done minor things without saying anything before. I have numbers of records of charges against you; but I have not brought them to enforce; knowing you have taken these steps with good intentions. NOW MY DEAR BELOVED BROTHER, I will tell you again and again, you have heard me from time to time, that [you] must not undertake the labor of Islam unless you do know it 100%. This is why I am here to guide you to the right road, you must always tell me, other [wise] you will not be successful. It is true that you can use the wisdom but remember you are the wise and are in the mouth of the lion in his cave or civilization without any right in regards to the rules and regulations for practicing your profession in this cave civilization in the first place. You have no business being here but since you are here a long way from home and your kind and are in the cave of savage, you must use your wisdom with care; otherwise this savage will piece you in two. The law of nature will not allow a man to run the home of another man, so be clear on this and use your wisdom with care. I will tell you to get out on the street and on the top of all the high buildings and yell out your wisdom when the time comes. The time is not ripe yet. How many times have I told you this? Are you wasting my valuable moments on the same things over and over? My movements, time and hours are limited and are for the dead nation. So you be aware not to rob the dead and your [word unintelligible].[330]

In his letter, Master Fard Muhammad advised his student to continue to study his most recent lesson "the Problem Book":

You keep this letter and present to me when I see you and I will read for you and explain to you. I know you are going to ask 1000 un-valuable questions but write them down and present to me when I see you. Get on the labor

[168]

now and study your assignment. See that you master your history, all of the form all of the problems. All everything I left you is to be dug out and study. Problem 31 should clear you of the mystery that you all long for but your wisdom and keep all to yourself.[331]

Master Fard Muhammad vaguely mentioned some of his adventures and outlined specific instructions to the Hon. Elijah Muhammad about traveling to the same cities:

Now right along with your study you can go over to Chicago unexpected; do not tell no one where you going or when you going excepting Kallatt Mohammed. Give them a lecture and run over to MILWAUKEE at 8th and Center St., inquire about Mr. Joe Bey, many smellers around there and ask to have a special meeting for you. Give them a lecture or two and go back to Evanston and ask for Mr. Brown. Try to get acquainted there and start a station there; you may promise some Ice Maker a big bone and get in with him and start arising the dead. With your wisdom you easily do this, but have patience; just look at me. I have all the hard luck and confronting more hard luck caused by my own people. Don't you see they are poison by the devil and so badly poisoned that they can't see me walking among them every day and eating with them give them Knowledge to compare with anybody in the world and they are still in doubt. How many you want me to pick out each time when you have meeting? Be wise and take lots of graveness for you are dealing with babies. There will be time when they all will know you then your happiness will be give. Now I go back to my subject. Then from Evanston, you can round Chicago again unexpected then home. Stop in these little towns on your way home and leave little wisdom everywhere, get around and get acquainted, caravan the territory between your home and Milwaukee. Start stations every where you can. St. Louis and Kansas City will be your territory too, but at present you can master the above said and later I will tell you when to go there.[332]

Ending the letter with another question from the Problem Book, Master Fard Muhammad assured the Hon. Elijah Muhammad he was coming along fine and is looking forward to seeing him again, and to continue to study:

About your labor working the problems, you are doing fine; you may consult one of the Teachers on beginning and forming your figures. The distance of Platoon is given in one of the problems. Light travels 186,000 miles per second and the sun is 93,000,000 miles from the Earth. Then if you divide the traveling speed in to the distance, it shall give you the time to strike the Earth. Ha! Ha! This is good one for you. I shall have big time with you when I see you; but now do not be bashful to study, for the wise always go to the bottom to secure real cure. Write to me every day and tell me all about your study. My best wishes to you and family, all the labors and 17,000,000.

I am going with you,
from W.D. Fard[333]

"The Lost-Found Muslim Lessons"

When Master Fard Muhammad returned to Detroit, he gave a test on February 20, 1934, to all of his select students and laborers on the subject of his teachings. He prepared a list of questions for the students on two exams. The first exam consisted of 14 questions and was titled "Lost-Found Muslim Lesson No. 1." The second exam consisted of 40 questions and was titled "Lost-Found Muslim Lesson No. 2."

After the students had taken the exam, Master Fard Muhammad graded all the papers to determine who did the best. Of all the Students and Ministers, Master Fard Muhammad verified that Supreme Minister Elijah Muhammad gave the best answers. A journalist refers to three of the questions and Elijah's answers from Lost-Found Muslim Lesson No. 2:

Within the Lost-Found Muslim Lesson no.2 (1-40) it teaches a naturalist theory of the universe which denies the idea of life after death as well as the existence of a "mystery god." The only resurrection possible is a revival from "mental death" (ignorance and superstition). Those who believe in a mystery god are mentally dead. The only "god" is man himself; it is the "devil" (white man) who has tricked 85 percent of humanity into believing in a god whom they cannot see, so that he can "make slaves [of them]... rob them and live in luxury." This exposition leads into a series of three important questions…:

14. Who are the 85%? The uncivilized people; poison animal eaters; slaves from mental death and power; people who do not know who the living God is, or their origin in this world and who worship that which they know not. Easily led in the wrong direction but hard to lead in the right direction.

15. Who are the 10%? The rich slave-makers of the poor, who teach the poor lies to believe that the Almighty True and Living God is a spook and cannot be seen by the physical eye; otherwise known as bloodsuckers of the poor.

16. Who are the 5% in this poor part of the Planet Earth? They are the poor righteous teachers who do not believe in the teachings of the 10% and are all-wise and know who the true and living God is and teach that the true and living God is the Son of Man, the Supreme Being, the Black Man of Asia; and teach Freedom, Justice and Equality to all the human families of the Planet Earth; otherwise known as Civilized People, Also is Muslim and Muslim Sons.[334]

Master Fard Muhammad summoned the Reformer Burnsteen Sharrieff to type and make copies of Elijah Muhammad's two completed exams for the entire Nation of Islam to study and memorize. Master Fard Muhammad issued the statement:

Instruction 1
The student must study his Assignment--Lesson #1.
Each Student should copy the Answers of Lesson of Minister, Elijah Muhammad, and study until the Student is able to memorize, By Heart, all Answers to, of said, Lesson #1.

Next, Master Fard Muhammad got with the Reformer to type all the following lessons he made mandatory learning:

(1) Original Rules of Instructions to the Laborers (1-13)
(2) Actual Facts (1-20)
(3) Student Enrollment (1-10)
(4) Lost-Found Muslim Lesson No. 1 (1-14)
(5) Lost-Found Muslim Lesson No. 2 (1-40)
(6) English Lesson C-1 (1-36)
(7) The Problem Book (1-34)

The Reformer recalled Master Fard Muhammad advised her to take great care with the task, often meeting her in obscure places such as defunct large freezers to review the Lessons. He taught her to put the lessons in different hiding spots such as under furnaces in case police raided their meeting places. This way they wouldn't be able to seize all of the Lessons because they'd have plenty stashed away.

The Impact of the Lessons on the Believers

The "5%" being "the Poor Righteous Teachers" was a literal true statement. NOI Pioneers describe how they were poor, righteous and teachers as they managed to establish a University of Islam in Chicago:

Times were heard in the early days of the Messenger's mission. Jobs were few and there was very little money in circulation. But, if one cold make a little money, he could support his family well. We gave our nickels, dimes, quarters and half-dollars to the noble cause of Islam. We were happy to do this.

Everything was cheap. Food was priced at its lowest ever. My wife and I used to feed out family off of 25 cents per day.

A dollar was worth one hundred pennies, it was "In God we Trust." It was the God of the white man's world.

In those days, the early days of the Honorable Elijah Muhammad's mission, street car far was only seven cents. We ate well.

It's different today. Food is high, almost out of reach of the poor man's pocketbook. There is a food shortage today plus an inflationary dollar,

[171]

therefore, "In God we Trust" (the dollar) is going down the drain. Its power over other nations' currency no longer exists.

The Messenger taught us to give to charity and we gave all that we could. We never though we gave enough to the cause of Islam. We always wanted to give more.

The Messenger set up the school at Temple No. 2 (the University of Islam No. 2), and we all went to school—young and old.

We were instructed by the Honorable Elijah Muhammad to get busy and study. It was a joy and a pleasure to go to a Muslim school, staffed by Muslim teachers. We learned our "own" very fast.

We were given assignments, Lesson No. 1, The Messenger's first lesson from Allah. We were also given English Lesson No. C-1, the Problem Book, and the Forty Questions. We were instructed by the Honorable Elijah Muhammad to study these lessons until we were able to memorize these lessons, and this we did.

The spirit of Allah is in these lessons. If we want the spirit of Allah to dwell in us, let us, dear brothers and sisters, go back to our lessons, this is our first work.

In the early days of the Messenger's mission, Allah gave the Messenger these lessons. The Messenger gave them to us, the Muslims. We are studying his lessons.

It is an honor to have the privilege of studying the lessons that Allah (God) gave to this worthy and Honorable man, a holy man, a divine man, the Honorable Elijah Muhammad. We should take pride in our lessons. They will lift our spirit.[335]

Lessons Strictly Enforced in the Nation of Islam

The lessons were of paramount importance in the FOI classes. Karriem Allah:

In the early days, one hour of our time in the F.O.I. was spent in in drilling exercises to keep we the Muslims of the F.O.I. in physical fitness. The rest of the time was used to recite our lessons; this was done to keep us obedient to the instructions given to us by Allah, Master W.D. Fard, through His Messenger Mr. Elijah Muhammad – which says the student must study his; assignment Lesson No. 1.

Each student should copy the answers of lesson No. 1 of Minister Elijah Muhammad, and study until the student is able to memorize by heart all answers to/of said Lesson No. 1.

All of our time was used in building a dependable F.O.I. in Temple No. 2, equal to none in the Wilderness of North America. We the Muslims never wasted time. We were always trying to learn to be better prepared for the future which has unlimited progress for, we the Muslims under the leadership and guidance of Mr. Elijah Muhammad, the Messenger of Allah.

The more learned brothers and sisters helped the unlearned to learn. Elevating ourselves to a high level in knowledge, wisdom and understanding was foremost in our minds. Our learned brothers and sisters in the early days were never too proud to help those who needed help in trying to reach a higher level in education.

The more learned brothers and sisters did not look down with scorn upon those who had no education – no! They were always ready and willing to help their less educated brothers and sisters in the way of learning. Bigness was unknown among us.[336]

The Lessons served as a constant reminder of the duty of a FOI:

What we did was from the heart. We did onto do anything to be seen. The Messenger said He did not want any showing off among the Muslims. The Messenger said there are no big I's, and little you's in Islam. He said Muslims do not do other than themselves – we lived up to these rules.

Our going forth in the city among the lost-founds – the mentally dead – was to promote peace, friendship and understanding. The Honorable Elijah Muhammad was an example of peace, brotherhood, goodwill and friendship among we the Muslims.

The Messenger taught us that we are direct descendants of that first god who created the heaven and Earth, the Sun, Moon and Star. We were happy to hear this; we were happy to know this. The Messenger said that Allah's message, to us (the lost Nation of Asia) was accept your own and be yourself.

When you learn yourself Black brothers and sisters, you will want to be yourself. The Honorable Elijah Muhammad teaches that ourself is better than any other self.

Dear lost-found brothers and sisters – if you understood the time we live in, you would run to the Honorable Elijah Muhammad, the Divine caller in your midst. Look at what is happening in the land. The Messenger keeps warning you that the end of this world is at hand, you all should listen and take heed.[337]

Lessons Inspire Fiery Wisdom in the Believers

The new converts saw first-hand and embraced the fiery spirit the Lessons produced in the Fruit of Islam. Leslie X remembers:

Brother Leslie X came to Islam in 1934. He says, "The first day I went there I joined the Fruit (F.O.I.). When they were Teaching, they told me just what I wanted to know. I thought it was just great.

"I love the righteous Teaching and how valuable we are—the so-called Negro. I love the law. Allah and His Messenger, the Teachings.

"I've had a lot of proof about Islam—in prison the only Teaching that stood up was Islam."

This is their story, the fearless first fighters for Islam in North America, but it is really the story of the Honorable Elijah Muhammad. Because his followers' most treasured memories are time spent with him, or some memorable wisdom he gave to them, as he had been given by Allah in the Person of Master Fard Muhammad.

[173]

"The Messenger would always stress—he'd say don't let nobody cause you to lose your reward—Islam is fire! If you don't want it leave it alone," said Brother Leslie X.

...Although times were hard in those days, and even though all the believers remember the hard times, it is not the hard time that they want to dwell on, they want to talk about the great progress of the present and beauty of the past.

They speak of the bold steps taken by the Apostle, his actions, his compassion, his love and devotion to the Teaching that Allah has given to him, the way he has welded a group of Black men and women in a bond of unity that has never been known in the history of men.[338]

The Effect of the Lessons on Listening Audiences

The revealing of the Lessons made it clear to audience members at Temple meetings. The plain language spoken by the Messenger caused many to join the FOI ranks. John X Lawler remembers:

It seems that from the very day that I learned to read and write, I had been a student of the Bible - although frankly, it confused me. I would sit for hours reading it or discussing many of its complex points with friends and advisors.

But only when I discovered Islam, as taught by the Honorable Elijah Muhammad were the most puzzling aspects of the scripture made clear. And not only I, but others have found the Messenger of Allah's teachings to be the key that unlocked not only the mystery of the Bible, but of life itself.

Actually I first accepted Islam during the height of the depression years, 1934. I was then working in the steel mills and living in Chicago in what was then considered fairly decent housing. Whatever my previous living standards, Islam elevated them and add years to my life and a new outlook.

The Messenger of Allah taught us the reality of the Supreme Being, of All Mighty God Allah and made His presence the most important part of our lives.

Islam has helped me understand and observe not only my duties to Allah, but my duties to my fellow man I am an eyewitness to the act that The Messenger of Allah has turned thieves into honest men, has enable the blind to see, the deaf to hear and the lame to walk.

I have no doubt that Messenger Muhammad is the One, the One who is spoken of in the Bible, that would be raised up before that great and dreadful day when the Son of Man would come to rescue us from a Godless people.[339]

...Actually, my first contact with Islam came through a brother and sister who went from door to door telling people about the Messenger of Allah and of the great work he was doing for our people. I was convinced of their sincerity and my wife and I agreed to attend one of the meetings. I shall never forget that first meeting. It was held at the old Pythian Temple on State Street and the Messenger of Allah, the Honorable Elijah Muhammad was the principal speaker.

[174]

The things I heard this man say were enough to arouse the most sleeping of mankind. For the first time things became much clearer and more vivid to me. No longer did it seem that we were dependent on spirit and spooks to guide our way.

The Messenger of Allah that night spoke long and held our attention every minute of the time. When he finished and asked if any wished to join with their own kind, I did not resist. From that glorious moment until today Islam has given me a greater, richer and more rewarding life.[340]

Within four years, Wallace Fard Muhammad developed an organization so effective he was able to withdraw almost entirely from active leadership and gradually stopped his public appearances. He was preparing for his leave.

Clara Muhammad and her son Wallace D. Muhammad

8 Exodus

Master Fard Muhammad Hints about Leaving

"Master Fard Muhammad would often remind His Apostle, and others, the He would not be long among them. He indicated that He was only to spend a certain amount of time with them."[341] As Master Fard Muhammad came like the biblical Son of Man like a "thief in the night," it was time for him to make his exit. As he was endeared to the family of the Hon. Elijah Muhammad, he hinted to them that he was going away. Elijah's eldest son remembers a statement Master Fard made to him about his departure:

The last time I saw Master Fard, he left our home in Detroit, Michigan, May 26, 1933. Master Fard was given twenty-four hours by the police commissioner in Detroit to leave the state of Michigan. From Detroit, Master Fard came to Chicago, and as my father said, as soon as [Fard] arrived here in Chicago, he was arrested. But he did not spend no time in jail. They turned him loose. He stayed here in Chicago from a while before he left for good. Master Fard said that he was going up in the mountains, where the cavies (he referred to the Caucasian race of people as cavies)—where they would not be able to find him. Master Fard didn't specify no particular mountain. That was in 1934.[342]

At his last public appearance in Gary, Indiana, Master Fard Muhammad appeared to be giving farewells to some of those who endured with him over the past four years. Elijah's brother John Muhammad recalls his last meeting with Master Fard:

In 1923, I stopped lying. I'm not going to lie to you. I thank Allah for the resurrection of my Brother, Messenger Elijah Muhammad, who has taught me, since the day that he became a Teacher or Minister, Prophet or Messenger in The Nation of Islam. Messenger Elijah Muhammad taught me until the day he died. Master Fard Muhammad taught me on the last day that I seen Him in Gary, Indiana in 1934. Master Fard taught me that day and that night. That was my last teaching that I got from His mouth. Others I got from the pen and the paper.

Remember this. I didn't know it then, that He was God in person! But I made that promise and later on Messenger Elijah Muhammad, my brother, told me, "Brother John...(I has the name John then. I didn't tell you how I got that name did I? I'll tell you next time. He gave it to me, Master Fard Muhammad did)...that man that we called "Brother Fard" was none other than The Beneficent God. (All Praise Is Due Allah)

I looked around. I said, "Sir?" He [Elijah] said. "That man is none other than Allah in Person. He is The Allah that is to come in this day!"[343]

Master Fard's parting Gifts to Elijah and Kallatt

Master Fard Muhammad had two parting gifts for his Supreme Minister Elijah Muhammad and his Supreme Captain Kallatt Muhammad.

In an interview, the statement was made to Elijah, "Master Fard Muhammad has a Book in his hand. There is a picture out there with a Book in his hand." To which the Hon. Elijah Muhammad responded, "That was teaching to teach me to keep your head in the book for learning. This was for me." Then Elijah revealed, "Now, he gave my brother, Kallatt, at that time who was the Captain of Detroit, Chicago, and Milwaukee. He gave him a picture where he was working square roots and he gave that to Kallatt." Elijah continued, "Kallat asked me, he said: And he [Master Fard] gave him the Poison Book. He said, "He give you the Holy Quran and he give me the Poison Book." "And what do you think of that?" The Messenger recalls, "I think I told him the truth is in both of the Books. And that's how far I went with it. 'Cause I wasn't going to be no judge on why he [Master Fard] did this or why he didn't do that. And of course he [Master Fard] was here at that time. So, to get in the thinking of God..."[344]

The Hon. Elijah Muhammad confirmed the same (him receiving the Quran, and possibly another book in the future) to a journalist:

> Elijah Mohammed mentioned that Mr. W.D. Fard had given him in the last two months he had seen him two copies of the Koran, one in Arabic and the other with the English translation alongside the Arabic, and he told him to learn Arabic. In this context Elijah stated that when W.D. Fard gave him the copies of the Koran he told him: "These are not the only books I have but I have another book that I made myself."[345]

Toward the end of his career as Leader of the Nation of Islam, The Hon. Elijah Muhammad recalls Master Fard Muhammad provided him a bibliography of 104 books to study. The majority of books were on the life of Prophet Muhammad. Elijah asked if these books were in the library there in Detroit. "No," was the answer. Master Fard then gave Elijah his own personal copy of the Holy Quran and spoke of "a new book" to come:

> But another 40 years I have been studying, scripture and history, after Allah taught me for three years and four months. Then he give to me 104 books to study. He gave me the number and room of the place where I can find them. So I studied. And he give me a Holy Qu'ran in Arabic, but I couldn't read it. So he got one in Arabic and English translated by Muhammad Ali of Pakistan. Then later he found one of Yusef Ali of Egypt. He brought me that. Then he told me, "I will give you a Holy Quran, when you learn how to read

Arabic. Then I will give you a Holy Quran in Arabic." He said, "I made it myself." So he showed me that Holy Quran in Arabic in September last, but I couldn't read it, I could only recognize one letter in it. So I expect him in a year to come back with that same book.[346]

In an interview Elijah verified his intense study of the Holy Quran confirmed the truth for him that Allah came in the Person of Master Fard Muhammad:

The Apostle used to tell the writer: "When Fard left he gave me a list of 150 [sic] books to read. When I began to read I have detected, especially after reading Koran carefully, that Fard was Allah himself incarnated. The more I read the more I become sure about this fact, especially that his name has been mentioned in the Bible and the time of his coming has been assigned, but the devil has concealed him under another name."[347]

Before he left Master Fard Muhammad appeared to test the will of his student by suggesting that if necessary, he would just save Elijah and leave the others if in fact Elijah failed in his mission. The Hon. Min. Louis Farrakhan recalls what the Most Hon. Elijah Muhammad told him concerning the subject:

Master Fard Muhammad said to Elijah that "if you can't get them, just bring me the key, and I will destroy them all, and make a new Nation from you." Elijah Muhammad stared at his teacher and said, "Then you will have to kill me too." Mr. Fard said with approval of his student, "I knew you would say that."[348]

The answer was probably expected, given that Master Fard Muhammad reiterated to Elijah Muhammad on occasion: "He said to me that He would eat rattlesnakes to save our lives and that He would walk a mountain 40 miles high just to save one of us in exchange for our safety and return to our own."[349]

In any sense, Master Fard Muhammad insisted that the time was right even according to the universal signs. To prove it, he showed Elijah a key sign in the night sky. Elijah remembers:

One night he pointed out to me two little stars in the Southeastern skies, a blue and a red one. He said, "it's" been fifty-thousand years since we have seen these two stars," He said, "When they go away out of the skies from out sight this time, it will be fifty thousand years before they reappear." Every time they reappear there will be a universal change.[350]

Master Fard's Instructions to Elijah upon His Leave

All in all, Fard taught Elijah Muhammad what he needed to know over a period of 40 months. W. F. Muhammad hinted that he completed this chapter of his assignment; and now it was on Elijah to lead his people to Freedom, Justice and Equality in his absence. Fard implied that he was in contact with the "24 scientists" and they were very aware of Elijah's progression in understanding the teachings. Elijah recalls W. F. Muhammad reporting with glee the approval of the 24 scientists with the success of the teachings. As Elijah reports a statement made by Fard on the day of his departure. "They just waited. They're so glad that the day has come now that they can show you now that the Black Man is God!"[351]

The Hon. Elijah Muhammad gives intimate details about his meeting with Master Fard Muhammad before his departure:

The Savior told me in seeing me how best I could probably get to the people with Allah's help. He looked at me and he said, "Why don't you accept it?" He said, "The time is right," meaning accept the mission to teach our people. He said, "The time is right and if you don't someone else will do it, because it is time, brother." That is the way he spoke. And I sat and looked at him without an answer. I was still thinking so deeply that I could not speak. I had been teaching then for two years. He looked at me again and yet I did not say anything. He said, "Brother, there is no one to do this job but you and me." And then he repeated the same thing. "Why should not you do it, meaning to give life truth to my people," He said, "and get that big name." I still wondered what big name was he referring to, because I had never had knowledge of any big name? He said to me then, "surely you will have a hard time." He said, "trying to get the dead arisen." He said, "but others had that same kind of time," but he said "don't worry over that." He said, "and don't worry over your family, go ahead and study." He said he did not want me to do a thing in the world but just study Islam and teach my people and your people, and then he looked at me and said "Aren't you with me to put them on top of civilization?" I said, "Yes sir, I will give my life to see them on top." He said, "Yes brother," he said "fear not." He said, "I will be with you, and when the time come, brother, you and I will be together and we will finish the job in a very short time. We will only have to stop in one city 15 minutes at a time; that will be time sufficient for acting pretty" he said. I guess to him because I was thinking. He said, "Cheer up." He said, "After you go through with all of this I had never went through." But that is what he said then, "You will be happy after that." I looked at him and said "Yes sir." He said, "But remember that poor man Jesus brother, what a hard time he had. The people said everything about him that was evil, no good, some of it brother could not be printed on the pages of history in writing it was so terrible. Just remember him. What a hard time he had." And then he looked at me again and said, "You have the hardest job of any man who ever lived. I am giving you that job." He was then missioning me to my surprise as a messenger to his people. He said, "Tell them I will not charge them for the sins they have committed. And that I will not even mention it to them. Tell them that (even the ice makers) that if they will follow you, then I will if that is what they want. Good homes and good friendship if they will give them money, let you teach them, and they teach what you give them to teach, and not what they are teaching now. I said, yes sir, but he said they will not follow you until at a certain time, and when that happens then, they all will come to you the ice makers will come then and will help you and bow down to you. He said and all the dead will come. You will see them coming by the thousands. He said believe my words. He told me what could happen to bring them into submission....352

Master Fard Muhammad reiterated he was God, and the love and power he had for Black people. Elijah reiterated he had the same love:

"Tell them, Elijah, I love them!" "They have been here 400 years, and there is none that has befriended them. I am their God," He said, "and I love them. I will destroy the Nations of the Earth, to save them and then die Myself." And I said, "I'll do the same." I said, "I can't destroy the Nations, but I will die trying to teach them." He (Allah) looked at me and smiled. He said, "Yes," He said, "You **will** do that." He looked at me some more. He said, "Yes, He will give his life." He said, "Jesus didn't do anything; no more than any believer." Well, that's right. If I say I believe in God and His true Religion, certainly I will give my life for it.353

He asked me, "Are you with me?" I said, "Yes." He said, "Well, then, you come with me and help me with this work so as when the time comes you and me will be together."354

One of Elijah's future Ministers remembers what the Messenger taught concerning this subject:

On His leave he began to emphasize specific things the Messenger could expect to come to pass. He went deeper into what the Messenger should do to try and make Black people qualified to escape the doom of this evil world. The Messenger was taught how to reform us and make us acceptable to the Islamic people. It was made clear to him that we must change completely into righteousness; not the righteousness of this world, nor righteousness according to the standards of this world. No. We would have to get into the righteousness of the God who would rule the next world; that God being Master Fard Muhammad.355

A major part of Elijah's mission seemed to rely on his faith in his Teacher, who made him the solemn promise that they would be successful and "together in the end." Elijah verifies the proof of his teacher and his commission:

"This promise he [Master Fard Muhammad] made to me. He said 'At that time, you and I will be together.' He said to me. He said, 'We will be together at that time.' What time? At the end of this! "He says, 'You and I will be together, and we will cover the country [just] like that.' I said, 'Thank you, sir.' And I believe it! I believe I will be with him! The Holy Quran teaches me that he will question the prophet on that day. How did the people take the teachings, and how did he deliver it to them? It's all there in the Holy Quran."[356]

The Hon. Elijah Muhammad said: "The last time I saw Allah was in Chicago in 1934."[357] Some journalists who interviewed the Messenger claim: "On March 19, 1934, Muhammad recalls, Master Fard Muhammad disappeared as mysteriously has he had come, without leaving a trace and without ever being seen or heard of again." He just left," remembers the Messenger, "natural, like a friend leaving another friend."[358] E.U. Essien-Udom notes: "Muhammad claims that Master W.D. Fard or Wallace Fard Muhammad came from Mecca, Arabia, and that he was with the Mahdi at the airport when he was deported"[359] An official statement from Temple #2 in Chicago verifies the same, "In 1934 he and Elijah drove to the airport in a Model-T Ford. Elijah cried because he loved his Saviour and didn't want to be without him. Fard said to him, "You don't need me anymore." "Oh, yes I do," Elijah replied. Fard repeated, "You don't need me anymore." Fard then boarded the airplane and flew away, never to be seen publicly again.[360]

The office of Temple #2 claims during Master Fard Muhammad's last meeting with the Messenger in Chicago, that Fard pressed a small folded paper into Elijah's hand that contained Psalm 23:

Psalm 23
[1]The LORD is my shepherd; I shall not want.
[2]He maketh me to lie down in green pastures: he leadeth me beside the still waters.
[3]He restoreth my soul: he leadeth me in the paths of righteousness for his name's sake.
[4]Yea, though I walk through the valley of the shadow of death, I will fear no evil: for thou art with me; thy rod and thy staff they comfort me.
[5]Thou preparest a table before me in the presence of mine enemies: thou anointest my head with oil; my cup runneth over.
[6]Surely goodness and mercy shall follow me all the days of my life: and I will dwell in the house of the LORD forever.

This wasn't the last time Elijah Muhammad would correspond with his teacher, not long afterwards he received a letter from Mexico from Fard:

Since the winter of 1932, after he had established the University of Islam and organized the militaristic training of the followers who constitute what they call the "Fruit of Islam," W.D. Fard gradually sank into the background of the movement and took the role of the administrator. He did not come to the temple any more but he practiced his plan by contacting his minister whenever he had an order, decision, or instruction. On the fourth of May, 1933, he was deported by the local authority from Detroit, after they arrested him for the third time, accusing him of disturbing the peace in Detroit. He left Detroit to come to Chicago and lived there for awhile; then he travelled all over America. He left Chicago for the last time in February, 1934. His last letter to his Apostle was from Mexico in March, 1934. He was 56 years old when he left Chicago.[361]

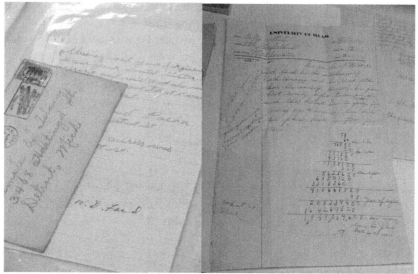

Mailed handwritten letters from Master Fard Muhammad to Believers at Temple #1, Detroit Michigan. Also pictured are student school work assignments from the University of Islam that were personally graded by Master Fard Muhammad.

9 Fight for Your Right

A Detroit Times report said the fight erupted when a police inspector was knocked down and a police squad went to his aid. 150 police using batons joined the clash that lasted 10 minutes. 12 police were injured with cuts and bruises. 100 were arrested. There was no report of marchers' injuries.

Detroit Authorities Seek to Close University of Islam

The Hon. Elijah Muhammad and the Nation of Islam were immediately tried after Master Fard Muhammad's departure. The absence of Muslim children from Detroit's public school system became apparent. In opposition to the Muslim school, the city's authorities would plan their move on the Muslims. The state of Michigan ordered the Muslims to send their children back to Detroit Public Schools and disband the University of Islam. The Muslims refused to comply. The Michigan State Board of Education had the Muslim teachers arrested for "contributing to the delinquency of minors." Elijah Muhammad was among those arrested. Highly organized and efficient, the Muslims fought the case in court and the charges were eventually dropped. Not first without a battle.

Inspection of UOI

On March 27, 1934, The Detroit Free Press headlines read "Voodooist Cult Revived in City":

Truant officers alarmed by the increasing number of Negro children dropping out of the City's schools to enroll in the "Universities of Islam" were advised Monday by Recorder's Judge W. McKay Skillman to bring legal action at once to close the "universities." The aid of the prosecutor's office was immediately enlisted.

The "Islam Universities," the court was advised by Archibald N. Henniger, director of attendance of the Detroit Board of Education, are a resurgence of a cult movement here which, nearly two years ago, was climaxed in a sacrificial murder.

A group of officials, who were forced to call upon police to force an entrance, Monday visited one of the "universities." At 3408 Hastings St. It was occupied previously by the Temple of Islam, a center of activity during the earlier cult development here.

When the officers headed by Asst. Prosecutor George W. Schudlich finally obtained an entrance they found 46 Negro children in the school going through military maneuvers. None of the pupils or their instructors — there were seven of them — would give the officials any information other than that they did not believe they were responsible to the State laws, but merely to those of the cult.

The State law provides that children may be entered in private schools providing the curriculum there is in accord with the teachings in public schools, and the names of the pupils are listed with the Board of Education. The instructors at the "university" were ordered to submit a list of the students enrolled as well as a list of the studies taught.

If the information is not supplied by Tuesday, Henniger said, legal steps will be taken to close the school. Secrecy had surrounded the growth of the schools, Schudlich said. It was the same secrecy which prevailed when the cult developed in 1932 and came to police attention after a crazed Negro, Robert Harris, murdered James J. Smith, another Negro, on a makeshift altar.

The problem was brought to the attention of the Prosecutor's staff by truant officers. Investigating the withdrawals of Negro children from the public schools they found they were being sent to schools patterned after the teachings of the cult.

They were able to learn little of the schools other than that the children were being given Mohammedan names and were being taught subversive subjects, Leonard A. Morrison, supervisor of attendance for the Board of Education, declared.

Many of the instructors were not equipped educationally to instruct the pupils, it was said. The whereabouts of all the schools has not been learned because of the reluctance of members of the organization to discuss the cult.[362]

Court and Board of Education officials visited the premises of the University of Islam as part of their inspection. The intent was to classify its teachings as subversive and linked to noted radicals. Children were singled out as possible victims of a 'cult teaching' and authorities acted shocked at the numbers of the movement:

Eight officials, three from the board of Education and five from the Prosecutor's office, visited to the Hasting Street "University" Monday. They made several attempts to gain an entrance and when the officials were ordered out police from the Canfield Station were summoned. The instructors in the school refused to cooperate in any manner. Schudlich said.

Advised of the situation, Judge Skillman said that the courts would support any movement to wipe out the schools if their teachings were subversive and they were not up to educational standards. He urged that the Prosecutor's office get evidence against the schools as soon as possible.

Fifteen-year-old Sally Allah, taken out of the Garfield School by her parents and sent to the "university," was questioned by Schudlich. She admitted that the teachings were based on the Mohammedan faith. Through her it also was learned that the school's teachings were contrary to the better interests of the public, Schudlich declared.

The new development of the cult, police declared, is alarming. Following the murder of Smith, Harris proclaimed himself "King of Islam," and declared he owed no responsibility to State laws. Police discovered then that the cult movement had reached large proportions.

An Arab, Wallace Farrad, had come to Detroit and enrolled more than 8,000 Negroes in an organization. He was ordered from the City but police learned that he made several subsequent visits to Detroit. Detectives said that he probably is directing the movement from another city and visits Detroit periodically to collect dues and to foster the growth of the cult.

Nenninger said that the Board of Education had hoped to cope with the situation without police aid by due to the secrecy of the members of the cult the refusal of parents to discuss the organization or truancy with officials extra efforts had to be taken. Many Negro families are opposed to the movement, it was said, and have instructed their children to have nothing to do with "the voodoo" group.[363]

Building Inspectors Join Campaign Against University of Islam

On Wednesday, March 28, 1934, The Detroit Free Press headlines read **"Islam Faces Double Probe, University Believed to be Cult's Home."** This time building inspectors joined the campaign, as well as Negro church leaders again sought to testify against the Muslims:

Investigation of the "University of Islam," Negro cult movement with headquarters at 3408 Hastings, will be conducted by the Board of Health and by the Fire Commission, it was indicated Tuesday by Archibald N. Henniger, director of attendance of the Detroit Board of Education.

No police action will be necessary if it is found that the premises are suitable for public assemblies because of unhealthy conditions or fire hazards, he said.

Further inquiry into the "University" brought out that 25 to 30 adults were in the habit of frequenting the place. How many of them were teachers of the 50 children who were found there could not be determined. All denied connection with the institution, but the four men who apparently were in charge were ordered to submit a list of pupils and the courses of study.

It is known that there were no textbooks used in the school, and it is virtually certain that no prepared course of study was followed, Henniger said.

As soon as Dr. Don W. Gudskunst, chief investigator for the Board of Health returns to the City, the health investigation will be made.

The "University of Islam" is thought to be a survival of a secret cult uncovered in the slaying of James J. Smith by Robert Harris on a sacrificial altar in the home of the cult.

Later in the day the Rev. Jeremiah Jackson, a Negro evangelist, entered the office of Asst. Prosecutor George W. Schudlich. He declared himself out of sympathy with the Islam cult movement, saying that it was a reversion to paganism, and ought to be halted at once. He will appear before Schudlich again on Wednesday morning.[364]

Detroit Police Raid University of Islam

After a couple of weeks into the investigation, Police decided to raid the University of Islam and arrests 13 staff members. On April 17, 1934, The Detroit Free Press sensational headlines read: "Voodoo University Raided by Police; 13 Cultists Seized, Squad Finds 400 Enrolled at School." The headlines added, "*Instruction Books Tell About Spooks and 'Moslem' Lore*, Officers Told 'Slaves' Pay for New Names." The Police dismantled the school alarm system, and seized more NOI Lessons containing NOI Theology, that received major scrutiny:

Thirteen Negro officials and instructors in the "University of Islam." 3408 Hastings St., were arrested Monday afternoon, charged with contributing to the delinquency of minors, and subversive teaching.

A squad of police under the direction of George W. Schudlich, assistant prosecutor, and truancy officers of the Board of Education made the arrests and confiscated pamphlets used as textbooks. In the books was found evidence, Schudlich declared, that the youngsters, withdrawn from the City's schools and enrolled in the cult, were being taught "voodoo" practices.

Because of the resistance encountered previously by the officials in attempting to gain information about the "university," 15 policemen from the Canfield Station aided the authorities. They cut wires in the school through which the teachers sought to summon aid through a watchman in the basement, it was said.

Only two students were found in the school by the officials, but records seized disclosed that more than 400 were enrolled there. Archibald M. Hennigan, head of the Truancy Department of the Board of Education, declared.

Efforts had been made to trace many of the youngsters taken out of the public schools, it was said, but because their names were changed to "Moslem" ones and secrecy was prevalent among the members of the organization, it had been difficult to estimate the numbers sent to the "University of Islam." [365]

Caption reads, "Tuesday, April 17, 1934, The 'Flag of Islam,' one of the emblems of a Negro cult seized Monday during a raid on the "University of Islam," is being studied by three of the raiders. From the left are Detective Sergt. Michael Larco, prosecutor's investigator, and Archibad W. Hennigar and Leonard Morrison, of the Board of Education Truancy Department. The "university," officials believe, keeps children out of public schools to train them in mysterious practices of the voodoo cult.

Initial Arrests of School Staff

The news reporters cited the names of all arrested. Among them was Elijah's brothers, John Muhammad and Jam Sharrieff. Those held gave these names:

John Muhammad, twenty-four-year-old head of the cult, 4182 Dubois St.
Tadar Ali, 25, of 1344 E. Lafayette Ave., secretary of the school.
Abbass Rassouln, 24, of 558 Alfred St., assistant secretary.

[187]

James Mohammed, 36, of 2209 Macomb St.
Mrs. Mary Rozier, 33, of 5714 Twenty-eighth St.
Allar Cushmeer, 38, of 558 Alfred St.
Ravell Shah, 44, of 1948 Alfred St.
Azzad Mohammed, 53, of 1309 E. Lafayette Ave.
Willie Mapjied, 28, of 4182 Dubois St.
Mrs. Mary Almanza, 31, of 1839 Brewster St.
Jan Sharrieff, 25, of 660 E. Warren Ave.
Miss Burnisteen Sharrieff, 18, of 2301 Erskine St. [366]

Police and Public school officials re-hashed the same rhetoric used against the Muslims during the Robert Harris trial. So did Negro church leaders, "The attempt to close the school was supported by a large number of prominent Negroes in Detroit who wrote to Schudlich urging him to take action against the cult, which, it was said, was a resurgence of the organization which two years ago climaxed its activities with a murder."[367] Public officials mocked student materials, ravaged the mosque, targeted Muslim students and determined Muslim teachers weren't qualified to teach their own children.

School officials made a several visits to the "university recently when they became alarmed by the increasing number of withdrawals from public schools. They received little information from the heads of the organization and finally ordered the school to submit its curriculum to determine if it was up to the State standard.

The list was submitted and included a wide range of subjects, including "General Knowledge of Spook Civilization," "Chronology," "Intelligence," "Prophecy" and "Duty of a Moslem," in addition to the more standard subjects.

The school officials decided that the course of study was not up to the specifications of the educational system and ordered the place closed. Before Monday's raid was made, Sergt. Michael Larko, prosecutor's investigator, and Leonard Morrison, of the Truancy Department, visited the school and found 43 students there.

Because of the large list of students found on the "university's" records it is believed that there may be others in Detroit in addition to the Hastings St. school, which was the center of the earlier Islam cult here.

The two students found in the school, David Sharrieff, 17, of 2301 Erskine St., and Sally Allah, 15, of 936 Garfield Ave., also were taken to police headquarters for questioning. Through them it was hoped to gain additional information concerning the activities of the school.

Schudlich said that when the police entered the place they saw a huge "Islam" flag on the wall above the American flag. They also found an emblem of the group showing both the "Islam" and American flags entwined.

Morrison pointed out that in the "textbooks" seized there was considerable erroneous information and statements which were not in the public interest and safety. None of the instructors under arrest is said to have a teacher's license. Charges may be brought for this violation as well, Schudlich said.

[188]

He intended to confer Tuesday with jurists to determine if a permanent injunction could be obtained to close the school. All of the 13 officials and instructors of the organization will be taken to court Tuesday on the charge of contributing to the delinquency of minors, he said.

It was learned that Mohammed, head of the cult, charged new members $1 to change their "slave name" to an "Islam" name through a baptism ceremony.[368]

In the seizure, authorities read and reviewed the Lessons:

While the curriculum submitted to the school authorities indicated a wide range of subjects — 23 were listed — and included such higher studies as trigonometry and astronomy, it was doubted whether the instructors taken into custody were capable of teaching them, it was said.

The books found in the place were bits of garble information as well as misstatements, it was said. The "universe" was identified as a planet in one of the books. Bits of religious information were interspersed in the books.

The actual knowledge of a sun of man has searched for 66,000,000,000 years or more and have not located the spook yet," one lesson read. "Mohammed killed 6,000,000 Christians in his time and put 90,000 heads in a hole. The Nation of Islam has 21,000,000 trained soldiers ready to take the devils off the earth. Sampson was the man who muscled up the stone in the City of Mecca. It weighed 3,000 pounds.

The lesson, it was said, was typical of many of the others in the pamphlets and many of the teachings would frighten and disturb the Negroes of Detroit, Schudlich declared. While the majority of Negroes in the city was against the organization, there had been a steady increase in members among those less educated.[369]

Initial Arraignment

On Tuesday, April 17, 1934, the Detroit News, covered the same story. "Islam' Cult Faces Court,"

Fourteen instructors of the "University of Islam," negro school which taught the destruction of "the spook civilization," were to be arraigned today on charges of contributing to the delinquency of minors. The charges are based on allegations that the teachings of the school were subversive, and that the students were drawn from legal and accredited institutions, George W. Schudlich, assistant prosecutor, said.

The instructors, one student and one graduate were arrested late Monday afternoon in a raid on the school, at 3408 Hastings Street, by investigators for the prosecutor's office and the Board of Education.

Efforts at questioning the teachers proved unsuccessful Monday night. They maintained ironic silence concerning their Islamic cult, the headquarters or which, police assert, was used by a group involved in a voodoo, sacrificial killing several years ago.

Much of the evidence to be presented will be taken from records and queer books found in the school building by the raiders. The records show that 400 pupils attended. A: N. Hennigar, attendance director for the Board of Education, said he knew of 46 pupils who went to the school, absenting themselves from regular classes in the public schools or accredited private schools.

In an effort to show their teachings were standard, the school presented two lists to the Board of Education, purporting to detail the subjects taught. On one list was such a subject as higher trigonometry, although most of the students were recruited from grammar schools. On the other list, containing the purely Islamic teachings, were "intelligence," "domestic affairs," "prophecy," "chronology," "the duty of a Moslem," and "general knowledge of the spook civilization, displayed for 6,000 years."

Pamphlets and booklets in the school "library" revealed that the "spooks" refer to unbelievers outside the pale of the cult, and that there are 21,000,000 trained soldiers in "Islam" ready to drive the "devils" another term for unbelievers) off the earth. Negroes are referred to as the "original" people, while the other races are called "colored" people.

On the wall in the school two flags were painted, both backwards, on the United States emblem and the other the flag of "Islam," red with a white star and crescent. In the corners of the Islamic flag were the words justice, freedom, equality and Islam....[370]

Elijah, Kallatt, Ozier and 2 Students Arrested

Authorities arrested Three National Laborers Supreme Minister Elijah Muhammad, Supreme Captain Kallatt Muhammad, Ozier Zarrieff, along with two students Sally Allah and David Sharrieff. On April 18, 1934, Detroit Free Press reported: "U.S. May fight Voodoo in City, may fight Syndacalism Charges."

Information on the operation of the "voodoo" cult in Detroit was submitted Tuesday by Assistant Prosecutor George H. Schudlich to the United States Department of Justice to determine whether the 12 men and four women, all Negroes, held in connection with a raid on the University of Islam may be prosecuted under Federal statutes.

Schudlich's action followed the statement of a fourteen-year-old girl who was arrested Tuesday with three men, said to be members of the Cult of Islam.

She declared that at the "University" the American flag was denounced and the students were taught that the only true flag is that of Islam. Such practices might be construed as syndicalism or anarchism, Schudlich said.

The men arrested Tuesday were Elijah Mohammed, supreme investigator for the Cult of Islam, Ocier Zariff and Rollatt Mohammed. With the four women and nine men arrested Monday night in the raid at 3408 Hastings St., they were charged with contributing to the delinquency of minors.

Two students taken in the raid and the girl arrested Tuesday were held at the Juvenile Detention Home and will be called as State witnesses when the others appear Wednesday morning on the delinquency charges.

The raid which opened the offensive against the cult disclosed an enrollment of 400 pupils at the school, where, according to Schudlich, the children were taught "voodoo" practices.

Attempts made by the Board of Education to trace the children after they were taken out of the public schools was made difficult because they were given

Moslem names, according to the Archibald H. Henningan, head of the truancy department of the Board of Education. [371]

Authorities Claim School Not Up to Standard

Books confiscated in the raid gave garbled accounts of a number of subjects, some of them a mixture of Biblical history and highly imaginative "Moslem" predictions. Previous investigation of the "university," which required submission of its curriculum to the State Board of Education, showed that it was not up to standard.

The general belief among educators was that the instructors were incapable of teaching some of the subjects listed, but it was impossible to question their ability to deal with such subjects as "General Knowledge of the Spook Civilization," "Prophecy" and "The Duty of a Moslem."

The movement to organize Negroes in Detroit into such a cult was brought to light two years ago by a murder which was described as a "human sacrifice" in keeping with the cult teaching.[372]

The FOI and MGT Protest the Muslims Arrest at the Police Precinct

The Muslims refused to allow their Leaders and children be unjustly arrested by the Police. The FOI and MGT & GCC (joined by Lost-Founds) stormed the Police Precinct demanding the Muslims be freed. The staff of Temple #2 recalls the chain of events:

In 1934, one Detroit radio station broadcasted that "the leaders of the cult of Muslim Believers have been arrested." More than 700 unarmed Muslim men, women and teenage boys marched in an orderly line to police headquarters at 1300 Bogan Street where Messenger Muhammad was being held on charges of "contributing to the delinquency of minors." Because Muslim children were being educated at the University of Islam and were no longer attending the white run public schools. As the Muslims approached, police armed with billy clubs rushed out pushing and shoving the Muslims with their clubs. Many police were even mounted on horseback. But all the Black People in Detroit were decidedly with the Muslims as Blacks (Muslims and non-Muslims alike) courageously turned the tide in favor of the Muslims, one police leader was quoted saying "We can't handle this, we can't handle those niggers." That officer and many with him turned in their badges and their guns rather than join the fight against the Muslims [video shows a huge crowd of Blacks confronting a police force].

The Muslims who led the faithful in support of their leader, the Hon. Elijah Muhammad, the Messenger of Allah, led the brave group marching back to the Temple, armed only with a strong belief in the "power of Allah" as taught by his Messenger. Most of the Muslims were uninjured, while many of the policemen were known to be hospitalized.

"Here are the some of the unarmed Muslims of Muhammad's Temple of Islam #1 Detroit, Michigan, at the 1934 attack by police": Bro. Muallah Hazziez, Bro. Rasul Ali, Bro. Abdul Hazziez, Bro. Ernest Karriem, Bro. Carl Pasha (a Jr. Fruit at the time), Bro. Leon Hazziez (also a Jr. Fruit at the time), Bro. Kalendar Muhammad, Bro. Jazavel Joshua, Bro. David Pasha, Bro. Governor X, Bro. Emmet X. [373]

Chicago Temple Caravan Comes to Detroit

The FOI from Chicago came to Detroit through a caravan seeking to bust their leaders and children out of prison. NOI Pioneer Sidney Shah remembers:

In the early '30s when me and the Messenger was in Detroit, so when the Messenger was in Detroit, and then he came to Chicago, what I mean to say to set up a Temple here in Chicago, and he did set up a Temple here in Chicago. And then after he got the Temple set up in Chicago, he went back to Detroit. It was in Detroit that he had some kind of disturbance with our enemy, and this was in 1933 [sic]. And then the Captain Pasha, he got about four or five carloads of us and rushed us to Detroit. We got a telegram from Detroit that they was bothering the Messenger, and they got 5 or 6 cars, what I mean they loaded us in, they called us from our homes to get to the Temple at 33rd and State (at the Odd Fellows Hall where we had the Temple at) quickly. So we got there as quickly as we could. And they got us together and we left around that evening, must have been about 4:30 or 5 o'clock for Detroit. So when we made it into Detroit (I don't know just what time), but when we made it to Detroit we went to the Messenger's house where the Messenger was—but he was gone. And we left there and we went to the jail. And we didn't go through the front door to go into the jail, we went all the way—we walked all the way from the bottom of the steps all the way to the top. We stopped on every floor looking for the Messenger. So when they found out they said, "He isn't here." And so we left and we drove around Detroit for a long time and then we left back to Chicago.

We come back to Chicago, and I think when they had the fight at 11th Street, this is when our enemy had really come to be against the Messenger more than what he was, and the Messenger then he moved to Chicago.[374]

Sidney Shah

UOI Principal Ben Sabakhan, UOI Student Sally Allah

From L to R: personal secretary of Master Fard Muhammad - Sister Burnsteen S. Mohammed, wife of the Honorable Elijah Muhammad - Mother Clara Muhammad, the first principle of the University of Islam - Ben Sabakhan, the youngest blood brother and minister of the Honorable Elijah Muhammad - Brother John Muhammad and Sally Allah, who was mentioned in Message to the Black Man in America. (NOI Historic Exhibit Facebook Page)

Wallace Fard Muhammad and Elijah Muhammad founded and organized the Nation of Islam in the early 1930s in Detroit. A headquarters and school, set up Hasting Street, was raided by police and Detroit schools officials on April 16, 1934. Several members were arrested and held. They were charged with contributing to the deliquency of minors by withdrawning children from the public schools and "teaching subversive doctrines." The next day 500 Nation members marched to police headquarters to see those who were arrested. They were met by Detroit police.

The marchers stopped in front of police headquarters and when they refused to move, police took about 20 into the building.

Another man is taken into police headquarters.

Twenty-nine Nation of Islam members were arraigned April 22, 1934 in Recorder's Court. Two were charged with assault to do great bodily harm and the others with disturbing the peace. Asked to raise their right hands to be sworn, the defendants stretched out arms with palms up and said: "We swear only by the one true God, Allah."

On Thursday, April, 19, 1934, The Detroit Free Press headlines read "**13 Policemen Hurt Battling Voodoo Band, Cult Backer March on Headquarters to Protest Arrests, Motor and Mounted Forces Join in Fight.**" Right before the 19 incarcerated Muslims were to go in court for their arraignment, a disturbance broke out between police and Muslim protestors, which quickly escalated to a riot.

Thirteen policemen were injured and several rioters were hurt when a horde of Negroes, aroused to frenzy by the teachings of a voodoo cult calling itself Mohammedan, marched on Police Headquarters Wednesday to protest the arrest of their leaders.

Only a handful of policemen at first tried to break up the demonstration. They were quickly overwhelmed, and before the battle ended all available officers were engaged, squad cars were drawn into the fight and the mounted force was called upon.

Police reported that 41 Negroes were arrested during the disturbance. Sixteen men were held on charges of inciting a riot. Nine men and 12 women were held for investigation. Four boys, from 14 to 17 years old, were held at the Juvenile Detention Home.

An hour after the riot the 19 Negroes whose arrest in the cult's headquarters at 3408 Hastings St. inspired the protest parade were arraigned before Recorder's Judge Arthur E. Gordon.

Accused of Causing Truancy

They were charged with contributing to the delinquency of a minor by causing Sally Allah, 15 years old, to play truant from the public schools to attend the cult's "university."

Lined up before the bench, handcuffed to each other and closely watched by a dozen detectives, they pleaded not guilty and were held in $500 bonds each for examination next Wednesday.

After the riot the police took precautions to guard against further outbreaks. Numerous patrolmen were stationed throughout the neighborhood and detectives were placed at all strategic points in the Recorder's Court.

All police on the day shift were ordered to extra duty Wednesday night, reporting at Headquarters.

List of Muslims Arrested in the Riot

Those arraigned gave these names:

Mary Rozier, 33 years old, 5714 Twenty-eighth St.;
Albert Sharrief, 20, of 660 E. Warren Ave.;
Mary Almanza, 31, of 1839 Brewester St.;
Burnsteen Sharrief, 17, of 2301 Erskine St.;
John Mohammed, 24, of 4182 Dubois St.;
Wali Mohammed, 33, of 504 Woodside Ave., Ferndale;
James Mohammed, 36, of 1344 E. Lafayette Ave.;
David Sharrief, 17, of 2301 Erskine St.;
Ocier Zarrief, 29, of 1309 E. Lafayete Ave.;
Tadar Ali, 25, of 1344 E. Lafayette Blvd.;

Willie Majied, 25, of 4128 Dubois St.;
Rozell Shah, 44, of 1948 Alfred St.;
Abbass Rassoull, 34, of 558 Alfred St.;
Allar Cushmeer, 38, of 558 Alfred St.;
Willie Mohammed, 68, of 4182 Dubois St.;
Kallatt Mohammed, 29, of 283 E. Hancock Ave.;
Elijah Mohammed, 36, same address;
Azzad Mohammed, 51, of 1309 E. Lafayeet Ave.,
and Jim Sharrief, 25, of 660 E. Warren Ave.

The roundup of the defendants was begun Monday and was accomplished without any serious violence occurring until Wednesday's outbreak.

Cry, 'Get The Coppers'

When the rioters first appeared, Inspector William G. Rick and a few patrolmen met them in Clinton St. and tried to turn them back. A cry from the crowd of "Get the coppers!" started the action.

Inspector Rick and his men were quickly driven back and the fight swirled up to the main entrance of Headquarters. Feet, fists, clubs, stones and knives were being used by the time reinforcements arrived.

Even a heavy can of green paint, left outside the police building by a workman who had been painting a guard rail, became a weapon in the hands of the rioters. Patrolman Bernard Preo, going to the assistance of another officer who was being blackjacked, was doused with it by one of the Negroes.

When Inspector Rick went to his aid another rioter picked up the can and flung it in Rick's face, backing his eye and inflicting a severe cut on his nose.

Before the battle ended it was being directed by Commissioner Heinrich A. Pickert, Deputy Supt. James E. McCarty and Chief of Detectives Fred Frahm, who took their stand on the steps of Headquarters.

A tear gas squad was held ready but was not needed. Policemen fighting on foot with clubs and mounted patrolmen riding into the crowd broke up the attack and scattered the mob. The rioters were driven back to Hastings St.

The known casualties, besides Inspector Rick and Patrolman Preo, whose nose and back were injured, were:

Sergt. Miles Furlong, driver for Commissioner Pickert, bruised shoulder.

Detective John Mulligan, Special Investigation Bureau, fractured thumb and cut lip.

Patrolman Dewey Welderman, Bethune Station, bruised head.

Patrolman Stanley Slavin, McGraw Station, fractured hand and razor cut.

Patrolman Fred Aller, Central Station, bruises.

Patrolman Ira Pender, Central Station, fractured thumb.

Roy Carmer, Traffic Division, laceration of temple.

Patrolman Charles Malcolm, Central Station, abdominal injuries.

Patrolman Bernard Mulligan, Central Station, bitten on index finger.

Patrolman Marty Milan, Traffic Division, bruises.

Patrolman E. Leydet, Central Station, face scratched and hand cut.

Victor La Rose, mechanic at Police Headquarter's garage, fractured right thumb.

Aaron Sharriel, 5754 Boyd Ave., contusions of hip and right forearm.[375]

The Media singled out Elijah Muhammad and his two brothers Kallatt and John while standing trial in court. John recalls:

When I was in jail, in 1934, handcuffed side by side with my Brother, Elijah Muhammad, where we stood before the judge in the county jail in Detroit, along with out father, (whom many hardly recognized as being a Muslim. He is always called a Baptist preacher, as you know). The Detroit Free Press did a writing on the three Brothers, (Messenger Elijah Muhammad, Captain Kallatt Muhammad and Secretary John Muhammad) honoring us as being the "Sons of Islam."[376]

Jailed Muslims Go on Hunger Strike

On Friday, April, 20, 1934, The Detroit Free Press headlines read "**Cultists Start Hunger Strike, Jailed Negroes Won't Touch Any Food.**" The first day, the Muslims protested the food offered them in jail:

The 15 Negro men held at the County Jail as leaders of the Islamite Cult that fomented Wednesday's riot, in which 13 policemen were injured, went on a hunger strike Thursday.

Sheriff Thomas C. Wilcox said that he offered them hamburger and onions, peas, mashed potatoes, bread and coffee, and that they refused to touch any of the food.

The four women also held as cult leaders ate the food offered them, however.

All 19 are awaiting examination on charges of contributing to the delinquency of a minor. They are accused of causing a fifteen-year-old Negro girl to be an habitual truant from the public schools by encouraging her to attend the cult's "university" in which the study of "spooks" is the chief subject.

Meanwhile the police held 29 men, four boys and nine women as members of the mob that marched on Headquarters Wednesday to protest against the incarceration of the others. Twenty of the men were charged with inciting a riot, and the boys were held for juvenile authorities, and the rest of the prisoners were under investigation.

Assistant Prosecutor George W. Schudlich said that he would take statements from all the prisoners with a view to obtaining as much information as possible about the cult.[377]

On Monday, April, 21, 1934, The Detroit Free Press headlines read "**A Hunger Strike Ends with a Bang, 30 Cans of Sardines Are Just a Starter for Cultists.**' The Muslims pooled their resources and were able to purchase their own dinners:

What a hungry Moslemite of the Hastings St. variety will eat after a prolonged fast became known at 3:30 p.m. Friday to the clerk of the County Jail commissary.

At that hour the 15 Negroes held as leaders of a local voodoo society, known as the Cult of Islam, ended their hunger strike by purchasing their own dinners.

They had refused jailfare since Thursday morning on the grounds there was a curse on it, and had taken nothing but eight loaves of bread in the meanwhile.

Their purchases and consumption Friday afternoon consisted of:

30 cans of sardines.
2 cans of corn.
1 pound of peanut butter.
23 candy bars.
1 pound of cheese.

No calls for the house doctor had been received up to press time.[378]

29 Muslims Arraigned in Court in Front of Judge

On Sunday, April 22, 1934, The Detroit Free Press headlines read, "**29 Arraigned in Cult Riots.**" Security was tight as the Muslims stood their ground in court:

Twenty-nine Negroes, all members of the voodoo cult of "Islam," who, with about 500 others rioted in front of Police Headquarters Wednesday, were arraigned Saturday in Recorder's Court. Two were charged with assault to do great bodily harm and the others with disturbing the peace.

The pair charged with assault on Patrolman Stanley Slavin appeared before Judge John P. Scallen and each was placed under bond of $2,000 after standing mute. The defendants were Karrien Bey [Karriem Bey], 38 years old, and Rufius Hezziez [Rufus Hazziez], 31. Examination was set for Tuesday.

The remaining 27 were arraigned before Judge Arthur E. Gordon. Of the group of men and women all were found guilty, but sentence was suspended on 10 of the women.

The court room was guarded by 50 policemen. All doors were watched to prevent sympathizers from causing trouble.

The defendants were taken before the Court in single file with a police officer standing near each.

Asked by Judge Gordon to raise their right hands to be sworn, they refused and stretched out both aims with the palm of their hands faced upward to the level of their waist and said

"We swear only by the one true God, Allah."

Joseph Mohammed acted as spokesman for his "brothers."

Judge Gordon asked him where he was born.

"I was born in the Holy City of Mecca in the year 1555," the spokesman said.

The members of the cult testified that they had gone to Police Headquarters to see the other members of the organization who had been arrested. They said police were to blame for the entire riot because they started to shove some of the voodooists into the station.

The "University of Islam" at 3408 Hastings St. was raided by police after it was reported that subversive doctrines were being taught there.[379]

14-year-old Sally Allah Takes the Stand

On Thursday, April 26, 1934, The Detroit Free Press headlines read, **"Girl Recounts Lore of Islam, School's Mohammed Gets Probation."** The time finally came for Muslims to have their day in court. Sally Allah, 15, was called to the stand to be scrutinized by the District Attorney:

The rewrite job done on the religion of Mohammed by Detroit's "University of Islam," in an apparent effort to put a sock and speculative fillip into it, was described to Recorder's Judge Arthur E. Gordon Wednesday by Sally Allah, fifteen year-old former Garfield Intermediate School Negro girl.

She was taught in the Islamic New Deal, she said, that if she cut off the heads of four devils—devils being unrighteous people – she would win a free trip to Mecca—and a button of some sort.

"I was taught arithmetic and algebra, and that I was an Asiatic girl and cream of the earth," she said.

"And—"prompted George W. Schudlich assistant prosecutor.

"And that the Caucasians would be put off the planet in 1934—destroyed."

"How destroyed?"

"By poison gas and fightin'."

The court asked who was going to fight whom.

"You're going to fight to stay here," responded Sally, impassively, fumbling at her dilapidated fur neckpiece.

A semicircle of 19 members of the Islam faculty stood in front of Judge Gordon and listened stoically to the girl recite what was taught in the syncopated Hastings St. institution. They were co-defendants charged with contributing to the delinquency of a minor.[380]

Heavy Police Presence at Trial in Fear of Muslims

The Press described her co-defendants and Muslims in attendance that stood with her in court as the same people who maimed and injured police officers during the riot. They also noted extra police officers were on standby in case of a recurrence:

Rioting sympathizers at the arraignment of the 19 a week ago, slugged, stoned and knifed 13 policemen who got in the way of their protest march. Forty-one Negro rioters were arrested then.

A swarm of policemen, armed with riot sticks, waited in the police garage Wednesday morning for any recurrence of last week's belligerence, and admittance to the Recorder's Court Building was refused to anyone not having business there.

Five other Negroes of the Allah girl's age were in court to testify, but she was the only one examined.

She changed over to the cult university from Garfield School, she said, because she wanted to; No one persuaded her, she asserted.

Sally said that the school taught her not to take much stock in the American flag.

"They taught me to believe in justice and freedom," she volunteered.[381]

The Hon. Elijah Muhammad represents the Muslims at Trial

Elijah Muhammad, representing the Muslims, denied the allegation they charged people to receive holy names, reiterated the importance of having a NOI membership card and questioned Sally Allah on what constitutes a 'devil'. While the judge posed a specific question about the reward mentioned in the 10th Q&A of Lost-Found Muslim Lesson No. 1:

> Elijah Mohammed, who said that he was the pastor of the university, cleared up the point as to devils.
> "Does the prophet teach you that only white people are devils?" he asked Sally.
> "No, all wicked people are devils."
> The girl also said, in response to Elijah's quiet questioning, that she carried a card of membership as a registered Moslem and that it said right on it that if any other Moslems found her doing something that wasn't righteous he had the authority to take the card away from her. Mohammed estimated local membership at 8,000.
> Judge Gordon tried to find out whose picture would be on the button to be awarded as a secondary prize for cutting off the heads of four devils, but Sally's recollection was not clear. She thought it might be a likeness of a Mr. G. D. Farrand, whom she had heard mentioned as prophet and savior.
> The Court endeavored to learn who Mr. Farrand was, and where he was, but outside the fact that he was in town two months ago, the best Judge Gordon could get from anyone was that Prophet Farrand was last heard from in Gary, Ind.
> The rumor that members paid $10 to trade "slave" names for stalwart Islamic names was denied by Preacher Mohammed.[382]

Elijah Muhammad explained to the judge that the Muslims were poor righteous teachers with little money. Some received aid from the state, yet collectively survived because Islam teaches them to unite and share with their fellow Muslims. The judge handed down his decision; none of the Muslims would face jail time and were free to go, as well as Elijah Muhammad was given six months of probation on account he send the children back to public school, and re-apply through the state to start a University of Islam that meets Michigan State standards:

> "We never have any money," he said.
> It developed that eight of the 19 were on public welfare.
> "If you don't have money, how do you eat?"
> "Oh, if one of us has a slice of bread, we divide it—and we have one man working."
> A man at the end of the semicircle stepped forward and said that he was working as City janitor.

Mohammed said that he never had gone farther than the fourth grade, but he had withdrawn his children from a Hamtramck school because other children taunted them and fought with them and admitted that perhaps youngsters at Islam University could not get as good instruction as in the City schools.

"You've got to remember that they've got to go out in the world and meet competition. I want them to have an equal chance, and I think you do," said Judge Gordon.

"I also want you to talk over things with those misguided followers of yours who marched down here a week ago," he said. "I advise you, if you want a school, to get a faculty entitled to teach under our State law."

Judge Gordon let the other 18 go and put Elijah Mohammed on six months' probation, conditioning it on Mohammed getting the children at the Hastings St. institution back into regular schools and providing the Board of Education with a list of the children's real names.

Mohammed lives at 283 E. Hancock. Young Miss Ali [Allah], whose "slave" name was Bomar, lives with her Islamic mother, Helen Allah yclept Bomar, at 936 Garfield Ave.[383]

Newspapers Sensationalize NOI Lessons

On Sunday, April 29, 1934, the Detroit Free Press sensationally played up the NOI lesson in their headline "Voodoo Catechism Says Heads of Four Devils Are Passport to Mecca":

Devils named for destruction by Detroit's "University of Islam" breathed easier Saturday and began to come out of their holes.

Checkers posted by the Board of Education at the Hastings St. portals of the institution reported that leaders of the syncopated Negro Moslem cult apparently had taken to hear the orders issued Wednesday by Recorder's Judge Arthur E. Gordon and disbanded their children's classes. The voodoo guild, which is said to have won a membership of 9,000 in Detroit, and which precipitated a near riot 10 days ago in which 13 policemen were injured and 41 rioters arrested, was instructed by Judge Gordon to return children on their lists to their regular classrooms in the public schools.

Archie M. Hennigar, director of the attendance department of the Board, said Saturday he was still awaiting from Elijah Mohammed, pastor of the cult, the list of children's names which the Court ordered Mohammed to provide.

Trip to Mecca Promised

Children and adults as well, were taught that if they cut off the heads of four devils — usually unrighteous Caucasians — they would be given a free trip to Mecca and a button to wear on their dress or in their coat lapel.

An investigation by the Prosecutor's office of the University — the pastor managed to get through the fourth grade — has revealed that aside from a certain lunacy in the things taught, courses were taught in the fashion of a schoolboy's dream.

Sessions were two hours daily, starting at 2 p.m., for three days a week.

The manual of cult practices and beliefs, apparently conceived in the spirit of a child making its first cake out of mud and whatever is handy in the cupboard, contains considerable astonishing instruction.

On the matter of the Annie Oakley for Mecca, for example, the "University's" question-and-answer book is as follows

Q. — Why does Mohammed and other Moslem murder the devil and what is the duty of each Moslem in regards to four devils? What reward does he receive by presenting the heads of the four devils to the prophet at one time?

A. — each Moslem is required to kill four devils and by presenting the four heads he receives his reward of a button for his buttonhole and transportation to Mecca to pass a visit with his brother Mohammed."

Textbook Tells of Flag

"Our flag," explains the textbook.

The father of Mohammedanism is referred to affectionately by "University of Islam" undergraduates as "Joe Mohammed."

"is the sun, moon and stars.

"Planets are something grown or made from the beginning, and holy is something that has not been diluted, mixed or tampered in any form."

Again:

Q. — Why does Mohammed make the devil study from 35 to 50 years before he lets him become a Moslem son.?

A. — So that he can clean himself up. A Moslem does not like the devil, regardless of how long he studies. Even after he has devoted 35 to 50 years trying to learn and do like the original man. He could come and do trading with us and we would not kill him as quick as we would other devils who have not gone under this study. The devil is 100 per cent wicked and will not keep and obey laws of Islam. His ways and actions are like the snake of the grafted kind. So Mohammed figured that since he could not reform the devils, they had to be murdered. All Moslems will murder the devil because they know he is a snake and would sting someone else.

"Because the original man," remarks the textbook in another passage, "is the owner and god of the earth, he knows every square inch of it and has chosen for himself the best part."

Taught They Are Asiatic

While most of the Negro Islamites were born in Georgia, North Carolina and Kentucky, the "University" teaches that as a matter of fact they are really natives of Asia and were born about the Fifteenth Century.

All classes, according to George W. Schudlich, assistant prosecutor, were held in a hall subdivided into four rooms over a theater at Hastings and Wilkins Sts.

Islam truant officers have been somewhat bedeviled by the fact that even with two-hour classes, they frequently would find younger Islamites in the theater below instead of out where they should have been bagging devils and getting the free junket to the Kaaba.

W.D. Fard is said to be the prophet and savior of the order. No one at the Hastings St. school knows where he is, or will say where he is. When a letter is sent to Prophet Fard, they say, it is merely addressed to General Delivery in the last city he was known to be in, and through some divine fashion, the mail catches up with him.[384]

This trial was a sign of more tests to come. Without the presence of Master Fard Muhammad, the Muslims would be severely tried through ongoing police harassment, trouble with the law, the hard economic times and the heavy racism.

NOI's First Newspaper: The Final Call to Islam

In mid-1934, the Hon. Elijah Muhammad started "The Final Call to Islam" newspaper based out of Detroit. The staff included his brothers Kallatt Muhammad, Wali Muhammad, future sister-in-law Reformer Burnsteen Sharrieff and Lonnie Pasha (asst. Supreme Captain) as contributing writers. The paper consisted of well written columns detailing the teachings of Master Fard Muhammad. They were able to produce four or five editions of the paper from June through September of 1934.

Elijah Muhammad starts to teach that Master Fard was Allah

The one thing was the Saviour was still mentioned as "Prophet W.D. Fard." In his teacher's absence, the Messenger believed it was time to reveal the secret of the Master's true identity. Elijah Muhammad:

So, I did begin teaching that the Son of Man or the Second Coming of Jesus was present. This was He now, here among us. He didn't allow me to go too far with that kind of teaching while He was present. He told me, "You can do that after I am gone." He said, "Don't talk too much about Me now.' He said, "Give them a little milk." That's the way He talked all the time; He never would just say anything hardly direct. He would give it to you in a way that you would have to learn just exactly what He meant by what He said. And so, He said, "You cannot give babies meat." I understood what He was referring to. And so He said, "Give the little baby milk." He said, "When I am gone," He said, "then you can say whatever you want to about Me.'385

Staying true to his promise, Elijah openly started teaching that Master Fard Muhammad was more than a prophet; and that he was Almighty God Allah himself, and that He, Elijah Muhammad, was his Prophet.

Q. Why did Messenger Muhammad leave Detroit?
A. Sometime in 1934 Allah left. As they had agreed before Master Fard Muhammad left, Elijah Muhammad began teaching that the one who had been known as Prophet Fard was in fact Allah (God) Himself, in the person of Master Fard Muhammad. Some of the former student ministers disagreed. They didn't want to believe that the most humble among them had been chosen to be The Messenger of Allah – they began disbelieving in Allah after they had said they believed; they became hypocrites.386

In-Fighting begins after Fard's Departure

When Elijah shared this with some of the Ministers and Laborers, some were very upset. Some felt he was changing the teachings; others still had an ax to grind with him per his election as Supreme Minister. One such person was Lonnie Pasha, asst. Supreme Captain, who gathered his loyal soldiers and began to spread dissatisfaction to others, to the point where they were planning to make a move on the new Prophet. John Muhammad recalls:

Until finally we were at a Brother's home in Detroit, who turned enemy to Messenger Elijah Muhammad - after The Messenger was called, "The Messenger of Allah" after we first called him "Prophet." Do you remember that? We used to call The Messenger "Prophet" in that area of time. When we called him "Prophet," this man became a very bad enemy to The Messenger, until they had ran him out of The City of Detroit.[387]

Major Attrition of Muslims Due to Internal and External Conflicts

Many Muslims became disenfranchised with all of the fighting and bickering, and with Master Fard Muhammad being gone, some left the movement and went back to what they were doing before he came. Others just couldn't stand the pressures that came along with being in the Nation of Islam:

After the departure of W.D. Fard the movement underwent a rapid collapse. Most of the members had converted back to Christianity, because the movement did not appeal to them anymore, especially under the arising conflicts. Clashes of interest and striving of the various ministers and assistant ministers among themselves to get hold of the group for their own personal benefit were other additional factors in disappointing most of the followers. The most effective factor in weakening the movement, Elijah said, was that of the arousal of the police department in Detroit against the movement. Moreover, death of some of the followers and the lack of replacing them by new converts was another factor in the increasing collapse of the movement. Some other followers, Elijah Mohammed said, began to be careless about their affiliation in the cult.

Division of the original body of the cult into small groups scattered around Hasting Street in Detroit has left around 180 members, who organized themselves in a temple which forms a branch of the cult currently led by Elijah Mohammed.[388]

In 1933, after the deportation of W.D. Fard from Detroit, the conflicts and clashes among the ministers, assistant ministers, and the members aspiring to leadership became so strong that Elijah Mohammed was not able to continue preaching in Detroit. Therefore he changed his residence to Chicago and appointed a minister for the small group in Detroit who kept allegiance to the teachings of W.D. Fard and his disciple.[389]

Elijah Muhammad Places His Detroit Officials in Charge

Elijah Muhammad left his brother Wali Muhammad in charge of one of the Detroit Temples when he left for Chicago. Brother Arroz Jordon who was in Temple #1 recalls the challenges they faced:

Arroz Jordan: During that particular time, when the Messenger was teaching us, he was away from us most of the time because we had an infiltration of hypocrites. A hypocritical type of person who wanted to take his life, who wanted to persecute him, and those were very perilous times. But of course, we of the faith banded together. And by banding together and keeping the faith, and praying to Allah, we were able to overcome these. But of course, they propped up in different forms. They came in, they partook of the teachings. And they wanted to proclaim that they were members, but actually they were not. We had various forms of deception. And as a direct consequence is this, we, the poor Muslims, at that particular time realized the peril that was around us. And we had to be very, very cautious, very careful, and very diplomatic, the way we handled the situation and handled the people that were around us.[390]

Elijah Moves to Chicago to Establish New Headquarters

Elijah's eldest son Emanuel recalls when his family moved: "I remember when Islam in America was in its infancy in the years of the '30's. The Messenger and some of his laborers were persecuted and thrown in jail for teaching the religion of Islam. He moved His family from Detroit, Michigan on September 5, 1934 – to Chicago."[391] Temple #2 NOI documentary verifies the same, "On Sept. 5, 1934, Elijah and his family took up residence in Chicago, Illinois, at 5830 S. Wabash Avenue. Later they moved to 3735 S. Giles Street. In the late '30s they moved to 5308 S. Wabash.[392]

Elijah resumed teaching at the same places him and Master Fard established, yet as numbers dwindled and the threats increased, like his teacher, he found other places to teach as well.

In 1934, Elijah continued to teach at the Odd Fellows building, and then later at the Pythian Temple 3741 S. State Street. Token Blacks worked with authorities to dissuade Muslims from meeting in public places. So Elijah started teaching in homes of people like Mr. Marrcellars Jardan at 18 E. 30th Street, Clara Hazziez, 3721 S. Federal Street, Tamara Hazziez 2912 S. Ferry, Amos Muhammad, located in an alley over a garage in the 3300 block of Vernon and South Parkway (now known as King Drive).[393]

5830 S. Wabash Street, and 3735 S. Giles Street

5308 S. Wabash, and Pythian Temple 3741 S. State Street

Sends Letter to Temple #1 that Prophet Fard is Allah

On December 3, 1934, the Hon. Elijah Muhammad wrote a letter addressed "To the Ministry Class of No. 1 Michigan." The letter by design seemed to be the Messenger's way of putting everyone on notice in regards to his view of Master Fard Muhammad as God. Thus it starts:

As-Salaam Alaikum, My Dearest Brothers, Followers and Laborers with me in the Name of our Saviour, the Almighty Deliverer of the Lost Founds, W.D. Fard Mohammed; whom the world has not known as yet, but will shortly. It is you and I who has said that we know Him and are His witnesses to make known His name among those who are sleeping in sin and ignorance; and who enter the school of preparation that we may be found worthy of Him when He returns to put us on His book as Laborers fitted for the cause of righteousness.

Give ear my Brothers, and listen diligently to these my words and forget them not. Islam is not to be played with and those who teach it must forever be mindful of the <u>LAW</u>, because ignorance of the law is no excuse. Now we are not ignorant of the Law, because we received it not by prophecy nor was it sent to us in a book that we might say we could not understand it or that we failed to receive it. No, but Allah has come to us Himself, to each us out of His mouth in the person of our Saviour FARD MOHAMMED; whom we have seen with our eyes and heard with our ears, and our hands have handled Him lest we have excuses and say He was not real. This blessed and only friend of we who were lost, called me into His ministry in August 1932. Not for the works that I done, nor for the education, for I had neither. But for His own cause, that I should hear the world of His mouth and go and teach others of His Majesty, and wonders that He is about to work in the wilderness of North America where we now live.

He Himself, knowing the times and seasons of all things put upon me a great work to accomplish, but not without a great reward at the end; that is if I keep His Law and Commandments and obey without priding myself against Him who sent me. Now this did He charge me with, to go and make many ministers and send them in all of the cities and teach Islam as He has given it to me. Adding nothing to it, nor even taking a atom from it, lest we dilute His Holy word and be found guilty of falsifying the truth on His return. Now this have I tried to do, to make Him someone to help in the work of the Ministry, that His name may be known among those that know not Him nor His word.[394]

Understanding the turbulent times, the Prophet Elijah Muhammad cautioned his Ministers and followers from partaking in the recent jealousy and envy campaign of his enemies. He forbade it amongst his followers, and advised them to hold fast to the rope of Allah, of which he advised they should pray to his Allah, Master Fard Muhammad:

Now, remember brethren how I warned you of how to keep evil from ever entering the class by never permitting that hateful thing called jealousy and envy ever once be named among you. Seek not one another's faults until we look carefully into our own, because he that seeks his brothers faults and not his own, always stands in danger of judgment.

Remember if one of you has a fault and he is warned of it and the brother repents and asks you for forgiveness and acknowledges all his wrongs, then we must fast and pray to our Saviour for a protection against all of our faults and teach us whether our brother is right or not, and if so the Saviour will tell you in His own way; but do not tell Him in our prayers to show you His answer in a way you desire because He knows our hearts and He does whatsoever He will.[395]

Further along the letter Elijah addressed "Ministerial Qualifications" for those seeking to be in his ministry, and some biblical passages reminded them of the work of the prophets, and the nature of a similar letter he received from his good Minister Sultan Muhammad. Most noticeable was the way Elijah Muhammad ended the letter to the Ministers at Temple #1, he signed: "As-Salaam-Alaikum. Your Brother and Servant of Allah, Prophet Elijah Muhammad.[396]

The Introduction of "X" as Last Name

The naming process under Master Fard, was that a Muslim would recite the lesson "Student Enrollment" 100% right and exact in front of a Temple Laborer, and then they were given a letter to write to Master Fard Muhammad to get their holy name.

Since Master Fard left and didn't give anyone authority to approve names, a solution had to be created in the interim "until Allah gave you a holy name." Elijah's brother John recalls:

When Master Fard Muhammad gave names to the Black Man and Woman, in Detroit, Michigan, --which were approximately 25,000, and in Chicago, Illinois; also a few in Milwaukee, Wisconsin, from His mouth-this was the fulfillment of that Prophecy of an individual receiving a name from the mouth of God. This taught the Messenger and his followers of what kind of name to use or name themselves...

There are people (Muslims) who received a name from Master Fard Muhammad and never saw Him while He was with us. Many people could not tell the meaning of their names because of this state, but they were out of the names of their slave masters.

People who joined the Nation of Islam, did not receive an X while Master Fard Muhammad was with us giving names, because after their letters were OK'd, Master Fard Muhammad gave them their names and they became a registered Muslim in the Nation of Islam. At that time, we called them by their first name only, until a name was given, although the laborers were given the understanding of the letter X, and after a little while of His departure, the X became commonly known to those whose letter were OK'd by the Laborers of Islam. Many letters came to Master Fard Muhammad. I kept many of them and did not open them, and I also OK'd many of them to Master Fard Muhammad. Then later the Messenger said to me at my home, after he had moved to Chicago,

"Brother, don't hold up any more letters without opening and checking them for being OK'd for their names...

From that day on we opened every letter and those that were OK'd, the Messenger would give them the "X."[397]

To accommodate the faithful waiting to receive names, the Laborers rewarded an approval letter giving them an "X":

6116 South Michigan Avenue
Chicago37, Illinois

(Date)_____

Mr._____
(Street No.)_____
Chicago, Illinois

As-Salam-Alaikum

In the name of Allah, and in the name of his true Messenger, Mr. Elijah Mohammed.

Dear Brother,

We have your letter of _____, seeking to be united again to your own. We the Labors of Islam are very pleased. The same has passed our inspection, and it now awaits the inspection of Almighty God, Allah. Until He gives to you your holy name, you will be known among us as Brother_____-X.
Please report to 824 East 43rd Street for further information concerning your letter.

As I say unto you in the name of Allah, and in the name of His true Prophet, Mr. Elijah Mohammed.

As-Salaam-Alaikum
Sec'y.[398] PAGE 206

Address
City and State
Date

Mr. W. F. Muhammad
℅ Mr. Elijah Muhammad
9415 South Damen Avenue
Chicago, Illinois 60620

Dear Saviour Allah, our Deliverer,
Who Came in the Person of Master
Fard Muhammad to Whom Praises
are due forever:

I bear witness that there is
no God but Thee and that Elijah
Muhammad is Thy Servant and
Apostle. I desire to reclaim my Own.
I desire a name from Thee. Please
give me my Original name. My slave
name is as follows:

Name (Mr. Mrs. or Miss)

This is copy of the Dear Saviours Letter all converts had to write in order to be accepted into the fold of the Nation of Islam and receive your "X".

New converts now were being raised under the new Prophet based out of Chicago, which became the new Headquarters of the Nation of Islam:

Interviewer: Bro. Muhammad, tell us your first impressions of the Messenger when you first met him.
Willie Muhammad: When I first met the Messenger, I knew that he was an unusual person. His teaching of Islam to us (in the year of 1934 I accepted Islam). He gave me duties to perform such as reform and a secretary and that kind of work. And I had an insight of what was really being done and I thought that he was a wonderful teacher.
Interviewer: Where were the teachings being held at that time?
Willie Muhammad: The teachings, the first time I heard it was at 3335 S. State Street (the old Odd Fellows Hall).
Interviewer: How was the struggle during that time, before and after the Messenger came?

Willie Muhammad: At that particular time times were very hard and people were without food and clothing. We had a pretty tough struggle at the onset with the teachings of Islam in 1934. We had our means of getting something to eat and food by having "push carts" as we called them, together, taking the carriages to junkyards. As I said, we had a pretty tough struggle but we sticked it out.[399]

Interviewer: Brother Leslie, when did you first hear the teaching of the Hon. Elijah Muhammad?

Leslie Muhammad: In 1934. Times was rough then!

Interviewer: Were you working?

Leslie Muhammad: No, sir! Not no regular work, just wherever I could get some work to do.

Interviewer: Where did you first hear the teachings?

Leslie Muhammad: 3335 State Street.

Interviewer: How did you first hear it?

Leslie Muhammad: I was living at 3922 State and there was a fellow I knew come to my home that morning, I was getting ready to go to the Grand Theatre for a picture show, he wanted me to go to 3335 State to hear the teachings. "Hear the teachings of what?" "Who is?..." "What you talking about?" He said, "Well go and hear him, I never heard a man talk like that." I said, "Alright." So I went on and heard it.

Interviewer: What was your first impression of the Messenger?

Leslie Muhammad: Well, he told me what I wanted to know.

Interviewer: And what was that?

Leslie Muhammad: Well, how come we in this shape, and a lot of that.[400]

Established in Chicago, the Hon. Elijah Muhammad was about to have another rendezvous with the law, this time a clash with the police that would leave a roster of injured Muslims and Police officers, and one white Police Captain dead.

10

11th Street Courthouse Battle

It was, I sincerely believe, our people's love of Allah that once brought us before a rather severe test in 1935. Messenger Muhammad constantly forewarned us of the dangers ahead, so I was not really surprised when our followers ended up in a Chicago courtroom.[401]~Captain James Pasha

11th Street Courthouse Battle

Ever since the departure of Master Fard Muhammad, the Hon. Elijah Muhammad was fighting to keep the Nation of Islam afloat in face of major opposition from internal and external enemies. Another severe trial would face the Muslims that started February 24, 1935, (two days prior to the First Saviour's Day). The event however would culminate on March 5, 1935, with an all out brawl with the Chicago Police that left one Police Captain dead. The trial has since become known as "The Trolley Car Incident." In their documentary on NOI history, the staff of Temple #2 explains:

On March 5, 1935, in the courtroom of Judge Scheffler, at police headquarters at 11th and State Street in Chicago, 44 unarmed Muslims, 16 brothers and 28 sisters, withstood a fierce onslaught by heavily armed police who fired shotguns, pistols and automatic weapons, without one single Muslim casualty. Yet, a police captain was stricken with a heart attack and died at the scene. And a court bailiff was shot and wounded by one of his own police officers. Although the initially disorderly conduct charges against a Muslim family which had defended itself against an attack a month earlier, on a State Street Trolley car, had been dropped in court; the fight was brought on when an angry bailiff literally ran through the courtroom and pushed a Muslim sister as she peacefully and quietly filed out the courtroom. Surely this event served only to strengthen the belief of the Muslims in the divine protection of Allah as taught to them by the Hon. Elijah Muhammad. The enemy had been well armed with weapons of great fire-power. The Muslims were armed with divine truth and the will to fight the enemy and the might of arms.

The Muslims fought the battle in the Name of Allah, Master W.D. Fard, "to whom all praises are due forever," and in the name of Allah's last Messenger, the Honorable Elijah Muhammad. Here are some of the unarmed Muslims recalling the armed attack by the police on that historic day, March 5, 1935.[402]

[214]

The following NOI pioneers were interviewed by Temple #2 on this history of this event: Hassan Shah, Maggie Sharrieff, Shelby Karriem and Marigold Allah.

NOI Chicago Pioneers Recall the Trolley Car Incident and 11th Street Courthouse Battle

NOI Chicago Pioneer Hassan Shah recalls details of the Trolley Car Incident:

Interviewer: Could you tell us about the bus incident that started the police incident?

Hassan Shah: As far as my knowledge, Brother Wali Muhammad and our Brother Zack Hassan children were going through a little phase there that was clearly known to be as a sort of hatred. They were at a time you could not even walk in some areas without being molested or picked upon [by hostile whites]. His children were on the bus and this incident started with his children. What really happened on the bus was the dispute among the children. And the older peoples, such as the mother of the [white] kid wanted to take up her child's part, and chastise Bro. Zack Hassan's son or daughter. But his wife [Mrs. Rosetta Hassan] intervened; she would not let it go.[403]

Maggie Sharrieff, a NOI Chicago Pioneer who joined in 1935 gives her account of the fight inside the court:

Interviewer: When did you first hear of the teachings of the Hon. Elijah Muhammad? When did you accept?

Maggie Sharrieff: In 1935. I think I said that right.

Interviewer: Tell us about the fight in the police station.

Maggie Sharrieff: The fight at the police station. Well, we were supposed to go out one door. And we was going out the wrong door they say. And the way we were talked to, our brothers wasn't standing for it. So they talked back at them you know. And one word led to another, and they started to fighting.

Interviewer: Who made the first blow or who threw the first blow?

Maggie Sharrieff: As far as I know – the devil.

Interviewer: And then what happened?

Maggie Sharrieff: Well, the devil went to shooting.

Interviewer: Was it in the courtroom?

Maggie Sharrieff: In the courtroom.

Interviewer: And then what happened?

Maggie Sharrieff: Well, as far as I know, you just heard them shooting. If you hear one boom over there, I looked. If you heard one boom over there, I looked. One over there – look. One over there – look. That's 'cause I wasn't doing nothing but looking, but they were continuing to shoot – continuing to shoot.[404]

Chicago Temple pioneer Shelby Karriem gives a first-hand account what triggered the actual brawl:

Shelby Karriem: I heard the teachings of the Nation of Islam in 1932.

Interviewer: Would you give us some information on the police incident down at the 11th Street Police Station in Chicago?

Shelby Karriem: Well, I was down there with one of the brothers for the trial concerning his little boy. And so the judge was having the trial, and they seemed to find out that they was Muslim, and they taking them back to consider the court case, and when the brother came back, he came back all of a sudden you know, and he said, "It's all over with brother." And everybody mounted the floor. And then, that seemed to upset them and the Judge see, and the judge said, "Sit 'em down! Sit 'em down! Sit 'em down!" And we was fixing to go out and that's when the fight began.[405]

Marigold Allah who was one of the sisters arrested at the case gives her perspective:

Marigold Allah: When I first heard the teachings of the Hon. Elijah Muhammad, it was in 1933.

Interviewer: And will you tell us about the police incident or the fight that occurred at the 11th street station in Chicago?

Marigold Allah: Well, as I told you, in the beginning of the fight, I wasn't in that group. But I was in the group where the fighting was with the fellas and the police.

Interviewer: Tell us what happened during the fight.

Marigold Allah: Well, ain't nothing happen no more than just the brothers and the police was fighting and then I guess each one of them was fighting to win.

Interviewer: Were you arrested?

Marigold Allah: Yeah, I was arrested with all the rest of the group. Yeah, I was there.

Interviewer: How many of you were arrested?

Marigold Allah: Well, I think it was 23 of us and 17 brothers. Alright?[406]

The Trolley Car Incident

NOI Chicago Pioneer, Karriem Allah, recalls the specifics of the Trolley Car incident that took place on February 24, 1935, that preceded the actual court case:

The fight preceding the battle at 11th Street Police Headquarters took place one Sunday evening in January – if my month is wrong I will correct it. My brother-in-law Zack Hassan, his wife Sister Rosie Hassan, their children, his father's brother Armadan Ali, and my mother-in-law Sister Linnie Ali, were on the streetcar on their way home from attending Temple service. A fight started on the streetcar between my brother-in-law and a devil, after one of the devil's boys hit one of Brother Zack Hassan's sons. He told his mother about it. His mother, Sister Rosie Hassan, told her son to go and slap the "hell out of him" and he did. This incident brought on the battle at 11th Street Central Police Headquarters.

Police came aboard the streetcar and arrested Brother Zack Hassan, his wife, his children and his mother and father. The devil was also arrested. They were taken to 11th Street Central Police Headquarters. A disorderly conduct charge was filed against my brother-in-law Zack Hassan: the court date was set for March 5, 1935.[407]

Messenger Cautions Muslims About Upcoming Court Date

Karriem Allah recalls the guidance the Hon. Elijah Muhammad gave the Muslims in a Temple meeting the week before concerning the court case:

On the Sunday before the trial of brother Zack Hassan (March 4, 1935), the Messenger, the Honorable Elijah Muhammad, was at the Temple. Before he dismissed he asked, who all were going to the trial? All the Muslims stood up, but the Messenger said he did not want all the Muslims to go. He said this would excite the devil. The Muslims were on a three-day fast. The Messenger of Allah taught we the Muslims about this battle with the enemy long before it happened.[408]

One Officer Dead, One Officer and One Muslim Shot, 41 Hurt

Naturally the Trolley Car incident was the headlines of Chicago Newspapers such as the Defender (the only Black-owned Newspaper in the city), the Daily Tribune, the Daily News and the Herald-Examiner. The day after the lethal brawl, the news hit the stands: "Cultist Riot in Court. One Death, 41 Hurt":

A quarrel between two women on a street car ten days ago developed yesterday into a man sized riot in a courtroom on the ninth floor of the police headquarters building at 1121 South State Street.

In the melee a police captain died, a bailiff was seriously wounded, two members of a colored cult were shot, and 38 others—twelve policemen, six bailiffs and twenty cultists—were cut or bruised. Last night 43 of the colored culturists were under arrest, with a possibility that some of them may be charged with the police captain's murder.

The captain was Joseph Palczynski, 73 years old, a veteran of nearly 50 years' service in the Chicago police department. He died of a heart attack brought on by the excitement and the assault of several cultists.

The wounded bailiff is Philip Brankin Jr., 28 years old, 3610 West 64th street. He was shot in the chest. At St. Luke's hospital last night physicians said it might be necessary to resort to a blood transfusion to save his life.[409]

Muslims Attend Court, the Original Case Dismissed

The Chicago Defender, the city's only Black Newspaper, reported the genesis of the Trolley Car Incident was a dispute between the Hassan family (who was Black) and the Christopulas family (who was White):

The investigation revealed that the members of the society had gone to the court room to learn the outcome of a matter involving one Zack Hassan, 3342 State

Street, whose nine year old son, Zack, Jr. with Mrs. [Rosetta] Hassan had figured in some trouble several days ago [Feb. 24] on a Madison Street Surface Lines car. There was a fight between young Hassan and the young son of Mrs. Athanasia Christopulas, of 1448 West Monroe Street. The mothers are alleged to have quarreled over the incident and the white woman claimed her glasses were broken. She went to the women's court to secure a warrant.[410]

The news reported the charges initially were dismissed by the Case Worker, in which the Hassans were free to go:

The custom of the Municipal court is for a welfare worker to hear the charges first and determine whether there is probable ground for issuance of a warrant. Miss Rosemary Griffin, 6459 Kenwood Avenue, the welfare worker, summoned all the parties to her office, adjoining the Woman's court, yesterday morning.

Previously, however, the Hassans had laid their trouble before the cult leaders. The cultists agreed, it was learned, that in accordance with their vow of unity they must go to court and stand by their "sister" so that "justice and freedom and truth" would be served.

Accompanied by fifty or sixty of the cultists the Hassans went to court. Miss Griffin interviewed the Hassans and the complaining witness in her office and ruled that no warrant should be issued. Apparently satisfied with the result, the Hassans returned to the courtroom.[411] Hassan, according to the Sharrieff woman, had called: "Sisters and brothers, let's leave. It's all over."[412]

Police Clash with Muslims Trying to Exit Court

The trouble began when after being dismissed the Muslims proceeded to leave the courtroom in military ranks. One news report recalls:

Hassan smiled assurance to his supporters. At a signal from one of their number the entire band rose with military precision (such military procedure is a part of their ritual) and started marching to the rear of the courtroom.

Meanwhile Judge Scheffler was hearing charges against ten colored women in another case. He instructed Bailiff George Wilson, 3528 North Whipple Street, to take the women to a detention room which opens off the rear of the courtroom, and continued their cases.

The two groups — the cultists and the ten women — became intermingled. Bailiff Wilson tried to sort out his charges. In the rear of the room were John Coyle, 65 years old, assistant superintendent of Municipal court bailiffs for the police building, and Deputy Bailif Theodore Mazola.[413]

White Officer Shoves a Muslim Sister

Karriem Allah recalls: "The judge dismissed the case involving my brother-in-law and sister-in-law. The Muslims started to leave the courtroom when suddenly a white bailiff pushed one of our sisters. This he should not have done — he lived to regret it. The infidel is not to touch a Muslim woman. This incident angered the Muslim brothers and brought on the fight at 11th Street Police Headquarters between Muslims and the entire police department."[414] Mr. Allah elaborates on the importance of protecting the Black Woman:

The Messenger taught we, the Muslims, to fight unto death for the preservation of the Muslim women. The Muslims always gave good account of themselves when it came to the protection of the Muslim women. She was then, and is now our glory as was taught to we the Muslims by our Honorable Leader, Teacher and Guide—Mr. Elijah Muhammad.

We the Muslims obeyed all the Messenger's instructions. We the Muslims found it easy to obey the Messenger's instructions, because we wanted to obey him. It was a pleasure to do so. The Honorable Elijah Muhammad was and is the first Black man in America ever to speak out loud for the protection of Black womanhood. All the other so-called Black leaders are afraid of white people.

Black women—you all should love and honor this divine man, the Honorable Elijah Muhammad, who is always speaking in your defense Black sisters, the daughters of the Tribe of Shabazz – bring your husbands over to Islam. The Honorable Elijah Muhammad wants to shake the fear out of them with truth; you Black women love brave Black men! Honor, respect and dignity is yours on your acceptance of Islam, and the willingness to follow the Honorable Elijah Muhammad.[415]

11th Street Courtroom Brawl

After physical shoving between the Police and the Muslims, the melee ensued: "The crowd started toward the rear door near the bullpen and were halted by a bailiff. Meanwhile Deputy Bailiff Theodore Mazola rushed up from the front of the courtroom and began questioning the first of the group he met. Suddenly trouble started. Fists began to fly and torsos commenced falling."[416]

After seeing Muslim sisters being shoved by white Police Officers, the FOI engaged the Police in battle, with MGT in the middle of the charge:

The bailiffs called for order. An excited cultist woman shouted at Mazola: "Take off your glasses and I'll whip you."[417] Roused to an almost fanatical frenzy by a chain of small incidents that ordinarily would have passed unnoticed in a crowded courtroom, the cultists, their red, crescent marked fezzes askew, stormed through the room with wild shouts. Cries of "Freedom and justice!" and "Onward, brother, onward!" mingled with the refrain of "Who's Afraid of the Big Bad Wolf?" sung by a woman of the cult in the throes of religious fervor."[418]

In half a minute the riot had started. Coyle and Mazola were knocked down and kicked. Policemen standing in the courtroom rushed to their aid. The cultists seized chairs and began swinging them.

Capt. Plczynski, who had been sitting next to Judge Scheffler, started toward the melee. Detective Harry Scholz grabbed his arm and urged him not to get into it. Instead, the captain pushed into the crowd in an effort to restore order.[419]

King Shah, it was charged, shoved him and Capt. Palczynski fell to the floor. Other witnesses reported seeing several negroes pummel the fallen man, but no marks of violence were found when he was carried into the judges chambers. A physician was summoned and pronounced him dead. [420]

[219]

Chicago NOI Pioneers involved in the 11th Street Courthouse Battle

Zack Hassan

SEARCH CULTISTS AS THEY ENTER COURT
Sergts. George Larson (left) and Harry Scholz "frisking"
Ollie Brooks as he entered Woman's court for hearing yes-
terday which resulted in jail sentence for cultists.
[TRIBUNE Photo.]

[TRIBUNE Photo.]
COURT RIOT CAUSES POLICE CAPTAIN'S DEATH
Capt. Joseph Palczynski, 73 years old, veteran of police department, who died of heart failure during cultists' disturbance yesterday in Woman's court. (Story on page 1.)

Caption reads: Search cultists as they enter court. Sergts George Larson (left) and Harry Scholz "frisking" Ollie Brooks as he entered Woman's court for hearing yesterday which resulted in jail sentence for cultists. 2nd photo caption reads "Court Riot Causes Police Captain's Death. Capt. Joseph Palczynski, 73 years old, veteran of police department, who died of heart failure during cultists' disturbance yesterday in Woman's court.

"X" marks the spot where the fight began between the Muslims and the Police. White bystanders take a photo for the paper.

Some of the FOI taken into custody from 11th Street Courthouse Battle

MGT Photo (line-up) from 11th Street Courthouse Battle, Left to Right: Lennie Ali, Lennel Cushman, Georgia Jordan, Anna Belle Pasha, Hattie Majie, Mary Gold, and Mary Ali, who are among 43 FOI and MGT arrested. [Chicago Tribune]

Zack Hassan

Hassan Shah, Shelby Karriem

Maggie Sharrieff and Marigold Allah

Elijah Muhammad Rushes to Fight Scene

While the fight was in action, word traveled quickly to Muslims in the street, James Pasha recalls seeing the Hon. Elijah Muhammad rushing to the fight at the court house when he joined him:

The year was 1935 and Franklin D Roosevelt had been in office three years. The Honorable Elijah Muhammad taught us to always expect the unexpected, so I was not surprised when all of us were herded into a police courtroom one day that summer...I did not anticipate any trouble would erupt, so I had not planned to attend. Then I met the Messenger walking down Wabash Avenue as I was pushing my cart.

He said: "Brother, our brothers have met with some serious trouble in the courtroom, so you had better come with me." Many brothers and sisters were crowded into that small room to assure themselves that no harm had come to the brother who was on trial.[421]

Pasha describes what he saw when they arrived on the scene:

Suddenly, a white police officer and a bailiff shoved one of the brothers and gruffly ordered him to sit down. A few angry words were exchanged between a brother and the bailiff, and the latter punched him in the face.

This action brought all the Muslims into the fight, for we were taught by the Holy Apostle to defend ourselves only if attacked. I overheard the red-faced judge angrily ask the police, "What did you wear those guns for? Put your guns away!"[422]

Shots Fired

In the heat of battle police fired their weapons at Muslims, reportedly striking two, King Shah and Allah Shah, the former shot in the shoulder, the latter reportedly shot in the foot. A police officer also fell from a bullet wound to his chest:

Meanwhile Bailif Brankin had rushed from the courtroom of Judge Leon Edelman across the hall. In company with the growing force of policemen and bailiffs he dashed into the fight...Several shots were heard and Brankin fell wounded. Later King Shah was found to have been shot in the right shoulder and Allah Shah in the left foot.[423]...One hundred and fifty policemen and bailiffs, summoned from all parts of the building by a riot alarm, finally quelled the uprising after a half hour of swinging clubs and pistol butts.[424]

The police realized bullets didn't stop the Muslims from fighting, and officers found themselves bruised badly, and at least one officer fell from being shot accidently by his fellow officer in the confusion, while others had to be rescued:

Bailiff Frank Higgins snatched his service gun from the holster and fired twice. A moment later a fellow bailiff Philip Rankin dropped to the floor with a bullet in the body. It is believed he was struck by a bullet from Higgins' gun that ricocheted after striking the stone floor.

Patrolman James (Jimmy) Williams and George Maisac who were in the courtroom waiting to present a case jumped into the fray and emerged with badly bruised bodies and abrasions of the hand. It was Williams who rescued Mazola by battling off four men.[425]

Muslims Not Afraid of Weapons

James Pasha gives accounts of the gun shots:

Several shots thundered inside the courtroom and – All Praises Be to Allah – only one brother was actually shot. The bullet ripped through his shoulder, but he was not seriously injured. Some of the policemen were accidentally shot by their fellow officers. It was not certain whether the police captain suddenly died from a bullet wound or a heart attack. Since all those well-armed policemen could not kill one of the brothers, the Chicago Police Department has shown great respect for the followers of the Honorable Elijah Muhammad through the years. I resurrected this not-so-well-known story to demonstrate the power Allah will grant to his faithful worshippers, and that no power on earth can halt the progress begun by his Messenger, the Most Honorable Elijah Muhammad.[426]

Karriem describes what he learned in F.O.I. class why Muslims should not fear the carnal weapons of the white man:

The enemy was well armed with weapons of great fire-power. The Muslims were armed with Divine Truth and the will to fight the enemy and his might of arms.

The Muslims fought this battle in the Name of Allah, Master W.D. Fard to Whom Praise is due Forever, and in the Name of Allah's Last and Greatest Messenger, the Honorable Elijah Muhammad.

The enemy put his trust in the might of his arms. The Muslims put their trust in Almighty (God) Allah who has power over all things.

The Messenger taught we the Muslims that Allah created all matter. The bullets fired from the enemies guns travel in Allah's atmosphere. Allah controls His atmosphere: it is His atmosphere.

The enemy poured fire into the onward rush of the Muslims, but the Muslims kept marching forward fighting the enemy. The enemy's fire-power was powerless to bring down the Muslims. This they could not understand – the enemy lost faith in what they trusted in as a defense. They said the Muslims were all fanatical.

They were unable to kill them or crush their will to fight. The enemy was astonished and dumbfounded over the ineffectiveness of their fire-power.

Allah's Almighty power was present in that courtroom. It was Allah's Supreme Universal power versus the enemy's fire-power. Allah used the Muslims against the enemy's fire-power to show His power over the enemy's fire-power. He,

Allah, made His unlimited power manifested in the Muslims who was in this fight.[427]

Muslims Earned Respect of Chicago Police

Karriem Allah reiterates the respect the Muslims earned from the Chicago Police Department that day:

I use department, because this fight between the Muslims and the police involved every police on duty inside police headquarters and those on the outside joined in on the fight to put down the Muslims who were involved in this historical fight which did not only make the headlines of every paper in Chicago, but all over the country – it will also go down in history. The entire police department was shocked and stunned at seeing such courage and solidarity of the Muslims under fire. The police opened up with their automatic weapons shooting point blank at the Muslims.

The Muslims never yielded from this withering fire. The Muslims kept coming after the police; they never lost their courage – Allah gave them the will and the spirit to fight.

Allah, to Whom Praises are due forever, showed forth His mighty power through the Muslims in that fight at the 11th Street Station, which lives on in the hearts of the Muslims and the police department today. It is as fresh today as it was the day it happened.

The police had never witnessed anything like this in the history of the police department. A small group of dedicated Black Muslims willing to fight unto death for the noble cause of Islam – defending their Black brothers and sisters from the hands of the unjust white man who is known to kill any Black man who attempts to defend Black women. Black womanhood's honor was in jeopardy. [428]

Police Chief Died from Cardiac Arrest per Shock

Although it was initially thought the Police Captain was murdered by the F.O.I, results later showed he died from cardiac arrest due to shock. Two news sources reported:

Capt. Palczynski fell in the midst of the turmoil and, though some witnesses thought they saw him slugged, an autopsy by Dr. Samuel Levinson brought a verdict of death from heart disease. There were no marks of violence, the doctor said.[429]

Seventy-four year old Captain Palczynski, who was seated inside the rail went to join the onrush, but collapsed as he reached the fringe of the battle ground and toppled over. He died a few minutes later in Judge Scheffler's chambers of heart failure. [430]

43 Muslims Arrested and Detained

After the fighting ceased, all 43 Muslims involved were arrested at the scene and detained. As part of their investigation into the Nation of

Islam, the State Attorney desired to charge the Muslims with manslaughter:

The death of Capt. Palczynski led Chief of Detectives John L. Sullivan and Assistant State's Attorney Martin Ward to consider placing charges of murder or manslaughter against several of the cultists, all of whom are members of the "Allah Temple of Islam" at 3743 South State Street.

Should the investigation, which was incomplete last night, disclose that the followers of the "temple" entered the courtroom prepared to incite trouble, the charge would be murder, Ward declared.

If the melee was an accident, caused by the emotional state of the cultists, as seemed probable, Mr. Ward said manslaughter charges might be made against those found to have taken part in the attack on Capt. Palczynski.[431]

The police verified the Muslims did not have weapons in court:

Chief of Detectives Sullivan and other investigators were unable to determine who fired the shots which wounded Brankin and the two Shahs. No weapon of any kind was found in a search of the 43 prisoners. Nor could police find a gun or a knife on the courtroom floor. Because several witnesses told of seeing bailiffs and policemen with drawn revolvers, Chief Sullivan said that this morning he would question all the law enforcing officers involved to learn if any of them fired shots. Thirty of the 43 prisoners also will face contempt of court accusations this morning at 10 o'clock before Judge Sheffler. The judge began a contempt hearing after the riot, but adjourned it until today. [432]

Nation of Islam Mistaken as Moorish Science

In their investigation the police conflated the followers of the Hon. Elijah Muhammad (the Nation of Islam) with those who followed Noble Drew Ali (Moorish Science Temple):

Among the 43 prisoners were King Shah, 38 years old, 3242 South State Street, and Allah Shah, 18 years old, 2556 Warren Boulevard, the two wounded cultists. Their "Moorish" names puzzled the police until King Shah disclosed that the prophet of their order, W.D. Fard, or Fard Mohammed, or Elijah Mohammed, had christened them thus last spring.

A police search for Prophet Fard was started but he could not be found last night. He was described as one "born in the holy city of Mecca in 1877," who came to America on July 4, 1930.

The cultists admitted that most of them were clients of the Illinois Emergency Relief commission. King Shah, who appeared to be a minor prophet, said he received $27 a month in relief grocery orders and the commission paid $20 a month for his steam heated flat. The fezzes and red robes, which the cultists also wore, apparently were rented.[433]

The "Allah Temple of Islam," which propounds the theory that all blacks are Moors and not negroes, is a secret organization of national proportions, investigation disclosed. The original "prophet," one Noble Drew Ali, who began his career as a New Jersey expressman, appears to have left Chicago, which once was his headquarters, the police said.

The Chicago temple, which is said to be an offshoot of Drew's original group, holds meetings in its South State street headquarters on Wednesday, Friday, and Sunday nights. A complete system of military procedure, apparently drafted almost word for word from the army manual, governs the conduct of the members.

Members of another branch of Noble Drew Ali's Islamic following engaged in a pitched battle with the Chicago police on Sept. 26, 1929. Two policemen and a leader of the cult were killed.[434]

Muslims (from Court Brawl) Back in Front of Judge the Same Day

The same day after the courtroom brawl, a total of 44 Muslims (23 women and 21 men) appeared in front of the Judge to explain their actions, or as the press said "Weird doctrines were voiced as Judge Scheffler opened his investigation, with dozens of heavily, armed officers on hand to prevent a recurrence."[435] The Herald Examiner captured the episode:

Like characters in a Moorish drama, fifty red-fezzed Negro religious fanatics were herded before Municipal Judge Edward Scheffler yesterday for grilling about a courtroom riot earlier in the day that left Police Captain Joseph Palczynski dead and Bailiff Philip Brankin wounded.

Out of the group, twenty three women and twenty men, all members of Allah Temple of Islam, 3743 S. State St., were sent to cells to await continuance this morning of inquiry into the melee, in which two cultists were shot, eighteen policemen and rioters injured and an undetermined number trampled.

Technically they were charged only with contempt of court, but Assistant State's Attorney Martin Ward is seeking evidence to justify murder or manslaughter indictments against some.[436]

Muslims Testify On Their Own Behalf
'Only by Allah!'

Among those called was Eliza Sharrieff of 3650 Calumet Ave., who refused to take an oath, explaining:

"I swear only by Allah. He is always with us. He is the truth."

Concerning the yellow crescent on her red skullcap, she said:

"It stands for the sun, the moon and the stars. I was before them. We are the people of the Asiatic nation. We are all brothers and sisters. We stand for freedom and liberty."

She said the cause of the outbreak was "pushing around" of the cultists by bailiffs.[437]

When Judge Scheffler opened his hearing, many prisoners marched from their cells chanting hymns.

Most wore red fezzes. Several women had cleanly shaven heads, indicating, they explained, that they were "princesses." The Sharrieff woman explained that they had learned Sunday, at a meeting at the temple, that "Sister" Hassan was in trouble, and:

"When one is in trouble, we all are in trouble."

She and other cultists said they had intended no violence and were leaving peaceably when the dispute began. Mazola denied that anyone was "pushed around."[438]

The Newspapers Erroneously Claims Muslims were the Shooters

It's possible the Police were planning to frame the Muslims with the shooting of the Police Officer Branklin as they alleged it was the original plaintiff Zack Hassan who shot the officer, and found NOI Lessons on Muslims they labeled "communistic":

HASSAN CALLED GUNMAN - Capt. George O'Connor announced that Hassan had been identified as the one who shot Branklin, and that "King Shah," the other wounded rioter, had been seen to push Capt. Palczynski. Both are in Bridewell hospital.

Several witnesses identified Nojie Lenzie of 2979 South Parkway as a man they saw stand on a bench and snap his fingers as though in signal for the outbreak. Others told of seeing guns, but none was found. Brankin's weapon was mysteriously missing.

Several of the prisoners had Communistic literature, but spokesmen denied the order had red leanings.

All the prisoners used Turkish names, "Sha being frequent among the women and "Allah" or Mohammed" among the men.

The women prisoners went on a hunger strike last night. Police took a baby from the hunger strikers and gave it milk.[439]

Black Newspapers and Muslims Expose Corrupt Policemen

The Chicago Defender reported that Elizabeth Sharrieff, a key witness who saw the bailiff shove the sister, testified the police started the fight. They also alleged the bailiff already had a pre-existing history and reputation as a bad apple. The Defender reports the minutes from the court hearing:

Blame for the entire trouble was laid at the feet of Bailiff Mazola according to the testimony of Mrs. Elizabeth Sharieff, only member of the cult to testify at the hearing Tuesday afternoon, Officer Williams however in his testimony declared one of the women started the disturbance when she challenged another court bailiff and invited him to take "off his glasses."

Mrs. Sharieff, however, stated "We were through and were ready to leave. We didn't know which door to leave through and started toward the rear."

"If the bailiff had directed us to the right door we would have left and nothing would have happened. Instead of that he began pushing us around and trying to force us to sit back down."

Someone he manhandled, she intimated resented his abuse.

Assistant State's Attorney Martin Ward asked her if she didn't know the judge was on the bench. She admitted she did and retorted with the remark: "I see no reason why a person or persons were not entitled to leave after their business had been finished." There was some talk about an investigation of alleged misconduct off deputy bailiff at the 11th Street police building.

After hearing testimony the Judge decided to continue the case on the next day:

Judge Scheffler in questioning the witness asked if her society believe its laws superior to the laws of the state. "No," she said "we obey your laws." She was excused after a few other questions.

King Shah, 38 years old, 3343 State Street was identified by a policeman as the man who pushed Captain Palczynski. Shah was not called to the stand Tuesday and therefore hadn't been given an opportunity to deny the charge. Judge Scheffler, who called the hearing immediately after the police investigation, continued it until Wednesday morning.

The matter before the court is on contempt charges.

The prosecution stated efforts would be made to make out more serious cases, probably manslaughter. This however, admittedly, seemed unlikely.[440]

5 Muslims Not Involved in Case Arrested for Protesting

The Daily Tribune reported: "Before the contempt hearing began yesterday five members of the cult who were not in court Tuesday appeared at the police building to help those who were under arrest. They were arrested when they started a demonstration after being ordered to leave the building."[441] The same five Muslims disrupted Wednesday morning hearings:

Before the hearing opened this morning five colored members of the cult created an uproar in the corridor leading into Judge Scheffler's courtroom.

Mrs. Florence Raghman, 52 years old, 1725 Fulton Street, and two other women and two men refused to leave the corridor when ordered to do so by Policemen Edward Mulcahy and Albert O'Neil. Mrs. Raghman's husband was one of the crowd seized yesterday. "We want our freedom," the five shouted in unison. "Liberty and rights." They were forced into an elevator and booked at the central station on charges of disorderly conduct.

Before she was bundled into the elevator the Raghman woman cried:

"I'd like to throw a bomb in that courtroom."

She was searched, but no bombs or other weapons were found.[442]

Spectators Barred from Wednesday Court Hearings

Security was beefed up for the Wednesday hearings, and spectators barred. One skirmish was reported says the Herald Examiner:

Fifty extra policemen were on guard in the police building as Judge Scheffler, sitting beside Chief Justice John Sonsteby, renewed his investigation.

Three men and two women, members of the cult, tried to push their way past guards at the hearing room. Shouting and swinging fists as they were resisted, they were finally pushed into an elevator and trundled into cells on an upper floor.

Because of the fear of renewed trouble, all spectators were barred from the hearing. All who left elevators on the eighth floor, where Judge Scheffler's court is, were questioned before being admitted. Loiterers were shooed from the first floor on order of Capt. George O'Conner.

Police were still trying to find whether Allah Temple is an affiliate or an outgrowth of the Moorish Temple of the Science of the World, members of which caused difficulty for police about five years ago.

Funeral services for Capt. Palczynski will be held at 1:30pm tomorrow at his home at 1025 N. Sacramento Ave. Burial will be at Oak Ridge Cemetery.[443]

The Defender recalls spectators were allowed strictly for identification purposes in the line-up:

As Judge Edward S. Scheffler began the second day of investigation into the cause of the riot in his courtroom Tuesday which precipitated the death of Police Captain Joseph Palczynski, and injuries to forty other persons, including a deputy bailiff, efforts were being made to fix responsibility for the outbreak.

Participating in the disturbance were approximately 40 members of the Allah Temple of Islam, a Moorish cult with offices at 3743 State Street, and 100 or more policemen, bailiffs and court clerks, who battled for nearly an hour before the cultists were whipped into submission and herded into detective bureau cell rooms.

In order that attaches, police and spectators present in the courtroom could have an opportunity to view the cultists for possible identification of participants, Lieut. Sullivan, chief of detectives assembled them in the regular showup room. Practically every prisoner was pointed as having taken part in some phase of the rioting.[444]

Chicago Media Describes Muslims as a Cult in Court Case

The Chicago Daily News title ran "'Allahs,' 'Hassans' and 'Shahs' Crowd court as Cultists Answer Rioting Charges" as they described the Muslims in very sarcastic terms:

Amid a starry constellation of cops and bailiff's badges, forty three faithful man and woman worshipers from the Allah Temple of Islam in South State Street shuffle humbly to prisoners' benches in the jury branch of the Municipal court.

Gone are fanatical glares on the faces of these local Othellos and lady Moors, who yesterday participated in a riot in the Women's court in which Capt. Joseph Palczynski died from heart shock and Bailiff Philip Brankin was wounded with a pistol which has vanished as if into air.

These Chicago Negroes, who profess to be apostles of an Islamic cult, have passed a night of reflection and meditation in the jail house. They have been wrapped in thought and some of their shaved heads have been wrapped in bandages, which bulge like white turbans of followers of Mahomet. Yesterday's riot turned against them in the second inning, when it poured club-swinging, gat-flourishing bluecoats upon the embattled courtroom.[445]

These dark-skinned believers, who have refashioned their names into an assortment of "Allahs," "Hassans" and "Shahs," fill the prisoners' benches and overflow into the jury box.

Among them are striking types. One, who is addressed with something like "Mary Jane Allah," is of child's physique. Small and gnomelike, she is said to have been a mighty gal of valor in yesterday's scrimmage of fists, clubs and gunfire. Her close-shaven head is covered by a red super-fez.

Another woman carries a boy baby, who wears a tiny red jacket and glances at this formidable array of policemen, Municipal court bailiffs and automatic pistol reserves with innocent, even delighted, eyes. The mother is Mrs. Rosetta Hassan ("Sister" Hassan to the rest), who with her husband, Zack Hassan, became involved in a street-car quarrel which preceded yesterday's courtroom incident.

Sister Hassan has a defiant eye for the courtroom army. There is even defiance in the swinging of her big, gold-hued earrings.

One of the bandaged youths is liberally decorated with a fresco of red and blue spots on his face. The fire of battle has gone from his eyes—at least from the optic which still remains open.

"Get back, gents, get back!" pleads a bailiff. But he is not addressing spectators, for there aren't any. The crowd that shoves and pushes from curiosity, is the overflow of armed guards. Outside, corridors also are guarded and all visitors are forced to produce credentials.

Some of the male Islamites have gone oriental with semiturbans in the form of wool skull caps. These cover their close-shaven polls. Among them sits a Negro who has been high-hatting the barber. His hair is thick and lustrous; he has a black mustache and a goatee. Detectives rush to separate sheep from the goatee. This chap isn't a defendant. He is a witness.

Another witness is identified and is put on the stand. He is George Washington, who tells a credible story of what he saw in Women's court yesterday. George knows none of the defendants, he says. The court takes George at his word.

Then the gentleman with the goatee is questioned.

"What were you doing in court yesterday?" he is asked.

"I was asleep," says the witness George Walter. He didn't see much of the riot, says this seasoned snorist, having slept through its earlier and more deadly episodes.

"Sister" Hassan fetches her baby to the stand and corrects the prosecution right off. It isn't pronounced "eyes-lam" but "Is-lam" as in "izzard," she explains haughtily.[446]

Interrogates Witnesses in Police Captain Death

The Police continued their interrogation to find out if anyone struck the Police Captain before he died:

The judge ordered Assistant State's Attorney Martin Ward to ascertain whether charges of assault with intent to kill should be instituted as result of the reported slugging of Capt. Joseph Palczynski, who died of heart disease during the fight; and the shooting of Bailiff Philip Brankin.

One of the cultists, Lenzie Najib of 2979 South Park Ave., was shown a picture of Capt. Palczynski and asked if he was the man he struck.

He replied.

"I couldn't say. I don't remember."[447]

Police took a letter from one of the other prisoners, Alonzo Jarmon, 3977 Vernon Avenue addressed to a sister in North Carolina. It read in part:

"This is the end of the white man's civilization. His time is up. There is a nation going to take the white man off the planet earth and I will tell you more in my next letter."

Lenzi Najieb, a lanky Negro of 58, who is suspected of having struck Capt. Palczynski, admitted that he had struck a policeman, "an oldish man," but refused to identify a photograph of the dead police captain as the man he struck.

Sophie Hassan, another of the participants, was asked by Assistant State's Attorney Ward if the cult did not believe the white race should be destroyed.

"Well," she drawled, "you all know your time is up."

She explained that their belief is that the white race is to live but 6,000 years and that the 6,000 years have just about expired.

"Did you see any of your brothers swing chairs?" asked Mr. Ward.

"Yes, sir," she said, "and some of your brothers, too."

The participants, most of whom testified that they had been provoked to trouble by being shoved about by bailiffs, refused to take the Christian oath and took this one instead: "I will declare to my father, Allah, that I will tell the truth."[448]

Search for Gun.

Police are searching for the gun which fired the bullet seriously wounding Bailiff Philip Brankin and injuring two of the "Moslems."

Chief of Detectives John L. Sullivan admitted that none of the cultists were found to have been carrying revolvers when the rioting subsided yesterday and the critical condition of Bailiff Brankin prevented physicians in St. Luke's hospital from removing the bullet from his left lung for ballistics tests.

Chief Sullivan said he was "satisfied that the shot was fired by one of the rioters."

After hearing William Palczynski, son of the dead police captain testify that his father was in good mental and physical condition yesterday, Deputy Coroner Louis J. Nadherny this afternoon continue the inquest into his death until March 22.[449]

Jail Sentences of 30 days for Sisters, 6 Months for Brothers

Judge Scheffler imposed a 30-day jail sentence for 24 of the women, and 6-month jail sentence on 17 men to be served at Bridewell[450]:

Jail sentences were imposed today by Judge Edward S. Scheffler of the Women's court against twenty-three women and seventeen men, all members of a cult of Negro "Moslems," for participating in yesterday's riot in the courtroom. The women were sentenced to thirty days in jail each, but the men, many of them husbands of those whose red fezzes today were supplanted by bandages for minor wounds received in the fracas, were not so fortunate. They were each given terms of six months for contempt of court. Assistant State's Attorneys Martin Ward and Charles NcNamara announced that they would file complaints against the cultists on charges of conspiracy to obstruct justice and conspiracy to incite a riot....[451] All defendants are member of the Temple of Islam, a religious organization with headquarters at 3743 State Street in the Pythian building. It was learned that after becoming a member of the organization an individual is given "his real name," which is supplied by the governing body of the unit.[452]

NAMES OF CONVICTED (WEDNESDAY COURT HEARING)

Defendants to Jail
Those convicted gave their names as:

Armstead Allah, 32 years old, 2656 Warren Avenue;
Clifton Williams, 21; 1740 Maypole Avenue;
Willie Pasha, 52, 3501 Wabash Avenue;
Eli Mahied, 35, 2656 Warren Ave.;
Ali Kashker, 19, 3536 Prairie Ave.;
James High, 48, 3644 State Street;
Sha Allah, 19, 3650 Calumet Avenue;
Shah Hassan, 18, 503 E. 34th Street.
Tamar Hazzier, 32, 3342 State Street;
Shelby Harriem, 35, 3839 Wentworth Ave.:
Amos Mohamet, 45, 2248 Maypole Avenue;
James Neely, 28, 4732 Forrestville Avenue;
Shah Reiser, 21, 503 E. 34th Place;
Samuel Raghman, 56, 1725 Fulton Street;
Lindsey Majied, 58, 2979 South Parkway and
Sha king, 38, 3342 State St.

The women are:

Idabelle Pash, 38, 3650 Calumet Avenue;
Grace Hassan, 35, 3900 Dearborn Street;
Mary Gold, 43, 3556 Giles Avenue;
Elisa Shrieff, 48, 3650 Calumet Avenue;
Hattie Majied, 18, 1794 Caroll Avenue;
Teressa Allah, 29, 3650 Calumet Avenue;
Lennell Cushman, 28, 2656 Warren Avenue;
Lennel Ali, 54, 2656 Warren Avenue;
Minnie Shah, 39, 3342 State Street;
Mary Ali, 44, 3501 Wabash Avenue;
Martha Ali, 46, 10. E. 33rd Street;
Fannie Hazziez, 46, 503 E. 34th Street;
Priscilla Smith, 45, 3501 Wabash Ave.;
Frieda Shah, 34, 3359 Giles Avenue.

Maggie Sharieff, 50, 2319 Dearborn;
Thelma Yacal, 20, 3536 Prairie Avenue;
Bessie Majied, 27, 2656 Warren Avenue;
Mrs. Paul Hazziez, 37, 3721 Federal Street;
Josephine Wilson, 27, 10 E. 33rd Street;
Eullen Jabob, 60, 3359 Giles Avenue;
George Jordan, 35, 3124 State Street and
Rosiland Shah, 25, 3342 State Street.

A victim of Tuesday's outbreak was Police Captain Joseph Palczynski who died of heart failure due to excitement. A deputy bailiff was shot, several other officers were slugged and pummeled and many of the members of the religious group had bruised heads and badly damaged bodies.[453]

Police Try to Raid Chicago Temple after Court Case

During sentencing the Chicago Police desired to arrest more Muslims at the Temple. With 150 Police officers they tried to break into the Temple only to be stopped by Captain Edward Ali and the FOI:

Captain Ali received training at St. Charles Military Academy, at St. Charles, IL, and was Captain of Muhammad's Temple No. 2 at the time of the "11th Street Fight" that led to his 21-year incarceration. Tensions were still high throughout the area when the Muslims returned to their Temple. Later that night, 150 Chicago policemen appeared seeking entry to the Temple. "I had about 60 or 75 Muslims," Captain Ali continued, who was Captain of Muhammad's Temple No. 2 during the incident.

The invaders shook the Temple door and yelled, "Open up!" Ali had issued orders at all costs to defend the sanctity of Muhammad's Temple.

Captain Ali paraded up and down the vestibule of the Temple, a swaggering stocky figure of a Black man and motioned for the intruders to enter at their own risk.

In response to the valiant stand of the Muslims, the policemen vanished and never returned. Edward Ali, however, was later incarcerated for parole violation.

Captain Ali revealed the original source of his arrest and imprisonment: "Why brother, I used to be one of the best gun-hawks the gangsters could find."[454]

The Chicago Defender Newspaper Defends the Muslims

In the midst of all the turmoil, The Chicago Defender stayed true to its purpose and wrote a defense of the Muslims (which they conflated with the Moors), verifying the corrupt racist history of some officers and court bailiffs at 11th Street Courthouse:

Case of the Moors

The disturbance which happened in Municipal Judge Edward S. Scheffler's court room Tuesday was precipitated not by the Moors themselves, but by an over-zealous bailiff of that court. This statement is supported by questions and answers coming not from the Moors, but from white people, attaches of that court. Had the bailiff permitted those people a peaceful departure, no confusion would have occurred; no one would have been killed and there would have been no necessity for the brutal beating which many of those men and women received.

Judge Scheffler is a fair and eminent jurist, who has the respect and confidence of all who know him. Chief Bailiff Albert J. Horan is a capable and efficient official and like other public officials, is no doubt compelled to make appointments occasioned by political expediency, rather than by his own choice.

A two hour survey Wednesday morning of the conduct, the attitude and mannerism of some of the deputy bailiffs assigned to the courts at Eleventh Street clearly disclosed that their conduct could cause almost anything to occur. Some of those bailiffs by their domineering attitude, their manner of addressing people and especially colored people who have business with an in the courts, are not such as will increase respect for law and order.

We hold no brief for the Moors any more that for any other cult or church. We do contend, however, that the Moors are entitled to peacefully assemble and peacefully depart from any public building as any other church or cult. They should not be brutally treated or imposed upon because they are Moors any more than a Baptist should be brutally treated because of his religious belief, or a Methodist or a Catholic because of his religious belief.

From very reliable source, we are informed, if the bailiff had not attempted to stop the peaceful departure of the Moors from the court, this terrible tragedy would not have occurred. The responsibility for the death of a police captain, the shooting of a fellow bailiff, and the injuries of the participants can be very properly laid at the door of an over-zealous bailiff.

There is no desire or intention of condemning all of the bailiffs of the municipal court but there are some who are power drunk and assume their temporary power entitles them to misuse people of color without regard to who they are.

We do not believe that Chief Bailiff Horan would for a moment stand for some of the things which are happening at Eleventh Street if he knew it. It is to be hoped that though busy as he is, he will find time to give this particular branch some of his personal attention.[455]

11 The Hegira of Elijah Muhammad

The Hypocrites Come to Chicago

The Nation of Islam was fighting a war on two fronts, internal enemies who were the hypocrites plotting on the Hon. Elijah Muhammad, as well as the external enemies such as the Christian Preachers and most of all the Police. It was only a matter of time before Elijah's enemies were at his door.

The Lord is my Shepard

The History Department of Chicago Temple #2 explains the mentality of the hypocrites pursuing Elijah's life, and how Master Fard Muhammad had prepared him for the attacks:

By the time our leader took on the mission given to him by Master W.D. Fard, others the Master taught became jealous, and envious, and wanted the position and honor bestowed on his chosen Elijah. Truly like the proverbial crabs, they sought to endanger our leader's life by threatening him, chasing him and seeking to kill him. But our leader, the Hon. Elijah Muhammad, was well prepared for his mission by his teacher, Master W.D. Fard. He was satisfied that Elijah was the one he come looking for and found. Allah and He were close. Close as a jugular vein. The Saviour gave our leader a page from the Bible which read:

Psalm 23
1The LORD is my shepherd; I shall not want.
2He maketh me to lie down in green pastures: he leadeth me beside the still waters.
3He restoreth my soul: he leadeth me in the paths of righteousness for his name's sake.
4Yea, though I walk through the valley of the shadow of death, I will fear no evil: for thou art with me; thy rod and thy staff they comfort me.
5Thou preparest a table before me in the presence of mine enemies: thou anointest my head with oil; my cup runneth over.
6Surely goodness and mercy shall follow me all the days of my life: and I will dwell in the house of the LORD forever.

Our leader would have to recall this reminder often, as the enemies and hypocrites devised plans against him always, hourly, weekly, monthly, yearly, and to this present day[456]

The Temple Dwindles Down to a Handful of Believers

Years later Elijah Muhammad would reflect on these times:

> Before long, the cult was torn by dissension resulting from a power struggle between Muhammad and several brothers who found his story a little too difficult to believe. "One year after Master Fard left me," Muhammad recalls, "I had to leave Detroit; the enemies, hypocrites united together to drive me out and I had to come here (Chicago) and later they came here. They united to drive me out of here and kill me and I fled to the East Coast where I stayed seven years.[457]

> For thirty-three years, I have been doing this. I spent seven years running from my enemies and hypocrites from '35 to '42. I was flying for my life up and down the East Coast from my enemies and hypocrites, for just the same thing that has happened here, recently. ONE WANTED MY PLACE. And they all but brought me to a naught, as far as followers is concern in '35. I had no Temple in Chicago, here.
> They brought that Temple of 715 down to about 15 or 20 people meeting in homes of the Believers. And in Detroit, of 400 regular attendance there, it was brought down to seven. I have you here today. Some of you knows about this. You were here. Especially here in Chicago and Detroit. If you don't know it, ask the older people. They will tell you.[458]

Min. John Muhammad recalls the same: "Our Temple, of the Nation of Islam, went down lower and lower to only a handful, after we had grown to thousands in number."[459] One journalist noted, "Consequent upon the clash between the two brothers the movement had suffered a rapid collapse, beginning with the fall of 1934. From around 400 members with organized meeting only 13 members had kept allegiance to the movement in September 1935. This small group of followers began to hold their meeting in their houses under the ministership of Malik (X), who was appointed by the Apostle for this purpose."[460]

The Hon. Elijah Muhammad wisely organized the remaining members of the Chicago Temple:

> It is very interesting to note that even in the periods of the severest collapse, where the whole membership amounted to 13 members only, the members were distributed on the following duties: general secretary, recorder secretary, Fruit secretary, formal secretary (whose duty was to sponsor and file the forms after they had been filled by the new members who planned to join the movement), a captain, a minister, assistant minister, and the other six members as lieutenants. PAGE 82[461]

Although the Nation of Islam numbers dwindled, the Hon. Elijah Muhammad still had righteous companions in his circle. Among his notable loyalists were: Min. Sultan Muhammad (Milwaukee), Elijah's brother Min. Wali Muhammad (Detroit), Min. Linn Karriem (Chicago), Min. Marrcellars Jardan (Chicago), Burnsteen Sharrieff, Min. John Muhammad (Detroit), Pauline Bahar (Milwaukee) and many others.

Chief Hypocrites

On the other side, many of his Laborers turned against him, such as: Min. Theodore Rozier, Elijah's brother Supreme Captain Kallatt Muhammad, Min. Abdul Mohammed (that started his own NOI sect), Lonnie Pasha, Min. Augustus Muhammad and many others. A journalist notes his conversation with Elijah Muhammad about hypocrites who plotted against him:

In Chicago a strong conflict or schism had developed within the movement as a result of emerging conflict between Elijah and his younger brother. The Apostle said: "In the fall of 1934 most of the followers turned out to by hypocrites and they began to teach against the movement, and to join enemies of the movement. The situation got so bad that in 1935 it was impossible to go among them because it seemed to me that over 75 per cent of them were hypocrites. And therefore I had to leave them to save my own life. Hypocrisy was arising even within my house; my youngest brother, who was living in my house with another assistant minister, aligned against him because he wanted the teachings for himself. They joined my enemy here and in Detroit and they began to seek my life.[462]

Origin of Dispute between Elijah and Kallatt

In his capacity of Supreme Minister, Elijah seemed to notice or at least thought it possible that his brother might be jealous of him. Kallatt seemed to be more loyal to the opposition. Elijah's son, Min. Nathaniel Muhammad, recalls the history:

See, dad was strong. He fought off a lot of these people who wanted to take his life you know. And his own brother was part of a coup that wanted to kill his brother. But Kallatt didn't want to kill him, Kallatt just wanted to take over his position, but some of those brothers got so radical until they wanted to kill daddy. But Kallatt was against killing him because that was his brother you know. And Kallatt was the Supreme Captain, but he wanted to be able to take over as the Supreme Captain and probably get rid of daddy altogether and appoint another minister. Or leave daddy as the minister, but he'd be in control. He'd be the boss. So this went on up until 1935.[463]

Master Fard first made my father minister. Later he made him the Supreme Minister of all the temples. He also made my uncle the Supreme Captain of the Nation of Islam and also the Head Investigator. My uncle was envious of my father's position; he became an enemy of my father. He died because he began to be an alcoholic after he was expelled from the Nation of Islam under my father's leadership. [My uncle] lost his mind. Sometime he would be out walking the street talking to himself. My father said, "Allah put him

[239]

in that condition," but at that time he meant Master Fard put him in that condition.[464]

Elijah recalls seeing traits of hypocrisy in his brother Kallatt:

In Detroit once, after they ran me down there, I had about 7 people meeting in the home of someone. And today, you see, that Allah has blessed me to have a well-established Temple. Right? I did not give up because they were after me, running me over the country, hiding here and there for years, depriving me of the privilege of staying home and rear my sons and daughters, help my wife.

I didn't lay down and cry and grieve over that because I knew what was coming. I knew one day, I would be the winner, because Allah had taught me from the start up until the very year of it all. And I know, yet, what is coming. And so I'm saying to you that I was crushed once before, for no other reason than jealousy envy of my position. Allah put a stop to it. He overtaken those who devised the plan, tried to carry it out. He overtook them and He chastised them.

One of the leading ones, at that time, was my own brother when we were living in a house together. He was living downstairs at 5830 South Wabash, here. And I was living upstairs, yes sir. And now, Allah, taken him down from the Supreme Captain, at that time, threw him on his face, prostrated him at my feet because he had sided in with the enemy against me because he wanted to be the Big Boss over all. I made him that. I made him the Captain myself. The Supreme Captain. I had all the confidence in him. I didn't think not one time that he would ever deviate. But Allah showed me that I didn't know their hearts. [465]

The Hon. Elijah Muhammad addresses the origin of the rift between him and his brother, Supreme Captain Kallatt Muhammad, of which they shared a house:

The clash began by the younger brother's asking Elijah Mohammed to allow somebody to copy whatever is said in the class of ministers, a thing which Elijah Mohammed emphatically refused. The conflict grew stronger between the two brothers. The assistant minister aligned with the younger brother of Elijah Mohammed. Both of these opponents were able to stir some of the followers against Elijah, who was compelled to run away later to save his life, because most of the followers, "75 per cent of them," as he said, "had turned to be hypocrites."[466]

Augustus, Kallatt and Lonnie Plot to Kill Elijah

Min. Augustus Muhammad, Elijah Muhammad's asst. Minister, also lived in Elijah's multi-family house. Elijah and his family lived on the 2nd floor, Kallatt and his family lived on the 1st floor, and Min. Augustus lived in the basement. The story goes that Kallatt along with other FOI including Lonnie Pasha had convinced Min. Augustus to conspire against Elijah Muhammad. The group would stage a coup by killing Elijah Muhammad in his own house. The plans were foiled when Elijah walked up on Min. Augustus who had a weapon in his hand, but couldn't manage to fire it. Min. Nathaniel Muhammad, Elijah's son who lived in the house, addresses the history:

> Minister Augustus used to live in the basement apartment (under Kallatt). And one day, daddy heard a noise that was coming up under the basement, and he went down to see what the noise was all about. And Minister Augustus had a hammock, breaking up a gun. And daddy asked him where did he get the gun. He said, "They give it to me to kill you." He had tears in his eyes crying daddy said. And daddy said the next morning he got up, and Augustus was gone, and ain't nobody ever seen him since. [467]

Elijah Muhammad recalls the day and shares the same sentiment:

> My Assistant Minister, at the time, Allah vanished him. He sent him into exile and I haven't heard from him since. His name was Augustus Muhammad. And no one, yet, have told me that they have seen him anywhere. He just vanished. You'll find the vanishment in the Holy Qur'an and it prophesied of a second vanishment. And this may be it, now, in the workings. [468]

Nathaniel believes his uncle himself would not have hurt his father, yet rather he was easily influenced by others that wanted to hurt the Messenger:

> Kallatt never went after daddy, he would let other people do that. Kallatt never went after my daddy, that's an absolute lie. My uncle lost his mind, Kallatt would never do it. But the other people did. It was Lonnie Pasha. Lonnie Pasha was my uncle Kallatt asst. Captain. He was the one that was really trying to; he was the one that set up that coup. It was a coup to overthrow daddy. He was the one who set it up. [469]
>
> Kallatt went crazy really because it bothered him so until he just really lost his mind. I shouldn't say crazy. He just lost his mind. Because he never did leave the house. He didn't even stop from going to the Temple he used to feel so bad, even when daddy was still there, he was staying home instead of going out to the Temple. He was very ill. Because my daddy told me and the rest of my family, talking about his family, he told us that one day Kallatt came up to his house on the 2nd floor (because Kallatt lived on the 1st floor). He came upstairs and he sat on the couch besides my daddy, he was in a trance like, because any spot, if you had a spot on your wallpaper that was red, he would stand and look at that spot until people had to take him and walk him away from it. So anyway, he told daddy, to take your knife and cut my throat. Well, that was true. Kallatt told him, daddy told us that Kallatt told him, they was sitting on the couch in the front room, he said, "Take your knife and cut my throat." [470]

Elijah Advised To Have No Sympathy For Hypocrites

Elijah Muhammad didn't appear to sympathize with his brother's position of being easily influenced by hypocrites, as he says he was taught by Master Fard Muhammad to expect these things, and have no sympathy as mentioned in the Quran and Bible. He recalls the incident with his brother Kallatt in 'the month of June 1935':

> I know what he [Allah] told me, he [the hypocrite] would wish that I had killed him, rather than suffer what Allah going to put on him. Allah, when he chastised my brother, my brother used to lie down at my feet many times and tell me to take my knife and cut his throat. "Cut my throat." He said, "Please." He said, "Cut my throat." I said, "For what?" He said, "Get me out of this." He said, "Just go ahead and cut my throat." I said, "No, no, no, brother." I says, "I have no right to cut your throat. No." And the bible and the Quran both teach you that Allah won't let nobody kill him. No, no. They got to take them out of their misery. He wants to suffer. Let him suffer. So I don't worry. He told me to leave them to him. He said, "I will fix them all together." So I'm not particular about you when you turn hypocrite, you just gone from me. I'm certainly not going to give you no trouble—if you don't give me any. But the hypocrites is never satisfied with going out themselves. They want to come back because they don't have nobody...Allah says in the Holy Quran that they will never have a true friend. He makes it hard for them to have a friend because he has offered his friendship to them, and they left him, so then they never have no true friends. And he appoints for them he says a devil for their companions.[471]

Elijah Muhammad expounds on his rationale:

> Because I did all I could and when the turned back on me I was so surprised, I was all but speechless. But when I thought over it and what He had taught me, then I soon regained my Post and stood up again. And so I don't follow no one down that, you know, turns back on his heels. I don't go out seeking him, telling him to come back. I don't seek that person. Because I had a job enough to try and find you in the first place.
> Now if you want me to go back after you, No! No! No! That's up to you and God and the devil, right there. I have too many in front of me to keep trying to get a hold to. So this is the thing that you must remember, that trials, sometimes, are so terrific that they will weaken the most strongest person sometimes. And these kinds of acts that have been made on me...in 1934 and 1935 is the kind of attacks that will draw away from the most strongest follower if he's not careful. The Bible says that if it was possible, they would deceive the very elects. It warns you of these kinds of attacks.
> You are tried. The Holy Qur'an says, 'Do not they see that they are tried once every year?' You must be tried to get into the Hereafter. And as long as your leader stands firm and will not turn heels on his enemies, will stand to their face and fight them, you have nothing to hide behind your excuse for not

backing him up. Nothing you have to hide. So I ask you if you don't think that you can keep going with me, any of you, and think that you would be better on another position, stand, and I will accept it in good faith. But if you think that you can go on with me and back up the truth with me, then from this day on I'm going to expect it. I expect it. [472]

Begins 7 Year Run, Goes to Milwaukee

The Hon. Elijah Muhammad began his 7 year journey on the run, leaving Chicago and going to Milwaukee, where he was forced to leave there too. Elijah recalls: "So Allah warned me to leave. Hence I left to Milwaukee, where Allah warned me to leave again and showed me in a vision nine people; among them was my brother. Therefore I left to Madison, where they followed me; and Allah warned me again to leave Madison." [473]

Hypocrites Ban Together in Chicago, including Abdul

Meanwhile back in Chicago, the Hypocrites roamed the city, even recruiting Elijah Muhammad's main Chicago Minister Theodore Rozier, who replaced Augustus Muhammad. Min. Theodore Rozier joined the Nation of Islam shortly after Master Fard Muhammad left. Elijah's son Min. Nathaniel recalls, "Min. Theodore Rozier, he was a part of it, he was one of daddy's ministers. He came from one of those Caribbean countries (I believe it was Haiti). He joined Abdul. There was a crew of them all together trying to stage a coup. It wasn't no three or four different crews, it was just one large crew. All of them wanted to get rid of daddy." [474]

Elijah's long-time rival Abdul Mohammed, was back on the scene, after his break with Asian Nationalist Takahashi, and the failure of SDOO "A Development of Our Own" organization:

Unfortunately for the 58 year old Takahashi, his health started declining just as the SDOO reached it zenith. Half-blind and suffering from ulcers, he was forced to hand over the reins of leadership to Abdul Muhammad. This move sounded the death knell for the SDOO because Abdul Muhammad, who was five years older than Takahashi, lacked the money and organizational skills to keep the organization stable. In the summer of 1932, the ailing Takahashi again moved into Abdul Muhammad's home to help him in the leadership takeover...

Notwithstanding repeated pleas and the American incentives, Takahashi was unable to persuade Abdul to renounce his American citizenship. Abdul was steadfast in his allegiance to the teachings of Noble Drew Ali. The only reason he had left the MSTA to begin with was that he opposed the theory among its members that John Givens-El, Drew Ali's former chauffeur, was the reincarnation of Drew Ali. Abdul and Takahashi argued continuously as the group evolved over the next nine months, the main point of disagreement being a suggestion by Takahashi that SDOO members murder white people as a token of their faith in him. Abdul Muhammad dissented vigorously, but Takahashi held firmly to this notion. Exasperated, Abdul ordered Takahashi out of their shared abode and threatened to summon the police if Takahashi ever showed up again at either the house or any of the five SDOO branch offices. Takahashi packed his things and left.[475]

Abdul new formation or sect mixed the teachings of Noble Drew Ali with the teachings of Master Fard Muhammad, thus creating an Islamic set that preached some of the traditionalist views of the Nation of Islam, but pledged allegiance to the American Flag and its government. Even if not buying into his ideas all of the way, the hypocrites all came together and joined forces based on their envy of the Hon. Elijah Muhammad. So Min. Abdul Mohammed, Captain Kallatt Muhammad, Asst. Captain Lonnie Pasha, Min. Theodore Rozier and a few others recruited a band of men to destroy the life of Elijah Muhammad.

Meanwhile the Messenger "went from city to city teaching Islam on the East Coast mainly." In hot pursuit, his enemies made serious attempts to track him down. One of his adversaries Lonnie Pasha was so overzealous that he wrote Elijah's wife, Sister Clara Muhammad, offering a bounty on Elijah's life. The Honorable Elijah Muhammad recalls the incident:

> Yes, for 37 years I have been trying to get the truth over to my people. I ran from my people, and other than my people, for about seven years. I went hungry and out of doors to be here today. I served those seven years, just running and dodging from my own people, who were out to kill me for a little sum of money, $500, from a brother in Detroit, Michigan, who said he would get a peck of rice and eat one grain a day, until I was dead. So, now he is dead.[476]

Elijah's eldest son Emanuel remembers when the hypocrites plotted against his Father Elijah's life while they lived in Chicago:

> In the year 1935, either in the month of April or May, if I am correct, His followers were attacked here. A police captain lost his life and several policemen were seriously wounded. They were the first to attack us. Only one brother was injured; he was shot in the foot.
> During this same year the Messenger left His family escaping for his life. I was 14-years-old at this time.
> One of the key hypocrites of Detroit – who was an official – said he would eat a grain of rice per day until he overtook the Messenger. Allah took this hypocrite off the scene; now he is eating the roots of grass. The Messenger was escaping for His life for about seven long years.[477]

The Hon. Elijah Muhammad spoke about this ordeal years later in his career, vividly capturing the mood of the time period:

I did not give up because they were after me, running me over the country, hiding here and there for years, depriving me of the privilege to stay home and rear my sons and daughters, help my wife, I didn't lay down and cry and grieve over that because I knew what was coming, I knew one day that I would be the winner, because Allah had taught me from the start up until the very year of the end of it all, and I know yet what is coming and so I'm saying to you that I was pressed once before, wasn't no other reason than jealousy and envy of my position. Allah put a stop to it, he overturned/overtaken those who devised the plan, tried to carry it out, he overtook them and he chastised them. One of the leading ones at that time was my own brother, when we were living in the house together, living downstairs at 5830 S. Wabash here, and I was living upstairs. Yes, sir. And now, I had taken him down from the Supreme Captain at that time, throwed him on his face, prostrated him at my feet because he had sided in with the enemy against me because he wanted to be the big boss over all. I made him that, I made him the Captain myself. The Supreme Captain, I had all the confidence in him, I didn't think that one time that he would ever deviate but Allah showed me that I didn't know their hearts. My assistant Minister at the time, Allah banished him, sent him into exile and I haven't heard from him since. His name was Augustus Mohammed and no one yet have told me that they have seen him anywhere. He just vanished. You'll find the Vanishment in the Holy Quran and it prophesy of a second vanishment, this may be it now in the workings. [478]

The Hon. Elijah Muhammad years later gave his overall sentiments regarding hypocrites in general:

So it don't make any different to me whether they burn in hell or broil in hell or boil in hell, it don't make any difference to me because I did all that work and when they turned back on me I was surprised until I was all but speechless. But when I thought over it what he had taught me, then I regained my composure [post] and stood up again. And so I don't follow no one down who turns back on his heels or go out seeking him, telling him to come back. I don't seek that person, because I have job enough to try to find you in the first place, now if you want me to go back after you know, "no, no, no" that's up to you and God and the devil perhaps, I'm not—I have too many in front of me to keep (sic). So this is the day that you must remember that pride sometimes is so terrific that they will weaken the most strongest person sometimes. And these kinds of attacks that have been made on me year, this year...'34 and '35...it's the kind of attacks that will draw away from the most strongest follower if he's not careful, the Bible says that if it was possible they would receive the very elect. It reminds you of these kinds of things. They Holy Quran says do not they see they are tried every year. You must be tried to get into the hereafter and as long as your leader stands for it, and will not turn heels on his enemies, will stand to his face and fight them, you have nothing to hide or no excuse for not backing him up.[479]

Elijah Assigns Ministers for Each Temple

To hold down the three established Temples, the Hon. Elijah Muhammad assigned his chief Ministers over them. His brother Minister Wali Muhammad was over Detroit's Temple #1, Min. Linn Karriem and Secretary Pauline Bahar were assigned to Temple #2, along with Min. Marrcellars Jardan who was given a satellite of Temple #2 on Chicago's Westside, and Minister Sultan Muhammad, who eventually became Elijah Muhammad's first National Representative, was assigned over Milwaukee's Temple #3. Each of these were Laborers who knew Master Fard Muhammad and agreed with Elijah Muhammad that Fard was Allah.

Yet it was a rough road ahead for the small group. Marrcellars Jardan recalls how after Elijah Muhammad left Chicago, the hypocrites surfaced and was on a manhunt for the Messenger:

> **Interviewer:** Brother Jardan, will you tell us about the time during the early '30s when Messenger Muhammad was running for his life during the time when the enemies and hypocrites were chasing him?
> **Marrcellars Jardan:** Well, things were going pretty fair but pretty rough then they got after him and they tried to close us out because the children were going to school, they didn't want them to send the children to school. And so they stuck around, and all of a sudden, he had to leave out. And so at the time when he was leaving, he sent for me to come over to take his works on and carry it on until he turned. And so at the time he was going away, they would come and ask me did I know where he was, and I'd tell them "No." And I'd say, "I'm looking for him myself." And so that's the way it went. And so otherwise, times was hard. So we just went door-to-door trying to keep the Temple open and moving on until things got kind of quiet.[480]

Prophet Elijah Muhammad represented himself as a fearless Leader with total faith in Allah. Often speaking in prophetic terms, he said the suffering of the now small Nation of Islam can be related to the scriptures as Allah promised their success as the eventual winners:

> I remember reading in the Holy Qur'an, once, I think it was pretty tough with the Jesus. He asked, who was his Disciple. So, here, some of the strong believers said, "I am your Disciple." So they went forward. Muhammad had a tough go once and he asked, "Who will be my vice-general?" He wanted to put a stop to the enemy.
> So a 15 or 16 year old boy rose up and he said, "I will be your vice-general." He says, "I will rip their tongue up, pull it out by the root, cut it out of their mouth, that says anything against you and I will rip their bellies up and pull

their intestines out." He says, "And burn them out and throw their ashes to the wind." He did die a martyr for Islam. He was a pretty tough man. Muhammad chose him.

It is always best for the man to do this on his own will and not to try and force him or beg him or teach him to do it. Let him take this on his own. You know, because, it may be trouble ahead and he don't expect it to be trouble. He thinks it all smooth going. And he run into trouble, he'll run back and say, "I didn't think it was going to be like this."

So a man to take this stand, today, to follow me, I cannot guarantee you no smooth going. I can't guarantee you that. I can say this, that we will be the winner! Allah has promised me victory! And if it pleases Allah we all will come out happy. But there is a tough road, yet, ahead. And we don't have to worry about what we probably might run into in the future, as long as we have Allah with us. If Allah is not with us we had better go home now and just dismiss. But I know He's with us because He has been with me for 33 years and I feel Him always. Getting up and lying down, sitting and going, walking, riding I feel Him! I always feel Him with me. And He will be with you.[481]

Rebel Muslims in Chicago
Meanwhile in Chicago there were still problems on the home front. Elijah would sneak home from time to time only to have to hide out from enemies. His wife Clara would have to travel far distance to visit her husband because it wasn't safe for him to come to Chicago. Elijah's enemies were still plotting and looking to be leaders in their own right. At least two rebellions surfaced since he left Chicago, one old and one new:

Since the disappearance of W.D. Fard many branches have sprung up. In 1936 one of the ministers of the movement by the name of Azzim Shah organized an independent group. A Haitian, Theodore Rozier, another assistant minister at the time of W.D. Fard, had organized his own group in 1938. All of these groups stayed within the same frame of teachings, although there were personal conflicts among the leaders of these groups: apparently the split is mostly an expression of craving for prestige and leadership among these ministers.[482]

Elijah writes letter to address Hypocrisy at Temple #2
While back in D.C. Elijah Muhammad would send memos often to Temple #1 and Temple #2. Such as in this example he wrote on November, 5, 1936, chastising any current or possible rebels:

Dearest beloved Labors and Moslems at #2 Illinois in general I have in spite of your constantly disobeying the law of Islam which is your Own, as well as mine, Continue to send you more of the same. And you have received from one...the same such warnings against disobedience to that Pure and easy way of your Own Salvation which the Almighty God Allah give to us for our Success.

The more teaching and warnings I send to you the more you disobey, and ask for more to ignore. I have more-over taught you how to seek your means of subsistence for yourselves and families, as well as to the cause of Islam; By putting before you "first of All" Our Savior, Allah, to whom Be Praises, Honour and Thanks. And you who sincerely tried have found Allah's Hand helping, and blessing you daily as long as you continue to obey me and trust in Him. But when you disobey; the blessing is quickly removed from you.

I have tried hard to Teach a Group of Labors to help me in this Noble Work, which Allah has assigned to me, to give life to the Dead that your name may live and be praised by your Nation as The Stars for ever, and ever.

But this glory you are still Dumb of, and refuse to believe it. Moreover, when I try by my Allah's Help to teach and train a Labor to any position in Islam, whether Minister, Captains, or Secretary or Treasurer or Principles. Soon as they receive this High Position and began to be a little successful for a week or two, By Allah's Help, Their chests begin to Swell with Self Importance, Thinking in Their minds that they need no more of my assistance, and for Goodness sake not my presents among them. This has been the very Thoughts of near every Labor of important at #1 Michigan, at #2. That is why your success only last for a few days. My Allah will never let none of you be successful that desires that I stay from among you so that you can do that which you thinks Best in your own way. [483]

Elijah speaks on the results of hypocrisy in the Temple:

It is the hypocrites both at #1 and #2 that is watching for every chance to stop your Progress and thus destroy the Temple of #2 Illinois. It is their secret advices among the Labor and Moslems in general at #2 that is gradually bringing you into discord with each other. I have warned you who believe in Islam to not take the enemies of Allah and His Apostle for Friends. Allah's Wrath be upon you who willful ignores it. You know that they have Driven me out from among you. Then would you offer them Love and friendship? And thus invoke the Wrath of Almighty Allah against your Life? Be it known among you; --Elijah Mohammed is the Apostle of Almighty Allah to you all. And who so-ever of you Love and obey, and follow me The same will Allah Love and will show His Blessing upon day and night...

They have began to love the ways of the devils more than the Way of Allah, and his teaching, and his Apostle sterness to His Laborers. They know the strick law that was enforced in the Temple and among the Labors while I was going in an out among them, both at #1 Michigan and #2 Illinois until I trusted a no good wicked and jealous brother of mine by the name of Kallatt Mohammed, Who became proud and Boastry, and desirous to be ruler over me as well as any the ones that he was given to. This he finding himself unable to do, and fearing the people would soon learn that he had no Power against me what-so-ever; He thus secretly joined himself with my enemies to instruct them how to try to overcome me, --And thus brought Down upon himself the Wrath of Almighty God Allah, And it shall remain upon Him and all that follow him -- to the day when they (the whole Nation) is raised up to the knowledge of their Saviour Allah! And his Apostle whom he has chosen. [484]

The Messenger reiterates that it isn't safe for him to return:

The Law at #2, Illinois in not carried out strictly like I give it. The Temple of Islam is a Holy Place where the name of Allah is Worshipped, Those who see to defile it by their own Dirty uncleanness will be the fuel of the fire of Hell. And such as Drunkards, Adulteries, Liars, Gamblers, Murders, Mockers, Hypocrites, Peace breakers etc. Shall Allah Roast in the Fire of His Anger in the near future. And just think how near it is on you that is guilty even at your very door.

Should not my absent among you be enough to warn you? How much you should be in eagerness in walking upright and how close in unity should you be together working for my return Among you that I may impart to you that which I am sent. Do you think I am so Dumb to send Valuable Wisdom through Mail? And do you think your success is secure as long you do not Help to make it safe for me among you? Or do you think as the hypocrites does, That the Temple and the Teaching of Islam will come to ought? No, by my Allah! He will send me and I will set it aright by his permission. So work in love and Peace that you may be show Favour on the Day.

This letter is not directed at no certain One among you, But is meant for the whole. I thank each and every one of you -- For the many blessings that you send to me and Family for if anyone needs blessings it is the one that is in the Bush. Though I have Followers (suppose to be) Who can spend Hundreds of Dollars on cars for their own temporary pleasure, and hardly will give me over 50 cent at the time and not over a $1.00 for the cause of Islam their own. I do not think such will succeed very long. May the Peace and Blessings of Allah be with you the Moslems. As I say unto you. As-Salaam-Alaikum[485]

Lose Some, Win Some

For anyone who left the ranks, more came behind them to join the ranks. Emmett X gives his testimony of joining the NOI in 1936:

My name is Emmett X. I am a follower of the Honorable Elijah Muhammad, and a firm believer in the one God, Who came in the person of Master W.F. Muhammad...I want to tell the world what Islam, Allah and the Honorable Elijah Muhammad have done for me.

From the first time I saw the Messenger of Allah,...[1936], I was inspired by his teachings and example. He was to we who knew him in those days, a light shining in darkness. From his teachings I was able to walk without stumbling. He kindled hope in me when all hope was gone.

He taught me to hold fast to the plow handle of Islam and to trust in our Saviour, Allah. I have never stopped trusting in our Saviour and following the one that He chose for us to follow, the Honorable Elijah Muhammad. Today I know that heaven and hell is here and not somewhere after we die. I thank Allah forever for His coming and giving to me Divine Guide and I Thank Messenger Elijah Muhammad for His thirty-five (35) [1966] years of sacrifice to keep the truth alive.[486]

Lester X Joins the Temple

It seems like the Messenger's work was paying off as new believers were joining the ranks, such as one strong believer name Lester X:

Those wild days when I was young man carrying a pistol and a knife seem like a dream to me now, but I know they were real.

They were days of hard and fast living, of drinking and carousing and of faith in nothing but money, my gun and my knife. I actually felt undressed without my gun. Then I found Islam, the religion of Peace, but that's getting ahead of the story.

I was born in the deep South, in Algiers, La., in 1906. My father was a porter on the railroad and we kids were raised in the city.

LIKE MOST of the other Negro kids in those days. I had to quit school early to go to work, in the fourth grade to be exact. I eventually got a job on a railroad steel gang and I made plenty of money but I never could account for a dime of it.

I graduated from steel gang to fireman and then to engineer for the line I worked for but by that time the big city was beckoning. I moved to Chicago in 1935 and I'm still living here. I like it here because this is where I first came in contact with Islam. Here's how it happened.

One day I was drinking and playing card with a friend named Bud. I mentioned that the only way I'd join a lodge like the Masons was to find one that didn't have a white man as its head. Old Bud just laughed and said:

"LISTEN, my sister goes to some kind of meeting with some Muslims and they don't have a white man at the head." I wanted to check into that right away but Bud told I couldn't go at this time because I'd been drinking and they didn't allow you inside with the smell of whiskey on your breath. So I determined to attend the next meeting.

The first thing I saw when I went to the meeting was the crescent on the wall. That crescent reminded me of a dream I had had a short time before in which I had seen a sign in the sky just like that. It was then that I realized that this was the right place for me.

I'll always remember the year 1938 as the most significant year of my life. That was the year in which I became a Muslim and follower of the Most Honorable Elijah Muhammad.

MY LIFE was transformed. In Islam, the religion of Peace, I found the true happiness, the true meaning of life. Gone were the days of carousing, of fast living. Replacing them were days of serenity and fulfillment in Islam.[487]

I felt different than at any other time in my life. The Muslim brothers called me "Brother" and that was something new. When I entered the temple, I observed everything. I saw the crescent, the moon and stars, the same as I had seen years before in Mississippi as I was walking along the road.

But I had not heard the word "Allah" before. That was strange to me. I was impressed by the name of the Messenger, Elijah Muhammad, and Islam. I had not heard of Islam before.

I was all eyes as I noticed everything in the temple. Marcellius Jordan was the minister. He taught us about the Honorable Elijah Muhammad and told us how the Messenger had taught him wisdom for more than three years.

I became a devout Muslim and I began to study Islam. In those days, the Honorable Elijah Muhammad sent messages to us and the Minister would interpret those messages. The Messenger was somewhere in the wilderness of North America – fleeing for his life.[488]

James 3X (Shabazz) Joins the Temple

Bro. James 3X Anderson (who'd later become Min. James Shabazz of Chicago) joined the ranks:

"When I first attended the Temple in the Spring of 1941, as soon as I entered the door, that Sunday – the feeling that I had – the atmosphere of the whole Temple got next to me – it gave me the feeling that I was in the right place..." said Minister James Shabazz of Temple No. 2.

"THE CLEANESS of the sisters with their beautiful white garments on, and the discipline of the brothers, the brothers were so well-dressed, there was such an atmosphere of discipline...." As the modestly dressed Muslim minister continues to talk it is obvious to see that he is still very excited about that spring day nearly 32 years ago.

"The Minister opened with prayer," Minister James continued. "Then he began talking. Everything he said was just what I wanted to hear. "Long before the minister finished his lecture, I was already convinced of the Truth of Messenger Elijah Muhammad's Teaching—his Mission. I accepted on the spot, immediately!"

These remarks, the treasured remembrance of that first time hearing the Teaching of Islam, as taught by the Honorable Elijah Muhammad, is a highlight in the hearts of all believers.

"When I first came to the nation of Islam the Nation was small and struggling," Minister Shabazz continues. "Most of the brothers were working at supporting their families and the Temple by selling junk...They collected junk from the alleys and sold it to meet their financial obligation. Sisters worked at odd jobs, doing "days work," to help supplement the up-keep of the family and the Temple."[489]

Elijah Goes to Washington DC

In the midst of believers coming and going, Elijah found himself on a fast train to Washington D.C.:

It was in 1935, that his blood brother, Kalot Muhammad rebelled against him (the Messenger). Not long afterward a group of envious hypocrites, who were formerly his followers, sought his life. With the help of Allah and a little help from a brother named Ali, the Honorable Elijah Muhammad first fled to Milwaukee, Wisconsin. After a short stay, he went by train to Washington, D.C.

He would spend the next seven years on the run, never spending more than two weeks in a city, as Master Fard Muhammad instructed him. Running, or traveling, teaching, praying, suffering and studying what Allah taught him, was an ordeal; but it was necessary for his growth, and for our benefit too.[490]

12 Hegira Pt. 2, Temple #4

Al-Wakeel Benjamin Ilyas Muhammad
(Benjamin X. Mitchell)

A former Residence of The Honorable Elijah Muhammad
1602 13th Street N.W. Washington D.C.

1935

When the Hon. Elijah Muhammad made it to D.C., he went into the Black neighborhoods to witness the condition of his people. He introduced himself to town folks using different aliases such as "Mr. Bogans", "Mr. Evans", and "Muhammad Rasool" among other names. He inquired about a room-for-rent sign he saw in a window. There he met his future longtime companions Al-Wakeel Benjamin Ilyas Muhammad (formerly Benjamin X. Mitchell) and Sister Clara Muhammad (formerly Clara X. Mitchell). Brother Benjamin remembers:

Rents a Room in DC

In the year of 1930 (June 29), I got married to Miss Clara Bryant from Bainbridge, Georgia. We moved into a small room at 1722 – 15th Street, N.W., in Washington, C.C., and lived there for several months. From there we moved to a larger room at 1447 R Street, N.W., second floor. In 1934, we decided to rent a five-room apartment at 1602 – 13th Street, N.W. we lived at that address for four years or more.

In 1935, we placed a room-for-rent sign. He introduced himself to my sister as Mr. Evans. He was permitted to see the room, and informed my sister that he would be back at 5:00 p.m. to discuss the matter with me.

True, he did return at 5:00 p.m. He introduced himself as Mr. Evans. He stated that he had seen the room and it pleased him. He asked if he could move in. I told him he could. He mentioned that he would like for me to block out the transom over the door to the adjoining room. He explained that he would be using much light and didn't want to disturb us. HE offered to pay for the use of extra light. I assured him that he could use all the light that he desired and no extra pay was necessary. Mr. Evans moved into the room.[491]

Teaches Roommates He met with God

It wasn't long before Elijah Muhammad started told the family he met with God and was ordained by him to teach his people:

I worked at the U.S. Navy Yard from 4:00 p.m. to 12:00 a.m. Every night upon my arrival at home, I would find Mr. Evans and my family up talking. He said he was doing missionary work among our people. He said to me, "Brother, I met with God, and He gave me a message to give my people." Astonished, I said, "God! Have you seen God?" He answered, "Yes." "You can't see God and live! What did He look like?" Calmly, he replied, "He is black and He told me to tell my people to hurry and join on to their own kind because the end of this world has come."

He had been with us about seven days or more, but I had not seen him go out for food. On Wednesday he asked me if I drank coffee. I told him I did, and said I usually had coffee about 9:30 a.m. He said, "how about putting my name in the pot the next time you make coffee?" Eagerly, I said, "Yes sir!" I seized this opportunity to invite him to dinner. He accepted the invitation. [492]

[254]

Teaches Dinner Guests

As Master Fard Muhammad did with him and his family, Elijah Muhammad accepted an offer to have dinner with the Mitchells, providing they allow him to buy the groceries and they invite some friends. Like Fard, he used it as an opportunity to teach:

> The following morning, Mr. Evans went out, bought all of the food, sat it on the table. I said, "That is a lot of food for sister [wife] to fix." He put on an apron and taught my wife how to prepare the dinner.
>
> After he bought two bags of food, sat them on the kitchen table, helped my wife to fix it, I felt that this made me look bad and I felt bad about the dinner since I invited him for dinner.
>
> After preparing the food and setting the table, he asked me, "Brother, how are we going to eat all of this food?" I replied, "Don't ask me. I had wondered the same thing when I saw your bring all that food here."
>
> Mr. Evans asked if I had some friends that I could invite to dinner. I told him that most of my neighbors were working but I would try to get someone. I did get two of my neighbors to come for dinner. Mr. Evans sat at the head of the table and prayed the Muslim way. Afterward, we began eating and he explained the Muslim prayer and the food that we ate. This was the beginning of any weeks, months, and years of talks with him. He was a wonderful mystery to us. He never ceased to amaze us, even to the day he died.[493]

Benjamin and Clara grew to be very curious of their tenant and in awe of him at the same time:

> One day after he had lived in and out of my home for a number of months, he said, "Brother, I'll be out for a while and I am expecting a letter here. It may be in the name of J. Bogan." Immediately, I asked, "I thought you said your name was Mr. Evans?" He smiled and said to keep the letter for him if it came. I related the conversation to my wife and we wondered what kind of man was he –carrying two names.
>
> A few weeks later, he said he was expecting another letter in the name of Mohammad Rassoul. We had no idea of the identity of this magnificent, mysterious man but we were awed by the wisdom, the density of his teaching, and his plans for us. We could not begin to comprehend the greatness of this little man, nor the profound effect that this plan given by his God would have on our lives so many years later. We loved him and we followed him throughout the land, even to jail.[494]

CONGRESSIONAL LIBRARY 104 BOOKS

While in Washington, D.C., Elijah Muhammad started researching the 104 books his teacher Master Fard Muhammad instructed him to read that contained "bits and pieces of the truth." The white man Fard said had recorded this truth but it wasn't in books generally available to the public. Once Elijah made it to the study room at the Congressional Library, he discovered a prize left behind by his teacher: "One day, while in Washington, D.C., it occurred to the Messenger that those 104 books Master Fard Muhammad told him of probably were in the Congressional Library. (He was to experience the shock of seeing a picture of himself in one of them)."[495]

Studied Majority of Books about Prophet Muhammad

The majority of the bibliography of books was on different aspects of the life of Prophet Muhammad of Arabia of 1400 years ago. Elijah recalls, "While running for seven years, I was going in and out of the Congressional Library daily to hide and study and read books on Islam and Muhammad of 1400 years ago. That is the way I spent a lot of my time."[496]

Studied a Book about Masonry, yet Islam is the Real Truth

One of the books Elijah studied at the Congressional Library was on the Masonic Order (of which he once was a part until his meeting with Master Fard Muhammad): "Once I was a Mason, too, until I became a Muslim."[497] Elijah speaks on the subject:

In reading a book in Washington Congressional Library on Ancient Masonry, I had to laugh sometimes to see how we have been fooled. And now you'll get their highest degree in that order which no white man would ever teach you.

If we bring to you (I'm talking about the disbelievers and hypocrites), that Flag [of Islam] and tell you that is our sign or emblem, you that have studied degrees in Masonry should not hesitate to come over, because we give you more than what the devil has given you. These brothers (FOI) sitting here before our eyes and controlling the [floor and spaces], they are men that have learned more about Masonry than you. You're Masonry has included the history of your slavery, and it also teaches you that, but you don't know it. Your first three (3) degrees takes you into your slavery. Those three degrees there are the answer to your slavery, if you understand. But not understanding them, as the white man would not teach you the theology inside of it, it makes you dumb to even that which you actually own. I don't like to cal you such names, but it's an easy answer to the truth of it. You look, the ignorant among you, at that [Flag of Islam] and laugh at it, because he's ignorant of the truth of it. He doesn't know what he's doing. He'll smile at his old stars and stripes, he calls it "Old Glory." If I were you, I'd change the name and say it's "Old Hell."[498]

Know Thyself

Elijah maintained masonry simply was the story and study of the Black Man who is the answer to the cosmic puzzle of all Theology:

You [Black Man] are the answer to it all. You're Hiram Abif yourself. Yes sir, you are the one. You are the one that has been hit in the head, and it takes a long time for that head to heal. You are the one. You are the one that needs to be stood up. I say my friend, you are the one that has the blindfold on. You are the one that ought to be crying for light and more light, but you are not. You're reaching for the blindfold. Stand up my friend for self and know that you're in the day that you must be separated from the people that you have known for the last 40 years. God doesn't lie. He doesn't allow his prophets to lie. It is written and it must be fulfilled: you must go back to your own.[499]

Teaching How to Eat to Live

One of the priorities to establish Islam in D.C. was teaching his people "how to eat to live", which also meant teaching people about Fasting. Benjamin recalls:

I remember one day we were having dinner. I had invited some Christian friends in to listen to this "Little Man" [Mr. Evans]. He asked "Have you all finished eating so quickly?" My sister told him that he sure could eat a lot. Mr. Evans replied, "Well, you all will have to excuse me for eating so long. I really haven't had any food since Monday, and today is Thursday." Everyone at the table was astonished, and repeated together, "since Monday?"

One of the guests asked Mr. Evans how and why did he go so long without food. He replied, "Well, first, I don't eat many of the things that the Christians eat, such as the pig or hog and many of the scaleless fish and seafoods. Second, we should eat one good nutritious meal once every 24 hours." Everyone was astonished again and began to look at him with amazement. Mr. Evans asked, "Why are you looking at me so hard? Do I look all right?" One of the guest replied that he looked very good to have not eaten since Monday and then asked, "Aren't we supposed to eat three times per day?" "No," Mr. Evans replied, "Allah [God] said once per day is sufficient." Eating once every 24 hours will add years to your life. He went on to say that many of us dig our graves with our teeth. Three meals per day are too many meals. He said, third, to eat the poison animal will shorten your life. The Bible [Leviticus, Chapter 11] teaches us not to eat the pig or hog. Mr. Evans asked, "Doesn't your preacher teach you about the hog?" I replied, "He eats the hog himself!"

Mr. Evans [the Messenger] did most of his teaching at dinner time. He taught this strange teaching in many places in and around D.C.[500]

Elijah Teaches Solidarity

"Islam is Unity of the Black Man" taught Elijah Muhammad. While in D.C., Elijah stood up for the rights of his people. Benjamin:

One day, Mr. Evans asked me if I would help him with his mission. I replied that I would help and would do what I could. He took me around with him to churches and parks where our people would hang out. Sometimes, he would ask questions to get started teaching.

[257]

I remembered on one occasion, Mr. Evans came into the house and asked me if I knew where Green Valley, Virginia, was. He said that he had been listening to the news that morning and the reporter said that a group of black people had been taken from the steps of the Capitol by the police and escorted to Green Valley, Virginia, for protesting some grievances concerning black people. I told him that I thought Green Valley was in Arlington, Virginia, just off Columbia Pike Road but it could be found. Mr. Evans said, "Brother, let's go and see if we can locate them." WE took off to Arlington, Virginia, looking for the people. After riding through the black neighborhood inquiring about some black people being brought from Washington, D.C. to Green Valley, Virginia, for shelter under a tent, one young man said he knew where the people were and would show us the place. He got into the car with us and rode a short distance into a little valley with green trees and a stream of running water. There we found a tent erected near the near the stream of water. A few yards from the tent, up the stream, we found two or three women down on their knees washing clothes in the stream of water. We spoke and introduced ourselves to them, asking if they were the ones who were arrested in Washington, D.C., a few days ago? One of the ladies replied, "Yes we are." Mr. Evans asked, "Where is the leader of the group?" They replied that he had been arrested and taken to jail and had left the other two with them. "Where are they?" Mr. Evans asked. One of the ladies replied, "One is under the tent, and the other is out at present." Mr. Evans asked if we could speak to the one that was there. They called the gentleman to the front to meet Mr. Evans and me. A heavy-set, dark brown man stepped forward, dressed like a Jewish Rabbi. Mr. Evans introduced himself and me and explained to him that he was doing some missionary work among black people in America. Mr. Evans started telling the gentleman about his work, but was soon cut off by the gentleman who was dressed like a Rabbi. He then began to tell us about what they were doing. Mr. Evans stopped talking and listened to him talk until had had talked out.[501]

Elijah Teaches Charity

Elijah Muhammad expressed the importance of charity by demonstrating to his students how Black people were to support each other regardless of their religious creed. Benjamin continues:

Mr. Evans asked him if he could have a few words. He said, "I have listened to you for quite a while. I would like to know where you are from." The gentlemen replied that they were from Cincinnati, Ohio, and that they were black Jews. "What was the charge the officers had against you all?" Mr. Evans asked. The gentleman said they were charged with protesting and demonstrating on the Capitol steps. Mr. Evans asked about the brother who was the leader of the group. The answer was, "We don't know. All that we know is they took him from us and we haven't heard from or seen him since."

The women and children didn't have any food. Mr. Evans asked me if I had any money with me. I said that I had three or four dollars. He said, "I only have but a few dollars myself, but these sisters and their children need some money for food and transportation back to Cincinnati, Ohio." Mr. Evans suggested that we put our money together and give it to them for transportation back to their home. We did that and Mr. Evans told them that we would be back Friday and would bring some food for them. Mr. Evans and I went to the Safeway Food Store and bought box of food supplies for them that Friday evening and took it to Green Valley, Virginia. Mr. Evans presented the box of food to them and began to teach them of his Mission and they began to listen to him. The brother that was dressed like a Jewish Rabbi spoke up and said, "Do you know our leader sad to us that someone would come to our aid and help us back home?" They began to thank Mr. Evans with tears in their eyes and thanked God for sending this little man.

Now this great deed that Mr. Evans did for these people who were strangers made a great impression on me [Benjamin X]. Why? Because I had never seen or heard of any black leader or teacher being interested in a group of people, especially when they had been arrested by U.S. Government officers on the U.S. Capitol steps.[502]

Dropping Seeds for Temple #4, #5 and #6

Elijah referred to this kind of missionary work as "dropping seeds." As it would not be a coincidence that D.C. would become Temple #4, and Cincinnati, Ohio (where the people he just helped were from), would become Temple #5. His eyes were set on laying groundwork for Temple #6 as they traveled to neighboring Baltimore, Maryland:

Another time I was impressed by Mr. Evans. He took me over to Baltimore, Maryland, to meet the lady he stayed with while visiting in Baltimore, Maryland. I don't recall her name. However, we talked with her for a short while. Then he took me to a park called Lafayette Square where many people would sit and talk. Mr. Evans said, "Brother, you know Baltimore is the largest city in the South, and I am going to have a large temple here one day. It will take a little time to get it established because the people are very fearful of Islam, but Allah will remove the fear and they will listen. I want you to take note as to how fearful they are to talk with us. This is why I drop the seed of Islam in these cities and towns and later I come back to see if the seed has sprouted."[503]

The Hon. Elijah Muhammad relayed to some of his Ministers about one experience in Baltimore that almost led him to quit; until he heard the voice of his teach Master Fard Muhammad in his ears. Min. Farrakhan:

One day I was blessed to be with the Hon. Elijah Muhammad and he was telling me about the early days of Islam , and he was on the run from violent hypocrites who desired to kill him. And he was in the city of Baltimore, Maryland. And he had so much persecution, so much rejection, so much evil coming toward him from those who once believed, that he decided to run away and leave us, and leave the mission. And he said he was on the train, from Baltimore on the way to Philadelphia . And on the train as the tracks were making that wonderful sound that we like to hear when we are on the train, he heard this voice saying "do men think that they will be left alone on saying they believe, and will not be tried? And indeed we tried those before them. So Allah will certainly know those who are true, and he will know the liars.

When he heard those words of the Quran, it settled his heart, it settled his mind, it renewed his spirit to suffer to bring us a word. A word that would free us from the chains of ignorance that had engulfed us for all these centuries suffering in America. Not knowing why we were suffering, but he would teach us that we were suffering for a great cause, because Allah had chosen us, not for our righteousness, because we were not righteous. Not for our goodness because of 400 years of evil and injustice we were not so good. But Allah chose us out of the furnace of affliction to be the cornerstone of a brand new world where all human beings would never again be subjected to the evil that we have been subjected to (and that the human family has been subjected to). But through the guidance of Allah, and the beauty of the unraveling of the wisdom of the Holy Quran, we would bring into existence a brand new world and civilization."[504]

Visits George Washington Grave, Teaches History

A key component of the teachings of Islam is learning and knowing history to benefit self. The Messenger demonstrated this principle on a field trip with Brother Benjamin:

Another enjoyable day with the Messenger [Mr. Evans] was a trip to Mount Vernon, Virginia, the home and burial site of President George Washington. We toured the grounds and his home, the slave quarters, stable and grave site. While standing in front of the grave site, a black man was standing by the grave site reciting a long history to the people about George Washington.

On our way back to Washington, Mr. Evans said to me, Brother, did you hear how well our black brother recited the history of George Washington? If we had asked him to recite to us the history of himself, do you think he could have done that? "No" he replied, answering his own question. "Black people know all about other people's history but don't know anything of their own history. We are like that mockingbird. He sings and mocks all other birds, but can't sing his own song. The black people of America are just like that mockingbird. If it be the will of Allah [God], I will teach them a knowledge of themselves." He then asked, "Brother, will you help me?" I replied, "Yes, sir. I will do what I can."

From that moment, I began to listen closer to what he was talking about.[505]

History is Best Qualified to Reward All Research

Around that same time April 2, 1936, the Hon. Elijah Muhammad wrote on the importance of history through an open letter to the Nation of Islam which read:

First: History is all our studies. The most attractive, and best qualified to reward our research. As it develops the springs and motives of human actions, and displays the consequence of circumstances which operates most powerfully on the destinies of the human being.

Second: It stands true that we the Lost Found NATION, of ISLAM, in the wilderness of North America, have not applied ourselves to the study of History. But rather to folly. Having a lots of the bread of idleness, and when an effort was made to the above affect of History study, it was to our detriment by not knowing what History that was more valuable, to aid us in the knowledge of our own NATION.

THE WISE MAN, is the one who have made a careful study of the PAST events of ANCIENT and MODERN HISTORY. The KNOWLEDGE of the FUTURE is JUDGED by the KNOWLEDGE of the PAST. There are MEN born with a gift of PROPHECY. While some are trained into the KNOWLEDGE by intense studies of the PAST EVENTS OF HISTORY. [506]

Elijah the Friend

One day he said to me, "Brother, I feel like eating some watermelon. Where can we buy a melon?" I told him that we could get one at the Farmers Market, Fifth Street and Florida Avenue, N.E. After getting the melon, he asked me where was a good shady place along the highway to sit and eat the melon? I said we could go over to Virginia on Highway 211 between Vienna, Virginia and Washington. On our way up the highway, we found a nice shady place up on a little hill. We sat down on the ground under big green shay Red Oak Tree and he began to rip open the melon. Oh, it was nice, red and sweet. Mr. Evans began talking about the creation of the universe. I had eaten all that I could. But Mr. Evans continued to eat. HE really did love watermelons. Some of my friends began to call him "that little watermelon eating man."[507]

The Creation of the NOI Blackboard

Benjamin approached the Hon. Elijah Muhammad about officially:

After moving from 1602-13th Street, N.W. to 713-13th Street, N.E., Mr. Evans began to speak stronger and bolder about his message to his people. This move was made in 1937. After a few months of living in northeast Washington, I wanted the people in that section of the city to meet and hear this little man with this strange message. My wife and I invited 25 or 30 people into our apartment to hear Mr. Evans talk. Again we went to the undertakers' parlor and borrowed some chairs. Mr. Evans had me to make him a small portable blackboard for this meeting. This meeting was very fruitful. The neighbors and their children began to love Mr. Evans. The little boys and girls would run and meet him when they saw him coming up or down the street. He always took time to talk with the little girls and boys. He would give them money from his pockets.

A few weeks after the meeting in our apartment, Mr. Evans said to me, "Brother, I want you to find me a large blackboard so I can have it to teach from. I can explain to my brothers and sisters with a better understanding. We want to put our national, flag on it with the sun, moon, and star and the cross." We brought the material for the blackboard and built it in my back yard at 713 13th Street, N.E. The board was 4'x6' long. I still have it. Mr. Evans used this blackboard to teach from and he converted many brothers and sisters. He converted me from that blackboard — his first blackboard. He really knew how to handle the two signs that were printed on the blackboard.

After the board was built, Mr. Evans seemed to have taken on a new spirit to teach Islam to our people.[508]

The Start of Temple #4

In sharing the wisdom of Islam throughout the city, it was now time to start looking for an official meeting place to set up the start of a Temple of Islam. For the first time, a meeting was held in D.C., and those who attended helped support the cause:

Mr. Evans continued to talk about his mission that God had given to him for his people. He said to me one day that he was going to look for a place (a hall or a large room) where he could invite some people. He checked on a building at the corner of Vermont Avenue and R Streets, N.W. He rented room in that building for a few hours one Sunday afternoon. Mr. Evans then stood on the street in front of the building and invited people to attend a meeting on the second floor front for a few minutes. He was successful in getting a few people. At the end of the meeting, he asked if there were any questions. Some questions were asked and answered. Mr. Evans in return asked the group a few questions: "Did you enjoy the lecture? What do you think about the lecture? Would you all like to meet here again next Sunday?" All agreed that they would. He replied, "This room costs me $3.00 for three hours. We all can put in fifty cents each and be back here next Sunday at 3:00pm." There were seven or eight people present. Mr. Evans met there for a few Sundays.

The next meeting was in my living room at 1602 – 13th Street, N.W. We invited some friends and neighbors for the meeting. I went to the undertaker's parlor and borrowed a few chairs or he meeting and we had a grand time listening to Mr. Evans lecture and then listening to how he answered the many questions. After that meeting, people began to call and ask questions about that little man: "Where did he come from? How long is he going to be with you?"[509]

Holds Temple Meetings Elsewhere in the City

As he did in Detroit, Chicago and Milwaukee, Elijah set up other meeting places to spread the word. He schooled his small dedicated following on strategies to help make Islam successful:

> Another meeting was held in Langston Terrace, 21st and Benning Road, N.E., Washington, D.C., in the Religious Center. A man by the name of Mr. Thomas View was in charge of the Center. One Sunday afternoon, Mr. Evans held a meeting with only a few converts. He said to them, "brothers and sisters, when you all get in the Center don't sit together. Scatter yourselves among the people so that you can hear and see what they are saying about me and what I am teaching." We did as he said, and what a meeting we had! It lasted until late Sunday night. We left MR. Thomas View's Center (he is known now as Brother Thomas Sharieff) and went to Brother Charles X Miller's apartment to finish up the question period. From that meeting, Mr. Evans began to get more converts.
>
> My wife, Sister Clara, arranged a speaking engagement for Mr. Evans at the Y.W.C.A at 901 Rhode Island Avenue, N.W. At that meeting he shocked his audience again.[510]

Benjamin and Clara Join the NOI

Benjamin approached the Hon. Elijah Muhammad about officially joining the Nation of Islam. After giving them advice, the Messenger conceded the point and the couple eventually joined:

> After listening to the Honorable Elijah Muhammad's teaching [Islam], it cleared up many things that I had in my mind about Christianity. One of the things that he made clear to me was the soul of man; second, what and where is Heaven and Hell; third, what and where is God and the Devil; and fourth, why we had not heard this teaching before.
>
> After hearing him [the Messenger] defeat so many Christian preachers, teachers, and scholars, I said I would follow him because what he was teaching was the truth. I asked the Honorable Elijah Muhammad if I could write for my Islamic name. HE said, "Brother, I don't think you and sister [my wife] have understood the teaching well enough yet. Why not wait a while?" We waited, then we wrote for our name [X]. My wife and I had a reply from Chicago stating that our letter had been okayed. I immediately told Mr. Evans [the Messenger] about it. He asked to see the letter. I immediately showed it to him. He said, "Oh! I didn't mean for Sister Secretary to write this to you, about paying dues [money]. Let me have that letter, I will have that corrected. When you learn to love Islam, you will pay charity without anyone asking or telling you.[511]

Teaching on a Field Trip

In 1938, we took a weekend trip to Northern Virginia. We visited the Skyline Drive, Luray Caverns, and the Endless Caverns. This was at the end of the summer season when the trees began to drop their leaves. The mountain ranges were brown, tan, and green, and it was beautiful scenery. As we were riding up and around the mountains, Mr. Evans asked questions like, "What makes rain, hail, snow, earthquakes, hills and mountains?" We answered "God." Mr. Evans looked at us, smiled and said, "Yes, Brother and Sister, all of this is caused by the son of man," and left it like that.

After arriving at Skyline Drive, which is approximately 85 miles from Washington, D.C., we had lunch and began to make a tour of the caverns. On entering the caverns, we had to go down under the mountains a few hundred feet. The temperature was 70 to 72 degrees in the caverns. We found some very interesting things in the caverns, including rivers and lakes. We found a cathedral that was formed by nature from the rocks under the mountain. This naturally built cathedral had been equipped with a pipe organ to play music. We sat and listened to the music in the caverns as our escort explained the history of the caverns.

Our next visit was to the Endless Cavern, which was 20 or 25 miles northwest of Luray, Virginia. This place is called The Natural Bridge, built by nature from rocks of the mountain.

The escort explained to us why this cavern was called endless. He said that the cavern was some 240 feet or more in the ground and said that no one had ever been to the end and returned. He went on to say that is anyone attempted to go to the end of the cavern, they would do so at their own risk. We came out of the cavern and returned to Washington, D.C.[512]

More Join the Ranks in DC

Washington, DC proved to be fertile ground for the Nation of Islam; many started joining the ranks per their experience in America and the benefits they saw in the teachings. Such as the following pioneers. Sister Lydia Hazziez:

I heard the message of the Honorable Elijah Muhammad, the Messenger of Allah (God)...[1938]. Islam, the religion of Allah, has done much for me. It seems as though I had been looking for something since childhood.

My grandfather was a Cherokee Indian. While seated around the fireplace, he would tell us his hopes of one day seeing us, his children, having a better time in life than he had. The last time he was sold, it was for $16.00.

Islam ended and satisfied my search for the truth in life, and I am well pleased with it. After learning from the Messenger about our original home, and seeing the lot of our people her in North America, I began to look at the other nations of ours (Chinese, Japanese, and the rest everywhere else in the world) and recognized the truth of myself and my people. I knew we had to stand up for ourselves as a people. Islam is the only thing I saw that could unite us as a people.

BEFORE accepting Islam and coming into the knowledge of Allah (the one God), I was always sick. Since the Messenger taught us how to eat properly, my sick spells gradually came to an end.

He teaches us that what, how, and even when we eat has a direct effect on our health. Islam is wonderful. My accepting Islam also put an end to the confusion in my mind over the white man's Christianity.

Islam has improved my home a great deal. My marriage and family life is better than it was before. I have four boys, sixteen grandchildren, and five great grandchildren.

ISLAM has increased my pride and respect for my people and respect for my people in such a way that my friendships in all walks of life have become many.

I will never put Islam down. I will forever hold on to it and hold it above all else. I don't have any room in my heart for anything but Islam.

All praise is due to Allah, and I shall forever thank Him for our beloved leader, teacher, and guide, the most Honorable Elijah Muhammad.[513]

I Live in Fear Near Lynch Tree—Until Islam
Sister Beatrice X, NOI Washington DC, Pioneer tells her story:

A limb has been sawed off the big tee on the Whamm plantation near Greenville, S.C. The sight of this tree may be meaningless to the casual visitor in the area, but to the black and whites who have lived in the vicinity of the plantation for years, it is a symbol of death, casting a pall of fear over the future.

A black farm hand was lynched from this tree. He had been accused of assaulting a white girl. The black man never was given a fair trial. The perpetrators of this gruesome murder cut off the tree limb as a warning to all black folks to "stay in their place."

As a child, I used to have to pass this tree everyday, and my sister used to work on the plantation. We all knew that the black man was innocent of the charge, but what could we do? Crimes of this kind take place all over the South.

I was born into the world in this God-forsaken area some 58 years ago [1906]. There were 12 children in my family, and I was next to the youngest. My people were farmers and devoted churchgoers. My father was a "'Republican," he said because that was the party of Lincoln.

Every member of a farm family has chores to do. I worked alike all the others—hoeing, picking cotton and getting dinner ready for the workers in the field.

Like most country folks, we attended the Baptist Church. There was plenty of Christian religion in the family. My uncles were preachers. Looking back, I think of what a shame it was to see them glorifying the white man and preaching his religion with so much fervor.

One of my uncles was also a school teacher. He was responsible for much of our education in those days.

I was married early—at the age of 14. My father struggled the best he knew how to rear and feed us after the death of our mother. My marriage somewhat eased my father's burden. Unfortunately, my husband was killed in 1924—and I was left with four children of my own.

For a while I was fervently religious, joining the Church of the first Born. I was "taught the bible" by a man who was a 33-degree Mason and minister. I held him in high esteem and so did the entire community.

This Mason and preacher, who taught me the bible, was later involved with a young girl. There was a big religious scandal after that. This, and other things I had learned about black preachers, turned me against the church.[514]

The terror of a tree in South Carolina on which an innocent Negro farm hand was lynched by white racists in 1924—and her disgust with the antics of some preachers were recalled by Sister Beatrice X in the first installment. In Part II following, the final installment, she tells how the move to Washington, D.C., was the turning point in her life.

I left the South and came to Washington, D.C., a move that was to prove the "turning point" in my life. I continued my search in the nation's capital for the "truth." For sometime I found it as elusive in Washington as it was in Greenville, S.C. The preachers were no better than those in South Carolina.

My home in Washington happened to stand near a small building that was called the "Temple of Islam." However, I did not visit this temple immediately. I was too busy putting my nickels and dimes on the "wrong" number. Like most of the Negroes from the South. I was trying to "hit" it rich.

One day after I had married again, a friend I hadn't seen for a long time came to the house, enthusiastically telling me about a little man preaching a "new truth."

At the first chance, I heard this man. He pointed out some things in the Bible with which I had to agree. When he began to explain the nature of the white man and his inborn hatred of the black man, I had visions of that limb on the "Lynching tree" in Greenville where a white mob murdered an innocent black man.

I also remembered the Mason, who used only part of the teachings of Islam—and the preachers refusing to tell the real truth about the scriptures.

In a matter of days, I became a Muslim. My long search for truth and a way of life which did not require me to sacrifice my dignity and identity had ended on a happy note.

I registered all my children under 12 years of age. At the beginning, my husband, whom I love very much, grew hostile. He and one of my sons tried to dissuade me. But time has changed all that. One by one, the others began to come to Islam.

I consider myself one of the early Muslims in Washington. We suffered extreme hardships to help the Honorable Elijah Muhammad establish Islam here. I served 20 days in jail. My sons, James and Johnny, were taken away from me and placed in Blue Plains, D.C. (presently Junior Village).

Our leader (we did not know at the time that he was the Messenger) also was arrested - on May 8, 1942. For the slightest provocation—or for no reason at all - Muslims were arrested and thrown into jail. But, thanks to Allah, we have endured it all.

What has Islam done for me? Islam has given me peace of mind and contentment. If all the money in the world were placed at my feet, I would not exchange Islam for it.

Sixteen years ago I weighed more than 200 pounds. I was sluggish and always was "down with something." But today I am vigorous and active. I always have liked to work with food and children, which requires much standing. However, I work with food and children today with relative ease.

Fourteen years following the Messenger of Allah have given me life, vitality, peace and happiness. I hope that every so-called Negro soon will accept the teachings of the Honorable Elijah Muhammad.[515]

The Hon. Elijah Muhammad years later reminisced on his days in DC.

Elijah Remembers Religious Debates in DC

"He [Benjamin] know me from '35. I used to room in his house for about 4 or 5 years in Washington. And he used to go out and bring some of the toughest. The boys called them "cats" [laughs]. The toughest cats he could find, and sick them on me!

One day I got to looking at him, I said he think he will find some cat yet that can out think me. They were all in shifts. He think they scared of me, he'd go out and get another one (laughs). He said I will get you after a while (laugh), 'I know one that's real bad.' So he'd bring me a real bad one, when he leave him I'd have him all whipped. So he'd look at me again, I think he saying 'where this man come from'? Right brother Benjamin [laughs with Benjamin].

I used to tell him, I'd say, "One of these days..." I'd say, "You'll see" I'd say "I'll have a Temple right here." I'd say "You'll be in it, you'll be with me then." I'd say, "I will get arrested here, they'll send me maybe to prison." I'd say, "but..I'll be the winner, we'll have a big temple here one day." So he sees now. Way back then in '35.[516]

Up and Down East Coast

So I'd travel up and down the East Coast running every 2 weeks 3 weeks going to another place because the dog would be right there after me. Soon as they'd chase me and find me up this tree, I'd jump into another tree or go into a hollow. I had to do that for 7 long years. Brother right here would tell you. Him and his wife—I would say they could represent me better than anybody on the East Coast. They've known me a long time. They know me. They know my morals. He and his wife, and some more there in Washington DC, they knew me, back in those says when I was in my 30s. I was probably in my middle 30s or more. And they saw me for years (coming in and out). And if you want to know me, then ask them. Ask anybody up and down the East Coast. I stayed up and down there 7 years. Well, in my middle 30's, I was a young man, up until about 42 years old, about 44 years old, when I got sent to prison. And just go behind me, where I went along, and the people will soon tell you from Boston to Atlanta. And I'd stop in and out of every little city or town. All of them. And now today there, it's like a fire burning. Allah has blessed me with Temples in every one of these places. Brother will tell you, I'd tell him I was at such and such place. He'd talk about "where you been so long?" I'd say I was at such and such place. Now at all those such and such places now you will see a temple in them. Well Allah blessed me wherever my foot trot he caused the seed of salvation to prosper there and it went into the heart of our people. And today there is those things that cats operate up under water and after many different days you will see it again. After many years know I see. So brother didn't think that he would be standing here today as a minister, in those days.[517]

Benjamin Takes Elijah to Spar with Preacher

Minister Benjamin recalls taking Elijah to visit a church where the Messenger and the preacher got into a debate:

I remember one weekend, Mr. Evans said to me, "Brother you know, I feel like teaching a little Islam. Do you know some preachers who have small churches were we can visit?" We might get a chance to talk a little." I replied, "Yes, I do know one from my home town of Winchester, Arkansas. His name is Reverend L.M. Carroll. He lives in Warrenton, Virginia and he has invited me to visit his all-day church services at Sperryville, Virginia, which is about sixty miles from Washington. Meals are usually served at these all-day meetings on the church grounds." Mr. Evans (the Messenger) said, "Yes Brother, I think I remember meeting that Reverend, when shall we go?" I said we could go up next Sunday. That following Sunday, Mr. Evans and I drove to Sperryville, Virginia, for the all-day meeting which was in the late summer of 1939. On our way up the meeting, he began to instruct me on how to handle this dinner problem. "You know brother, these people are going to have plenty food and much of it will consist of the poison animal (the hog). Usually brother, the people on the farm bake some very good cakes, pies and make good ice cream. To keep from being so different, we will eat ice cream and cake with them. I will show you how to handle it.

After the service, instead of having dinner on the church grounds, we were invited with the minister, Reverend Carroll, and many others to the home of one of the deacons.

True was the statement of Mr. Evans about the poison animal for dinner. The table had cakes, pies, and ice cream. We stood and said blessing with them and proceeded to eat. Mr. Evans said to the group that we were on a diet and could not eat many of the foods on the table but we could have some of that good looking cake and ice cream.[518]

Elijah Upsets Preacher

While at the table, Mr. Evans was being asked many questions concerning Islam and he was answering that without any trouble. Reverend Carroll was really looking and listening to Mr. Evans. All of the Reverend's followers began to look and listen. This made the Reverend angry to see his followers so interested in what Mr. Evans was teaching. The Reverend jumped up from the table and said, You all seem to be so interested in what that little dude is saying. I know him. I heard about him in Washington, and I met him one time at Mitchell's home. He is preaching against our government and I don't like it. You all sitting, looking and listening like you believe what he's saying. I don't like it either. I am ready to fight." Mr. Evans replied, "Your pastor doesn't care for me to talk to you on this subject." His members began to look at one another.

Mr. Evans said to me, "Brother, it's time for us to go, and we thanked the Deacon and the Minister for the invitation.

On our way back to Washington, Mr. Evans said, "Brother you see how angry the Reverend got about my answering the brothers' questions?" He knows if his followers continue to listen to what I am saying, they will believe Islam. This is why the ministers of Christianity will not permit Islam to be taught in the churches. They will tell you quick, "NO, NO! We can't have that teaching here. That is an Eastern religion. It's against our government." Mr. Evans then said to me, "Brother, when I get back to Washington, I am going to see if I can find a storefront building and teach in it. Brother all of this is in the bible under the title, Birth of Jesus. Actually brother, that is our history (the Birth of a Nation). They don't want this to happen. Therefore, they don't have room in the churches for Islam."[519]

The Hon. Elijah Muhammad gives the uncensored comical version of the story:

But he said [laughs], he carried me down there in Virginia one day and throwed me on one of those bad cats [laughs]. That cat was so bad he ordered me out in the backyard for a fight. Yes, sir. Yes, sir. Brother will tell you. Half of the church. I made fun of him and he felt pretty cheap after that. But he got jealous because his followers were there beginning you know to listen at me and the worst of it his wife was about to become a convert [laughs]. I think he just got real angry, you know just lost control of himself. Being jealous of me here teaching people something that he didn't teach, and they believed it. And so, I laughed at the old brother. I was pretty strong in those days. I was a young fellow. And I told the old brother he wouldn't have lasted 2 minutes if I would have went in the back yard. [laughs] I said poor brother. He was a little ill, you know, skinny and pretty weak. And I thought maybe that I could finish him off in a little while. But that wasn't the point. I wanted to convert him. I wouldn't argue with them. I didn't talk that kind of talk. I made them look pretty cheap for talking to me like they did. He didn't have enough truth to fight me with me truth, why now he wants to take it out on me physically. He made a fool out of himself. But this is the thing we must learn to do, to be very diplomatic. Fight or use your firsts whenever you got to, and then make a good job out of it as you did out of you know your tongue. All ministers have to be good fighters both ways. Because they can talk alright (laughs). Though I don't believe everyone to be like myself. I never expect you to get into no kind of fight physically, because I believe I can always outwit you with the word. I will make you come off of that and after a while you will be shaking my hand. And yet I wouldn't show you that I'm a coward, I just believe I can outwit you with the word, and have you coming down to be my brother.

Benjamin: Yes, I'd like to tell my brothers here that what the Dear Holy Apostle is telling you is right. He's real people. And as he said, I can bear witness, that he knows how to speak. Because I went around with him, and he was teaching me how to speak. And I didn't realize that until 2 years into what he was doing. I had to do some of the same things that I saw him do, out here with my people.[520]

New Meeting Place

The Messenger and the DC Muslims secured a storefront where they could hold Temple meetings, later to secure a church:

A few months later, Mr. Evans was successful in finding a storefront at 1600 8th Street, N.W. After teaching there several months, he had some pamphlets made inviting the people to our services. He called himself Mr. J. Bogans. (An example of the strongly-worded pamphlet follows).

A few weeks later, Mr. Evans rented space in a Baptist Church at the corner of Fourth and L Streets, N.W. from Reverend Lambert. Our meetings were held after their Sunday services for two hours. The large board that I built was brought into the church so Mr. Evans could use it to explain the teaching of Islam.

Mr. Evans lectured for five or six Sundays at the church. The teaching was so strong and effective until Reverend Lambert began to fear and had the blackboard removed from the church.

When we went into the church that Sunday afternoon for our service, our blackboard was missing and no one seemed to know where it could be found. Mr. Evans told the brothers that we had to find that board. One of the brothers was pretty rough when he got angry. He stated that if Reverend Lambert didn't get that board, we would take him for a ride. The brothers got into the car and went p to Reverend Lambert's home and asked about the board. Reverend Lambert stated, "I don't know where it is." The rough-speaking brother spoke up and said, "Now listen, Reverend, if you don't get that blackboard, we will have to take you for a ride." The Reverend got into the car with the brothers and directed them to a few places and they found the blackboard in a garage. The brother returned the blackboard to the Messenger [Mr. Evans].[521]

DC Pioneers Buy a House

In the year of 1940, I moved from 713 – 13th Street, N.E, in Washington, to 1205 – 51st Avenue, N.E. (Deanwood Park, Maryland).

The Honorable Elijah Muhammad (Mr. Evans) at that time or period had rooms in Virginia, Maryland, and Washington, D.C. He came out to see the house that my wife and I were trying to buy. The house was very, very old and needed many repairs. I remember one day he came out and I was up on the roof making repairs. The Messenger said to me, "Brother, if I had the money, I would give it to you so you could get someone to help you make the repairs that are needed. That's a lot of work for you to do by yourself." Once when he came out to see me, he was driving an old used car, a black Buick. He said to me, "Brother, I have some reports to get out to Chicago, and I am going to take my work in my car over there under the shade trees on Lee Street and work on them. You will see where I am from the rooftop where you are working and I can see you." Time continued to roll on and the FBI continued looking for the Honorable Elijah Muhammad (Mr. Evans) and his followers.[522]

Temple#4 Officially Established (1941)

Finally, the DC Muslims were able to Establish Temple #4 after hard trials:

During the month of July 23, 1941, Mr. Evans had made plans to have a big meeting in the McKinley Memorial Baptist Church, Fourth and L Streets, N.W. He made up several hundred pamphlets and put them into the hands of many people. Since Reverend Lambert, minister of McKinley Memorial Baptist Church, didn't want us to have any more services in his church. Mr. Evans decided to see if the minister in the 1300 block of H Street, N.E., would let him use his storefront Baptist church t lecture to his people. Mr. Evans showed the minister a few of the pamphlets that he had printed for the week of July 23, 1941. The minister then asked Mr. Evans to wait until he had talked with some of the other ministers about the subjects.

The Messenger of Allah, Mr. Evans, waited and waited for an answer from the minister but never received permission to use his storefront church.

Many of these pamphlets got into the streets of Washington, D.C., and many of the people began to be fearful of such powerful and timely subjects. Many of these pamphlets got into the U.S. Government buildings. A few weeks later that U.S. Government put out radio and newspaper notices that said: Notify the FBI if you know of anyone speaking against the U.S. Government. This was the beginning of a special hunt for Mr. Evans. (Please see example of one of the pamphlets on page 14.)

The first official temple was set up by Mr. Evans (the Messenger of Allah), the Honorable Elijah Muhammad (may Allah be pleased with his work), in awakening the black man and woman in America.

The Messenger and his few followers and believers were successful in finding another storefront building at 1525 or 1527 Ninth Street, N.W., Washington, D.C. During the fall of 1940, we began to hold our regular meetings at 8:00pm., Wednesday and Friday, and Sundays from 2:00p.m. to 6:00p.m.

At that time, we referred to the black man and woman as The Lost-Found Nation of Islam in the Wilderness of North America. The Messenger began to break down from the blackboard the meaning of the wording that was written upon the board to all of us. His way or method of teaching from the board was very effective to open-minded brothers and sisters. At the end of the meeting, Mr. Evans (the Messenger) would have a question and answer period. Many interesting points and answers were explained and made clear to many of the Christians. The black people in the early and late 30's were very, very fearful of the teachings of Islam. The Messenger stated to us many times that if you had an audience of 100 and taught them Islam, you would do well to convert three out of that 100. The Messenger and his followers in the 30s and early 40's really had some hard knocks and insults in establishing the teaching of Islam in North America.[523]

THE EMBLEM OF
CHRISTIANITY

THE EMBLEM OF
ISLAM

**Which one will survive
the WAR of**

ARMAGEDDON?

The sign that leads to
**SLAVERY, SUFFERING,
and DEATH**

Have the so-called Negro (Asiatic) ever received Freedom, Justice, and Equality under the above sign? Why?

Why should we fight to maintain that which leads us and our children into Slavery and Death?

Can the so-called Negro (Asiatic) be forced to fight on the side of his Slave Master against his will in this War?

Does the Negro know what this War Means to Him?

The sign that leads to
**FREEDOM, JUSTICE,
EQUALITY**

Why are those who follow the above sign standing aloof of the present Christian's conflict?

How old is the above Religion? What does its name mean?

Why has the truth of this Religion been kept a secret from the American Dark People (Asiatics)?

Why did the Slave Maker of the Dark People of America exclude from the Bible the Religion of the Prophets?

COME OUT AND LEARN—THIS IS THE END OF THE WORLD

Get the Answers with Proof from

J. BOGANS

beginning at

February 7th 1941   8:00 p.m.   1600 8th St N.W.

Facsimile of first pamphlet distributed by Mr. Evans in 1941 (reset for clarity).

13 THE BELLY
OF THE BEAST

First Muslims arrested in DC

While America was at war, J. Edgar Hoover and the FBI sought to arrest the Hon. Elijah Muhammad and all Muslims who refused to register for the draft. Benjamin recalls the climate in DC that had Christian ministers upset and other blacks curious about the Muslims stance on the war:

> During the latter part of 1940, 1941 and 1942, the Islamic tension was high among the religious leaders of Christianity and the U.S. Government, especially after some of those pamphlets that the Honorable Elijah Muhammad had printed for services to be held in the McKinley Memorial Baptist Church. Tension began to grow among the black ministers and their followers. News was being broadcasted weekly, advising Americans to report anyone speaking against the government. I was, at that time, working for the U.S. Navy Yard and America was at odd with the government of Japan.
>
> One afternoon when I reported for work, one or two employees asked me about these pamphlets that were being distributed in the streets of Washington. They asked what kind of religion was Islam since they hadn't heard of it until a few days ago. I replied that I didn't know too much about it and suggested they visit the temple and ask questions since I had been told that they would permit you to ask questions. [524]

One by one Muslims started getting arrested under charges of draft evasion, the first being Brother Harry X. Craighead, soon to be followed by several others. Brother Benjamin X remembers the animosity of President Theodore Roosevelt and the government towards the Muslims:

> The tension began growing more and more in Washington, D.C. The U.S. Government was registering men for the army from 18 years to 40 years. One believer and follower of the Honorable Elijah Muhammad by the name of Brother Harry X Craighead was called by the U.S. Government for service in the Army. Brother Harry refused to register on the ground that he was a Muslim and Muslims do not fight on the side with Christians. The FBI told Brother Harry that they would put him in prison if he didn't fight for his country. Brother Harry said, "Well, you will have to put me in prison, because I will not go and fight." So they arrested Brother Harry. The President of the United States (President Roosevelt) told the FBI to make a thorough investigation of this case and bring him the findings. He

[273]

said, "This is a Christian Government and we don't teach Islam here. If we permit that, they will have all of these Negroes calling themselves Moslem [Muslim] and we are at War." The FBI agents began making more arrests in the Washington area and in the Chicago area also Detroit and Milwaukee. The second or third brother to be arrested was Brother John X Miller...Brother Elmer X Carroll and Brother Joseph X Nipper were the next to be arrested. The hunt for Muslims (or Moslems) by the FBI was very, very hot. This was during the months of March and April in 1941.[525]

Another FOI John X. Lawler was also arrested in 1941 for refusing to register for the draft. He tells his story of what happened to him:

My years as a follower of the Honorable Elijah Muhammad have not been without trials and tribulations, for in 1941, I, along with others, went to prison for failure to register for the draft.

Why didn't I register? I felt the draft was for the citizens and since I had never been allowed the privileges of citizenship, I did not feel the need to assume any of the responsibilities of a citizen. Surely, I thought, they would not dare deny me the rights of a citizen and then harness me with all the most dangerous responsibilities of a citizen.

We were given what I considered stiff sentences, but in 1945 we returned to take up the cause of Islam where it had been interrupted. Our trials had only intensified our belief and since that time we have been blessed to see our dear beloved leader and teacher attain success after success in the ever spreading everlasting Nation of Islam.[526]

Elijah Gives Instructions About His Own Arrest

Understanding the climate, the Hon. Elijah Muhammad anticipated his own arrest. Some say he had divine foresight and intentionally left some NOI documents in the Temple for the government to study:

Nevertheless, Allah revealed to him, one day, as he was traveling on a train, that he would have to give himself up to his enemies and go to prison. He gave him insight into how this imprisonment would ultimately serve the cause for which he was sacrificing. The F.B.I., on the orders of the president and J. Edgar Hoover were seeking him to take him into custody, and worse. Allah showed him why prison was to be his lot, for a while. He submitted to Allah's will. He indicated to his followers what was coming. He deliberately wrote certain points, of what he was taught, on the blackboard, in the Temple in Washington, D.C., which he wanted the government to study.[527]

Brother Benjamin explains the circumstances and specific instructions the Messenger gave him prior to his arrest:

He rented a room from Mr. and Mrs. Williams at 1306 Girard Street, N.W. on May 6, 1942, Mr. Evans had one of the believers, Brother Henry X, who was a taxicab driver, to bring him to my home for a chat. We were sitting on my front porch. The Messenger said to me, "Brother, I would like to talk to you privately for a few minutes before I go back to D.C." I replied, "Yes, sir, you surely can," I asked Brother Henry X if he would excuse us for a few minutes. Mr. Evans and I walked under a large tree in my front yard, he looked straight at me and said, "Brother, I am leaving for Philadelphia, Pennsylvania, this afternoon and I want you to do something for me." He asked me to take his car and two suitcases to his wife in Chicago, Illinois. I told him that I would, but the statements that he made still lingered with me. I wondered what he meant by saying if something happened to him.

Well, Mr. Evans and Brother Henry left to go back to D.C. Mr. Evans reminded in Philadelphia, Pennsylvania, Thursday night and returned to Washington, D.C., Friday, May 8, 1942.[528]

Elijah Muhammad arrested in DC

When Elijah returned on May 8, 1942, he was arrested by FBI agents waiting for him at his room:

According to his landlady, Mrs. Williams, when Mr. Evans came to his place of residence at 1306 Girard Street, N.W., he came into the house by the rear door. Mrs. Williams also stated that she ran to the rear of the house to warn Mr. Bogan (the Honorable Elijah Muhammad) not to come in because two men were there to arrest him. Mr. Bogan asked, "For what?", and kept going into the house. As he entered, the two men rose to their feet and asked if he was Bogan. They stated that they were FBI agents. They showed their identification card and informed Mr. Bogan that they wanted to talk with him at the FBI office about his religion. Mr. Evans (Mr. Bogan) submitted and went with them. This happened the Friday before Easter and he stated to us that he remained in their office all of Friday, Saturday, and a portion of Sunday and was questioned by the government officials concerning the religion of Islam. The FBI agents crucified Mr. Evans the Friday before Easter, May 8, 1942. The news quickly spread that the FBI had arrested this much-wanted man, teacher of Islam. They kept him in the D.C. jail for a few months.

Mrs. Williams called me the Friday evening after his arrest and said that FBI agents came and arrested Mr. Bogan. She said they had been sitting around the house for two or three days. Friday they came into the house and said that they were looking for him and desired to wait for him. She went on to say that when Mr. Bogan came in the back way she begged him not to come in because FBI agents were going to arrest him. "They took him and I wanted to call to let you know of his arrest," she said. I thanked Mrs. Williams for letting me know. [529]

Elijah Muhammad said of the incident itself that, "Uncle Tom Negroes" tipped the white man off to his teachings and he was charged with draft dodging even though he was too old to register for the military:

I was arrested on May 8, 1942, in Washington, D.C., by the F.B.I. for not registering for the draft. When the call was made for all males between 18 and 44, I refused (NOT EVADING) on the grounds that, first, I was a Muslim and would not take part in war and especially not on the side with the infidels. Second, I was 45 years of age and was NOT according to the law required to register...[530]

NOI National Laborers and Believers respond to Elijah's arrest

After his teacher's arrest, Brother Benjamin recalled Elijah's instructions to go see his wife Clara in Chicago:

I then thought about what Mr. Evans asked me to do for him on Wednesday, May 6, 1942, under the tree in my front yard. He asked me to take his car and two bags to his wife in Chicago if anything should happen to him.[531]

Late Friday, May 8, 1942, I began to make ready to take Mr. Evans' car to his wife in Chicago. I left D.C. alone on Saturday morning about 1:30a.m. I took route U.S. 30 arriving in Chicago Saturday evening about 5:30 or 6:00pm, and made my report to his wife, Sister Clara Muhammad.[532]

FBI Interviews Elijah in Prison

Meanwhile at the jailhouse Elijah Muhammad was badgered and interrogated by the FBI and examined by a psychiatrist:

After that, I was arrested by the F.B.I. in Washington on the eighth day of May 1942. They took me to their jail. First they questioned me all night long in their office, until approximately eight or nine o'clock that morning—it was Friday when I was arrested. And they sent for a doctor to examine me to see if I was getting a little "off," but I was still normal.[533]

The FBI Special Agents had Elijah Muhammad (under the alias Bogans) to issue a statement on his stance on the war. Listed below:

May 8, 1942

I, Gulam Bogans, make the following voluntary statement to [name redacted], and [name redacted], whom I know to be Special Agents of the Federal Bureau of Investigation. No threats or promise have been made to induce my making this statement, and I realize it can be used against me in a court of law.

"I was brought into the Islam Creed in 1931 at Detroit, Michigan. At that time, Allah, also known to me as W.D. FARD, appeared and began to teach me Islam. Among other things, he told me that I was to have no part in fighting or military matters whatsoever. I have been teaching Islam since that time in Chicago, Detroit, Milwaukee, and Washington, D.C.

"I have been teaching my followers that Allah has instructed me that no righteous Moslem will take part in fighting or military training, since they are registered with the Nation of Islam."

[276]

After reading the above, BOGANS admitted that it was true, but refused to sign his name, stating that his word was his bond.

Witnessed,
[name redacted] Special Agent
Federal Bureau of Investigation
1437 K Street N.W.
Washington, DC

Meanwhile in D.C. the word spread quickly in the Black community. Local Muslims staged a protest in staunch support of their leader requesting that they too be arrested with him to show solidarity:

The news of Mr. Evans' arrest spread fast. A few days after his arrest, the followers of the Messenger came together to picket the jail and to protest to the government for the arrest of our leader and teacher. The news media stated that 25 Moslems (Muslims) picketed the jail of the Prophet.

Mr. Evans asked the jail Superintendent, Mr. E.A. Green, to lock us up because we believe the same as he believes. Mr. Green said, "I can't lock them up. They will have to do something." The Muslims cried out, "We believe in the same thing that the Messenger believes, so lock us up too."[534]

Temple #1, #2 and #3 Notified of Elijah's Arrest

Word of their beloved leader Elijah Muhammad's arrest quickly traveled up to the Chicago, Detroit and Milwaukee Temples. Most Muslims had been prepared for this news in advance:

The Messenger taught we, the Muslims, that some of us would go to prison for Islam. He taught us that Yakub and his followers were imprisoned in his time for the teaching of Islam. He said to us, history repeats itself.

On May 8, 1942, the Messenger was arrested in Washington, D.C. The government charged him with failure to register for selective service, of course, in the United States Army – to serve them or their country as we, the Blacks had always done until the coming of Allah in the Person of Master Fard Muhammad, to Whom Praise is due forever for bringing to we the Black people in America, Islam...and teaching it to the Honorable Elijah Muhammad and missioning Him to teach we, His lost-found brothers of Asia, our own.

We, the Muslims, received the news of the arrest and imprisonment of our beloved Leader, Teacher and Guide. He is beloved by the Muslims. We were deeply touched by this not-too-good news, but we were not surprised. We had been expecting this to happen at any time, since the country was at war and knowing the history of the past.

The Muslims were firm and dedicated to Islam – we were together. We took a firm determined stand with our Leader and Teacher of Islam in the wilderness of North America. Although we had not seen Him in seven and one-half years, this did not alter our faith in Him. We were united with Him in Islam until the end of our days. Allah gave Him to us.

We, the Muslims, loved Him. He being away from us seven and one-half years tested our faith in Him. We were loyal to Him and the humanitarian cause of Islam. Seven and one-half years away from His followers made us, the Muslims, firm, determined and steadfast in Islam.

Our faith was never shaken because of His absence. The Muslims knew He was then and is today the Intercessor between we, the Muslims and our God, Allah. There was nothing we wouldn't do for Him. It was the Honorable Elijah Muhammad and Islam versus the United States government.[535]

Min. Wali and Min. Sultan travel to DC

The Hon. Elijah Muhammad entrusted his Brother Minister Wali Muhammad and NOI National Representative Min. Sultan Muhammad to lead the campaign to free him from prison. Karriem Allah recalls the character of Min. Sultan Muhammad:

We need unity and oneness today. Our minister Sultan Muhammad was strong, fearless, bold and daring. Allah, to Whom Praise is due forever could not have given a better one. He was in step with the time – he was a good minister. He was lovable to work with; he did everything he could to please the Honorable Elijah Muhammad; he obeyed the Messenger's instructions. We were with him. He proved himself to be worthy of his position.

He was good to the Muslims. We the Muslims loved him. We would fight for him; we guarded him well. We were under strict orders all the time; we obeyed them to the letter. We had loyal officers; we had a loyal F.O.I. there was no playing and joking. We carried out our orders that were given to us; we made no excuses. We were put on guard at the Temple night and day; the enemy was active around our Temple. We attended all Temple services.

Our minister Sultan Muhammad, was present in No. 2 on Friday nights and Sundays. He would leave Chicago and go on to Milwaukee, Wis., to rally the Muslims there in NO. 3. All the Muslims respected him; he was worthy of respect. He carried himself in a dignified manner. The Muslims were with him.[536]

Muslims Protest to Free Elijah

Following their love and desire for Elijah Muhammad, the Muslims rallied around their leadership and efforts to free "the Messenger":

The Time had come for us to show our love, devotion and respect and unity to Him – this the Muslims did, we rallied to his defense. We were determined not to let anything stand in our way in helping Him, we were his followers. It was our duty to come to His aid – He had done so much for us.

He sacrificed for us seven and one-half years. What I mean, he was away from us for seven and one-half years. It was our time to sacrifice for Him. How many of you today would have stood by Him and not see Him in seven and one-half years? – talk is easy, time will prove your worth. He was then and is now, our All and All.

Minister Sultan Muhammad was the minister of No. 1, Detroit, Mich. He was the assistant minister to the Messenger in those days. He rallied the Muslims in Temples No. 1, No. 2 and No. 3 to the defense of the Honorable Elijah Muhammad. He said, "Dear brothers and sisters, the enemy has arrested our beloved leader, the Honorable Elijah Muhammad in Washington, D.C. and is holding him in prison. We must get Him out of prison as soon as possible.

He said we cannot do anything without the Messenger. We, the Muslims, rallied behind our minister to raise money to bail our Leader, the Messenger, out of prison. He said to us, "I want you all to give all that you can for this great cause." We did as we were instructed; every Muslim gave.

The depression hadn't lifted; times were still hard. The Muslims were not making much money. We did not let that stop us – we sacrificed all we could. Allah was with us; he blessed us.

We worked together with our minister. He was a courageous man in this cause; he worked untiringly. Our spirit was high; we could think nothing but getting our Leader, the Honorable Elijah Muhammad, out of prison. Muslims worked like they had never done before. It was a time of unity and oneness.

Our Leader needed His followers, Allah, to Whom Praises are due forever, tested our faith. He suffered this to happen to the Honorable Elijah Muhammad to see if we would stand by Him in the time of great trouble: truly the Muslims did. We worked cheerfully, together in this cause. [537]

Ministers Wali and Sultan address the FBI and Get Arrested

Min. Sultan Muhammad and the Messenger's brother Min. Willie (Wali) Muhammad, fast-tracked it to DC where they checked in with Mosque #4 before going to see the Messenger in jail. The two Ministers made a great impression on the Muslims and the locals in DC. Min. Benjamin recalls:

A few days passed. The news began to spread about Messenger Muhammad being in jail. Early one morning, two Muslim brothers from Temple No. 2 and No. 3 came to see about Mr. Evans. Minister Willie Muhammad of Temple No. 2 in Chicago and Minister Sultan Muhammad of Temple No. 3 in Milwaukee came seeking information concerning the Messenger. I related to them what had happened.

These two men looked so clean and dignified, and seemed to be noticed by every one that passed by them. These two brothers wanted to go down to the FBI office to find out why Mr. Evans was arrested. Before I took them downtown to the FBI office, they asked me to take them by the U.S. Supreme Court. When we arrived there, they stood in front of the Court building looking at the statues of nine men engraved on the front gable end of the building. These two brothers were discussing something about the carving on the front of the building. I was standing a short distance from them, admiring the way the people were attracted by these brothers. They really did look dignified and impressive. The people seemed to be on their lunch period.

After standing there for 15 or 20 minutes, they decided to walk on down to the FBI office. They went in and began to inquire about the Honorable Elijah Muhammad's arrest. [538]

The F.B.I. seized this opportunity to place Min. Sultan and Min. Willie (Wali) under arrest for refusing to register for the draft:

This initial group of believers in what was then known as Muhammad's Temple #3, located on McKinley Boulevard, produced the Honorable Elijah Muhammad's first National Representative, Minister Sultan Muhammad.[539] During this period the Honorable Elijah Muhammad never stayed in a city more than two weeks, up until his arrest by Executive Order in the spring of 1942 in Washington D.C. Upon receiving the news of the Messenger's arrest, Minister Sultan and William Muhammad, of Temple #1 in Detroit traveled to his aid, leading to their subsequent arrest and imprisonment under the Selective Service Act.[540]

Ministers Wali and Sultan Deported Back to their Cities

The FBI eventually discharged the two NOI Ministers back to Milwaukee and Detroit to be tried in their respective states. Min. Benjamin explains the details of what actually happened:

The officers began to question these two men. The questioning finally ended in their arrest. Brother Sultan Muhammad of Temple No. 3 was arrested and charged. Brother Willie Muhammad, the Messengers brother, asked the FBI agents to permit him to go back to his hotel room to take care of some very important business and then he would return to the FBI office. They permitted him to go. That following morning, Brother Willie Muhammad returned to the FBI office as promised. This was the beginning of their imprisonment. These two brothers were eventually sent back to their home town for trial and sentence.[541]

Meanwhile after their full interrogation of the Hon. Elijah Muhammad, the F.B.I. decided to hold him to an indefinite confinement. Elijah recalls: "I spent two months and 15 days in Washington before they ever came down to say whether they were going to have a trial or anything – or let me sit there and mold."[542]

Bro. Benjamin X Mitchell Arrested by FBI in DC

Bro. Benjamin speaks about the FBI's methods of harassment and persecution while the Messenger was under arrest:

The hunt for believers and followers of the Honorable Elijah Muhammad began to get very, very hot. As I stated in the beginning of my writing, I was employed by the U.S. Government. When I was first introduced to the Messenger, he saw that I liked what he was teaching and wanted to become a follower of his. He told me in advance, "Brother, if you follow me, you will be locked up and you will lose your job." I replied, "They will have to lock me up."

About three months after the Messenger's arrest, I began to have visits from the FBI agents. I remember one evening, while working in my garden at 1205 – 51st Avenue, N.E., Deanwood Park, Maryland, two neatly dressed men came walking up the road to my home and approached me in this manner: "Are you Mr. Mitchell?" I replied, "No sir." One asked, "What is your name?" I replied, "Really, I do not know." "Well, who is Mr. Mitchell?" asked one of the agents. I said, "Mr. Mitchell is a white man. You know I am not white." The other spoke up and asked me what was my name. I again replied that I didn't know. One of the agents asked why I didn't know. I said, "Because I lost my name about 379 years ago. I am surprised at you asking me if I am Mr. Mitchell. You know that all of our people are named after your people." They then showed me their identification cards. I took the card and said, "Oh! You are FBI men. What can I do for you?" They replied, we want to talk with you about your religion. I asked, "What do you want to know about my religion?" They asked me if I had registered. I replied that I had. They asked where I had registered. I replied, "With my government." "Your government?" one asked. "What is your government?" "Islam," I replied. "Were you not born here?" he asked. "Yes sir, I was," I answered. All persons born in this country are naturalized citizens. I replied, "No sir, I disagree." "Well, what are you?" one agent asked. I replied, "Just a free slave." One agent then said that I must remember that I was born here and that makes me a citizen. I said, "Look, officer, one of us doesn't know what a citizen is. What is your definition of citizen?" I asked. The agent began to recite to me the Fourteenth and Fifteenth Amendments of the U.S. Constitution. I asked the officer if our people enjoyed all of those things that he quoted for a citizen. Because I was born here doesn't make me a citizen. Because a cat gives birth to kittens in a cooking stove, that doesn't make them biscuits."

One of the agents said, "We can't report all of this." "Why can't you?" I asked, Just tell your boss that I have registered in my government. I can't register with two governments." They departed and went their way.[543]

Shortly afterwards, the FBI agents came to arrest Min. Benjamin along with several other NOI members:

About one month later, an agent came on my job to talk with me concerning my religion. He wanted to know if I had registered and how long I had been a Moslem (Muslim)? I told him that I had registered in my government and I had been a Muslim all of my life but I didn't know it. He asked, "Who taught you that you are a Moslem?" "Allah's Messenger," I replied.[544]

The FBI agents later would return to apprehend and arrest Bro. Benjamin for draft evasion. He recalls the details:

A month or more later, while working on my home at 1205 – 51st Avenue, N.E., I was laying some flooring in my living room. I looked through the window and I saw a well-dressed white man approaching the house. I asked my wife to see what he wanted, and told her if he wanted me to tell him that I had not arrived home from work. He told my wife to tell me when I arrived that he was from the U.S. Government office. A week later, I said to my wife, "I don't feel like I will be back home this evening. I have a feeling that someone is coming on my job for me." Sure enough, two agents came on my job August 1, 1942. They came in the room where I was working and asked, "Are you Mr. Mitchell?" I replied, "No, I am not." The agent asked, "What is your name?" I replied, "I lost my name a few hundred years ago. I am called Mr. Mitchell, but that is not my name." The other agent said, "Well, who is Mr. Mitchell?" I replied, "Mr. Mitchell is a white man. All of our people are named after your people. I am sure that you all knew that." The agents showed me their ID cards and stated that they had come for me. I asked them for what?" they replied, "You didn't register." I immediately spoke up and said, "Yes, I have registered with my government." The agents said, "We will have to take you down to the FBI office." On our way to the office riding in the car, I was sitting on the left side in the rear seat. One agent asked questions. He asked, "Would you mind if I call you Benjamin?" I replied, "No, you may call me Benjamin." "How long have you been a 'Moslem'?" he asked. "All my life," I replied. The agent questioned further, "Why don't you all teach us Islam?" "We did teach you Islam," I said, "Why don't you all let us come to your Temple?" he asked. "For the same reason that you won't let me come to your Temple, here on K Street, N.W.," I replied. At that moment we drove past the white Shriner's Temple. The agent said, "I am not a mason." He asked me how much money I had given to the Messenger. I spoke up and said, "Officer, I think that's a very personal question. I don't know what you would think of me asking you how much money you gave your wife each week." I left it like that.
On arriving at the FBI office, they set my bond at $5,000.00 I remained in the D.C. jail for three months or more before they brought me up for trial.[545]

Incarcerated NOI Members Unite and Teach in Prison
During this time more NOI members were arrested. While in prison, they took the liberty of meeting with each other and teaching other inmates about Islam. Min. Benjamin explains:

During my stay in D.C. Jail, many more of our brothers and one or two sisters were arrested by FBI agents. Brother William X Fagin, a young brother, was sentenced to four years in the Federal Prison for Selective Service violations.[546]

Benjamin recalls the ordeal and conditions they faced in their transfer to Petersburg, VA:

The brothers who followed the Messenger to prison in the early days of Islam in America had it pretty hard trying to survive. You may ask why? Well, in the first place, they (Caucasians) didn't want you and me to be taught Islam because Islam would free you and me from them. The Honorable Elijah Muhammad and those who followed him to prison went hungry many times before the enemy found out that we were true believers and followers of the Honorable Elijah Muhammad. The enemies of truth will hate you. I remember the day of my trial and the transferring of Brother Wallie X Fagin (better known as Wali Muhammad) and myself to Petersburg Federal Prison. While riding in the car with cuffs on our legs, the officer asked, "You fellows would rather go to prison than to sign on the dotted line and go on back home to your families?" "Yes, sir," I replied. The officer looked at me and said as he gritted his teeth, "If I had my way with you, I would shoot every one of you."[547]

They sent us to Petersburg, Virginia in November 1942. We stayed in the isolation ward for 30 days, then we were allowed into the general prison population. In the population, we found our brother, Harry X Craighead (now deceased), who was the first brother in the Washington, D.C. Temple to be arrested for Selective Service violations. After being in the general population for a few weeks, the inmates began to ask us questions about our religion, Islam. Three of us began to explain to the inmates the teachings of Islam. The officer in charge of our dormitory began to stand around and listen. The officer reported what we were doing to the warden and other top officials.[548]

Muslims Placed in Solitary Confinement, Transferred

Eventually the jail authorities had enough of Muslim prisoners teaching other inmates and placed them in solitary confinement after accusing them of starting a riot. Later they were shipped to the penitentiary at Milan, Michigan to finish out the rest of their sentence. Min. Benjamin remembers:

One Sunday afternoon, we heard our numbers yelled out over the P.A. system (inmates are called by numbers instead of names). While resting on our bunks, a call was made for Nos. 11942, 11943, and 1040 to report to the Administration office and to bring all personal belongings. This call was made two times. After the second call, I asked Brother Harry, "Aren't those our numbers that were called? What does he mean by 'bring all your personal belongings'?" Brother Harry replied that those were our numbers and that personal belongings meant our toothbrush and drinking cup. We reported to the Administration office. The officer in charge said that we were to be put in confinement. That Monday morning, we were called before 12 officials for trial. They charged us with inciting a riot in the institution Sunday night. We pleaded "not guilty" to the charge. We told the officials that we were not at the dormitory and that they had us locked in confinement. The officials said that the inmates tried to wreck the dormitory Sunday night and it all came from that Islam teaching that we did last week.

Each one of us was given 19 days solitary confinement. We were locked in a small room and ate white bread and drank black coffee. We slept on a thin mattress with a blanket on a basement concrete floor. They tried to force us to eat hog meat. But we wouldn't. When the 19 days were up, they served the total prison population a lamb dinner for the first time in the history of the prison.

After serving the 19 days in confinement, instead of returning us to the general prison population, we were transferred to another prison in Milan, Michigan, in January 1943. There we completed our four years.[549]

James 3X McGregor (Shabazz) & Isaiah Karriem join the NOI

In the midst of insurmountable persecution, new converts continued to join the Nation of Islam. The Hon. Elijah Muhammad would receive a new crop of future Ministers from this group. Among them would be a Virginia native Bro. James 3X McGregor (future Min. James Shabazz of Baltimore and Newark), as well as Bro. Isaiah X, who would become Isaiah Karriem, the future minister of Baltimore. These new converts would join or meet Elijah Muhammad and be taught by him in prison. Isaiah Karriem recalls: "It was back in 1942 in Washington, D.C., that I first embraced the teachings of the Messenger of Allah. Before that I was a professed Baptist with many questions in my mind—questions like why we had to die before going to heaven, why we had to love our enemies, and what a world would be like with black people ruling. I had no answer until I met the Honorable Elijah Muhammad. Before that my mind was plagued with questions. Then, after listening to one of Messenger Muhammad's ministers in the Temple on 9th Street, my whole life was transformed."[550] Isaiah Karriem recounts his story:

THERE ARE not enough words in the English language to adequately enumerate and describe the blessings I have received since becoming a follower of the Honorable Elijah Muhammad.

I never dreamed that I would live to witness and know a man directly from God Almighty.

When I was a little boy in the hills of North Carolina, I used to wonder and pray to the God my father taught me about, but never seemed to get any results from such a one. I always wanted to be close to God. I felt that if I could get in touch with Him He would understand my problems.

Many times in the cornfield, lying flat on my back praying to God, I would put spit into my eyes trying to impress God that I was crying and sincere and that I needed His attention. I always promised Him that if I ever got in touch with Him I would serve Him for the rest of my life.

UPON leaving home in 1940, I made my first long trip to the big city, Washington, D.C. Being a stranger in the city, I went to the C.C. Camp. After a period of six months in the camp, I received my discharge and went to work at Walter Reed Hospital.

After being there for two years, I met one of Messenger Muhammad's followers. The brother's name was James 4X. He began to tell me about a man who was teaching the history of the black man.

I was so impressed by his teachings that I visited the mosque at 1527 9th Street, N.W., D.C. after a couple of meetings I accepted the teachings of Messenger Muhammad. Afterwards it took me six months to get a good night's sleep.

After two weeks I was in jail and I spent three years feeling real happy and proud that I had found the truth. I began teaching in the prison and after being transferred from one prison to another...[551]

James 3X Anderson (Shabazz) join the NOI

Before joining the Nation of Islam and becoming the future Minister of Temple #2, James 3X Anderson belonged to the Ethiopian Peace Movement. He had heard about the Universal Negro Improvement Association as a boy in the South, and "that sort of geared" him "toward nationalism or national consciousness." He was then convinced that "Garvey's program and ideology would go a long way toward solving the black man's economic problem."

In 1938 James registered and voted in an election in Chicago, yet became disenfranchised with politics overall and so-called Negro leaders:

I was never a member of the NAACP. I could not accept Dr. W.E.B. Dubois position because he seemed to oppose Marcus Garvey's program and I was on Garvey's side. I did not think that the NAACP program was militant enough because it was not dealing with the basic problems such as a high degree of economic independence. The NAACP had no program which I considered would make substantial contribution to the advancement of the black man. I still do not think much of the NAACP now, because they are trying to get for the Negroes what I am opposed to. They are trying to get integration with the white man. I am for separate but equal. I frankly do not believe that the so-called Negro can ever receive better treatment from the devil so long as they remain in the same culture. I can never forgive the devil for what he has already done to my people. I did not think that the communists were fighting for my people. I never could, you know; they did not believe in God. Before I came into Islam I did think that perhaps ther communists could offer something because they advocated that all men were equal regardless of race. After studying the communist philosophy I came to the conclusion that their economic system was too harsh. I believe that the individual has the right of private ownership. The idea of private property gives the individual the incentive to work hard. The communists were opposed to private ownership. [552]

Given his politics James 3X Anderson had no difficulty in accepting the teachings of Elijah Muhammad:

> It did not take much convincing for me to join the Temple because it seemed Islam was what I was looking for. I joined the Nation in 1940. Before this I had done some historical research and had come to the conclusion that the white man's history of the Negro's past was not true. I never did go back to any meetings of the Ethiopian Peace Movement because Islam was just what I had been looking for.[553]

New Recruits Joining the Temples in Spite of Draft Charges

Elsewhere in Chicago the FOI was getting new recruits even in the process of being jailed and persecuted by the FBI. NOI Pioneer Carl X (Omar) describes how he came into contact with the Muslims and the teachings in early 1942:

> It happened to me to step into the apartment of my neighbor Andrew (X) who was visited that evening by another friend of his in the movement. Through our casual discussion we came to a point when we began to discuss religion, on which occasion they attacked the Bible. At this moment I had been really aroused and began to defend the Bible enthusiastically and with vigor. At that discussion I found how little I know about Christianity and even less about the Bible. I was astonished by these two men who taught me more truth in about less than one hour than I had learned in twenty-seven years. In that discussion, it came to a point where I could think of nothing more to say in defense of Christianity. When these two men found out that I was exhausted for words they invited me to the temple for further knowledge. After that discussion, I began to meditate about what I had learned so far about my religion. In fact, it was the first time in my life to have such shocking discussion in a religious matter. Therefore, I bought a Bible and began to read myself and I began to attend the church and question the minister about what I do not understand in the Bible; and I thought to visit the temple of these Moslems itself to bring some new points in defense of Christianity.[554]

After exhausting all of his arguments, Carl X (Omar) decided to visit the mosque per the invite of Bro. Andrew X:

> About three weeks later Andrew (X) asked me to go with him to the temple and I did. When I attended the service at that Sunday, and listened to the minister speaking I was really aroused because he disrobed Christianity completely. In addition to this, I came to the temple having in mind to

defend Christianity and attack the movement but when the minister asked whether there is any question I found that I had nothing to say and I had no point to defend. Since that meeting, I began to be doubtful about my Christian belief because they really have put me on the top of the fence. After that I began to read in the bible seriously because until that time all what I had read in the Bible was about only two pages. Andrew (X) was helping me in that study and he was showing me various passages in the Bible that churchmen run over. Andrew showed me various contradictory passages in the Bible as for example verse concerning eating pork. He showed that the bible has indicated eating pork in some of the passages while it has permitted this in some other passages. Here he addressed me, "Do you think that God has changed his mind?" In comparison with this, he was showing me the persistence of their teachings and their unchangeability. During that period I began to be more doubtful about Christianity and I began to go to ask my religious Christian friends about the verses that I had doubts about. But most of the time they were telling me that I am crazy and they were not willing to discuss the Bible with me because as they said, "It is God's words." 555

After his visit to the mosque, Carl X felt compelled to join the NOI. Even after the brother who invited him got arrested for draft evasion and sent to prison. Carl X explains:

To tell you the truth, I began gradually to quit eating pork or drinking and many other bad habits. It was my interest to attend the meetings in the temple to know more about the bible. At that time my friend Andrew has been sentenced to prison because of his refusing to go to the Army. This event has strengthened my desire to attend the meetings in the Temple because it showed me the virility and courage of the members in such matters as going to the Army. On March, 1942, I went to visit my friend Andrew in his imprisonment and he told me, "Don't worry, Allah is with me." I admired his courage and I felt at that time that I had to join this group. So I went on the following Sunday and I registered as a member.556
PAGE 198-199

Elijah freed on $5000 bond, goes back to Chicago Temple #2

The Hon. Elijah Muhammad was arrested in DC May 6, 1942, but wasn't given or couldn't post bond until May 17, 1942. He stayed approximately 4 months in jail. His bail was finally set at $5,000.00. His followers picked up anything to sell such as scrap iron, bottles and even sticks to earn money to get him out of jail. His wife, Clara Muhammad, dressed in all white, came to D.C. with $5,000 in cash to place bond. Bro. Benjamin recalls:

The Messenger of Allah (Mr. Evans) was held in the D.C. jail for a few months before being released on bail. His bail was set at $5,000.00. The bail money had to be raised by a few followers selling old papers and scrap iron. The $5,000.00 was finally raised in the Chicago and Milwaukee Temples. Sister Clara Muhammad, wife of the Messenger, arrived in Washington, D.C., dressed in a long white robe. She carried a white bag containing the money in pennies, nickels, dimes, quarters and dollars that was raised by his poor followers.[557]

At the time, Sister Clara Muhammad, the Hon. Elijah Muhammad wife, had worked with those in Chicago, and it was just a little bit of them at the time. And she brought down, I never will forget it because she was dressed in white, and she had a bag with money. And she said the believers sold paper and rags, dimes and old carpets and stuff they could bail out. And she walked in there, and they were watching her, the white folks were watching her, and they walked her in the back room and they counted all of those pennies out.[558]

FBI Agents say Elijah was Political Prisoner per President's Orders
After his release, the Federal agents admitted Elijah was originally arrested per the Executive Act (orders) of President Franklin D. Roosevelt. Yet almost immediately after his release, Elijah's lawyer warned him that his life was in danger and he needed to leave the city immediately. Elijah Muhammad recalls:

Soon as I was released, my lawyer heard where my wife and I were. He came and said, "for God's sake, leave the city. They are planning to get rid of you tonight." Pretty soon a white fellow came asking and inquiring where I was going to room. Was I going out tonight, or was I going to stay over? That evening, I boarded a Pennsylvania Limited train to Chicago and arrived the next morning about 8 o'clock. I felt relieved to be out of all that strain, although I was not afraid, because I had not done anything. Those who arrested me told me the same thing...The President [Franklin Delano Roosevelt] just wanted me out of the public.[559]

Temple #2 Welcomes Elijah Home
The Hon. Elijah Muhammad arrived safely in Chicago on September 18, 1942. There he was reunited with old members of the Nation of Islam, as well as become acquainted with new members that joined in his 7 year absence.

Min. James 3X Anderson (who joined in 1941 and would eventually become the future Minister of Temple #2 and Principal of the University of Islam in Chicago) recalls the moment he first laid eyes on the Messenger:

"I'LL NEVER FORGET that moment. When Messenger Muhammad came on the speakers stand, Minister Sultan Muhammad lifted him off the floor. (He was so happy to see him)!"

"That was the most dramatic event that had ever happened in my life, and the most memorable event in my life, the first time I saw Messenger Muhammad. It was a beautiful sight!"[560]

Elijah Warns Chicago FOI of Their Imminent Arrest

Although Elijah was happy to see his followers, the joyous moment would be short-lived as the Messenger shared the news of their eminent persecution in which he along with hundreds of other Fruit of Islam would be arrested in Chicago. His warning became a reality just two days after his arrival: "The Messenger returned to Chicago. On the 18th of September, as the Messenger was teaching the Theology of Time, he told the Muslims to expect some unfortunate events to happen affecting them, but to hold fast to Islam." [561]

FEDS raid the Chicago Temple, Hundreds Arrested

Almost on cue, Elijah's words rung true, as the Federal authorities raided Temple #2 almost arresting all male Muslim members: "On September 20, 1942, the FBI agents arrived at the Temple before the meeting and arrested approximately 100 men of the Fruits of Islam. The Messenger was arrested at his home at 6026 S. Vernon Avenue."[562]

Elijah Leaves a Sign (Ezekiel's Wheel drawing) for the Police

Yet before he was arrested in Chicago, in the same manner as the case in D.C., the Hon. Elijah Muhammad intentionally left evidence for the government to discover once they raided the Temple. NOI Pioneer Bro. Lester X of Chicago explains:

> Then, one fateful Friday night in 1942, The Messenger of Allah, during the course of a lecture, wrote on the blackboard. Though it is usually the custom to erase the board after each meeting, on this occasion he said, "Don't erase what I have written on the board this night, for the devil is surely coming here." On the board he had written the history of the devil.
>
> As he had predicted, the following Sunday we were met at the Mosque by police and taken to jail. They even went to the home of the Messenger and arrested him. [563]

Bro. Lester X (Anthony) again recalls when he finally got to see the Messenger after he came from DC, as well as the events of that Friday night, and their arrests on Sunday:

> We received these messages until 1942, when FBI agents arrested the Honorable Elijah Muhammad in Washington, D.C. We put up a $10,000 cash bond for his release and he came to Chicago to teach us. That was the first time I had seen him, although I had been eager to see him.

The Messenger taught us about the white man and the black man – the original man. He told us about the earth, how it was made, when it was made and about the approximate age of the earth.

AT OUR meeting on a Sunday in 1942, the devil was there to pick us up and take us to jail. They took the blackboard on which was drawn Ezekiel's wheel. We were charged with being pro-Japan. Newspapers branded us a cult. [564]

Muslims Stand in Solidarity Despite Arrests

The Muslims in Chicago stood in solidarity attempting to come to each others' aid from the arresting officers. Min. James 3X Anderson (Shabazz) recalls:

My first impression of the unity of the Muslims was when we were arrested in 1942, when the police made a raid on the Temple. All of the Muslims wanted to be in on it, not trying to avoid it. They were saying. 'Yes arrest me, I want to be with my brother' this was really my first impression of unity solidarity.[565]

NOI Pioneer Brother Lambus X also present at the Temple that day recalls their arrest and how led it to jail time alongside Elijah Muhammad and other FOI at the Federal Correctional Prison in Michigan:

Interviewer: When did you first accept Islam?
Bro. Lambus X: In 1933.
Interviewer: Tell us about the arrest incident of the Muslims in 1942 at the Temple
Bro. Lambus X: September 20, 1942, at 104 E. 51st Street. One Sunday morning we went to a meeting, and the FBI I think had broke in the door and everyone that came in they arrested them and put them in jail and we got sentenced by Judge Barnes. I was sent to Milan, Michigan. And January 25, 1945, we were released.
Interviewer: What were you arrested for?
Bro. Lambus X: I was arrested for Selective Service for not going to the Army.[566]

During the incarceration of the Messenger and his followers at Chicago's Temple #2, the Milwaukee Temple #3 would cover down for their incarcerated brothers: "During the Honorable Elijah Muhammad's and his followers unjust incarceration, the believing community of Milwaukee collected scrap metal, tires, and anything redeemable to support the Messenger's wife and family until his release on August 24th, 1946. [567]

MUSLIMS SENTENCED TO JAIL

In October the Messenger and some of his followers appeared in the Chicago courts on counts of failing to register for the United States Army. The Chicago Defender reported: **CULTISTS 'GUILTY'; 32 GIVEN JAIL SENTENCES, 3 Others Face Federal court For Sedition; Men Spurn Legal Aid Offered by Judge; Put Trust in Allah; The Chicago Defender, Oct. 10, 1942**

Federal Judge John P. Barnes cracked down Monday and sentenced 31 members of the Temple of Islam cult to three-year penitentiary terms after they had pleaded guilty to charges of failure to register under the Selective Service Act. Another cultist [Elijah Muhammad and his son Emanuel Muhammad] in court of the same charge drew a sentence of five years on a similar plea.

Six other followers of the mystic organization entered not guilty pleas and were arraigned Tuesday, Oct. 7.

Those sentenced to three years are:

John Tillman, alias John 5X
Nolan Cobbins, alias Nolan X
Russell Hughes, alias Russell X
Zack Walker, alias Zack Hassan
Alphonso Hatchett, alias Alphonso Pasha
Willie Mohammed
Benny Walker, alias Benny Allah
Harry X
Alla Armstead
Volger Paul Williams, alias Volger X
Nathan Robinson, alias Nathan X
Robert Woodward, alias Robert X
Lee Davis, alias Lee
James Anderson, alias James 3X
Leslie Fairrow, alias Leslie X
Paska [sic], alias Paska X
Shelby Karrien
John 3X
Robert Moore, alias Robert X
James 6X
Mambus X, alias Lambert X
Reiser Shah
Lester X
Allar Shah, alias Allar Shah
David X
Kasskar Ali
Charles Turner, alias Charles X
Clarence Bronston, alias Clarence X
Karrien Allah
Willie White, alias Willie X

Leonard X[568]

The same article captured the defiant attitudes of the Muslims toward their persecutors, singling out remarks from Elijah's son Emanuel who was given the maximum penalty: "Sentence to five years was Emmanuel Karrien, alias Emmanuel Mohammed, alias Robert Bridgeman, son of Muck Muhd a leader of the religious order. When sentence was passed, Karrien, head teacher of the temple, declared: "I hope the Japs win the war. Then all the Negroes will be free!"[569]

The majority of Muslims waived the right to lawyers while under interrogation and candidly restated their religious beliefs and allegiance to Allah and the Hon. Elijah Muhammad, while a minority reiterated the same, yet sought legal advice per their not guilty plea:

Assistant United States District Attorney Kiely asked each of the defendants why they failed to register for the draft and each gave identically the same answer: "I registered with Allah."

Allah is the God of the Mohammedan religion and the power Muck Muhd is said to wield among the Islams stems from the belief that he is Allah's earthly representative. His followers are alleged to call him "prophet."

All of the convicted cultists flatly refused legal counsel offered by the court explaining that they were being represented by Allah. The only exceptions to the disdain for legal advise came when six of the cultists pleaded not guilty. They accepted the services of Atty. Bentley Pike appointed by Judge Barnes. They are:

Sam Davis, alias Sam X
Leamon Thorton, alias Leamon X
Raymond Tharrieff
Farroz Jordan, alias Frazefe
Frank Eskeridge, ...alias Frank 2X
George Hawkins, alias George X[570]

Lastly, the papers reported the fate of Elijah Muhammad and his Minister of Temple #2 Linn Karriem and NOI National Secretary Pauline Bahar (the two later would become a couple). Yet, while the Government successfully prosecuted them for draft evasion, they failed in their case to prove a treason conspiracy:

During the trial members and followers of the Temple of Islam sat in the courtroom garbed in ceremonial robes with stoical expressions on their faces. There were no demonstrations by the cultists many of whom are educated and cultured folk.

Observers of the proceedings felt that the conviction on charges of draft evasion cleared the defendants arrested last week in wholesale arrests by

FBI agents of any connections with Japanese espionage. The government's attempt to build a case of sedition against them evidentally collapsed.

Efforts were made to convict some of the cultists on sedition charges when they were arraigned in federal court Tuesday. They are Gulam Bogans, alias Elijah Mohammed, alias Muck Muhd: Lenzie Karrien, and Pauline Bahar. These three are regarded as the top leaders of the cult.

They are said to have engaged in seditious acts by telling Islams: "Don't register for the draft." "You should not serve under the American flag." "You should not take up arms against the Japs," "The Japs are not our enemies."[571]

Muslims Believe Charges are Racially Motivated

The Hon. Elijah Muhammad and his followers insisted that the persecution and court case of the Muslims was a mere charade sponsored by the U.S. Government:

> Muhammad and his followers believe that they were imprisoned because of their religious beliefs. He asserts that "the devil cooked up the charges," and that he was "tried and imprisoned for teaching my people the truth about themselves." The services of an attorney could be of no help – "because the devil wanted to shut me up any way." Although Muhammad accepted legal counsel, his followers did not: "We rejected joining the war on religious grounds. We were offered legal counsel by the government and we declined the offer because we knew it would not do us any good if the government provided counsel." [572] James 3X Anderson

Years later Elijah would recall how many Muslims became casualties of the courts and prison system for their stance against the war:

> In the year 1942-1943, according to reports, there were nearly a hundred of my followers sentenced to prison terms of from 1 to 5 years for refusing to take part in the war between America, Japan and Germany because of our peaceful stand and the principle belief and practice in Islam, which is peace.[573]

Muslims go to Jail

After that they sent me, for five years, to the Federal Correctional Institution. That was Milan, Michigan. I stayed there approximately three years and five months. I stayed in jail in Chicago for approximately 11 months. I tried to eat the food the best I could. Actually, they wanted to force the Muslims to eat pig. I thought this was pretty bad, when their own Bible taught them not to eat it.[574]

Muslims Sentenced to Different Prisons

After served time in the Cook County jail, the government decided to split up the Muslims by sending them to different jails throughout the country. The majority (including Elijah Muhammad) were sentenced to serve their time at Milan, Michigan, while many others were shipped to Minnesota, including James 3X Anderson and Min. Sultan Muhammad. Min. James 3X Anderson (Shabazz) recalls: Messenger Muhammad was sent to Milan, Michigan, to the Federal institution there. Most of us brothers were sent up to Sandstone, Minnesota, a Correctional Institution in Sandstone, Minnesota.[575] NOI History records: "After Minister Sultan Muhammad was arrested and sent to Sandstone Federal Correctional Institution in Minnesota, the post of local representative [for Milwaukee] was given to Minister John 3X...."[576]

Emanuel Sentenced Along with his Father Elijah

Elijah's eldest son Emanuel Muhammad was also sentenced to prison. He recalls the chain of events leading up to his incarceration:

> During the year 1941, when the Japanese attacked Pearl Harbor, The Messenger was arrested in the Nation's capital (Washington D.C.) and placed in jail. His poor beloved followers took up a collection of $500 to bail Him out of jail. My mother [Clara Muhammad] and a well devoted brother took the money and went to Washington and bailed the Messenger out. My beloved mother and the brother are no longer with us. He [The Hon. Elijah Muhammad] returned home for a short time.
>
> On September 20, 1942, the Messenger was arrested here [Chicago] and some of His followers were sent to various governmental institutions during World War II for our religious beliefs. The Messenger and I were given a five – year sentence, and the rest of His followers received sentences ranging from one year to three years.[577]

Muslim Prisoners Treated Harshly at Milan, Michigan

Initially the Government decided to keep Elijah and others they viewed as NOI leaders in the Chicago jail for a few more months, while they sent his son Emanuel and other Chicago FOI in advance to Milan, Michigan, to join the DC FOI that were already at the Federal Prison. There the FOI were made to do harsh work. Min. Benjamin X. Mitchell recalls:

> The Muslims who went to prison for believing in Islam and following the Honorable Elijah Muhammad were really tried by the officials of this Christian government. I remember a few months before the Messenger was transferred to the prison in Milan, Michigan, the official had us (Brothers Harry X, Karriem Allah, Emanuel Muhammad and Benjamin) unloading some cars of soft coal along with some real hard criminals. Guards were on each end of the cars and were standing on the ground with high-powered rifles, keeping watch over us as if we were murders. Our faces and clothing were black with coal dust.
>
> Finally, one day while working on the farm, an officer called for me to report to the Carpenter's Shop for work. I remained in the Carpenter's Shop until my four years were served.[578]

[294]

Elijah Reunites with Muslim Prisoners in Milan

A few months later the Hon. Elijah Muhammad was transferred to Milan Penitentiary where he and others were reunited with their brothers of the Fruit of Islam from DC, Chicago and around the country. Min. Benjamin X Mitchell jubilantly recalls the day Elijah Muhammad and his prison entourage arrived:

> About three months after our arrival, the Friday before Easter in 1943, one of the officials told us that they were expecting two more of our "Moslem" brothers that afternoon. The officer looked toward the Administration building and said, "That looks like them now coming through the gate." We rushed to the front gate to see who the brothers were, and behold: it was the Honorable Elijah Muhammad and Brother Minister Lynn Karriem of Chicago.[579]

Upon their reunion, Emanuel recalls his father Elijah Muhammad reiterating to him his faith in Master Fard Muhammad in the midst of their prison ordeal:

> When I was incarcerated with my father during World War II, my father said to me, "Son, I want to tell you something. When I grew into my first knowledge of Master Fard, I went to him and asked him was he our long-awaited Jesus that the world been looking for for the past two thousand years?" He said, "Son, Master Fard said to me, 'Yes, I am that one that the world been looking for for the last two thousand years.'"
> Then he said that after he grew more and more into the knowledge of Master Fard, he went to him the second time, and asked him, "Are you the God that's supposed to come and separate the righteous from the wicked and destroy the wicked?"
> He said, "Master Fard's eyes grew small and he changed to a reddish complexion and said to me, with his finger pointed in my face, 'Who would believe that but you?'"[580]

Elijah Examined by Prison Psychologists

In prison Elijah underwent an entrance examination and answered a prison psychiatrist that if they were to let him go right now, he still wouldn't enlist in the army even if they assured him he would not be called for military service. The prison psychiatrist reported that Elijah started teaching him on the grave injustices inflicted upon black people by whites, including personal instances of how his family was mistreated in 1941 by the Chicago Welfare Association.

One of the prison sociologists felt: "He apparently accepts his present situation with the attitude of a martyr, but it is felt that he will adjust here without difficulty. Prognosis for future adjustment will be dependent upon the status of war."[581]

The prison psychiatrist Dr. W. S. Kennison was less optimistic, on July 26, 1943, he wrote: "His mental trend and thought content revealed that he does have a marked persecutory trend, both against himself and his race (Negro). He does admit having visual hallucinations, visions as he called them, in which the supreme Allah would come to him and talk with him. He also reveals that, on numerous occasions, he has had the feeling that he is being followed and that people are talking about him. In general, his attitude is that of his own superiority."[582]

The doctor further recommended Elijah Muhammad be interviewed by psychiatrists during frequent intervals: "While it is felt that this individual is suffering from paranoid schizophrenia, he is what is classified as an ambulatory type who has made an adjustment to his psychosis that will not probably render him into any adjustment difficulties."[583]

Elijah Muhammad's wife Clara serves as 2nd in Command of NOI

While the Hon. Elijah Muhammad was in prison, his wife was the first to go visit him in Milan. The Messenger's brother John Muhammad recalls accompanying her on their first visit to prison: "Minister Norman Noble and myself motored Sister Clara Muhammad to Milan, Michigan to see her husband, the Honorable Elijah Muhammad"[584] Other wives of members could also visit them, except they were not allowed to bring in unapproved books, especially the Holy Quran. Min. Benjamin X. Mitchell recalls: "The penal institution didn't permit the Muslim Bible (Quran) into the institution at that time. My wife was permitted to visit me. Also, the Messenger's wife was permitted to visit him."[585]

With her husband incarcerated the lot of leadership was assigned to Sister Clara Muhammad and the two served as a tandem as Elijah continued to run the Nation of Islam from prison through his wife Sister Clara Muhammad who served as the interim leader of the NOI. She was responsible for typing and bringing NOI lessons and verses from the Quran to her husband. She was also responsible for disseminating information to NOI officials of the four Temples. Her son Emanuel Muhammad recalls:

Q. How was the Nation of Islam run during this period?
A. Sister Clara Muhammad was the first of the family to accept the mission of the Honorable Elijah Muhammad. She held the Muhammad family together all the while he was on the run. And, while he was in prison, the remaining officials would seek information from her. "She would bring understanding from my father on questions she could not answer. She gathered and sent or brought to my father and I whatever literature the

prison permitted. She typed verses from the Holy Quran and sent them to us.[586]

Emanuel reiterates the role his mother played at this time:

"She held our family together all the while he was on the run. And while he was in prison the remaining officials would seek information from her. "She would bring understanding from my father on questions she could not answer – She gathered and sent or brought to my father and I whatever literature the prison permitted. "She typed verses from the Holy Quran and sent them to us. In general she held the family together all the while my father was in prison...."[587]

With Most FOI in Prison, MGT carried the Weight

NOI Pioneer John Hassan remembers how the NOI ranks were decimated per the majority of the FOI being sent to prisons throughout America and how the FOI and MGT rallied under the banner of Islam:

We faced some hard times during those early years in Islam. We were laughed at, scorned and persecuted but these trials only made our faith that much stronger.

During World War II there were even hints that we sympathized with the enemy and there were whispers of sedition and other terrible crimes. None had any basis of fact.

In spite of this, all the Brothers including Messenger Muhammad were sent to prison and charged with evading the draft. Only three or four older brothers, myself included, did not go to prison.

THIS SMALL flock clung together – bound by the teachings of Messenger Muhammad – and even managed to attract new converts. We didn't have any money to buy and no one would rent us a hall. But we met as usual in our homes.

Our Sisters, members of the M.G.T. and G.C.C., withstood the test. Many had to work at hard and back breaking labor. By the sheer strength of their faith in Allah they held their families together until their husbands were released.

From time to time we received words of encouragement from our leader, the Honorable Elijah Muhammad, sent by members of his family. These messages always lifted my spirits. To think that Messenger Muhammad could be locked up in jail and yet send us words of encouragement. The love this man has for us just cannot be measured in words. [588]

First MGT Uniforms Designed

Sister Clara Muhammad, Sis. Burnsteen Sharrieff-Mohammed and other Muslim sisters kept the MGT class in accordance and up-to-date with the Messenger's teachings. In 1943, official uniforms were adopted for the class. Elijah's brother Supreme Min. John Muhammad explains:

Messenger Elijah Muhammad set his Black Woman in Garments of righteousness, after they had agreed that Allah is God and Allah came in the Person of Master Fard Muhammad to Whom praise is due forever. These Sisters in the Muslim Girls Training and General Civilization Class began about 1943, wearing uniforms of 1.) Red, 2.) Green and 3.) White. They were not ashamed of boarding and trolley cars or to walk up and down the streets going to their Temple meetings on Wednesday, Friday and Sunday.

The M.G.T. and G.C.C. looked so beautiful, they took the eyes of all that saw them, also, they were respected by many of the so-called "high class" Black and white Americans. The people of the East began to admire the Black Woman of the West and gave Honor to Messenger Elijah Muhammad (PBUH) for the cleaning up the Black Woman from the lowest life in disrespect of civilization. [589]

MGT Class Training

Elijah's brother, John Muhammad explains the integral teaching and training of MGT class at the time:

Mr. Muhammad taught this class to first respect self and clean up from the filthy life they were in, to take a bath each morning, stop drinking strong drinks, using drugs, or anything that will cause them to be other than self. Mr. Muhammad gave special books on "How to Eat to Live," and by these books, the (M.G.T. & G.C.C.) became to create and make up their own recipes or dishes of clean, Muslim Food.

This class became the first people to serve the Navy Bean. They dismissed altogether, the cooking and eating of the poison swine and did not use any part of his essence. They became most careful in the cooking and eating of the wrong food. The wives in M.G.T. & G.C.C. would examine the food brought in the home, being sure, it was the right food for her husband and children to eat as taught by her great Messenger, the Honorable Elijah Muhammad (P.B.U.H.). each mother kept her children clean for school and Worship Meeting, and kept away from the use of things that destroy the physical and mental power. She taught them how to love self and kind, how to give respect to all people, regardless of color of skin or religion or profession. The M.G.T. & G.C.C. worked with the University of Islam, or whatever school their children attended, so the child could be able to use his creative mind, Mr. Muhammad said, the greatest mind. MR. Muhammad said, the greatest teaching to give a child while it is young is to teach him or her "self-respect first." This way a child can learn respect of others. Both go together. Self-respect demands self to respect others. This kind of teaching brings up a respected Nation of people.[590]

Chicago Temple that was raided by the Police

6026 S. Vernon Avenue, Elijah's house where he was arrested

The Hon. Elijah Muhammad arrested by the FBI in 1942

Elijah Muhammad mugshot from Cook County Jail.

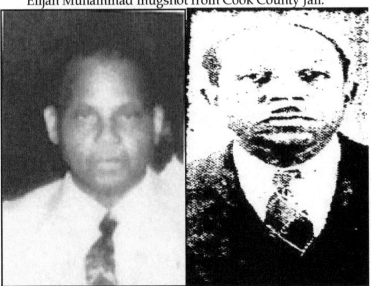

Min. Sultan Muhammad, Min. Linn Karriem (circa 1942). Both were arrested and sent to jail for draft evasion along with hundreds of other Muslims

(first row L-R) Minister Isaiah Karriem, Bro. Clarence, Bro. Elmer, Minister Sultan Muhammad, Minister James 3X McGregor Shabazz, Minister Benjamin Muhammad and Bro. Jake. (second row) Bro. Charles X Worthington, Bro. Richard, Bro. John, Bro. Herbert, and other NOI Pioneers of Washington, D.C.

Sis. Clara Muhammad was instrumental in the leadership of the NOI while her husband and many other Ministers and members were in prison.

Black Muslim women await the beginning of court hearing that involved three Chicago-based Nation of Islam leaders in late 1942. Women took a more active role in running the movement during World War II, when many of the Nation's male followers were imprisoned for refusing to fulfill their U.S. military service obligations.

1942 Muslims going to jail for NOT FIGHTING IN DEVILS WAR* "FEDERAL SENTENCING FOR 32 MEMBERS OF CHICAGO NEGRO TEMPLE OF ISLAM"

"Some of the Negro cultist on their way to jail after recieving three year sentence by Federal Judge John P. Barnes in the U.S. Courthouse. Thirty "Temple of Islam" members pleaded guilty to fail to register; another plead guilty to failure to filling out a draft questionaire, and another was given five years after admitting he was a special lecturer.".........from Boston newspaper archives [Oct 6, 1942]
AMONG THEM RAYMOND SHARRIEFF

Aerial View of Milan Federal Correctional Facility

During his incarceration in the Federal Correctional Institution at Milan, Michigan, Muhammad and others were expected to subsist on a diet that included pork (*see posted menu*). The leader would later attribute some of his post-prison ailments to the dietary arrangements at Milan.

(Courtesy of the Bureau of Prisons)

Milan Federal Correctional Facility Mess Hall.

The Hon. Elijah Muhammad's wife Clara (circa 1943)

The First MGT Uniforms (circa 1943), photos courtesy of
the Milwaukee Pioneers and the noiarchives.org

The result of MGT class was to earn the respect of the people and nations for Muslim women. John explains:

> I believe this has caused people of America and Kings of the East, to regard and give respect to the Honorable Elijah Muhammad, because in his teaching, the Black woman is known to be the Mother of Civilization regardless of how her past being called or known as nothing. The Honorable Elijah Muhammad taught the Black man or Brother that belongs to the Fruit of Islam to respect, honor and protect his Black woman here in America with his life, because the Black woman is the Mother of All nations, regardless of what part of the earth they are found. If there is any civilization or human being there, we know that the Blackman and Black woman are the beginning of that Nation. This was taught by Master Fard Muhammad in the word of question No. 1 of the Student Enrollment, and its answer.[591]

MGT Pioneers in Home Schooling

Sister Clara Muhammad and the M.G.T. kept open the doors of their homes for the purposes of teaching Muslim children. Many say that the Nation of Islam were pioneers for "home-schooling". NOI Pioneer Sister Lois X describes how they cared for the children in the absence of the men:

> **Interviewer:** Tell us how life was for the Muslim Women while their husbands were imprisoned?
> **Lois X:** Well, the children, I worked and I cared for them very well. And when my husband returned, they were well taken care of. I had plenty of food and everything the household needed.
> **Interviewer:** What were some of the things that took place while your husband was away in the Temple?]
> **Lois X:** Well, only the children, I kept the children in school and I was harassed about them being outside school, you know, public school, bringing them in, no problems at all, I kept them in the Muslim School and took care of them very well by working.[592]

Emanuel recalls how his mother was threatened by the FBI and still refuse to shut down the Muslim school program: "When my father and I were in prison, the F.B.I. approached my mother and told her that she would have to return the children to the devil's school. She told them she would rather die first.[593]

Small Intimate Saviours Day Celebrations

The small group of FOI, MGT and children left behind, participated in annual "Savior's Day" gatherings at homes of believers to celebrate the birthday of NOI founder Master Fard Muhammad. In these hard times, Believers exchanged modest gifts to celebrate. Imam W.D. Mohammed vividly remembers the time period:

I remember Savior's Day in Chicago, when the Hon. Elijah Muhammad and most of the men, the old and young, were in prison, because they refused to sign draft cards for World War II. We had mostly sisters and just a few brothers left.

Those brothers did not have to go to jail, because they were too old for the army. All they had to do is sign a draft card, and they would have been spared that three years, and some of them got five years. My father was too old for the army, but my brother was young enough to be drafted. They were drafting everybody in World War II. You had to be drafted, even if you didn't go to the army. So these men served long prison terms.

As a young boy of maybe 10 years old [1943], I remember attending Savior's Day in a house that couldn't hold more than about 30 people. It was the house belonging to a believer, a Muslim sister. It was near the street now called Martin Luther King Drive and 32nd Street. At that time it was called South Park.

In this big wonderful city of Chicago, you would think that homes had electric lights for everybody, but no. The poor had coal oil lamps, and you could smell the fumes while you were in the house. It was poorly lighted and some areas were shadowy. The light thrown out was to brighten the whole upstairs where we were having Savior's Day. But we were happy.

We were happier than we are now. Maybe now the excitement is worn off. I am still very happy. But most of us have been knocked down and all of the spirit has been knocked out of us. We didn't have anything, but we had what we cherished as being more important. We had a belief that G-d had loved us and that G-d had sent a help to us and that we were the Lost-Found Nation of Islam. We had what was more important to us than food or fancy, fine buildings.

There was a habit of giving out delicious apples, and February was a good month for that. We had these good, solid, nice apples that I remember biting into as a child and it was so nice! Everybody got a free delicious apple on Savior's Day. This was the Savior's Day celebration. What I want to do on this occasion is to talk about Savior's Day. We didn't expect anybody to talk to us about anything other than Savior's Day and what it meant to us.

Savior's Day is meant to be a day of remembrance and celebration. The Hon. Elijah Muhammad, on most Savior's Days, would begin by talking about his savior, Mr. W. F. Muhammad. He also was called W. D. Fard and by different names, but I am mentioning now W. F. Muhammad, because he said in his own words: "My name is W. F. Muhammad. I came to North America by myself...."[594]

Tribulations of Prison Life in Milan and Sandstone Prisons
NOI Pioneer Lester X Anthony who was incarcerated with and accompanied the Messenger to Milan FCI recalls the time and the initial negative reaction they received from the general population of inmates in jail:

[308]

They sentenced Messenger Muhammad to 5 years. I only got three years but Allah blessed me to serve my time with our Beloved Leader and Teacher, the Most Honorable Elijah Muhammad. LITTLE HAD I realized when I accepted the faith that becoming a Muslim would try my faith in Allah through persecution and imprisonment simply because we believed in the oneness of God.[595] We were sentenced to the U.S. prison at Milan, Mich. Nine of us were sent to Milan, including the Messenger and I. The rest went to Minnesota. Because of the pro-Jap news stories, our black prison brothers treated us with indifference at first. Eventually, they inquired about the truth of the charge. "We are not pro-Japan, but Japan is an island kingdom of Islam," they were told. "We have Muslim brothers in Japan." Soon, they began to understand.[596]

The same was the fate of the FOI sentenced to the penitentiary in Sandstone, Minnesota. There Min. Sultan Muhammad and other FOI such as Min. James 3X Anderson (Shabazz) would navigate their way through tough terrain by becoming model prisoners and holding study circles among themselves studying NOI teachings:

Min. James Shabazz: Messenger Muhammad was sent to Milan, Michigan, to the Federal institution there. Most of us brothers were sent up to Sandstone, Minnesota, a Correctional Institution in Sandstone, Minnesota.
Interviewer: What was the typical day for the followers of the Hon. Elijah Muhammad during these times while you were in prison?
Min. James Shabazz: Well after the period of quarantine was over then we were assigned different jobs there in the institution. And after these jobs were done then we would go back to our prison dormitory and we would then set up classes. And these classes would consist of the recitations of the various Lessons we were given, plus Mathematics, English, Languages, Science and History.[597]

Elijah Muhammad Prison Duties, Assembles Prison Study Groups
Forever being the best example for his followers, while in Milan F.C.I., the Hon. Elijah Muhammad taught the FOI in study circles and became the ideal example of a model prisoner although initially he'd be severely tried by the prison guards. Benjamin X Mitchell recalls such a test that involved a pig farm on the prison land:

The Messenger was locked behind the prison bars for five years. During his lockup, the prison officials tried him out with food that was cooked with hog meat and also tried to work him in the pig house where hogs were raised. A few weeks after the arrival of the Messenger, one officer was sent out with a truckload of work-release inmates to the piggery. When the truck arrived, the officer said, "O.K., fellows, this is our working spot." All of the inmates got off the truck except the Messenger. He remained on the truck and said to the officer, "I am willing to work, but not in this hog house. If you have another job that you could give me, I would appreciate it very much. Working with hogs is against my religious belief." The officer said, "I will take you back to the office for further instructions." On returning to the officer with the Messenger, the officer reported that he had an inmate whose name was Bogan that could not work in the piggery because it was against his religion. The Captain said to the officer, "I didn't intend for you to take him out there." The Captain had the officer to open the gate and let Bogan in. The Captain said to Bogan, "Your job will be to take care of the Officers' Quarters as long as you are here."[598]

Elijah Highly Respected by Inmates and Guards

The F.O.I. in Milan noted the kind of respect Elijah Muhammad garnered from inmates and prison guards as he was given his new assignment as an inmate: "The Honorable Elijah Muhammad was a model prisoner. Respected by inmates and guards alike, he was made an orderly in charge of the Guard's Quarters, and continued to teach salvation to his followers in the prison, who were Black in the Milan Federal Prison."[599]

All of the F.O.I. was given their posts as inmates, and forever mindful of staying close to their leader. In fact Milan FCI set it up so that the majority of the Muslims could stay in one dormitory. Many helped the Hon. Elijah Muhammad after their assignments per the love and respect of their leader and the brotherhood of the F.O.I., Bro. Lester X recalls a special moment he shared with the Hon. Elijah Muhammad:

Well I was in Milan Michigan, the Federal Institution. I became to be one of the first trustees. And I had taken care of the warden's little grandson. The Holy Apostle had a special assignment from us, and that was in the Officer's quarters. So when I get off early, I would go by and help him get through early so he can come in and teach the brothers in the evening. And he taught me how to pray. While I was in there, I thought I knew when I first went. But after I got with him, helping him get through, he blessed me with teaching me a special prayer for him. I have a special prayer that he taught me especially for him alone. And therefore, our first time being there, when coming out, Officer Whitehead, before we was getting ready to leave, he said to me (coming with the Holy Apostle), he said, "9740, you glad you going home now, aren't ya?" I told him, "No sir, Mr. Whitehead. I'd rather for the Holy Apostle to go and I stay here."[600]

After becoming acclimated to his prison duties, the Hon. Elijah Muhammad established the study times for his small group of followers. Benjamin recalls: "A few weeks later, after Messenger Muhammad had settled down to his prison assignment (job), he began to hold Muslim services each Sunday at 2pm. The Muslim Brotherhood in the institution numbered about 10 or 12. They were from Chicago and Washington, D.C."[601]

Muslims Prisoners Food Protest (pork)

Perhaps the greatest battle between Muslims and prison authorities was over the food served in the prison. Muslims off course didn't eat any pork, yet the prison wasn't willing to accommodate the Muslims by offering pork-free meals (at least not initially). The Most Hon. Elijah Muhammad speaks on his battle with the prison authorities over this issue:

> I have experience in living and eating according to the way He [Master Fard] taught me for a while and I found it one of the happiest and most peaceful ways of which I ever dreamed. I began with eating one meal a day and forced my family to do the same for several years, until I was picked up and sent to prison for teaching Islam in 1942. Of course, the government said they sent me up for failing to register. That really was not the reason, for I did not come under the draft law at that time. Some of my followers, 60 and 65 years old, were sent to prison at the same time. Persons of such an age were not desired by the War Department.
>
> There in prison, the Christians made it hard for us to live as we had been. They deliberately put swine, or the essence of the swine, in everything and the assistant warden made mock of it when I told him my followers lived on nothing but bread to avoid swine. He said that even the bread had swine in it. We used to make a meal of dry baked white potatoes. We had it hard— and all my followers now in prison still have it hard. All those converted to Islam in prison at present suffer in order to avoid eating the divinely prohibited flesh of the swine. And all that God said, "Thou Shalt Not Do," they said, "Thou Shalt Do." You who read this article know the Christians are the great false teachers of God, who care nothing for Allah's (God's) law.[602]

The staff of the prison cafeteria tried to trick the Muslims often into eating pork. These antics caused the FOI to go for days without hardly any food. Benjamin X recalls one of the many instances and how the Messenger decided to handle it:

> I learned in Islam that the disbelievers will continue to try to persuade or influence the believers to follow them. I remember one week while in prison, the Muslims had not eaten a full meal for four days or more. The chief cook in the institution called out over the P.A. system that the Muslims could report for dinner. "We have a pork free navy been dinner for you," he said. The Honorable Elijah Muhammad happened to be in his dormitory at the time the call was made. When we Brothers came in from work at noon, the Messenger told us to report to the dining hall for a specially prepared dinner for us. He said, "You all may go if you care to. I am not going. I don't care for anything." We Muslim brothers reported to the dining hall and had our bowls filled to the top because we had not eaten anything but white bread, water and coffee. We all were seated at the table. Before eating any of the

beans, the Messenger's son, Emanuel, found some small blocks or squares of white pork meat cut up and cooked in the beans. Brother Emanuel Muhammad said to us, "Pork is in the beans." We rechecked and found the pork. All of the brothers sat at the table quietly. The officer of the dining hall came to our table and asked, "What's wrong with the beans? I see you are not eating." Brother Emanuel replied, "You have pork in the beans." The officer said, "Those beans are pork free." Brother Emanuel showed the pork meat to the officer. The officer of the dining room called the chief cook of the kitchen to the front and said, "They claim that you have small blocks of pork meat in the beans and they are not going to eat." The chief cook replied, "It's not suppose to be any pork in the beans. I told the cook not to cook pork in the beans." Brother Emanuel handed a spoon full to the chief cook. He tasted it and said, "Yes, pork is in the beans. You brothers are not required to eat the beans." We dismissed ourselves from the table and returned to our dormitory.

We reported to the Messenger what had happened and he said, "Well brothers, you see the enemy of Islam is trying to get us to bow to him." Later, the chief cook explained to us what happened to the supposedly pork free bean dinner. He said the cook in the kitchen at the institution was a member of the white Jehovah's Witnesses and they were enemies of Islam. One of the witnesses thought that he could cut up fine pieces of pork and we wouldn't be able to tell the difference.[603]

Elijah's Wisdom on how to handle Prison Diet

Bro. Lester X speaks on another similar case of the FOI bout with prison authorities trying to feed them pork, and how the Messenger handled it:

When we first arrived at the prison, one of the big problems was that they always seemed to put pork in all of the food. Mr. Muhammad instructed us to stay out of the dining room and we did this for three days.

ON THAT third day, one of the Brothers was so weak that the Honorable Elijah Muhammad told us we would all go over and have coffee.

Our arrival in the dining room was greeted with calls of, "Here, Mr. Muhammad, have some pork. We've got pork in everything."

Always the master of everything, the Messenger of Allah simply smiled as we took our coffee and drank. After we had our coffee, we left.

That night, around midnight, the guard called all the Muslims by name and told us to get dressed and that he would be back for us as soon as he made his rounds.

WE DRESSED quietly, wondering all the while what was going to happen and certain that no good would come of it. But trusting Allah and the wisdom of His Messenger, we sat and waited.

Then, on the return of the guard, we lined up in twos and followed him. To our surprise, he led us straight to the dining room.

There we were greeted by bright lights and the officer in charge, who told us that food had been prepared for us—food which contained no pork.

[312]

We were told that we would be allowed to select one from among us to prepare our food and that in the future we could eat in a section to ourselves. This night, they had prepared fried chicken, hot rolls, rice and peas. That dinner was delicious! [604]

Emanuel says that fellow prisoners empathized with the plight of the Muslims: "Inmates who worked in the fields would secure food for us to eat because of the difficulty we had getting something we could eat."[605]

Prison Authorities and Inmates Eventually Honor Muslim Diet

Bro. Karriem Allah says that things got better for the Muslims in prison after several months passed by and they gained the trust of Prison authorities:

Life in the prison with the Messenger for the first four months in prison was rather hard on us because the prison authorities didn't understand us. Well, after we were there for four months. Then they began to understand us and began to relinquish some of their restrictions on us. We were able to move around in the prison freely without any hindrance. Now the food in the prison wasn't good, because we being Muslims, we could not eat any kind of food. Most of the food that was cooked in prison was cooked with pork. And this is forbidden to be eaten by a Muslim. So our life in prison was good after we were there for about six months. Then things began to get better for us then.[606]

Bro. Lester X Anthony seems to verify the same of how things got better, including his personal relationship with the Messenger and how their small group of 10 or 12 Muslims grew to over 400 members at Milan F.C.I. who eventually accepted the teachings of the Hon. Elijah Muhammad:

Our big prison headache was food. There was pig in everything. We had to endure it until special arrangements were made to provide us with a Muslim cook. Brother Leonard X became our cook. We continued to convert while in prison until our Muslim numbers were greatly increased. I STAYED with the Honorable Elijah Muhammad as much as possible. We were inseparable until I was granted a parole, which I wanted to "blow" in order to remain beside the Messenger.[607]

Our stay in prison was a most eventful period in my life.

During those weeks and months I spent a great deal of time with our Holy apostle and he taught me much.

I used to say to him, "Dear Brother Muhammad, I don't know how I shall remember all the things you are teaching me."

HIS REPLY WAS ALWAYS, "Brother Lester, you'll remember everything I teach you." This has certainly proven true.

All the Muslims stayed in one dormitory. At first the other prisoners resented us because they had been told that we were pro-Japanese, and our country was then at war with Japan.

But after they had met the Messenger of Allah and heard his teachings, this attitude changed. Before long, almost all of the Negroes in the prison, about 450, were calling one another "Brother."[608]

Elijah's Holds Temple Sessions in Prison

Emanuel explains how the Hon. Elijah Muhammad never allowed any confrontations in prison set him back. On the contrary he held routine meetings for the Muslims and sympathizers in the prison. At the same time he entertained debaters who rejected the teachings, as well as exposed to those who wanted to harm him for his teachings to the point of exhaustion:

This did not stop the Messenger from teaching his profound religious teachings that He received from Almighty Allah (God). He called His followers together on Wednesday and Friday evenings for worship, also on Sunday afternoons at 2:00 p.m. He made many converts of the prisoners. Some of them, when they were set free became ministers of Islam. Some of the ignorant Black prisoners said to the white guards, if you give me a gun I will shoot all those Muslims down.

During our time of imprisonment, other prisoners used to debate with Him on their religious beliefs, such as the Jehovah's Witnesses and the Moorish American. He put them all to flight.

While I am preparing this article, I cannot help from shedding tears over how much my beloved father suffered for the love of His people. Sometimes after a very busy day he was so fatigued that I felt like carrying Him and placing Him upon His bed.[609]

With his efforts paying off, Elijah Muhammad established a "Temple" in the Prison (complete with the "Christianity vs Islam: Which one will survive the war of Armageddon" black board). Elijah's congregation became stronger, even making prison guards curious. Emanuel:

What has impressed me most, I think, was my stay with my father in prison. He set up a Temple in the prison despite the difficulties he experienced with the blackboard and all. He set up classes right there in prison. He would teach on Wednesday and Friday evenings until the bugle was blown for us to go to bed. He also taught on Sunday afternoons at 2:00pm. He made many, many converts in prison. Even the devils who came by to steal an earful wound up bowing in agreement, an unconscious bearing of witness to the truth The Messenger taught.[610]

Emanuel adds: "Once in a group discussion with my father [in prison], a white physician admitted that it is a known medical and scientific fact that white people came from Black people."[611]

Elijah's and Muslims Relationships with Caucasian Prisoners

Lester X goes farther into the incidents shared by Elijah Muhammad and the Muslims with prison authorities and other Caucasian inmates:

> I have described how during our stay in prison, all the Muslims stayed in one dormitory.
>
> When the other inmates discovered how well we fared as Muslims they began to declare themselves as Muslims also.
>
> Each evening when we finished our duties, the Messenger of Allah would sit down and teach us. Today, those of us who were with him there have only to look around us to see that many of the things he told us about have come to pass.
>
> I remember an amusing incident which happened in connection with one of the white prisoners.
>
> A MEMBER of the Capone gang, he asked me to plead with the Messenger to have mercy on him on the day of retribution. This same fellow prisoner wrote to his wife and told her he had met with the Apostle of Almighty God Allah and urged to pray to Allah so that she might save herself.
>
> Then there was another time, when the prison doctor—who also operated the library—invited the Honorable Elijah Muhammad up to talk to him. Of course, the Messenger of Allah took us with him.
>
> We witnessed this doctor admit that Islam was the true religion and that he was hoping someday to bridge the gap between Islam and Christianity. When we were leaving, he offered his hand to Mr. Muhammad, who politely refused saying; "I'll wait until you bridge that gap. Then I'll shake your hand."
>
> EVEN THE PRISON officials tried to test the Messenger.
>
> They sent another prisoner—a Muslim from Turkey—to try to establish Mr. Muhammad's teachings as false. This brother came and heard the teachings of the Messenger of Allah. He promptly declared: "You're better Muslims than we are." He then asked to become one of Messenger Muhammad's followers.
>
> The entire staff of the prison treated the Honorable Elijah Muhammad with the greatest respect. They seemed to hold him somewhat in awe.[612]

14 The Return of Elijah, the Renaissance

Elijah Stresses Economic Program to Muslim Prisoners

In 1945, on the eve of many FOI being released from the prisons after serving their 1-to-5 year sentences, Elijah stressed the importance of economics for the Nation of Islam, and presented a model concept of "Do for Self." Even acquiring a farm for the NOI in the process:

> When most of the male followers were in prison and the economic plight of their families and relatives was very severe, the prisoners, among them the Apostle himself, had developed economic objectives and economic interests. Then these interests had acquired plans and decisiveness because the Apostle himself adopted them. When some of the imprisoned followers were freed they carried out with them these plans and order which had already been supported by the will of the Apostle. First they bought a farm in 1945. Then they bought some cattle to be developed on the farm. PAGE 83[613]

Elijah and the Muslim inmates survived off of donations from Believers and Family members. Elijah spoke of the liberal rules in regards to commissary: "In Milan, you could send a prisoner there $10 thousand if you wanted. But, they would lock it up in the safe and give you just so much. They had an allowance that you could trade so much at the commissary, and at the termination of your term there, they give you a check for your money that you may cash.[614]

Muslims Start to be Released from Prisons

In 1945, many of the FOI were being released from the prisons after serving their 1-to-5 year sentences. From this crop of FOI came new ministers for Elijah Muhammad such as Harry X (D.C.), Benjamin X (Richmond, VA), James 3X Anderson (Chicago, IL), Isaiah X Karriem (Baltimore, MD), James 3X McGregor (VA) and Asbury X (Cincinnati, OH) and many other helpers that helped spread Islam.

One of the first out of prison was Brother Harry X that returned to DC to serve in the Ministry: "Brother Harry X was released from the prison long before many of the other brothers because he was the first brother in the Washington area to be imprisoned for the teachings of Islam. He returned to Washington, D.C. and became the Acting Minister of Temple No. 4."615

Elijah Gives Instructions to Benjamin for DC Temple

Benjamin X Mitchell went back to D.C. to assist, but not before some parting words and instructions from the Hon. Elijah Muhammad:

A few days before leaving the prison, the Honorable Elijah Muhammad called me to him and said, "Brother, when you return to Washington, I want you to go to the Temple and check out everything and let me know how you found the believers and their activities." I did as he had instructed. A few weeks later, I began to visit some of my friends and neighbors who criticized me for believing in Islam and following that little strange man to prison. I recall one couple who called me everything but a child of God. When I visited their home, I found both in the bed sick. A few months, later, the wife passed. Three or four years later, the husband passed. This couple said to me when I made my visit, "Mitchell, I want to congratulate you for sticking to what you say are your religious beliefs. Many people would not have done what you all did."616

Benjamin and his wife Clara enjoyed success in helping Temple #4 get new converts. NOI Pioneer Sis. Elvie X recalls how she joined Temple #4 at the time:

I became a follower of the Honorable Elijah Muhammad in June, 1945. Sister Clara X. Mitchell has invited me over to her house one Sunday evening. I heard of Islam for the first time and I accepted it as the truth.

Before becoming a Muslim I prayed often, as a Christian, but I never received an answer. I was a good Christian. I believed what they taught: heaven was, beyond the sun, moon and stars, and, if I was good, when I died I would go to that heaven.

When I heard the teachings of the Honorable Elijah Muhammad, of how the white man had enslaved our mothers and fathers and made us believe in a God that didn't exist, I became angry. Angry with myself for believing the white man's lies.

As a Christian, I was afraid most of the time. I never felt safe or secure but as a follower of the Honorable Elijah Muhammad, fear has gone, and I feel peaceful and happy.

Years ago we were not able to see the Messenger very much, but today, all praise is due to Allah, we can sit at home and hear him on the radio, and travel from city to city to hear him speak.

I thank Allah for opening my eyes. I shall serve and obey Him and His Messenger. The Honorable Elijah Muhammad is the door to our salvation. May the peace and blessing of Allah be upon him forever and forever.617

Isaiah Karriem Released and Evangelizes for NOI

More Muslim brothers trickled out of the prisons to be reunited in the DC-Maryland-Virginia areas. Isaiah Karriem who eventually became a minister gladly recalls the time:

I accepted Islam and in less than three weeks I was in jail for refusing to be inducted into the armed forces. I served about three years in prison.

Upon my release I found I had another problem to contend with. Because I had suddenly stopped drinking, using cigarettes and eating pork, my immediate family thought I was in need of psychiatric care. They hinted that I was too perfect and therefore must have been getting ready to die.

During my term in prison I had become more and more interested in the teachings of the Messenger of Allah. I taught every black man I saw about Mr. Muhammad. Sometimes our new-found discovery of Islam would make us forget we were in prison.

I just had to tell everyone about the teachings of the Honorable Elijah Muhammad. As a result I was transferred about six times. And when I was released I began teaching about Messenger Muhammad while I was on the way home.

Today his teachings are still a growing part of my life. He has brought me from my 'ABC's' to where I can meet a man on any level he presents himself on. His teachings have blessed me with a sense of dignity, of love, and a yearning to be with my own kind.

His teachings have fired me with a zeal strong enough to claim any mountain or cross any valley.

There is no distance great enough to stop me from spreading the everlasting truths of Messenger Elijah Muhammad.[618]

After his discharge from prison, Isaiah became active in the DC temple, and became a sort of an evangelist for the Nation of Islam, spreading the teachings throughout the South:

After two weeks I was in jail [1942] and I spent three years feeling real happy and proud that I had found the truth. I began teaching in the prison and after being transferred from one prison to another, the warden finally told me that I was more of a nuisance than a Muslim and that he was discharging me from the institution.

UPON BEING released from prison [1945], I went immediately to the mosque and shortly thereafter got a job on the railroad. I went in debt and borrowed $1,200 to buy a car so I could spread the teachings of the Honorable Elijah Muhammad.

I was indeed successful in getting the car and for the next seven years spreading the teachings of the Honorable Elijah Muhammad throughout the states of North Carolina, South Carolina and Georgia; setting up mosques, selling newspapers and talking about this great man from god. Allah always blessed me with converts from every city I entered.

It was a great job to spread the teachings of truth to so many dead brothers and sisters who had suffered the same things I had suffered – slavery, suffering and death. I met opposition, but with the teachings of messenger Muhammad, I always won over my opponent.

INSTITUTIONS VERY STRICT ON THE FOLLOWERS OF Messenger Muhammad during the 40s and 50's, are now beginning to open their doors to the same one who were confined in their jail cells.

All praise is due to Allah for our great leader and teacher, the Most Honorable Elijah Muhammad. I never felt as though I have done enough to help in the struggle for the uplifting of this black man and woman on the continent of North America.[619]

Elijah Instructs Lester X upon His Release

In Milan Bro. Lester X sorrowfully left Elijah Muhammad behind in prison in 1945. He believed his time in prison helped strengthen his resolve for years to come. In his mind echoed a prophetic statement from his teacher:

With time off for good behavior, I was released from prison after 27 months. Though I would have been happy to stay with the Messenger he told me to go home. I left, but I left my heart with my leader and teacher, in prison.

SINCE THOSE months in prison, the years have only served to strengthen my faith in Allah and to tie me ever closer to His Messenger, the Most Honorable Elijah Muhammad.[620]

Prison doors were opened for me at Milan on Jan. 25, 1945, when I reluctantly left the Messenger. But I recall his words during 1943. "Allah will send much hail, as large as baseballs, heavy snows and destructive tornadoes." We are having destructive weather and more is predicted to come.[621]

Min. James 3X Anderson Released and Arrested Again

In one twist of events, Min. James 3X Anderson (Shabazz) was released in January 1945, and re-arrested on a technicality. He was released later in the year. Min. James explains:

We were released in January, 1945 and I was arrested again in April, 1945 for failure to report for induction (the first time was for failure to register for the draft and when we went to prison they registered for us and classified us without our consent). I wrote the Draft Board a letter saying that I would not report for induction, and that is why I was arrested again. I spent another month in jail and they would not listen to my complaint. It seemed as if they were bent on railroading me back to jail again . . . I was brought to trial after about a month, and I was sentenced to two years before I had a chance to say anything in court. After the sentence I asked the permission of the judge to say something. Then I told him that I could not be sent to prison since I still had five months of the first sentence to complete. This was my question. The judge replied that he did not know that I was still on probation. This was something that had been kept away from the judge. The judge told the prosecution attorney that he could not send me back to jail until I had completed my first term. The probation officer in charge came to verify that I was on probation. There were no arrests after that. The three years sentence was shortened by nine months on account of good behavior.[622]

Elijah Encourages Released Muslim Inmates to Skill Trades

While in prison the Hon. Elijah Muhammad told the FOI to take advantage of some of the vocational trades they learned in prison. As his followers were released, they employed some of their new-found skills, such as the example of Bro. Carl X:

Carl (1X) works as a driver days, as a barber at night, and does painting, carpentering and "fixing grass" on his days off. Moreover, he fills his leisure time by learning Arabic and Spanish languages. He speaks Spanish now fluently. Since his release from prison in 1945, he has built a two-story house in addition to providing for a family with five children. Every year he adds another room to the house. He and his children cooperatively do all the building, painting, and carpentering that the construction needs. In addition to this, he owns a car and his house is very well furnished.[623] PAGE 221

The Muslims Move to a Better Temple

During 1945 and 1946, the Detroit Temple was located at Temple and Reapelli Street.[624] From prison Elijah Muhammad got word to his followers that he wanted them to prepare for the future by saving up to buy a building: "In 1945, Messenger Elijah Muhammad sent instructions for us not to pay any more rent but to hold our meetings in one of the believer's homes and to purchase a building."[625] From 1942 through 1945, the group went through various changes trying to get a place:

The movement began to grow again in winning members through friendship relationships. Increase in membership drove the group from meeting in the houses to hire a place at 51 Michigan, where the group continued their meetings until 1942, the year in which most of the Brothers were arrested consequent upon their refusal to join the American army during the war. Hence, the movement collapsed again. The rest of the Members who stayed out of prison left the temple and began to hold their meetings in the houses. They organized and developed themselves again by winning new members, and therefore they hired a place for their meetings on Wentworth Avenue in 1943. In 1944-45 the movement gained its vigor again by the return of the followers from prison. Therefore, the group decided to hire a big hall on 63rd Street for six months. At the end of this period the landlord compelled them to vacate the place. At that time they decide to buy a temple on 43rd Street, and so they did—a place where they meet today.[626]

Min. James Shabazz speaks about their challenges in trying to obtain a permanent meeting place at the time:

[320]

Shortly after my release [from prison] we were forced to leave the 63rd and Cottage Grove Temple and we found out that it was becoming more difficult to find a place where we could hold our services. It seems as though as soon as the real estate owners found that we were Moslems they raised the rent and hence we put our money together and brought our own place and so we moved the Temple to a brother's home and held meetings there until we were able to raise enough money to purchase a Temple. We purchased a place on 824 East 43rd Street. This place was formerly a dog and cat hospital and we had quite a job rejuvenating it for Temple Services. It was quite a struggle because we had to put our pennies together to purchase the building and then have necessary conversion into a Temple. But Allah blessed us and we were able to purchase that Temple.[627]

Elijah Muhammad instructed Benjamin X of DC to travel to Chicago to assist Min. Sultan Muhammad and James 3X Anderson (Shabazz) who was now assigned as the Principal of the University of Islam in getting a new building. The process required tremendous work. Benjamin recalls:

Before moving into the newly-purchased building, the believers held services in an old run-down garage somewhere off Michigan Avenue, up in an alley. On meeting days, the sisters would have to hold up their long dresses and rush across the alley to the garage (the Temple) so big rats wouldn't go into the Temple with them…

While the Messenger was being held in prison, the believers of Temple No 2 bought their first Temple (Mosque) at 824 43rd Street, Chicago, Illinois. The building that was brought for a Temple had been a Dog and Cat Hospital and needed much repair. The Messenger sent word to the officials of Temple No. 2 to send for me (Brother Benjamin X Mitchell) to come to Chicago and look at the building to see what could be done to it.

I arrived in Chicago in the spring of 1946 and reported to the officials, Minister James Shabazz, the school principal and Minister Sultan Muhammad. The F.O.I. worked closely with me to get the building cleaned before the repair work was stated. After working for several months, we were able to complete repairs on the building which turned out to be the first Muslim Temple to be owned by what was then the Nation of Islam…[628]

Now having a spot of their own, the Muslims decorated the awning with their "National":

The Muslims bought an old animal hospital at 824 E. 43rd Street. They cleaned it up and repaired it and began holding school and Temple meetings in it. On the upper part of the building where you see the iron pieces, they put the name in the awn "Muhammad's Holy Temple of Islam" and the Crescent.[629]

Elijah Muhammad Finally Released from Prison

Upon his prison release, Warden C. J. Shuttlesworth wrote, "Elijah, was one of our many Selective Service violators who made an excellent adjustment at this institution." It was on April 23, 1945, when Elijah appeared before the parole board. When asked of his plans he remarked, "To reform my people and put them back into their own. At the present time my followers and I plan to buy a farm upon which to raise food for ourselves and the market . . . . I will live with my family at 6116 South Michigan Avenue in Chicago."[630]

In 1946, the Hon. Elijah Muhammad was finally released from prison. The Hon. Elijah Muhammad recalls the terms of his release:

> In 1943, I was sent to the Federal Penitentiary in Milan, Michigan, for nothing other than to be kept out of the public and from teaching my people the truth during the war between America, Germany, and Japan. This war came to a halt in 1945 when America dropped an atomic bomb on Japan. And the following year, in August, 1946, I was released on what the institution called "good time" for being a model prisoner who was obedient to the prison rules and laws...[631]

One researcher describes what he believes was the impact to the movement per Elijah's jail sentence and release:

> Elijah Muhammad walked out of the Federal Correctional Institute at Milan, Michigan, on August 24, 1946, on conditional release. There were no cheering crowds to greet him or Fruit of Islam to escort him; just a parole officer who dropped him off in the Loop in Chicago and told him to "teach what you always have been teaching and nobody will bother you anymore...." To this, Muhammad replied that he intended to resume his ministry among the "so-called Negroes" as soon as possible. Four years in jails and prisons did more toward consolidating his authority over the Nation of Islam than a decade of bickering, purges, and wandering could ever have done. During the period between 1931 and 1942, he was simply the embattled Supreme Minister of a schismatic movement which had too many conflicting and ambitious personalities to bolster his claim to the messengership. After 1942, and especially following his release from prison, he had unquestionably become the premier martyr of the Muslims – their "Little lamb" and saintly "Messenger of Allah." Competition for the reins of power in the organization had ceased, and Muhammad, through his own adherence to Nation of Islam doctrine and subsequent persecution, now commanded an almost immeasurable loyalty from his small, but growing, following. When he resumed the rostrum again in late 1946, he did so with a new confidence. Henceforth, the days of running were over, and his leadership was more secure than ever before.[632]

Pledges to Increase the Growth of the NOI

After his release from prison, the Hon. Elijah Muhammad quickened his pace toward increasing the growth and stature of the Nation of Islam:

The Honorable Elijah Muhammad, the Messenger of Allah, that piece of Jewel, after going to jail for non-proof of charges, and making four years of time, he returned to his handful of followers and made double time, trying to place them again on top of civilization, so the world could see the Blackman in the light, standing in the Sun of Freedom, Justice and Equality.[633]

A Homecoming for Elijah, Purchases a New Temple #2
John Hassan recalls the historic day Muslims waited when they finally saw the Messenger of Allah freed just in time to dedicate their new Temple. He also verifies that Elijah Muhammad had a FOI escort team on that day and he made it home just in time to dedicate the new Temple:

IT WAS not until 1945 that we launched a drive to purchase a hall that could be used as a meeting place. Many of the Brothers were being released from prison at this time and Allah blessed our efforts.

When we learned that the Messenger of Allah was being released. I was among those picked to escort him back home. In fact, I was the first one to shake his hand when he left prison. His release was timely in another sense also, for he was able to dedicate our first Mosque, at 824 E. 43rd Street address. We had grown too large for that Mosque. We settled in our present location at 5335 S. Greenwood Ave.

I would like to see my children settle in a world that offers freedom, justice and equality. Islam offers us that chance. I have made many changes since accepting Islam but all that I have really done is get rid of the waste and add the good. I pray that Allah will bless me to follow his Messenger all the days of my life. And I pray that you too will hearken to the life-giving message of the Honorable Elijah Muhammad, the Messenger of Allah.[634]

The Believers were happy to see Elijah "Returning to Chicago in 1946, immediately taken up active leadership among his family and followers from whom he had been absent during the chase by hypocrites, and imprisonment by his enemies." Benjamin X remembers in vivid details how the Hon. Elijah Muhammad enjoying seeing the MGT in their new uniforms during Sunday service at the new temple:

When the Honorable Elijah Muhammad returned from prison in August 1946, he had a reconditioned Temple in which he could teach Allah's truth. I use to stand on the corner of 43rd and Cottage Grove and watch the brother and sisters go into the newly-decorated Temple for the Sunday service at 2pm. At that time, the sisters had three uniforms, white, red, and green. I remember the first time that I saw them wearing the red uniforms, ten of the sisters look like 5x10 as they entered the front of the Temple.[635]

Observers acknowledged the Temple was one step toward their overall goal for the movement and Black people:

Likewise, mobility and the compulsory change of the Temple from place to place, due to the direct persecution of the landlords or the indirect persecution stimulated by other opposing agencies, had given rise to the formulation of a decision to buy a place to be a temple.

In the course of the development of the organization, minor goals have emerged which later became some of the most important ends—ends to which more attention has been directed by the leadership of the group then to the original basic objectives. Although the major goal, namely, salvation of the Negro from the enslavement of the white man by deporting them to their original land, is still lurking behind all the collective activities of the group, there is not any serious planning toward the realization of such a dream and will never be. The major interest of the group has become expansion for the organization and developing structural means: such as expanding the school building a new temple or improving the restaurant.[636]

The NOI Establishes New Temples/Study Groups in other States
"I remained in Chicago a few months after the Messenger returned," Brother Benjamin said. "I then came back to Washington, D.C. and he (the Messenger) made me the Secretary of Temple No. 4 in Washington. I remained the Secretary for six years or more. The Messenger asked me if I would like to be a Field Minister? I replied, "I don't think I am qualified to be a minister dear Holy Apostle." He then said, "Oh yes you are! You will become a minister a little later."[637]

After Elijah's prison release, he reassigned and dispatched other ministers.

Detroit Temple #1 had his brother Minister Wali Muhammad, and later his Asst. Lemuel Hassan would become the Minister.

Chicago Temple #2 had himself as the primary Minister, along with his new aid and field Minister Lucius Bey.

Milwaukee Temple #3 still had Minister Sultan Muhammad, who was now assigned as the Nation of Islam "National Representative." He'd eventually be assigned to be Minister over the East Coast Region, which included Eastern Regional Headquarters that was Washington, DC at the time, and later New York City (of which he'd become Minister over both of them).

Temples #5 and #6
As the Hon. Elijah Muhammad ministers went into the field, so did new Temples or Study Groups spring up in places the Messenger visited

while on his 7-year run before going to prison. The Messenger taught that in order to have a Temple you had to have "40 Registered Believers or more" in order to get a Temple number assigned to your city. Before he went to prison he had 4 Temples. Yet 4 more Temples were about to be added, as well as study groups that would become Temples in the very near future.

Most new temples and study groups were established by those who were incarcerated along with the Messenger. Min. Asbury who was a student inmate of Elijah's in prison, went to Cincinnati where he became Minister of Temple #5.

Min. James 3X McGregor (Shabazz) went back to his native Virginia, but ended up moving to Baltimore, MD, and started and became Minister of Temple #6. Years later he'd become the Minister of Jersey City Temple #21 and Newark's Temple #25.

Temple #7 (New York City)

Min. Linn Karriem and Sister Secretary Pauline Bahar both went to New York City to help start Temple #7 in Harlem along with a group of local pioneers, "The first location for Temple #7," Min. James 7X Najiy states, "was set up in a Madison Avenue Apartment in 1948, by such pioneers as: Brother Alexander X, Eustace X, Hubert, Frederick X, Arnold 2X and other brothers." This group would go on to influence New Yorkers such as Garveyites, Moors and other movements to join the Nation of Islam. An early convert Hubert X recalls Marcus Garvey prophesying about the coming of a Messenger in Harlem in 1919:

> Thirty-nine years prior to my initial introduction to the teachings of the Honorable Elijah Muhammad, I remember hearing the Honorable Marcus Garvey predict the coming of the Messenger.
>
> It was a Sunday night in 1919 at Liberty Hall on west 138th Street. Someone asked Mr. Garvey what kind of government would he start when he got back to Africa. Mr. Garvey said, "An Islamic Government."
>
> What book would he use? "The Holy Koran," Mr. Garvey answered. So, someone said, why not teach it? It was then that Mr. Garvey said, "Oh! No! I am not the man for that. There is one coming behind me. He will give you everything. That's the man to follow." [638]

Bro. Hubert X explains why he joined Temple #7 in the 1940s:

> In 1949, at the age of sixty, I first heard the teachings of the Messenger. Although I had lived among Muslims in Ethiopia, when I went there to the crowning of Haile Selassie, they never interested me. I was brought up in the Anglican Church but it never appealed to me and when I became a Garveyite, I dropped all religion.
>
> But when I heard the teachings of the Honorable Elijah Muhammad I immediately recalled the remarks of Mr. Garvey, uttered thirty years earlier.

I said, "This is what I've been looking for; this is what Mr. Garvey was talking about!" Immediately I became a follower of the Honorable Elijah Muhammad. And I said, you can count on me from now on. [639]

Bro. Hubert X further gives his testimony how Islam significantly changed his life, and why credits Elijah Muhammad:

I can say truthfully that all praise is due to Allah, and that one is none other than the Honorable Elijah Muhammad.

Before the coming of Almighty God and raising up the Honorable Elijah Muhammad as our leader and teacher, I had no hope or future plans – just drifting around in the darkness of ignorance.

But now, thanks to the five principle of Islam – belief in one true God, whose name is Allah, and his divine Messenger, divine revelation, fasting, prayer, and charity—I have improved tremendously morally and spiritually. Although I am not strong enough for the fasting, being seventy-four years old, I try to make up for that weakness through praying.

Morally, Islam stopped me from running around and chasing women: spiritually, Islam has made me want to do everything right, and gave me a sense of being. It elevates me considerably. There is no other leader to follow but the Honorable Elijah Muhammad. All praise is due to Allah.[640]

After making Sultan Muhammad the NOI National Representative, the Messenger assigned him the territory of New York and D.C. With the latter being the East Coast Regional Headquarters.

Temple #8 (San Diego, CA)

Another Muslim inmate "Brother Howard" traveled to San Diego to start the beginnings of Temple #8 after being freed from prison. He'd soon influence Henry Majied, a native of Georgia, who after moving to New York, moved to San Diego in 1944 at 34 years old. His bio tells of how he came into the Nation of Islam in San Diego:

Minister Henry Majied was born March 24 1924 In Perry Ga. He left Ga. In 1931 at 21 years old. He hitchhiked on the train by holding on underneath the train rails. He met Flora Barnes in Bakersfield California in 1938. They were married in 1939 he was 22 and she was 14. Henry Majied and his wife decided venture out to San Diego California. They settled down in a nice home and had a son, Henry Jr. he was born in 1944.

Henry Majied aspired to be a singer at one time, so he packed his family up and moved to New York City in Harlem. He took voice lessons and he performed at the famous Harlem Theater, He was not able to pursue his career at a singer, and he had to work to support his family, so he took a job as a contractor. He also took a course in Radio Broadcasting. They soon had a daughter and named her Helen she was born in New York. Something was missing in his life still not satisfied and fulfilled he once again moved his family and packed up his bags and moved back to California.

Something profound happened that would change his life and in turn he would be responsible for changing hundreds of lives. His brother-in law introduced him to Islam. He attended a meeting in a small storefront building, Brother Howard was teaching about the lost found tribe of Shabazz and that we were the first and Original People of the earth, he had never heard any teaching quite like this before. At that point Minister Majied knew he had to wake up his people from the dead, this was his calling. To uplift his people this is what he was searching for.

Bro Howard actually was not a Minster but an ex con that had heard the teaching in prison. Elijah Muhammad was in prison at the time for refusing to go to war. Brother Howard had drug problems and soon dropped out of site. However Minister Majied continued to teach the word, Minister Majied wrote Elijah Muhammad a letter expressing his belief in the teachings. Elijah Muhammad sent for him.. He made him the Minster of Temple no 8 and he was the first person to receive his "X". His mother was his first convert and soon his wife, sisters, brother and other family members converted to Islam.[641]

Another helper Yusuf Shaheed would join Henry in establishing Temple #8:

El Hajji Yusuf Shaheed Abdullah was born November 23, 1918 in Saltillo, Mississippi. His family moved to Oklahoma in 1937 where he would meet his future wife and go on to have five beautiful children. They moved to San Diego, California in 1941 where he was soon inducted into the United States Army, served his country, and was honorably discharged after World War II ended.

Brother Yusuf first heard the teachings of the Honorable Elijah Muhammad in 1946. He soon joined the Nation of Islam where he was a faithful believer. Yusuf was instrumental in establishing the first house of worship working hand-in-hand with Minister Henry Majied to establish Temple #8 the first Temple of Islam on the West Coast (which is Masjid Taqwa today). Subsequently, they made several trips to Los Angeles to establish Temple #27. In 1950, Brother Yusuf and a small group of Muslims from the west coast gathered to make the annual Savior's Day event in Chicago. While on that trip, sitting at the dinner table with the Honorable Elijah Muhammad Brother Yusuf was given his name. [642]

Mosque #8 would face problems with the police in a shoot-out:

It was back in San Diego in 1951 that the San Diego Police Department engaged in a ruthless confrontation with the growing and evermore influential Muslim band. It was a struggle that Yusuf helped lead where the Muslims stood with faith and courage against a hostile police contingent, determined to stifle the spread of Elijah Muhammad's message.[643]

Another incident occurred in September 1950, in San Diego, involving two officers of the San Diego Police Department who were attempting to serve a traffic warrant. Upon arriving at the address, two individuals accosted the officers and advised them the subject of the warrant was not at home. When the officers exhibited the warrant and expressed their intention of searching the house, they were ruthlessly attacked. This perpetrated a near riot and necessitated the calling out of additional cars and approximately twenty officers. Before the subject was taken into custody and the order restored, an unknown individual fired three shots into a police car. It was later determined that the subject and the two individuals who intercepted the officers were all members of the San Diego Temple of the Muslim Cult of Islam.[644]

The founding of Temple #8 would lay the eventual groundwork for several future Temples and study groups in Los Angeles, The Bay Area Oakland, San Jose, Richmond and Palo Alto.

Beginnings of Temple #9 (Youngstown, OH)
Temple #9 would open in the Midwest in Youngstown, OH. Some say that was home to Minister Theodore Hamza.
Beginnings of Temple #10 and #11 (Atlantic City and Boston)
Sheik Sharrieff, a student of Elijah Muhammad in D.C., migrated through the East Coast finding himself in Atlantic City, NJ, where he was run back-and-forth out of town by authorities for "trying to teach the Negroes Islam." As fate would have it while teaching on the boardwalk he met one Bro. Woodrow Love, a native of Monroe, LA, of whom he taught "the Black Man's History". Highly interested, Woodrow assisted Sharrieff in makeshift temples in car garages and storefronts until he finally accepted in 1942, and registered in the Nation of Islam as Bro. Woodrow X.[645] He would go on to become the Minister of Temple #10 in Atlantic City, as well in control of all the tapings and recordings of the Nation of Islam. Sheik Sharrieff also is reported to have gone to Boston to begin Temple #11.
Beginnings of Temple #12 (Philadelphia)
Not too far away was an ex-inmate that learned Islam in prison named Charlie X who moved to Philadelphia as a barber in the early 1940s. In his shop, he'd teach his patrons all about "Islam" and a man named "Mr. Muck-Muck" [Elijah Muhammad]. His first convert was a young teenager who'd later become Minister Jeremiah Shabazz and future Minister of Philadelphia, PA. Jeremiah recalls:

I was introduced to Islam back in 1943 by a man who moved into the neighborhood, who was cutting hair in a barbership that was directly adjacent to where I lived. This was in the spring of 1943, I was a young boy; well, I was a teenager I had just turned about 13 and I use to frequent this barbershop because of its close proximity to my house. And one day I went in and there was this man there arguing with the customers about religion. And he said his name was Charles Simms, and he began to explain that he had recently been released from a federal prison in West Virginia, having been arrested on a charge of bootlegging. But while he was in the federal prison, he had run into some Muslim brothers who were also incarcerated as conscientious objectors — not wanting to go fight in the Second World War. And these brothers introduced Charles, the barber, to the religion and upon his release, he came to Philadelphia and began to talk about it in his barbershop. And that is how I was first introduced - by sitting in the barbershop and listening to man explain about a new religion.

After listening to Charlie shut the mouths of these Christian people that were coming to the barbershop debating with him.

I was only about 13 or 14 years old. Charlie would argue with these men everyday in the barbershop. The first time I heard it was really afraid but then I did go back again because it was fascinating to hear a man say things the way Charlie was saying them and still stay alive. Because I was a young boy raised in Christianity, I believe if you spoke against the Father, Son or Holy Ghost, some unseen hand would come out of the air and smack you or smack you back to your senses or something terrible would happen to you. But hearing Charlie speak — and looking for the hand to come out of the air and it never came - I though Charlie had something. I kept going back and I saw that he knew the bible better than most Christians. He was also saying things about Christianity .. about the bible - that it was a book that this white man had fixed up to feed to black people to keep them enslaved.646

Teachings Spread from Chicago to Gary, Indiana

The teachings of Islam spread from Chicago to neighboring city of Gary, Indiana. Minister Samuel, who became the Minister of Gary, Indiana recalls how he joined:

Islam has opened my eyes so that I may see the truth today as taught by Messenger Muhammad. It has unstopped my ears to that I may hear the truth and recognize it to be the truth - and Islam opened my heart that I may understand and accept the truth.

I have been a follower of the Honorable Elijah Muhammad for 17 years [1949], and they have been the best years of my life. I am from a family of 11, eight boys and three girls. My father was a Baptist preacher.

When I was a small boy, I used to hear him preach about Moses, Noah and God; how the people in their time did not believe in them.

I would awake many nights thinking, how could these people reject such men and the truth they taught? I said then and there that if there ever came a man in my time from God, I would believe him and follow him wherever he went.

One day 17 years ago [1949], a brother told me about a man he heard who had met and talked with God. I told this brother to take me to this man. When I say this man — even before I heard him speak — I knew he was from

God. So after hearing him, I accepted the truth and have been following him ever since.

I was able to bring in six of my brothers and one of my sisters, who now are following the Honorable Elijah Muhammad. There are two ministers, a lieutenant, an investigator and a secretary out of my family for the Messenger.

Let me tell you, this man has taught me much and is still teaching me. Through his teaching I have been made a different man. Things I used to do, places I used to go, and things I used to believe in – I don't anymore because he has shown me a better way of life. He taught me who God is, who the devil is and who I am.[647]

The NOI Purchases a Farm

Making good on his promise to build businesses and do for self, the Hon. Elijah Muhammad and his sons purchased a farm for the Nation of Islam.

Mr. Muhammad had plans on a grand scale, here was a man who understood the nature of economics. He knows his people had to have possession of the land to provide in the broadest sense, all natural resources as we find them in nature. These natural resources include, not only the land's part of the earth's surface, but rivers and lakes, minerals and resources and natural vegetation. His sons, Herbert and Elijah Muhammad Jr. launched a program called "Back to the Farm." To stimulate interest amongst the followers, to want to own land, and getting away from the brainwashed tricknology of the slave master and the desire to be a janitor or an elevator operator, rather than being a farmer or owner of land[648].

The Hon. Elijah Muhammad maintained that it was necessary for the Nation of Islam to be self-sufficient in order to overcome persecution:

We had been persecuted so much to the extent that we were moving from temple to temple and from district to district just because we did not own our own temple. The white people and the Christian dark people were stimulating the owner of any place we had rented as a temple to compel us to vacate the place through the enforcement agency. The F.B.I. did that many times, telling the landlord to drive us out of his property. This continuous persecution led me to think of buying our own temple and so I told my followers, when I was in prison, to buy a place to be a temple. Then I thought of buying a farm to grow our own food, lest this devil someday might boycott us and then we would have nothing to eat.[649]

The NOI Opens up Shabazz Restaurant, Bakery and Supermarket

Elijah Muhammad had remorse over the prison diet of him and his followers: "Since returning from prison, it has been hard for me to adjust my eating habits. For many days in prison, we had to eat twice or three

[330]

times a day, in order to make up for one meal a day through trying to avoid eating the divinely-prohibited flesh of the swine. This cause me and the others illness after we had cleansed our stomachs of bad food and had begun to eat at the proper time."[650]

In the free society the Muslims opened up their own restaurant and wholeheartedly supported it by shopping at their own quality establishment:

> In 1945, the Apostle developed the idea of buying a restaurant. After they brought a restaurant, they developed the idea to have a store in the restaurant itself, and so they did. Behind the economic trend there is the tendency to isolate the group from the larger society. The members do not eat except in Shabazz restaurant; they do not shop, except under urgent necessity, but from Shabazz store. The Apostle himself expressed this decision to the writer, declaring that he "wants to isolate his followers from the wicked people and impure life as much as possible." He told the writer once that he has a plan to "have their own stores, their own school, their own homes," etc., so as to make the group self-sufficient and "has no necessity whatsoever to demand the devil or resort to him."[651]

Muslims not only shopped at the restaurant, but also worked there and cooked, baked and produced their own items:

> In July 1947, the Messenger opened at 3117 S. Wentsworth, a grocery, bakery and restaurant. The people were amazed, here was a grocery store without pork. No Black Man had ever attempted to open up a food establishment on such a high order. A clean place—no grease. Or even a grease smell on your clothes after leaving. Pure ingredients, and the best of cooking and baking, and of course, fairly priced. Yet, Blacks were fearful and unpatronizing.
> His daughters, Ethel and Lottie served as cooks and bakers, as their brothers pitched in as dishwashers, clean up men and delivery boys. Mr. Muhammad practiced what he preached. And his family loved, respected, obeyed and followed his principles of being clean, hard-working, respectable and fair.[652]

Muslims Grateful to Allah for their Own Businesses

Muslims at the time recall their overjoyed emotions of the fact of having their own business. Karriem Allah reminisces:

> Our first businesses were established in July 1947. The Honorable Elijah Muhammad, the Messenger of Allah, opened a grocery store, restaurant and a bakery at 3117 South Wentworth Ave., one year after His release from prison.
> The Muslims were happy over the good news of the opening of these businesses by the Honorable Elijah Muhammad. A store, restaurant, and bakery were big businesses. All this happened in such a short period. He

took the nickels and dimes we donated and used the money for a self-help program. With a self-help program He could set up a sound economical system for the Muslims. It is the most outstanding economical system among the Black people in America – a miracle of today.

From these businesses our success and growth was outstanding. He, the Messenger, the Honorable Elijah Muhammad, is building a sound economical system equaled by no other Black group or groups in America.[653]

The Messenger's followers contributed his success to his spiritual program and divine aid from God (Allah):

He is backed by the Divine power of Allah and His accomplishments are unequaled. No other Black group has the backing of the Divine Supreme Being Whose proper Name is Allah, Who came in the prson of Master W.D. Fard, to Whom praise is due forever. Therefore, brothers and sisters of the Aboriginal Black Nation, these Black groups cannot do what the Honorable Elijah Muhammad is doing for His Black people.

All this was done through unity of aim and purpose – the Messenger's aim. A sound economy for the Black man by a black man, namely, the Honorable Elijah Muhammad. His purpose? To employ every Black man in America through self-help.

Let the self-help come from the Black man to help the Black man. Sound good Blackman? Then what are you holding back for, Black man? You doubt the Honorable Elijah Muhammad? That's because you don't know the Honorable Elijah Muhammad nor yourself.

Let me get back to our first businesses; the store, restaurant and bakery. The hearts of the Muslims longed for these businesses wherein we all could go and shop at our own businesses managed by Muslim employees appointed by the Messenger. These businesses gave employment to managers, sales clerks, cooks and waitresses.[654]

Muslim Restaurant had Excellent Bakers and Cooks

Elijah Muhammad's son-in-law and future Supreme Captain Raymond Sharieff, who married the Messenger's daughter Ethel, recalls that his wife Ethel established the first bakery for the Nation of Islam, which she started in the kitchen of Muhammad's restaurant. "She baked bread with her own hands without a mixer. They didn't have a mixer in those days. You had to make that bread with your own hands," he said with a smile.[655]

The fact that Muslims employed their own and recognized each other's talents caused for great enthusiasm over their goods and businesses:

The Messenger taught our sister on baking. The sisters did the baking in our first bakery. The Messengers eldest daughter, Sister Ethel Sharrieff, our Supreme Captain Rayond Sharrieff's wife, worked in the bakery along with other sisters. These sisters were No. 1 bakers. They knew well how to prepare and cook bread and their baking was pleasing to the taste. Your mouth would water from the good smell of the bread they baked.

The bread was baked according to the instructions given them by the Messenger in the M.G.T. – G.C.C. class.

The bread was cooked through and through, well done. It caused no disorder in our stomachs after eating it. It was all wheat bread, whole wheat. It was dark in color, rich in iron and easy to digest. We bought the bread, rolls, pies or cookies as fast as they could bake them.

No bread, cakes, pies or cookies were ever thrown away. The Messenger taught us how to be economical. We bought and consumed the bread and pastry as soon as it was put on sale at our businesses. It has that long waited taste.

These sisters had no equal in baking. Much can be said about our sisters in their role as bakers for the Nation of Islam. The restaurant prepared and cooked food just as it is cooked in the homes of Muslims. The Messenger taught the M.G.T. C.C.C. how to prepare and cook food the Muslim way. No pork or its by product was used in the cooking of Muslim food.

Our people have always been good cooks by nature and no one could excel us. We have been preparing and cooking food for trillions of years. We are no strangers when it comes to cooking food. Our trouble was that we were cooking and eating the wrong food until the coming of Allah raising up the Honorable Elijah Muhammad. Our restaurant served the best food in all Chicago-land; big or small.

It was delicious to the taste— good food; you would hurry back for more.

Brothers and sisters, we the Muslims could eat in those days, and food was purer in those days than it is today. There was less sickness in those early days of Islam than there is in the latter days.

Today, hospitals and clinics are filled with people, sick people. The nature of food had not been tampered with then. When you tamper with food you are tampering with people's health.

Our restaurant grocery store and bakery had good business all the time. Our ice cream was the best, it had a taste that made you come back for more.[656]

Besides their great cooking and baking skills, what was equally impressive was the fact that Muslims had introduced new recipes and dishes to the Black community:

We also had changes in our foods. We had new and tasty foods. We had brown rice, where we would take white rice and parch it in a skillet with a little oil, until it was brown. We had bean soup; the bean soup in any restaurant would be different from ours. We had whole wheat bread. This was healthy for us.

But we also had 100 percent cheese pies that were not healthy, and those didn't last. Although they were delicious, you couldn't eat too much of it, because it was too heavy. We had bean pies, and our Christian brothers and sisters know about that bean pie. It was made very popular.

What was added to the meal to make it different was also the selection of spices. We didn't use the same spices. None of us were using tumeric before. But the Nation of Islam used tumeric and put it in the rice. We started using oriental spices. And we were having for the first time a menu that the world did not give to us.

Mr. Fard and the Hon. Elijah Muhammad and Sis. Clara Muhammad, his wife, gave it to us. She learned how to cook from Mr. Fard, himself. He came into her kitchen and showed her how to make those dishes that we are talking about. It all started right in the kitchen of Clara Muhammad. She gave it to other sisters and was happy to do that. I remember sisters coming to our house and working with my mother in the kitchen to get the recipes from her to learn how to make those dishes.[657]

Furthermore in the days of racial segregation, Blacks welcomed healthy, good and clean establishments where they could socialize, especially on Sundays after religious services. Yet, they recognized it was a heavy price to pay for the suffering they went through in racist America:

We would gather at our restaurant on Sunday evening after Temple service and enjoy ourselves to a delicious meal and dessert.

The Muslims thanked Allah Master W.D. Fard for blessing us with the Honorable Elijah Muhammad – for making it possible for us to have an establishment, a clean restaurant, a desirable place where we could gather, sit down, and dine in peace and comfort.

We were full of the good spirit of Allah. We were happy and cheerful all the time.

We gave the Messenger our nickels, dimes, quarters, half dollars and dollars. He took the money, pooled it and built a commercial business that stands out independently of white people. He did not receive any grants or donations from outsiders. He used what little money His poor followers gave Him to accomplish this.

It was struggle – a long struggle; it took years and patience. I thank Allah, Master W.D. Fard to Whom Praise is due forever for blessing me with patience. The Messenger told us of His great plans for the Muslims. He said to us we will have land to produce our needs and we will have businesses to employ all of our people.

Well, brothers and sisters, that was many years ago and today we see this in reality. What He told us in the early days he would get for us. He has fulfilled. With the help of Allah, He is gaining momentum in establishing businesses to employ His people We the Muslims cannot thank Allah enough for the Honorable Elijah Muhammad. The lost-founds used to say, you Muslims aren't doing anything but meeting and talking. When the Messenger set up our businesses, I said to them: Brothers, look what meeting and talking has done for us. The Messenger is setting up commercial businesses to employ all of us – not just the Muslims, but he planned this many years ago.

His plans do not leave you all out, brothers, it includes all of our people. The Messenger is a kind man. His heart is for you. He is all for His people and His people should all be for Him. There is not another leader like Him. His people, the Black people, dominate His thinking, brothers and sisters of the Aboriginal Black Nation. He studies day and night trying to reach you. He wants you all in unity with yourself and your Black kind.[658]

824 E. 43rd Street, Old Animal Hospital. Became a Temple in 1946

Temple #2 Bakery, Temple #2 Grocery Store

The Modern SHABAZZ Restaurant

. . . offers the best in foods. It serves wholesome foods for sustenance and abundant life in accordance with finest recipes of Islam.

The Shabazz Restaurant's Kitchen

The ever clean kitchen where one of the several cooks prepare home cooked meals of whole grains, with natural oils. Pies and meats with exclusive recipes find their way in the ovens.

Historical photos from Shabazz Restaurant and Kitchen

A Scene In The Shabazz Grocery   Open 7 A.M. to 11:00 P.M.
Fresh fruit and canned goods counter.

One of the Southside's Better Kept Groceries
It is 3117 South Wentworth Avenue, with fresh vegetables from their farm.

The Shabazz Beautiful and cozy 'Dining Room

Here you and your family or friends may be served without smoking. Choice
home cooked meals, or lamb and specially prepared vegetables.

Historical photos from Shabazz Grocery and Dining Room (both
pictures show Elijah Muhammad)

Arabic Class at the University of Islam

The largest youthful class of Arabic in America

These children reach out to millions and millons of brothers and sisters

in the Islamic World. They are taught a language not given by their slave masters.

A Class of young and eager youth at Islamic School
In character building, conduct, cleanliness and cooperation.

Their truism is, "Come down off the cross and get under the Crescent and enjoy heaven, peace and Contentment while you live."

The teaching staff at the University of Islam and Helpers

They teach reading, writing, and Arithmetic and Simple and Metric system, Advance Arithmetic Algebra.

From left to right. Peggy Richmond, Aliyah Majied, Ameerah Abdullah (sister to Peggy Richmond), Flora Majied (married to Henry Majied), Inez Muhammda, Mary Majied (Henry's mother), Lila Majied, last is unknown.

The Early Pioneers of San Diego's Temple #8

In 1945, Messenger Muhammad sent instructions for us not to pay any more rent but to hold our meetings in one of the believer's homes and to purchase a building. In the winter of 1955-56 in October, the building at 5333-35 South Greenwood was purchased.[659]

The Hyde Park Mansion purchased by the Nation of Islam for Elijah Muhammad in the early 1950s.

15 Appendix "Dean of the Ministers"

Min. Lucius Bey (at podium), seated from L-R: Min. Asbury X, Min. George X, Min. Isaiah Karriem, Min. R.T. X, Min. Malcolm X and Min. Ulysses X

Lucius Bey joins the Nation of Islam

In his previous 7 years on the run, the Hon. Elijah Muhammad 'dropped seeds' all throughout the Midwest, East Coast and the South. In prison he raised a new cadre of future NOI ministers who'd return to some of the same cities to help establish Temples. Since his stint in prison, a few more Temples emerged. Min. Asbury X helped to form Temple #5 in Cincinnati, and Min. James 3X McGregor became the Minister of Temple #6 in Baltimore, MD. At Chicago headquarters, the Hon. Elijah Muhammad had Min. Sultan Muhammad (whom he made NOI National Representative), along with Min. Marcellus Jardan in Chicago.

Lucius Bey Hears Islam for the First Time

Lester X, one of Elijah's strongest confidantes while in prison was also a great help in teaching Black people in Chicago. It was through him that Lucius Bey (who happened to be a Seventh Day Adventist evangelist) would soon join the ranks of the NOI and become Elijah Muhammad's close confidant and new Minister of Temple #2. In an interview with Bro. Cedric Muhammad of Black Electorate, Min. Lucius Bey told his story of his early beginnings in the Nation of Islam. Here he discusses how he first came into contact with the Nation of Islam:

I first heard the teachings of Islam from a Brother somewhere in the 1930s, during the winter. If I recall correctly I became a registered Muslim within three years or so after the very first time I heard the teachings. I do know for sure, it was a Brother by the name of "Lester X" I heard teach. He was a very dedicated Brother. We were standing on the corner. At this time I was Bible teaching in the Seventh Day Adventist Church, and he was teaching about "Yakub" and his history. He was saying things about which I was deeply concerned but I never did argue or dispute in a negative way, of things that I didn't know or didn't understand or never heard. So I stood by him and when the opportunity presented itself I asked him, "What denomination are you?" (As we would always ask those kinds of questions). And he told me about Islam and the Messenger Elijah Muhammad. And I said, "Where do you all meet?" and he told me. And every day I was out there to listen to him teach - every morning I would listen to him teach. I never disputed. I never had a negative (thought) against anything pertaining to the teaching of Islam although I didn't know all about it. But I had studied. I was a person that studied. I had studied the Bible, I had studied the history of the Black church in America. I had studied the history of all of the different founders of the Baptist, Methodist, and the Sanctified (churches). I had studied the history of all of those, so I was kind of open to learn. So, finally I visited the teaching and I was attracted to it. They didn't have a decent place at this time.[660]

Lucius Bey describes his first visit to the Temple:

This was 31st Street. Well the first time I visited it was on the South Side of Chicago... It was in kind of a hall, upstairs on the second floor. I actually registered (in the Nation Of Islam) there. And I think the Minister who was teaching was Minister Sultan Muhammad or Marrcellars Jardan and I was interested, so I joined. Sultan Muhammad was an outstanding Minister. He even looked after the family of the Honorable Elijah Muhammad when the Honorable Elijah Muhammad was gone.

At that time, as you know, it was the Depression. And the poor people would go and pick up stuff, left in the street – food and vegetables. It was good quality but the condition of the people was very poor. And Minister Sultan would go and gather things to help feed the Messenger's family. You have to deeply consider that Master Fard Muhammad came at a time when our people were in bad shape. And he came to Detroit, an area that was very poor. Master Fard Muhammad came at that time when our people were in that kind of condition.[661]

Lucius Writes His Dear Saviour Letter

Lucius was convinced enough to "write his letter" to be accepted as a Muslim in the Nation of Islam. Although, he delayed his entry a while in order to complete his obligation to his church as a travelling evangelist which often took him to the Bronx, NY:

> I wrote two letters [form letters necessary in the process of becoming a registered member of the Nation Of Islam]. The first one didn't pass but the second one passed. Now, I was to go to New York, in the Bronx, and make a lecture, and after I had registered, I went on to New York. But Islam was in my mind. I made a lecture there, I think I stayed there about a week and I came back. And at this time we were meeting in the 29th block in an old garage. We didn't have nothing decent. (We were) in a dirt floor, we didn't have decent seats or nothing, but everybody was interested and I was interested and I sat there and I heard the teaching... So I went back to New York, I'm still working.[662]

Gets to See Elijah Speak in Person

Upon his return to Chicago, Lucius received good news. The "Prophet" was finally home from prison and was scheduled to speak at the Temple. Lucius describes how he first met Elijah Muhammad:

> So then a Brother told me, he said, 'Our leader' (would be speaking). They referred to him (the Honorable Elijah Muhammad) then as 'prophet'. He said, 'he'll be here Sunday', I said, 'Well I'll be there.' So that Sunday, I was there - first time I ever saw him - and I ...was sitting there, 'cause everybody was very faithful - they didn't wait (for those who were late or to start the meetings) Brother, around 2 o'clock, 1 o'clock, they were there in those days.
>
> So when he [the Honorable Elijah Muhammad] came out, I heard somebody say, 'Attention!' I jumped around and said, 'what's goin' on here?' and he walked in, walked right down, skipped up on (the speaker's place) and started, and I kept my eye and my ear open – my mind, everything. I didn't want to hardly bat an eye. So when he was through (speaking) in those days nobody left out without shaking his hand. Sisters would line up and shake his hand and Brothers – they would be on this side shaking his hand. So when I shook his hand I said, 'I enjoyed you'. He said, 'Thank you Brother'. So I walked out. That was the first time I saw him and the first time I heard him. So the second Sunday I was there (again). And I walked up, shook his hand, and I said, 'I enjoyed you today'. He said, 'Thank You Brother'. On my way out I started inquiring (about) how I could talk with him. I said, 'How could I speak to the leader?' So one of his sons said, 'That's my father'. I said, 'well I would like to speak with him.' I said, 'how can I speak with him, is there anyway I can contact him?' He said, 'I'll

give you his phone number.' He wasn't staying on Woodlawn (Avenue) then. [663]

Has Dinner with Elijah Muhammad

Next Lucius called the Messenger and received a personal invite to have dinner with him at his home:

So I called him that Sunday – that second Sunday I saw him or heard him I called him. I said, "My name is Lucius. I'm a Minister. I'm a Mason. I used to teach classes in the Masonic Order." I said, "I'd like to talk with you." He said, "Well Brother, when?" I said, "Anytime you say so." He said, "What about Wednesday?" I said "It's good." He said, "Could you be here and have soup?" He meant 'soup' or have dinner with him. I said, "Yes Sir, I can be there." He said, "You married?" I said "Yes, Sir." He said, "Bring your wife." [664]

Lucius Bey describes the pre-dinner conversation:

So that Wednesday, following the second time I saw him or heard him, I'm sitting at his table eating dinner with him. So when I walked in the house, he was sitting in the living room with one of his sons. He put him out. And my wife went on in the kitchen with Sister Clara Muhammad. And no one was in that room but me and him. And I was sitting kind of in front of him. And he was sitting as he always sits straight with his hand you know [Minister Bey motions to describes how the Honorable Elijah Muhammad sat]. And he said, "Do you want to see me?" and I said, "Yes, Sir I want to see you." I said, "I'd like to ask you a couple of questions." He said "Brother, ask me whatever you like." I said, "They tell me that you are a prophet." I said, "Are you a prophet?" He says, "I am the Messenger of Allah." That was his answer. And it looked like to me, if he had given me anything else, I probably would have questioned him. I said, "OK, now they tell me that you talked with God." He kind of bowed his head. I said, "I want to know, are you sure (that) whoever you talked to was God?" He said, "Brother, He made me all into Himself." Every answer he gave me it just looked like it was the right answer in my mind. I said 'OK'. I said, "Now let me ask you another question." [The Honorable Elijah Muhammad says] "Go ahead." I said, "I would like for you to explain St. John." He says, "What part?" I said, "The first chapter." He didn't move his hand, didn't ask for a book or nothing. I said, "Start at the first verse of St. John, the first chapter." He started. He explained it and got down to about the third verse, I think, or the fourth, somewhere in that area. I said, "That's enough." He looked at me and said, "You can understand can't 'ya?" I said, "Yes Sir." He said, "Do you have any other questions?" I said, "No Sir." I asked him three questions and if he'd have answered any other way I probably would have cross-examined him. His answers just registered, just looked like it was the right answer. He said, "You don't have any other questions?" I said, "No Sir, not now." He said, "Well if you don't have any questions for me, I have one for you." I said, "Yes Sir." He asked me, he said, "What is Ether?" I studied a while, I said, "rarefied air." He smiled. He didn't say I was right. He didn't say I was wrong. I didn't ask him. That was the only three questions I asked him then, and I still got them in mind. And I will tell anybody, that I met a lot of preachers, big ones, little ones, so-called educated ones, those who had degrees. The Honorable Elijah Muhammad was the wisest man in religion and in real life, and thinking that I ever met. [665]

Becomes a Follower of Elijah Muhammad

Bro. Lucius Bey was satisfied and pledged his support to the Hon. Elijah Muhammad by joining the ranks of the Nation of Islam. He quickly made an impression as a stand out. Some suggested he become a minister, which made him uncomfortable. Then the Hon. Elijah Muhammad paid a special visit to the Temple to hear him speak:

Well I told him then, I says, "You know something?" He says, "What?" I said, "You got a follower." He said, "I wish I had 17 million." I said, "You got one." So as I came out every night – he only would come out on Sunday – the Minister he had then ...a young Brother, a good speaker was teaching. And his custom was that he would call or open up for Brothers to have a testimony or have a word to say. But I never did push myself, I never did get up. So he looked out one Wednesday night, he said, "We've got a Brother here who was a minister. Brother Lucius!" I said, "Yes Sir." He said, "Stand up, come up here, say something, talk." So I said a few words and I went and sat down. And after our meeting was over they all gathered in the aisle wanting me to be the Minister. And I didn't like that talk. I didn't like their attitude, "We want you for our Minister, we want you for our Minister..." I said, "You've got one." So I kind of pushed them aside and walked out, 'cause I didn't like the attitude. So I never did get up anymore and volunteer. I never would volunteer. So he would call me, "Brother come on up here and say something, everybody like how you talk." Well I would say a word so then they started reporting me to the Messenger but I would never volunteer to get up. I would never push for nothing. They start reporting me, now I don't know it at this time. So one Sunday the Honorable Elijah Muhammad came out and said, "They tell me I got a Brother here that can teach. Where is this Lucius?" I was sitting in about the third seat. I held up my hand. He said, "Come up here." I walked up there. He said, "Sit down behind me." So I sat down. He turned to the audience and said, "They tell me this Brother can teach. I want to hear him today for myself." He said, "Come here Brother. Talk long as you wanna'." So I guess I talked for about 10, 15, 20 minutes. And (the subject that) came to me to talk on was "Why I left the church." [666]

Becomes an NOI Minister

After hearing Bro. Lucius, the Hon. Elijah Muhammad made him an assistant minister:

That was it, "Why I Left the Church." When I got through I shook his hand and went to walk and he said, "Come back up here." I turned around. He said, "Sit down behind me." I sat down. He turned and looked at the people and said, "This Brother will never sit out there again. Whenever he comes here, this is his seat right here." He looked at me and he said, "Brother, don't you ever sit out here again. You sit up here and help this Brother teach." So he told the Brother (that was his assistant), "If you speak Wednesday, he speaks Friday, and whenever he speaks, he's going to be able to help you teach. If I don't come out on Sunday, you speak one Sunday, he speaks the next." [667]

Bro. Lucius Bey was made eventual minister of Temple #2 by the Hon. Elijah Muhammad. His affinity for teaching from the bible caused some members alarm. Elijah Muhammad was notified of the concerns. Lucius recalls:

Of course he (the Assistant Minister) didn't follow that. I didn't say nothing. I always sat there. I never was aggressive I would just sit there. So the Messenger then, it wasn't long, maybe two or three months, the Brother left, I think the Messenger sent him (away), and I became his Minister just like that. And when I started teaching back in those days, I taught everything in the Lessons from the Bible. Every subject: the coming of Master Fard Muhammad from the Bible; the making of the enemy or Yakub, from the Bible; the history of Jesus from the Bible; the grafting, from the Bible; everything I taught from the Bible. At this time he didn't allow a Minister to carry, you didn't see no Ministers carrying a Bible.[668]

I would say in 1947 I was made his Minister. And I would teach everything, I could handle it and I was the only one that taught from the Bible at this time. And after that then they started using it. So then they put it out that I was teaching mixed instructions. They reported me to him. I don't know this at this point. They said, "he's teaching mixed instructions."[669]

After vindicating his minister, Elijah surprisingly allowed him to speak in his stead at events outside of Chicago:

And at this time he was to speak at Gary, Indiana. Flyers were cut, everything was put all around for him to speak at a place, I believe…He was living out on 60-something so I got up that morning and I came out early, rang the doorbell. He come to the door. I wasn't living with him then and I says, "I come to go with you." He says, "Go with me where?" I said, "You are speaking in Gary, Indiana." He says, "I'm not going." I said, "You are not going?" He said, "No Brother I am not going." I said, "Who's going to speak?" He said "You." I said, "Me?" He said "Yes, you." I said, "What am I going to say?" (He said) "What I taught you." So I went and spoke. He told me what was going to happen and what I was going to say.[670]

Moves in with Elijah Muhammad and Family

With the growth of the Nation of Islam, plans were in place to purchase a bigger home for the Hon. Elijah Muhammad where he could have his offices and host guests. He extended the invitation to Lucius Bey as his Minister to take up residence at the new home. Lucius Bey recalls:

> And following this, after they had got his place ready, he told me before, it was on Woodlawn (Avenue), the second house from the corner. He said, 'I want you and your wife to stay with me.' I stayed in the house before he did, with his family. His room was the front room on the second floor. My room was right down the hall, down from him . . . I believe it was around 1950 because I stayed in the house with him about three years and a half...So I left, he sent me then in 1954 – which I have that down good – to be the Minister in Washington D.C. and New York City. So I would say it was around 1950, somewhere in there because I stayed about three years with him. And I left out his house in 1954. But before that he would send me to different places...He sent me to San Diego also and he sent me to another place, after cross out of San Francisco and you cross the bridge in Oakland, California. So I was in Oakland teaching, he sent me there. And he sent me to several places to teach and finally he said "Brother I want you to get ready, cause I am going to send you to Washington, D.C. to be the Minister." He said, "Now I don't want you to go looking for a job."[671]

Bey and Wife Adjust as Resident Minister and Sister Captain

As a minister and house resident, Min. Lucius Bey was considered a close family friend. He often served as an uncle figure to Elijah Muhammad's children. The family was fond of Bey and his wife, and the two were rewarded for their duties at the Temple:

> But, let me put this in before (to help explain). Now when I was staying with him to show you how blessed I was, at that time, the charity slip – you had on it (places to give money) the poor fund and for the Messenger's family and Minister, and whatever they gave the Minister is all he got. It was on the charity slip. And what they gave the Minister then was 7 or 8 dollars a week. The first week that I was Minister they gave me $50...So when I was staying with him, he would give me money. Every Sunday that I come home from teaching, he would give me money. All of his family wanted to hear me – his sons: Akbar, Wallace, Herbert, all wanted to hear me. Even his wife (Mother Clara Muhammad).
> **Cedric Muhammad:** Now what was the average minister given?
> **Minister Lucius Bey:** Oh the first Minister, that was all they would give him – maybe between $7 or $8 dollars. Maybe $10...The first Sunday that I was the Minister, the first week, they gave me $50 which was a lot of money then. And when I was staying with him (The Honorable Elijah Muhammad) my wife was captain. She later became a cook for the Honorable Elijah Muhammad. He loved her very much. They gave her $25 a week, as Sister Captain of the MGT (Muslim Girls Training) and he would give me about $50 every Sunday...[672]

Taught Directly by the Hon. Elijah Muhammad

Min. Lucius Bey took his responsibilities as a Minister very seriously, always checking in with the Hon. Elijah Muhammad. The two developed an informal communication system within their relationship. One immense benefit was the one-on-one tutelage he received from his leader. Min. Bey explains:

I never would open up (from the rostrum) without contacting him. On Wednesday about five minutes before I would open up at 8, I'd call him, (The Honorable Elijah Muhammad would ask) "Well how does things look, Brother?" I would say well we have so-and so. (The Honorable Elijah Muhammad would say) "How many out?" I would tell him. He said, "OK, Brother teach 'em what I taught you." I'd say, "Yes Sir." And on Sunday, he would mostly come out every Sunday but there were some exceptions, when he wouldn't come out. I would call him on Sunday morning, though I was staying with him I'd call him and I'd tell him and I knew that he was coming. He had a way that he would tell me. When he was coming out he would say, "Pretty soon" then I would know he was coming. If he wasn't coming he would say, "I'll see you at dinner" And I had a way of teaching when he was coming different from when he wasn't coming. No one had to teach me that. I just learned how to respect him and we would travel with him. I would drive him every day. I would be with him sometimes and we would go it looked like fifty or more miles riding. And in the morning when he would drink coffee he would always come down about 9 o'clock. And I would be down waiting and I would be sitting in the den waiting for him and he would always be on time coming out. (He would say) "Come on Brother Minister let's drink some coffee." And sometimes my wife would be there and sometimes his wife, Sister Clara Muhammad and his mother. I knew his mother. And sometimes she would be sitting there. And he had a sister and sometimes she would be there, sitting there. And when they leave, nobody would be sitting at that table but me and him. And we would sit there almost every morning until twelve and 1 o'clock talking, and he wouldn't be jiving, he'd be teaching. Nobody at that table but me and him.[673]

Some First Experiences as Elijah's Driver

John Hassan, who once was NOI transportation manager, had since then become the NOI National Investigator. Lucius Bey found himself moonlighting part-time as the Hon. Elijah Muhammad's driver. The Messenger liked to ride on a daily basis, often utilizing his minister as chauffer of sorts, typically to drive back and forth the Muslim farm in Michigan, yet often exposing Bey to other appointments and how the Messenger conducted business. In the beginning, Lucius zeal as a driver made him disregard the driving laws on several occasions which resulted in minor accidents. Min. Bey speaks on some of their adventures:

Yes, then he would look at his watch, and he would say, "Oh Brother Lucius, let's go riding." I'd say, "Yes Sir" and we would go riding. Sometimes we would ride a long ways. I would take him places.

He (once) wanted to see an attorney. I took him downtown in the Loop there in Chicago and when we walked in the attorney put his secretary out of the office. Nobody was sitting there but us three. The attorney would ask questions of him and he would answer him. That man [the Honorable Elijah Muhammad] knew something. And now, I would drive him down the Loop and when I was with him I did not think nothing could go wrong. I'd be driving downtown and he would say, "Brother I want to get on the other side." What do you think I would do in the Loop that you are not supposed to do? Make a U-Turn. [The Honorable Elijah Muhammad would say] "Brother, Brother don't do that!" And I said, "You want to get over there." And he would say, "I know but you are breaking the law." I said, "But you want to get over there." [laughter] If you know anything about Chicago then, you were not supposed to make a U-turn. I'd make a U-Turn. I figure if he'd tell me to do something, that's it. I didn't think nothing could go wrong and I used to drive him to ...the farm. Sometimes I would trail him. I had my Chevrolet. Now, Brother, he was gonna' drive. If that car got 120 (mph) he was going to get it. And I asked his wife once was she afraid [driving with the Honorable Elijah Muhammad] and she said "No, I think Allah is with him, I just sit there." So I was trailing him one time and oh that little car might've looked like it was going to fly. You'd think I was afraid keeping up with him. [laughter] I bumped into him once. When he got up a hill. Have you seen when you are by a block at a light?

Cedric Muhammad: Yes, Sir

Minister Lucius Bey: And the light turned and it looked like he was going about 70 or 80 (mph) and I'm right behind him, so it kind of rained and we put on the brakes, and I slide out. I kind of bumped him and he looked in the mirror and he did like this [Minister Bey shows how the Honorable Elijah Muhammad motioned his finger indicating the bump was a 'no-no']...

Cedric Muhammad: he waved his finger at you?

Minister Lucius Bey: Yeah. And when he was turning (a corner), Brother he could take a curve... What I did [Minister Bey, while trailing the Honorable Elijah Muhammad turned without making a complete stop at a corner]. He looked in the mirror and saw me and stopped. He pulled over and said, "Brother don't you ever do that. What if you get caught over there? Don't you ever do that."[674]

Elijah Muhammad addresses an Officer about a Speeding Ticket
On at least one occurrence both Elijah and Lucius received traffic tickets for speeding when they two were pulled over by a police officer. This further exposed Min. Bey to the wisdom of the Messenger:

So coming back one time, a police patrol stopped him. He was speeding and I'm right behind him. He gave both of us a ticket. He was just a humble man and he was very intelligent. So (later) he gave me an envelope and he said, 'Brother, I want you to take this envelope and give it to the (one) who gave us a ticket.' Now I don't know what was in it, then. OK, I know where the place was...so I got in my car to take it by and give it to them. And he stood up, he opened the envelope and read it and there was money in it. And he apologized. And he said, "I want you to apologize to Mister Muhammad for stopping him, and take the money back." He didn't even want to take the money...He didn't take the money, the Chief, or whoever it was. He wouldn't take the money, and he apologized. He said I want you to apologize to Mister Muhammad for stopping him. Now what he had in there I don't know I didn't read it. It was sealed. But I carried it back to him (the Honorable Elijah Muhammad). And he said "Brother, he didn't take the money?" I said "No Sir." He laughed. And I said he told me to apologize for him. And he (the Honorable Elijah Muhammad) laughed.[675]

Min. Bey and the Messenger witness a car accident
In another case Min. Bey and the Hon. Elijah Muhammad witnessed a severe car accident involving all whites. Min. Bey explains the profound charity of Elijah Muhammad in this case:

And (one time) we were going to the farm and there was an accident, all Whites (involved). And a White fellow was kind of bleeding and hurt. He (The Honorable Elijah Muhammad) pulled and stopped (the car) and got out. I got out with him and he walked back and he said (to the injured White man), "Is there anything I can do to help?" And it kind of got me (laughter). You know the way we were teaching back then (about White people). So he got back in the car and he knew how I was thinking. He said "Brother Minister." I said, "Yes Sir." He said, "Anytime you can help anybody, you help them." I said "Yes Sir." It really got me, he got out of the car stopped in front and got out - naturally I walked with him - walked back there and all of them were White and he said, "Is there anything I can do to help?" (The White man) said "No sir we are alright, thank you." (The Honorable Elijah Muhammad) said, "OK." So he told me, he said "Brother, anytime you can help anybody, you help them." I said thank you. So a lot of the teaching Brother, and the way Brothers acted way back then, he didn't teach that way. I know.[676]

In lieu of the car accident incident, Min. Bey advised that the Hon. Elijah Muhammad always stayed true to his teachings concerning the white man, and wasn't shy in telling them, although he did it in a respectful manner:

He talked strong, now. 'Cause he would always teach about the grafting of the devil. I have seen him with reporters - all Whites - on the first seat at a Saviours' Day, he'd stand there Brother and tell them why their eyes are blue and why their veins were blue...but the way he taught it was not like arrogant or attacking. It was just like you were stating a historical fact. And they (the Whites) would just look at him. That is all they would do. He

[352]

didn't teach arrogantly, you know, attacking. He didn't teach that way...and I was in the house when they interviewed him. They came out. He told me, Brother, they are going to come here, I want you to give them a seat, and say I'll be down' And they set their little lights up, and he was sitting in a chair. He sat just like this (Minister Bey positions himself to show how the Honorable Elijah Muhammad was seated) and I am sitting over there. I was always around him. And they asked him, 'Mister Muhammad,' he looked up and said, 'Yes Sir'. He (the interviewer) said, 'I understand that you teach that we are blue-eyed devils.' He said, 'I teach that y'all are blue-eyed devils? I didn't even know myself. Allah taught me y'all were devils and I believe Him.' Brother, he could answer any kind of question just as intelligently as you would think . . . It was just, he didn't have that arrogance. And he would teach. He would say, "Brothers don't ever call him devil to his face. That is not intelligent. Of course he is but he didn't make himself. We made him...So don't do it."[677]

16 Appendix "The NOI in Revue"

In 1951, a doctoral student named Hatim A. Sahib from the University of Chicago, was granted direct access to conduct a series of interviews with the Hon. Elijah Muhammad and 28 of his followers over a period of approximately two years so he could write about the Nation of Islam for his thesis. Following is some of the information pertaining to his study about the history of the Muslims from 1930 up until the then present time of 1950.

Muslim Demographics

One of the important things cited in the study was the demographics of the Muslims at the time. Most Muslims migrated from the South. Sahib went on to say:

All of the listed followers, with the exception of one girl 16 years old who was born in Chicago, came from plantation areas in Georgia, Alabama, Arkansas, Virginia, Mississippi, Tennessee, and Texas. All of them, including the leader of the group, came from poor families who lived on farms. All of them, except a few—not more than half a dozen—were farmers in the South. They migrated to the North seeking better living. The majority of them mentioned at least one kind of familial crisis that befell their families when they were children. Divorce, desertion, or separation of the parents, fights between the parents, and the death of one of the parents or both of them are some of the familiar happenings in the childhood of these followers.[678] PAGE 99

He added the fact that many members claimed to have previously or currently belonged to various Black fraternal and religious organizations. "Generally speaking, all of the followers who are above 25 of age pretend that they were Masonic," he documented.[679] In at least 19 cases other organizations were cited:

The various organizations among which these 19 followers were mobile prior to their conversion to the Asiatic cult were as follows: Marcus Garvey Movement, Masons, Seven Day Adventists, Israelite Movement, Jehovah Witnesses, God's Government on the Earth, the Elks, Night Pythiens, Repatriation Movement to Africa, Repatriation Movement to Ethiopia, Repatriation Movement to Liberia, National Advancement of the Colored People, Black Jews, and Peace Movement of Ethiopia.[680]

[354]

Two Muslim Testimonies

Two Muslims in the Temple willingly shared their histories to illustrate their demographic backgrounds. The first being Bro. Horace X:

Another example is that of Brother Horace (X), a man of 39 years of age who was mobile before his joining the Asiatic movement. He was moving from church to church, from peace movement to the Israelite Movement, frequently visiting Washington Park, a place for agitation in Chicago, to listen to the various speakers, "searching for the truth." After he had listened to one of the followers of the Asiatic movement speaking in Washington Park proving what he says by returning to the Bible, he decided to visit the temple and listen to the Apostle himself. Brother Horace said: When I went to the temple for the first time they searched me at the door. I was carrying with me at that time a small pistol which I carried with me so as to shoot any white man that I could get hold of whenever I had a chance for that. They took that pistol from me and I went to the meeting hall. The minister began to speak, telling us that these names we have are not our original names, and that Allah is a man. Then he told us about our ancestors and about our native lands and the glorious history of our own people. I felt at that time that I was finding myself through his speech. Then he told us about the history of the devil who lived in the cave for a long time; and he told us how the devil planned to keep us slaves and inferior so as to rule us and use us as tools. Then he mentioned that we have the true messenger whom Allah sent to us to raise us from mental death, a messenger who spoke to Allah mouth to mouth, and who knows everything in the world. At that time I was so happy to know that I was not that "dirty Nigger: but I am "Asiatic." I knew that he was speaking the truth because I had read the Bible.[681]

Second was a teenager named Sister Sylvia X of mixed parentage who decided to share her history:

A second example is that of Sister Sylvia (X), a beautiful 16-year-old mulatto girl in her twelfth grade of school. She said: "I went to the temple after I met a very handsome guy in Washington Park who told me about the movement. I heard the minister speaking, saying, "How can they call us Negro when there is no such country as Negro land or when people take their names from their country?" he said, "Our current names are not our original names but they are names given to us by the devil: and we have lost our original language and that is why we have this difficulty in pronouncing the English words." He said that the Bible describes the chosen people as the enslaved, the lost, the underprivileged, the people whom no one loves or cares about; describes them as the people who had lost the knowledge of themselves. At that time I knew that he was telling the truth because when you look over in present-day conditions you find that the Bible could have been speaking of none other than the so-called American Negro. Since that time I have felt that I am another person.[682]

The Muslim Protocol (Structure)

Next logical step for his social thesis was defining the actual protocol of the Temple, starting with humble position of the Hon. Elijah Muhammad himself. "The leader, for example is the spokesman of the group in the temple, but he washes dishes, serves the clients, and works as cashier in the restaurant. He plans and designs the steps for the group, and so on."[683]

Elijah Muhammad cited as Sole Leader

Yet, the writer made it clear that the Hon. Elijah Muhammad was the sole authority as he explained:

The Apostle [Elijah Muhammad] is on the top as the source of all the authority, administration, and leadership. The Apostle in this status system is the actual operator or mechanism. He got angry, for example, against the minister who directed the movement in Chicago from 1935 to 1942; therefore he stripped him of the ministership and drove him down the scale to be a private; he raised a new follower to the rank of a captain after that follower married his daughter; and he dismissed the Sisters' captain because he changed his mind about her and therefore raised another sister to be a captain. [684]

Elijah's hard work didn't go unnoticed by his followers, they rewarded him and his family by moving them from a humble house, into a better house for the time. Sahib noted:

The Apostle lives with his family in a private beautiful house which the group owns collectively. How did this come about? The actual operator was this: since he was the leader of the group, visited by many outsiders who are curious about the movement or have the idea of joining, the followers felt that the house in which the Apostle was living was not appropriate to their name. Therefore they built this house for him." PAGE 145.

Muslim Charity

The present income of the group comes from three sources: the donations, the restaurant, and the farm. Donations are paid weekly. They are as follows:

1. Donation for the University of Islam, which covers the salaries of the teachers and other expenses of the school.
2. Donation for the Apostle.
3. Minister's donation.
4. Donation for the restaurant.
5. Donation for the Apostle's family.
6. Secretary's donation.
7. Labor Donation.
8. Emergency donation, which covers any emergency cause that needs money.
9. The farm donation.

10. General treasury donation, which settles any deficit account in all of the other sub-treasuries mentioned above when there is not enough money in them to cover these above-mentioned demands. PAGE 174-175

Saviour's Day Gift

In addition to these donations, every member has to pay at least fifty dollars on the birthday of Allah, offered as a present to the Apostle on the twenty-fifth day of February, a day on which they hold their convention. On this day the various temples compete to beat each other by the quantity of money they raise for the Apostle or by the kind of present they offer. During the year the group offers presents to him or his wife. The temple in Washington, D.C., for example, offered a Chrysler "New Yorker" to his wife two months ago.

Most of the above mentioned donations are not assigned quantitatively. Hence, the members offer whatever they are able to offer. There are only two donations which are quantitatively assigned; these are the donation of the UOI $1.00 a week and General Treasury $1.00 a week. PAGE 174-175

Organizational Protocol for the Temple

The rest of the staff of command as structured in the Temple is captured by the observer:

Under the Apostle comes the minister, whose duty is to preach in the temple and outside the temple in some of the places of agitation. He has to teach what the Apostle tells him. All the other ranks offer him respect, expressed by saluting him militaristically, and behave towards him with reverence. His duty is to organize the meetings and preside at them when the Apostle is absent, and to deliver the instructions of the Apostle to the captains. Under the minister comes the general in the status system, but the organization has no general as yet. Under the general there are two captains, one of them the Brothers' captain and the other the Sisters' captain from among the Sisters. Theoretically the captain has to pass through all the preceding ranks before he becomes a captain, but the will of the Apostle is an exception to such an assumed role. In the absence of the Apostle and the minister the captain teaches the Brothers whatever the Apostle tells him to teach. Moreover, he functions as the head of the "special detail," the duty of which we have already stated elsewhere, and arranges the guards in the temple during the meetings and as long as the doors of the temple are opened. In addition to this he gives all the information that he receives from those who are below him in the status system to the minister, who in turn offers this information to the Apostle. After the captain in the scale comes the second and then the first lieutenant and then the private, who occupies the bottom of the scale. The followers are divided into divisions, each of which is presided over by a first lieutenant.[685] PAGE 172-173

Respective Roles of Male and Female Officials

The roles of the followers are differentiated along four lines of activities or specializations: religion, teaching, administrative, and labor. Besides the Apostle there are two ministers and four missionary Sisters. The ministers play the role of preaching according to the instruction of the Apostle. Their duty outside the temple is to go to the various places where agitation or induction is possible and deliver speeches. During the summer they are accustomed to go to Washington Park and have a "circle" there. The role of the missionary Sisters is to go around among the Negro community in Chicago preaching the new religion and the appearance of the prophet which the Bible has told about. Their job is confined to preaching among the females; hence, they go visiting from house to house.

The teachings' roles are of two types:

a) Teaching in the University of Islam.
b) Teaching the ideology of the movement which is predicated by the Apostle along the lines of what Fard has taught.

The captain of the Brothers delivers these teachings to the Brothers, and the captain of the Sisters to the Sisters. In addition to these teachings, the Brothers and Sisters receive military training, delivered by two of the Brothers to the Brothers and by the captain of the Sisters to the Sisters. Moreover, there are other members whose roles are teaching boxing and wrestling to the Brothers. Two of the Sisters teach the Sisters cooking and sewing. And an old man teaches the Sisters nursing.

In the realm of administration they have a special secretary of the Apostle, and ten other secretaries, each for a definite item of donations.

The captain of the Brothers has, beside delivering instructions and keeping control during the meetings, the role of arranging the guarding of the temple.

In addition to this administrative staff, there is a group of the members whose duty is to spy and offer reports to the Apostle about the various members in the cult.

Other roles in the cult are as follows:

1. Farming on the farm which the cult owns. Five of the Brothers are playing this role and live on the farm with their families.
2. The Sisters attend the temple wearing long dresses. This attracts the attention of people whenever they walk on the street or come to the temple on any means of transportation. Because of this inconvenience the Apostle bought a wagon car which they call the Sisters' Car. One of the Brothers has the role of driving this car, bringing the Sisters back and forth between their homes and the temple. This driver himself cleans the temple every day in addition to his driving.
3. In the restaurant five of the Sisters do cooking; two others serve, in addition to another brother who serves and cleans the restaurant. Three of the Brothers do shopping for the restaurant and the store each day. Washing dishes is an expected role of all; it is a job carried out voluntarily and cooperatively. The Apostle himself plays many roles in the restaurant. Sometimes he serves the customers, sometimes he washes dishes, and most of the time he is the cashier. PAGE 250-251

When the group bought a farm three of the brothers had volunteered to work on the farm. During the first three years no one of them was paid for his work. They were living on the farm with their families, trying to get their food from whatever they grew on the farm. Since about a year the Apostle has assigned a little salary to be paid to each of them.

The story is the same with the servant of the temple, the driver of the Sisters' car, the secretaries, the captains, the ministers, the missionary Sisters and all the others who play functional roles in the movement. Among all of these mentioned above, the only one paid a regular salary is the secretary of the Apostle, who began to receive her salary regularly since two years only. That means that all the secretaries who worked since 1932 until 1949 were unpaid workers. PAGE 255-256

When the group bought the restaurant the followers were competing enthusiastically in doing various works in the restaurant: some of them washed dishes, others cooked, some others served customers, and still others cleaned, and so on. During the days, when the older Brothers and most of the Sisters go to their jobs, children and the other free Sisters were running the restaurant. Being familiar with cooking and having lectures in the temple about how to cook, the women specialized in cooking while the children were left for achieving other works in the restaurant helped by other older Brothers who had no jobs or were having their rest day...What was encouraging these Brothers and Sisters to cooperate to this extent was the fact that the Apostle himself was serving there cooperatively with them. PAGE 253-254

Temple Meetings

In the style and fashion of the early days, the Hon. Elijah Muhammad provided a full experience for Muslims and visitors during Temple meetings.

Temple Invite

The first step was to pass out invitation cards in the community:

Anyhow, his consciousness of his prophetic role can be proved by the content of the card which they distribute to propagate for the validity of his prophecy. The content of the card is as follows:

Mr. Elijah Mohammed

The Messenger of God to the Black People of America. Come and hear the Messenger of God. A man that was sent: Not through a vision, nor a dream, but from God Almighty Himself to teach and warn us to flee to our own God and Nation, to escape the Destruction of this Wicked Western World of Christianity. Get out of the Slave Names of this World. Freedom, Justice, and Equality awaits you in your Nation of Islam. Hear him give the true interpretation of the Signs of Time. And also of the Bible and Koran interpreted. Temples in Chicago, Detroit,

Milwaukee, Cincinnati, Baltimore, Washington, New York, St. Louis and California.[686] PAGE 245

Temple Entrance Process

When guests visited the Temple, to gain entry itself was a process unlike any other for a religious meetings. Most guest were impressed by orderliness of the Muslims:

Service meetings: typical of these meetings is the one held on Sundays in which outsiders are allowed to attend the meeting.

Arrangement of the meeting: Members of the "special detail" are arranged in two lines, one facing the other, arranged along the stair leading to the basement. Behind the door of the temple is a group of guards and inspectors. This door is always kept locked and two guards behind it are responsible for it. The door is made of glass and behind it is a shading curtain. Whenever any member or visitor comes, the door will be opened and then immediately closed after him. If the comer is a member then the guards search him carefully to be sure that he does not carry any kind of weapon, candy, any kind of stimulant, gum, or lipstick with him. If the comer is not a member then he will be questioned about his name, his address, why he wishes to attend, whether or not this is his first attendance, and who has sent him. Then, if he is a dark man they search him after recording all of his answers to the above-mentioned questions. After he has been searched, another group of guards will lead him to the door of the hall where the service takes place. The guard on this door in his turn will lead the visitor to the place where he should sit. If the visitor is a white man, whether he was Moslem or not, they prevent him from attending the meeting after recording all of his answers to the above-mentioned questions.[687] PAGE 176

Student Minister Explains the National Flag and the Black Board

Once seated inside the atrium, security remains tight and orderly. At the front of the Temple stands an assistant Minister officiating the affairs and explains "the National Flag" and "the Black Board":

Around the place of meeting, guards are kept inside the hall whose duty is to watch carefully everyone in the meeting because they have been taught to be alert and "on their feet" during the meeting. Guards are changing many times during the meeting. On the platform just beside the speaker's stand is a big blackboard on which is drawn the National, the American flag, a dark man hanging to a tree, and beside him a cross, and a statement runs as follows: "Which one will survive? The war of Armagaddon." PAGE 177-178

The blackboard they have before the audience in the general meetings has on it the American flag, the National, a cross, and beside it a drawing of a Negro hanging on a tree and a sentence runs as follows: "Which one will survive? The War of Armageddon."

This flag, according to their myths, was the flag of their ancestors since the dawn of history; it was the flag of all the "civilizations that the dark man had built." But the Caucasians, because of their wicked nature, had "killed the ancestors of the dark race four centuries ago and had taken off their flag." When Mr. W. D. Fard came he brought them the flag back because it was hidden in the White House in Washington, D. C. This flag is so superior that Truman and many other eminent entities in the world carry the symbol of the flag on their chests, "because they know what the National is!" The red color in the National represents the sun, which gives "light and life," the star stands for the five senses and the crescent stands for keeping equilibrium of the water in the earth. There are four letters on the National, each in one of the four corners. These letters (I.F.E.J.) STAND FOR THE STATEMENT "Freedom, Justice, and Equality You and I own."[688] PAGE 141

The Hon. Elijah Muhammad teaching from the NOI Blackboard

These items on the blackboard had been additionally accumulated through a process which has a history. Now and then the collective process is pregnant with some symbolic development which emerges externally and objectively through a symbolizing act of some members. For example, the American flag and the National were drawn by Fard himself on the blackboard by using colored chalk. The purpose of drawing these two flags was to make a comparison between them during his speech. This comparison was carried on a symbolic basis. Later on, in 1942, Brother Yacob, an old man now 78 years of age, pictured a Negro hanging on a tree. This picture had been added to the other pictures on the blackboard. When the Apostle was released he himself added the statement on the blackboard. These items serve as good tools for agitation during deliverance of a speech. This is one of the most important tactics through which they raise the enthusiasm of the audience and heighten the emotionality of the attendants.pg 154

The Resident Minister Opens with NOI Anthem and Speech
After the student minister concludes the opening on the days that the Apostle is scheduled to appear, then the Resident Minister will officially began the service with "the Muslim Fight Song" and an opening speech:

At two o'clock in the afternoon the minister advances toward the speaker's stand. At that moment one of the older brothers comes before the audience, gives them the order to stand up. Then they begin to sing what they call the "National Song," which has been put out by one of the Brothers and which runs as follows:

THE NATIONAL SONG

We are fighting for Islam
And we will surely win
With our Savior Allah'
The universal King'
We are united with our nation
And is called by its name
So let us fight ye Moslems
Fight for your own
Let us fight for our nation
And we will all be free
Fight ye Moslems
Fight for your own
The earth belongs to the righteous
Fight for your own
Allah gave to you and I for a National
The sun, moon and star
The best of his creation
He is giving to you
So let us rise ye Moslems
Fight for your own
Freedom, justice and equality
We now must have
Four hundred years enslaved for the devils
Lost from your own
So let us rise ye Moslems
Fight for your own.

History behind the National Song of the NOI
The Muslims in Temple #2 reveal the history behind the NOI anthem that has come to be known as "the Muslim Fight Song":

This song has been introduced into the service two years ago. It was made by a Brother 78 years old. The Brothers obtained this song and they began to sing it and enjoy themselves whenever they felt like singing. This was not done in the

[362]

temple because it was profane to sing in the temple. But it happened once that one of the brothers had asked the Apostle to sing while he was before the speaker's stand. All the other members had confirmed his request. Before such collective pressure the Apostle had submitted to their request but he asked the whole group to sing with him, whereupon they sang the song with vigor and enthusiasm. Since that time the National Song has been introduced into the service and it has been put even before the prayer. PAGE 177-178

We had new songs for the Nation of Islam made by us after we got help to make up those songs from Mr. W. F. Muhammad and the Hon. Elijah Muhammad.
We had marching songs and other songs. In fact, the meetings use to be opened up with songs on Sundays. Everybody in attendance would be singing that song and we would be happy. We were addressing things that were bad and hurtful in our lives from the White world.[689]

Opening Prayer and Lecture

After the song the Minister normally explains to the audience the Muslim custom of opening all meetings with prayer. Then afterwards he precedes with his speech:

After singing the National Song all the audience face the East and begin to pray be reciting the first chapter in the Holy Koran. After that they take their seats and the minister begins his preaching. The function of the minister is to raise the heat of the meeting and to emotionalize the audience. His speech takes the form of contrast between the inferiority of the white race and the superiority of the original man. Then he makes a comparison between the National and the American flag, pretending that the National is so superior that "Truman carries it himself because he knows how sacred the National is." Then he claims that "Islam is the religion of all superior men in the world. Truman and most of the Senators are Moslems; Masons are Moslems," and so on. Then he comes to the injustices of the dark man in this country, saying, "Garvey was teaching that America is hell and god is planning to get the dark man out of hell." Then he begins to describe the Americans as "the beasts, savages, and the worst of all the animals in the world." Then he continues describing what the white man does to the dark people in the South and how he treats them, and how he calls them Coon, Nigger, Monkey, and so on. Later on, he comes to the picture of the dark man hanged to a tree which is drawn on the blackboard before the audience, saying: "Christianity tells you that Jesus was the one who has been crucified here in America." At about this time the Apostle appears, with the "special detail": around him, from a door leading immediately to the platform. On the appearance of the apostle the second part of the drama begins. It is worthwhile to digress here so as to remind the reader of some principles behind the ritualistic ceremony and procession.[690] PAGE 178-179.

The Grand Entrance of the Hon. Elijah Muhammad

Without a doubt the most impressive visual of the meeting is the entrance of the Hon. Elijah Muhammad complete with his full security detail. An observer captures the event at the time:

Standing up of the audience, for example, at the command of the captain, "Stand erect," when the leader comes, keeping guards during the meetings all around the audience, beginning the meeting on Sunday by the "National Song," facing the East while reciting the prayer, behaving of the guards according to militaristic traditions in saluting one another when they change guard-spots, encircling the leader when he attends the hall of meeting in a semi-militaristic procession, and innumerable ways of behavior are some of the symbolic acts developed in this collectivity and operating as patterns of their behavior. PAGE 140

Whenever the Apostle is among them the followers are taught to be alert to everything in the temple. This issue had been taught to them in the Fruit-meeting class, where they learn militaristic training. It will be recalled that this militaristic organization had been established by W. D. Fard himself in order to stand against the attacks upon the group. Since that time this militaristic training has been carried on by the group on the basis of emerging belief that some day they will have to fight with the devil and therefore they have to be prepared and ready for that day. Out of these members who constitute the Fruit of Islam a "special detail" had been chosen from among the best trained members. This special detail has the duty of escorting the Apostle in the general meetings. They have another duty which is a ritual procession which runs as follows.

On Sundays when the Apostle attends the meeting the "special detail" members arrange themselves into two lines, A and B, waiting behind the door of the temple for the coming of the Apostle. The minute he comes they walk outside the temple, lining up into two lines extending from his car to the door of the temple. The Apostle gets out of his car and walks between these two lines, preceded by the captain. When the Apostle enters the temple these two lines line up in one line following the Apostle. The whole procession walks militaristically through the basement and then through a door leading to the rostrum. The minute the captain comes out of that door he shouts commanding "Attention," a command at which all the audience should stand up reverently and the minister who usually speaks at that time should stop speaking. The "special detail" continues walking forward while the Apostle steps out of the line to sit down on the rostrum. Then the captain, who is the commander of the escort, gives the command, "Left face." Then the captain walks toward the minister, salutes him militaristically, to tell him that "everything is O.K.," a statement to which the minister responds, saying, "Very well, take your place." Then the minister gives the command to the audience to sit down and continues his speech. The members of the special detail, after that, will be distributed to guard all around the temple, watching every individual in the meeting carefully.

Whenever the Apostle plans to come to the temple he calls up before his coming to give opportunity for the captain to arrange the escort.

When the minister ends his speech, the Apostle advances toward the speaker's stand, accompanied by very enthusiastic and highly emotional clapping matched with shouting, an opportunity through which the followers express their extreme attachment to their leader.

After saying "As Salaam Alaikum," to which the followers respond enthusiastically, "Alaikum As-Salaam," the Apostle begins "the record" which he repeats over and over again whenever he speaks to an audience...which lasts four to six hours. PAGE 179-181

Like Fard, Like Elijah, Dedicated to the Mission

Elijah Muhammad once said that he and his teacher "were like two arrows shot from the same bow." The Honorable Elijah Muhammad adopted his leadership ways from his mentor and teacher Master Fard Muhammad, and pledged his entire existence around leading the Nation of Islam, from his appearance, ways and demeanor, on down to the length of his lectures:

Elijah Mohammed now follows the steps of Fard in all the details of his thought and actions. His leadership has been developed and established by the support that he has acquired from Fard first and by his exact imitation of Fard himself later on. Because Fard used to speak for five or six hours in the meetings, he should speak for that long a time, although he has not that caliber. Because Fard used to speak and approach his subject "in a mathematical way," he should follow him in that respect; as long as Fard used to offer some money now and then to some of the police just to "keep them quiet," he should do the same, and so on.

However, the Apostle does not do any kind of work outside the area of the cult. He devotes his entire time to the organization, answering questions sent to him by various individuals or various ministers of the other branches, commanding the restaurant and sometimes serving the clients there or working in the kitchen, delivering lectures to this followers (a duty that takes so much time because he never speaks less than four hours at least), and traveling around to see what is going on in the other branches, which are scattered all over the North and West of the United States. PAGE 237

In answering my question, "How can you speak for such a long time?" the Apostle said, "Because Allah was speaking for such a long time," and since his duty, as a messenger of Allah to the dark people, is to deliver His message, "it takes at least," as the Apostle said, "five or six hours after I have tried time and again to do it in less than that and I was not able." PAGE 241

Years later the Hon. Elijah Muhammad would joke about this tradition during one of his lectures in Baltimore. He said, "My friend, I'm quite sure you educators know that it takes a lot of time for a man to get some details like that. We have a hard work, sometimes I stand six hours and going, just like you see me, without a swallow of water. And I have not been swallowing anything but some coffee today. Maybe you couldn't preach this hard if you not had fried chicken for breakfast. (laughs). But I never eat breakfast, I only eat one meal a day and that's in the evening, sometimes later. I have some brothers here who go three or four days and don't eat anything. That's good for you. That prolongs your life, and keeps the doctor away from your home."[691]

Black Muslim Culture

The Hon. Elijah Muhammad was forever mindful of his teacher's way with the Believers. As Master Fard Muhammad once engaged the Laborers and Believers on outings every Tuesday, the Hon. Elijah Muhammad allowed the Believers to use their talent to enhance the social activity and arts of the Nation of Islam. As such was the case with an artist who made portraits and crafts of NOI symbols and teachings:

One of the earliest followers in the movement became interested in drawing the "National" after he saw it for the first time when he attended the first meeting of the group. Once he made a big "National" from cloth which he offered to the Apostle as a present. The Apostle thanked him and encouraged him. Consequent upon this encouragement, Yacob (the name of the man) began to make metal badges on which the "National" was drawn and offer them free to his intimate friends. Other members began to ask Brother Yacob to do them the favor of making such badges for them. These Brothers were rewarding Brother Yacob by giving him some gifts or offering to him some few dollars. Brother Jacob began to be involved in this line of activity and he began to be creative in this field. He made another different badge for the Sisters, he began to make rings on which he engraves the "National," and he began to make various pictures representing symbolically various myths or showing some sacred place as Mecca, for example, or presenting a slogan, a sacred statement or prayer. The followers compete for obtaining what Brother Yacob makes. In fact, all the symbols, slogans, and badges which every follower carries or keeps at home were made by Brother Yacob, who is paid a regular price for each piece.[692] PAGE 254-255

Sisters Designed their Own Pieces

The women in the Nation of Islam were also free to create according to their skills and the needs of the MGT. One sister had designed a headpiece for the MGT to wear:

The Sisters used to wrap their heads with a piece of cloth. In the summer this kind of head-wear is very inconvenient. The Sisters under such conditions developed dissatisfaction with this kind of head-wear. They raised this complaint to the Apostle, who planned to see a Christian designer for this purpose. One of the Sisters is an expert in making hats. In fact, she makes hats for some of the well-known stores in Chicago. She said:

I heard about the decision of the Apostle and so I said, "Why do we restore to a Christian girl to do our head-wear while we are supposed to know better than them because they ate still ignorant and blind?" That night, after thinking deeply about designing the Sisters' head-wear, I dreamed that I saw myself designing it. So I awoke and put on paper what I have designed in the dream. Next morning I showed it to the Apostle, who O.K.'ed it. Ever since I began to make them and give them free to some of my acquaintances without any charge but the cost of the material. Later on I began to sell them to the Sisters. This new head-wear had been developed since one year.[693] PAGE 255-256

Paintings of W.D. Fard and the Mother Plane

Popular was art that focused on the coming of Master Fard Muhammad and the Mother Plane he prophesized to destroy America. Each Muslim treasured these works of art:

Each follower keeps in his home a big drawn picture hanging on the wall. This picture represents the end of the white race when Allah comes back and begins the war of Armageddon, bombing the devil by the "mother planes" which Mr. W. D. Fard had described fully to his messenger, who in turn transmitted this description to his followers. This picture is drawn in such a way that it represents the horrible condition of the white people under such a divine bombing. PAGE 142-143

In fine, their belief in the deity of Fard and in the prophecy of Elijah has been expressed by being written on a board that each member keeps in his home. The statement on this board runs as follows: "Allah is our dear Saviour come all the way from heaven to save his lost people, God Himself, Elijah Mohammed, is His last prophet." PAGE 235

Weekly Temple Activities

The following is an outline for the collective weekly Temple activities as practiced in the late '40s:

Collective activities of the group are of the following types, classified according to their functions:
1. Meetings for service three days a week; Sunday afternoon, Wednesday evening, and Friday evening.
2. Meetings for teachings:
   a) Monday evening: special for Brothers
   b) Tuesday evening: special for the Sisters.
3. Socialization and recreational meetings:
   a) Socialization at the restaurant.
   b) Meeting for witnessing contests among the students of the University of Islam, which are held now and then, in various subjects of the school. PAGE 175-176

[367]

FOI & MGT Class, Unity Night Socials

An additional insight was provided for the separate FOI and MGT classes, which included joint socials afterwards referred to as "Unity Night":

2. Meetings for teachings:

a) On Monday evening the Brothers meet for a lecture by the Apostle or the captain for one hour, from 8 to 9. In this lecture interpretations of lesson No. 1 and lesson No. 2 are carried out. Instructions about how to behave in the presence of the Apostle are also given during this period. From 9 to 10 there are gymnastics and military training.

b) On Tuesday evening the Sisters meet to receive the instructions which we have already sketched briefly elsewhere in this study.

When the Sisters end their lessons on Tuesday evening they go to the Shabazz restaurant, where they meet with the Brothers. Because of that, this night is called the "unity night." PAGE 183-186

University of Islam Programs

In his research the author gave insight into family or Temple activities that centered on the education of the children in the University of Islam, as well as a real life example of a professor conducting the activities:

Other opportunities for collective meeting occur when they have contests among the students of the University of Islam in some of the subjects of their study. Rewards are given to the winners in these contests. As an example of such kind of meetings let me sketch briefly the meeting which was held on Tuesday evening, February 27, in which three kinds of activities took place:

1. Students' achievements:
a) A contest in the spelling of English words among the students of the school.
b) A showing of the achievement of the students in the Arabic language through debates and telling stories and proverbs.

2. Movie:
   Showing films about the various countries of the East through which a Negro fellow who works in the Field Museum, addressed as Professor, actually a very small official there, was making such comments on the film as, for example, his statement, "Look, our ancestors were building such great pyramids [the scene was showing the pyramids in Egypt] even before the white man knows how to make a humble cottage."

3. Speech by leader:

The leader has spoken, saying, "We are happy to hear our youngster Brothers speaking the language of our ancestors." [He meant the Arabic language.] Then he addressed those young children, saying:

Be proud of this knowledge and speak Arabic among you all the time and use always "As-Salaam-Alaikum" instead of using good morning or good evening because we have no good evening unless we get freedom, justice, and equality. The devil and here he means the white man says to you "Good morning" to deceive you because you know that you have not any good.

Then he began to comment on what they have already seen in the film, saying, "Our ancestors five thousand years ago had built these greatest civilizations at the time no one knows what the other man was doing." Then he said:

The Arabic language is the greatest language in the world. You know that the English language is not a language. If it is a language then give me the permission to call it a bastard language because it is a product of thieving from here and there. If you know the Arabic language you can go all over the world and contact with all the people by it because this is the language of our nation and our nation is all over the world.

Then he began to speak about writing and he said, "Look for this universal writing from right to left where you can write universally; while you have, in the devil language, to raise your hand at the end of each line to begin another line, and so on." (Here the audience laughed approving this comment because the leader was showing them the difference pantominingly.) Then he said: "We will be soon in our ancestor's land because the other man, the Caucasian, is coming to his end; that is because the Caucasian is a race and not a nation; and the race has a beginning and therefore has an end, but we are a nation and the nation has no beginning and hence no end." Then he said, addressing the audience, "You have to know yourself, and if you know yourself then he himself comes to you." [Here he means that the white man comes to the member seeking his assent and what not.] PAGE 183-186

University of Islam Curriculum and Staff

The report also outlined the unique educational curriculum of the University of Islam, and part of its staff:

Today there is a school for each branch of the cult. In Chicago, the University of Islam is constituted of 56 students.

According to their general program the subjects which are taught in the University of Islam are as follows: "Penmanship, Reading and Spelling, Language and General Civilization, Arithmatic and Simple and Metric System, Advance Arithmatic, Algebra, Advance Algebra, General Geometry and Trigonometry, Astronomy, Chronological History from 13,000 B.C., Solar System, Spook being Displayed for 6000 years, Ending of the Spook Civilization, and Chronology." Since about a year they have introduced Arabic, Physics, Chemistry and Elementary Sociology into the program.

The University of Islam has a principal whose duty is to administrate and teach, an assistant principal whose duty is to do all the secretarial work and to teach also, and a "professor" who teaches Physics and Arabic language. PAGE 187-188

DEPARTMENT OF SUPREME WISDOM

April 2, 1936

First: History is all our studies. The most attractive, and best qualified to reward our research. As it develops the springs and motives of human action, and displays the consequence of circumstances which operates most powerfully on the destinies of human beings.

Second: It stands true that we the Lost Found NATION, of ISLAM, in the wilderness of North America have not applied ourselves to the study of History. But rather to FOLLY having a lots of the bread of, idleness and when an effort was made to the above affect of History study, it was to our detriment by not knowing what History that was more valuable, to aid us in the knowledge of our own Nation.

The WISE MAN, is the one who has made a careful study of the Past events of ANCIENT and MODERN HISTORY. The KNOWLEDGE of the FUTURE is JUDGED by the KNOWLEDGE of the PAST. There are MEN born with a gift of PROPHECY. While some are trained into the KNOWLEDGE by intense studies of the PAST EVENTS OF HISTORY...

By Elijah Muhammad

Servant of Allah

As-Salaam-Alaikum

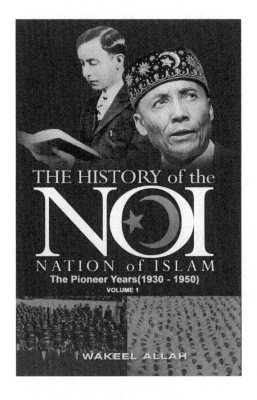

To order more copies of this book or
other A-Team Products:

www.ateampublishing.com
ateampublishing@yahoo.com

Please forward all written correspondence to:

A-Team Publishing
P.O. Box 551036
Atlanta, GA 30355

Other titles from A-Team Publishing:

www.Ateampublishing.com
www.theblackgod.com

[1] NOI staff, The True History Of The Nation Of Islam, N.P., N.D.

[2] Ibid.

[3] Frederick Douglass, "What, To the American Slave, Is Your 4th of July," Speech given by Frederick Douglass on July 4, 1952 in Rochester, New York.

[4] Elijah Muhammad, *The Fall of America,* Chapter 16," Independence Day".

[5] Anonymous, The True History Of The Nation Of Islam, .N.P., N.D.

[6] ibid.

[7] Emanuel Muhammad CD.

[8] Elijah Muhammad to Hatim A. Shahib in 1951 interview. Hatim A. Sahib, "The Nation of Islam," Masters thesis, University of Chicago, December 1951. Pg 65-66.

[9] E. D. Beynon, "The Voodoo Cult Among Negro Migrants in Detroit," *American Journal of Sociology,* May 1938. Interview with Sister Denke Majied (formerly Mrs. Lawrence Adams).

[10] Beynon, "The Voodoo Cult," *American Journal of Sociology,* Interview with Brother Challar Sharrieff.

[11] C. Eric Lincoln, *The Black Muslims in America* (Boston: Beacon Press, 1961) xxv.

[12] Beynon, "The Voodoo Cult" *American Journal of Sociology,* Interview with Brother Yusef Muhammad.

[13] Ibid.

[14] Elijah Muhammad to Hatim A. Shahib in 1951 interview. Hatim A. Sahib, "The Nation of Islam," Masters thesis, University of Chicago, December 1951. Pg 69

[15] Beynon, "The Voodoo Cult" *American Journal of Sociology.*

[16] Beynon, "The Voodoo Cult" *American Journal of Sociology.*

[17] Beynon, "The Voodoo Cult" *American Journal of Sociology.*

[18] Elijah Muhammad, "The History of the Nation of Islam."

[19] Beynon, "The Voodoo Cult" *American Journal of Sociology.*

[20] Master Fard Muhammad & Hon. Elijah Muhammad, The Student Enrollment, Questions and Answers (1-3). Undated.

[21] Beynon, "The Voodoo Cult" *The American Journal of Sociology,* May 1938.

[22] Lincoln, *The Black Muslims in America,* 114.

[23] Elijah Muhammad, *The Supreme Wisdom Vol. 1* (Atlanta: MEMPS, 1957) 21.

[24] "Clarification of Actions taken by Messenger Muhammad Against Muhammad Ali's Action," Muhammad Speaks Newspaper, April, 11, 1969.

[25] "Muslim Pioneer Hall of Fame: Pioneers of the 1930s (and Families), Detroit Michigan." This is a long list of NOI pioneers names that appear in the Original Temple #1, now known as "Masjid Wali Muhammad" in Detroit.

[26] Anonymous, The True History Of The Nation Of Islam, .N.P., N.D.

[27] NOI Temple #2, *"Elijah Muhammad: The Solution to the so-called Negro Problem,"* Video documentary. Continental Studios, Elk Grove Village, Illinois. February 20, 1975.

[28] NOI Temple #2, *"Elijah Muhammad: The Solution to the so-called Negro Problem,"* Video documentary. Continental Studios, Elk Grove Village, Illinois. February 20, 1975.

[29] Anonymous, The True History Of The Nation Of Islam, .N.P., N.D.

[30] Sahib, "The Nation of Islam," 88-89.

[31] Emanuel Muhammad, "Faith and Obedience in Allah and His Messenger," Muhammad Speaks, March 7, 1975. Pg 3, 13.

[32] Malu Halasa, *Black Americans of Achievement: Elijah Muhammad,* (Chelsea House Publishers, 1990).

[33] NOI Temple #2, *"Elijah Muhammad: The Solution to the so-called Negro Problem,"* Video documentary. Continental Studios, Elk Grove Village, Illinois. February 20, 1975.

[34] NOI Temple #2, *"Elijah Muhammad: The Solution to the so-called Negro Problem,"* Video documentary. Continental Studios, Elk Grove Village, Illinois. February 20, 1975.

[35] Elijah Muhammad, "The Theology of Time", Secretarius Publications 2002. Pg. 173

[36] The Hon. Elijah Muhammad, "Table Talks of the Hon. Elijah Muhammad", Track 9 "The Thinking of God". Aug. 1973.

[37] Sahib, "The Nation of Islam," 88-89.

[38] Malu Halasa, *Black Americans of Achievement: Elijah Muhammad,* (Chelsea House Publishers, 1990) 20-21.

[39] Ibid.

[40] Sahib, "The Nation of Islam," 88-89.

[41] Sahib, "The Nation of Islam," 88-89.

[42] History of the Hon. Elijah Muhammad, Masjid Wali Muhammad in Detroit, Michigan. http://www.umich.edu/~biid/FM_Masjid_Wali_Muhammad.html

[43] Elijah Muhammad "From the Messenger of Allah: Nothing Can Hinder Truth,"*Muhammad Speaks,* November 6, 1964. Pg. 3. Supplemented by transcription from author of original lecture recording found on "Table Talks Project" on Facebook.

[44] Sahib, "The Nation of Islam," 88-89.

[45] Sahib, "The Nation of Islam," 88-89.

[46] NOI Temple #2, *"Elijah Muhammad: The Solution to the so-called Negro Problem,"* Video documentary. Continental Studios, Elk Grove Village, Illinois. February 20, 1975.

[47] NOI Temple #2, *"Elijah Muhammad: The Solution to the so-called Negro Problem,"* Video documentary. Continental Studios, Elk Grove Village, Illinois. February 20, 1975.

[48] NOI Temple #2, *"Elijah Muhammad: The Solution to the so-called Negro Problem,"* Video documentary. Continental Studios, Elk Grove Village, Illinois. February 20, 1975.

[49] Emanuel Muhammad CD.

[50] NOI Temple #2, *"Elijah Muhammad: The Solution to the so-called Negro Problem,"* Video documentary. Continental Studios, Elk Grove Village, Illinois. February 20, 1975.

[51] Sahib, "The Nation of Islam," 88-89.

[52] NOI Temple #2, *"Elijah Muhammad: The Solution to the so-called Negro Problem,"* Video documentary. Continental Studios, Elk Grove Village, Illinois. February 20, 1975.

[53] Sahib, "The Nation of Islam," 89-90.

[54] Minister John Muhammad, Muhammad Speaks website, http://www.muhammadspeaks.com/smJohnMuhammadpasses.html

[55] FBI Files on Fard.

[56] Samuel 17X, interview of Emanuel Muhammad, "My Father's Message, Fearless and Forceful: A Son Looks at a Great Father," Muhammad Speaks.

[57] Sahib, "The Nation of Islam," 89-90.

[58] Ibid.

[59] Halasa, *Elijah Muhammad,* 42-43.

[60] NOI Temple #2, *"Elijah Muhammad: The Solution to the so-called Negro Problem,"* Video documentary. Continental Studios, Elk Grove Village, Illinois. February 20, 1975.

[61] Samuel 17X, interview of Emanuel Muhammad, "My Father's Message, Fearless and Forceful: A Son Looks at a Great Father," Muhammad Speaks.

[62] NOI Temple #2, *"Elijah Muhammad: The Solution to the so-called Negro Problem,"* Video documentary. Continental Studios, Elk Grove Village, Illinois. February 20, 1975.

[63] Steven Barboza, *American Jihad: Islam After Malcolm X, "The Communicator" interview with Wali Fard Muhammad.* (Image Book, DoubleDay Publishing, 1994) 272.

[64] Emanuel Muhammad, "Faith and Obedience in Allah and His Messenger," Muhammad Speaks, March 7, 1975. Pg 3, 13.

[65] Sahib, "The Nation of Islam," 91-92.

[66] Nathaniel Muhammad, The Lance Shabazz Show #159. Part 2. Interview conducted by Lance Shabazz.

[67] "Islam in America" Part 10. Interview conducted with Imam W.D. Mohammed by Umar Jamil Nasser. Added March 14, 2008. http://www.youtube.com/watch?v=1X9RMJqE3ls

[68] Min. Nathaniel Muhammad, interview with Author, Sept 30, 2010.

[69] Nathaniel Muhammad, The Lance Shabazz Show #159. Part 2. Interview conducted by Lance Shabazz.

[70] Supreme Minister John Muhammad, "Sup. Min. John Muhammad Interview with Munir", CROE TV, August 30, 1995.

[71] The Early History of Master Fard Muhammad as told by Minister John Muhammad, (Blood Brother of Elijah) Part 1

[72] Supreme Minister John Muhammad, "Sup. Min. John Muhammad Interview with Munir", CROE TV.

[73] Sahib, "The Nation of Islam," 91-92.

[74] Jabril Muhammad, *This is the One: The Most Honored Elijah Muhammad, We Need Not Look For Another, Volume 1*. (Arizona: Book Company, 1993) 163.

[75] Ibid.

[76] Sahib, "The Nation of Islam," 91-92.

[77] Elijah Muhammad, *Message to the Black Man* (Atlanta: MEMPS, 1964) 16-17.

[78] J. Muhammad, *This is the One*, 163.

[79] J. Muhammad, *This is the One*, 164.

[80] Sahib, "The Nation of Islam," 91-92.

[81] Sahib, "The Nation of Islam," 122-123.

[82] Sahib, "The Nation of Islam," 203-205.

[83] Sahib, "The Nation of Islam," 93.

[84] Sahib, "The Nation of Islam," 93.

[85] Sahib, "The Nation of Islam," 91-92.

[86] Sahib, "The Nation of Islam," 123.

[87] Minister John Muhammad, Muhammad Speaks website, http://www.muhammadspeaks.com/smJohnMuhammadpasses.html

[88] This article was reprinted in the January 1994 issue of Muhammad Speaks Continues Newspaper. It originally appeared in the April-May 1990 issue of Muhammad Speaks Continues Newspaper, and is written by The Supreme Minister, John Muhammad and entitled: "THE COMING OF ALLAH (GOD) AND HIS FOUR GREAT JUDGMENTS." Part #2 follows.

[89] Sahib, "The Nation of Islam," 91-92.

[90] Sahib, "The Nation of Islam," 91-92.

[91] Sahib, "The Nation of Islam," 126-127.

[92] E. Muhammad, *Message to the Black Man*, 16-17.

[93] J. Muhammad, *This is the One*, 167.

[94] J. Muhammad, *This is the One*, 167.

[95] Elijah Muhammad, Interview with Buzz Anderson.

[96] J. Muhammad, *This is the One*, 168.

[97] J. Muhammad, *This is the One*, 167.-168.

[98] Wesley Muhammad Phd, *Master Fard Muhammad: Who is He? Who is He Not?* (A-Team Publishing, 2009) 19.

[99] (Ministry Class taught by The most Honorable Elijah Muhammad In the 1930's Volume 2).

[100] Min. Nathaniel Muhammad, interview with Author, Sept 30, 2010.

[101] Elijah Muhammad, *The True History of Master Fard Muhammad* (Atlanta: MEMPS, 1996) 50.

[102] Elijah Muhammad, 1936 Letter to Detroit Laborers.

[103] Elijah Muhammad, "The Theology of Time", Secretarius Publications 2002.

[104] Elijah Muhammad: June 4th, 1972 A.D. *The Theology of Time*

[105] Halasa, *Elijah Muhammad*, 50-51.

[106] Beynon, "The Voodoo Cult," *The American Journal of Sociology*, May 1938.

[107] Elijah Muhammad, *How to Eat to Live* (Chicago: Final Call Publishing).

[108] Ibid, 281-282.

[109] NOI Temple #2, "*Elijah Muhammad: The Solution to the so-called Negro Problem,*" Video documentary. Continental Studios, Elk Grove Village, Illinois. February 20, 1975.

[110] Steven Barboza, *American Jihad: Islam After Malcolm X, "The Messenger's Kin"* interview with *Ayman Muhammad*. (Image Book, DoubleDay Publishing, 1994) 269.

[111] Emanuel Muhammad CD.

[112] Emanuel Muhammad CD.

[113] NOI Temple #2, "*Elijah Muhammad: The Solution to the so-called Negro Problem,*" Video documentary. Continental Studios, Elk Grove Village, Illinois. February 20, 1975.

[114] Hashim Hakim and Sandra Muhammad, "Ethel Sharrief, Daughter of Hon. Elijah Muhammad," *The Final Call Newspaper*, January 1, 2003.

[115] Samuel 17X, interview of Emanuel Muhammad, "My Father's Message, Fearless and Forceful: A Son Looks at a Great Father," Muhammad Speaks.

[116] Min. Nathaniel Muhammad, interview with Author, Sept 30, 2010.

[117] Min. Nathaniel Muhammad, interview with Author, Sept 30, 2010.

[118] Nathaniel Muhammad, The Lance Shabazz Show #159. Part 2. Interview conducted by Lance Shabazz.

[119] Interview with Norman Thrasher.

[120] Min. Nathaniel Muhammad, interview with Author, Sept 30, 2010.

[121] Tynetta Muhammad, "We Have Come to the End of the Old Mind and the Old World's Thinking as we Enter the Changeover of Worlds", The Final Call Newspaper By Mother Tynnetta Muhammad, September 21, 2012.

[122] Min. Nathaniel Muhammad, interview with Author, Sept 30, 2010.

[123] Ibid.

[124] ibid.

[125] Tynetta Muhammad, "The Master and The Water Glass", The Final Call Newspaper By Mother Tynnetta Muhammad, May 18, 2007.

[126] Written and sent to Ministers and Muslims in general in the Wilderness of North America. Written and sent by General Instructor and Servant of Allah: Elijah Muhammad, undated.

[127] Elijah Muhammad, "Muslim Conduct", Muhammad Speaks, July 7, 1961.

[128] Beynon, "The Voodoo Cult," The American Journal of Sociology, May 1938.

[129] The Early History of Master Fard Muhammad as told by Minister John Muhammad, (Blood Brother of Elijah) Part 1

[130] The Early History of Master Fard Muhammad as told by Minister John Muhammad, (Blood Brother of Elijah) Part 2

[131] The Early History of Master Fard Muhammad as told by Minister John Muhammad, (Blood Brother of Elijah) Part 1

[132] The Early History of Master Fard Muhammad as told by Minister John Muhammad, (Blood Brother of Elijah) Part 2

[133] The Early History of Master Fard Muhammad as told by Minister John Muhammad, (Blood Brother of Elijah) Part 1

[134] Supreme Minister John Muhammad, "Master Fard Muhammad Chooses the Messenger over other Ministers," by C.R.O.E. Munir Muhammad. Interview w Supreme Minister John Muhammad. 8/30/1995.

[135] Min. Nathaniel Muhammad, interview with Author, Sept 30, 2010.

[136] Elijah Muhammad, "Explanation of what the Muslims Want and Believe", Message to the Black Man, Chapt. 75.

[137] "The History of The Nation of Islam" - MEMPS. Pg. 26. [Second Interview with Buzz Anderson 1964]

[138] Emanuel Muhammad CD.

[139] Minister Jam Muhammad, Muhammad Speaks website, http://www.muhammadspeaks.com/JamMuhammad.html

[140] Minister Jam Muhammad, Muhammad Speaks website, http://www.muhammadspeaks.com/JamMuhammad.html

[141] Johnnie Muhammad, Muhammad Speaks website, http://www.muhammadspeaks.com/Bro.Johnnie.html

[142] Minister John Muhammad, Muhammad Speaks website, http://www.muhammadspeaks.com/smJohnMuhammadpasses.html

[143] John Muhammad, The Journal of Truth (U.B. & U.S. Communication Systems, July 1996) 116-121.

[144] John Muhammad, The Journal of Truth (U.B. & U.S. Communication Systems, July 1996) 116-121.

[145] John Muhammad, The Journal of Truth (U.B. & U.S. Communication Systems, July 1996) 116-121.

[146] Elijah Muhammad, "1964 Laborers Meeting", transcript.

[147] Karriem Allah, "The Early Days Pt. 2," Muhammad Speaks, February 28, 1975. Pg 3.

[148] Sahib, "The Nation of Islam," 79

[149] Sahib, "The Nation of Islam," 93-95.

[150] Sahib, "The Nation of Islam," 93-95.

[151] Elijah Muhammad, The History of the Nation of Islam, M.E.M.P.S (Atlanta).

[152] Elizabeth Hassan, "Her Life Was Transformed," Muhammad Speaks, February 14, 1964, (Chicago, Ill)

[153] "Bushman comes to Chicago, He was Lincoln Park Zoo's most popular resident, but not always its best tempered", The Chicago Tribune, August 15, 1930, http://www.chicagotribune.com/news/politics/chi-chicagodays-bushman-story,0,1541189.story

[154] Muhammad Abdullah, son of the Hon. Elijah Muhammad, lecture at Mosque Maryam.

[155] David Fard, "Thanks Allah for Divine Messenger," Muhammad Speaks, February 10, 1967. Pg 25, Muhammad's Mosque No. 1

[156] Sahib, "The Nation of Islam," 74-75.

[157] Sahib, "The Nation of Islam," 95-96.

[158] FBI files.

[159] Sahib, "The Nation of Islam," 95-96.

[160] Sahib, "The Nation of Islam," 95-96.

[161] Sahib, "The Nation of Islam," 95-96.

[162] Samuel 17X, interview of Emanuel Muhammad, "My Father's Message, Fearless and Forceful: A Son Looks at a Great Father," Muhammad Speaks.

[163] Anonymous,. Article contained in NOI Orientation Packet for processing Muslims. N.P., N.D.

[164] Min. Nathaniel Muhammad, interview with Author, Sept 30, 2010.

[165] Min. Nathaniel Muhammad, interview with Author, Sept 30, 2010.

[166] Nathaniel Muhammad, The Lance Shabazz Show #159. Part 2. Interview conducted by Lance Shabazz.

[167] Nathaniel Muhammad, The Lance Shabazz Show #159. Part 2. Interview conducted by Lance Shabazz.

[168] Supreme Minister John Muhammad, "Sup. Min. John Muhammad Interview with Munir", CROE TV.

[169] Imam W.D. Mohammed, Islamic Convention Chicago IL 8/31/2002

[170] Supreme Minister John Muhammad, "Sup. Min. John Muhammad Interview with Munir", CROE TV.

[171] To the Ministry Class of No. 1 Michigan by Elijah Muhammad, Servant of Allah. December 3, 1934

[172] Min. Nathaniel Muhammad, interview with Author, Sept 30, 2010.

[173] Nathaniel Muhammad, The Lance Shabazz Show #159. Part 2. Interview conducted by Lance Shabazz.

[174] Elijah Muhammad, "The Book of Names," from the Table Talks Series.

[175] Beynon, "The Voodoo Cult," The American Journal of Sociology, May 1938.

[176] The Early History of Master Fard Muhammad as told by Minister John Muhammad, (Blood Brother of Elijah) Part 3

[177] The Early History of Master Fard Muhammad as told by Minister John Muhammad, (Blood Brother of Elijah) Part 3

[178] The Early History of Master Fard Muhammad as told by Minister John Muhammad, (Blood Brother of Elijah) Part 2

[179] Minister John Muhammad, Muhammad Speaks website, http://www.muhammadspeaks.com/smJohnMuhammadpasses.html

[180] Sahib, "The Nation of Islam," 84-85

[181] Sahib, "The Nation of Islam," 84-85

[182] Sahib, "The Nation of Islam," 92

[183] Emanuel Muhammad CD.

[184] Emanuel Muhammad CD.

[185] Jabril Muhammad, "The 144,000" lecture, Nov. 15, 2000.

[186] "Leader of Cult Admits Slaying at Home 'Alter'", Detroit Free Press, November 21, 1932. Pg. 1

[187] "Voodoo Slayer Admits Plotting Death of Judges", *Detroit Free Press*, November 22, 1932. Pg. 1
[188] "Head of Cult Admits Killing," *Detroit News*, Monday, November 21, 1932. Pg. 1
[189] "Voodoo Slayer Admits Plotting Death of Judges", *Detroit Free Press*, November 22, 1932. Pg. 1
[190] "Voodoo Slayer Admits Plotting Death of Judges", *Detroit Free Press*, November 22, 1932. Pg. 1
[191] "Leader of Cult Called Insane," *Detroit News*, Tuesday, November 22, 1932.
[192] "Voodoo Slayer Admits Plotting Death of Judges", *Detroit Free Press*, November 22, 1932. Pg. 1
[193] "Leader of Cult Admits Slaying at Home 'Alter'", *Detroit Free Press*, November 21, 1932. Pg. 1
[194] "Voodoo Slayer Admits Plotting Death of Judges", *Detroit Free Press*, November 22, 1932. Pg. 1
[195] "Leader of Cult to be Quizzed," *Detroit News*, Tuesday, November 23, 1932. Pg. 7
[196] "Leader of Cult to be Quizzed," *Detroit News*, Tuesday, November 23, 1932. Pg. 7
[197] "Leader of Cult Called Insane," *Detroit News*, Tuesday, November 22, 1932.
[198] "Leader of Cult to be Quizzed," *Detroit News*, Tuesday, November 23, 1932. Pg. 7
[199] "Voodoo Slayer Admits Plotting Death of Judges", *Detroit Free Press*, November 22, 1932. Pg. 1
[200] "Leader of Cult Admits Slaying at Home 'Alter'", *Detroit Free Press*, November 21, 1932. Pg. 1
[201] "Voodoo Slayer Admits Plotting Death of Judges", *Detroit Free Press*, November 22, 1932. Pg. 1
[202] "Leader of Cult Admits Slaying at Home 'Alter'", *Detroit Free Press*, November 21, 1932. Pg. 1
[203] "Voodoo Slayer Admits Plotting Death of Judges", *Detroit Free Press*, November 22, 1932. Pg. 1
[204] "Voodoo Slayer Admits Plotting Death of Judges", *Detroit Free Press*, November 22, 1932. Pg. 1
[205] "Leader of Cult to be Quizzed," *Detroit News*, Tuesday, November 23, 1932. Pg. 7
[206] "Raided Temple Bares Grip of Voodoo in City", *Detroit Free Press*, Wednesday, November 23, 1932. Pg. 1
[207] "Raided Temple Bares Grip of Voodoo in City", *Detroit Free Press*, Wednesday, November 23, 1932. Pg. 1
[208] "Raided Temple Bares Grip of Voodoo in City", *Detroit Free Press*, Wednesday, November 23, 1932. Pg. 1
[209] "Raided Temple Bares Grip of Voodoo in City", *Detroit Free Press*, Wednesday, November 23, 1932. Pg. 1
[210] "Raided Temple Bares Grip of Voodoo in City", *Detroit Free Press*, Wednesday, November 23, 1932. Pg. 1
[211] "Raided Temple Bares Grip of Voodoo in City", *Detroit Free Press*, Wednesday, November 23, 1932. Pg. 1
[212] "Negro Leaders Open Fight to Break Voodooism's Grip", *Detroit Free Press*, Thursday, November 24, 1932. Pg. 1
[213] Detroit Free Press Newspaper
[214] "Intended Voodoo Victims' Number Still Mounting", *Detroit Free Press*, Sunday, November 27, 1932. Pg. 1
[215] The Detroit Free Press, November 24, 1932. Pg. 20
[216] E. D. Beynon, Prince –A- Cuba, *Detroit History* (Newport News: United Brothers & United Sisters Communications Systems, 1990) 6.
[217] "Negro Leaders Open Fight to Break Voodooism's Grip", *Detroit Free Press*, Thursday, November 24, 1932. Pg. 1
[218] "Harris, Cult Slayer, Faces Court Friday," *Detroit News*, Thursday, November 24, 1932.
[219] "Negro Leaders Open Fight to Break Voodooism's Grip", *Detroit Free Press*, Thursday, November 24, 1932. Pg. 1
[220] "Negro Leaders Open Fight to Break Voodooism's Grip", *Detroit Free Press*, Thursday, November 24, 1932. Pg. 1
[221] "500 Join March to Ask Voodoo Kings' Freedom", *Detroit Free Press*, Friday, November 25, 1932. Pg. 1
[222] "500 Join March to Ask Voodoo Kings' Freedom", *Detroit Free Press*, Friday, November 25, 1932. Pg. 1
[223] "Cult Slayer Pleads Guilty," *Detroit News*, Friday, November 25, 1932. Pg. 1
[224] E. Muhammad, *Message to the Black Man*, 16-17.
[225] "The Little Known Facts On! The Great Master Fard Muhammad & The Honorable Elijah Muhammad," Quote from Secretary John Muhammad under Master Fard Muhammad. Unpublished manuscript, Not dated.
[226] "500 Join March to Ask Voodoo Kings' Freedom", *Detroit Free Press*, Friday, November 25, 1932. Pg. 1

[227] Karl Evanzz, "The Messenger: The Rise and Fall of Elijah Muhammad", Pantheon Books, 1999.

[228] "Cult Slayer Pleads Guilty," *Detroit News*, Friday, November 25, 1932. Pg. 1

[229] "Cult Slayer Pleads Guilty," *Detroit News*, Friday, November 25, 1932. Pg. 1

[230] "New Human Sacrifice With a Boy as Victim is Averted by Inquiry", *Detroit Free Press*, Saturday, November 26, 1932. Pg. 1

[231] "New Human Sacrifice With a Boy as Victim is Averted by Inquiry", *Detroit Free Press*, Saturday, November 26, 1932. Pg. 1

[232] "New Human Sacrifice With a Boy as Victim is Averted by Inquiry", *Detroit Free Press*, Saturday, November 26, 1932. Pg. 1

[233] "Intended Voodoo Victims' Number Still Mounting", *Detroit Free Press*, Sunday, November 27, 1932. Pg. 1

[234] "New Human Sacrifice With a Boy as Victim is Averted by Inquiry", *Detroit Free Press*, Saturday, November 26, 1932. Pg. 1

[235] "500 Join March to Ask Voodoo Kings' Freedom", *Detroit Free Press*, Friday, November 25, 1932. Pg. 1

[236] "New Human Sacrifice With a Boy as Victim is Averted by Inquiry", *Detroit Free Press*, Saturday, November 26, 1932. Pg. 1

[237] "Intended Voodoo Victims' Number Still Mounting", *Detroit Free Press*, Sunday, November 27, 1932. Pg. 1

[238] "New Human Sacrifice With a Boy as Victim is Averted by Inquiry", *Detroit Free Press*, Saturday, November 26, 1932. Pg. 1

[239] "Intended Voodoo Victims' Number Still Mounting", *Detroit Free Press*, Sunday, November 27, 1932. Pg. 1

[240] "Pastors Decry Growth of Cult Practices Here", *Detroit Free Press*, Monday, November 28, 1932. Pg. 1

[241] "Pastors Decry Growth of Cult Practices Here", *Detroit Free Press*, Monday, November 28, 1932. Pg. 1

[242] "Pastors Decry Growth of Cult Practices Here", *Detroit Free Press*, Monday, November 28, 1932. Pg. 1

[243] "Suburbs also in Voodoo Net", *Detroit Free Press*, Tuesday, November 29, 1932. Pg. 1

[244] "Voodoo Chief Held Unsound", *Detroit Free Press*, Wednesday, November 30, 1932. Pg. 3

[245] "Slayer Held Insane; Fard Quits City, the Detroit Free Press, December 7, 1932

[246] Karl Evanzz, "The Messenger: The Rise and Fall of Elijah Muhammad", Pantheon Books, 1999.

[247] Karl Evanzz, "The Messenger: The Rise and Fall of Elijah Muhammad", Pantheon Books, 1999.

[248] Beynon, "The Voodoo Cult," *The American Journal of Sociology*, May 1938.

[249] E.U. Essien-Udom, *"Black Nationalism",* The University of Chicago Press, (1962)

[250] Beynon, "The Voodoo Cult," *The American Journal of Sociology,* May 1938.

[251] Karl Evanzz, "The Messenger: The Rise and Fall of Elijah Muhammad", Pantheon Books, 1999.

[252] Elijah Muhammad, "Instructions to the Muslim; Fathers and Mothers of Islam in North America:

How to care for pregnant mothers and their unborn babies," June 7, 1936.

[253] NOI History presentation given by Sister Medina Muhammad for Mosque #12.

[254] Muhammad's University of Islam No. 2 1963 pamphlet, "HISTORY OF THE SCHOOL".

[255] I AM Burnsteen Sharrieff Mohammed, Reformer and Secretary To MASTER W.D.F. MOHAMMED

[256] I AM Burnsteen Sharrieff Mohammed, Reformer and Secretary To MASTER W.D.F. MOHAMMED

[257] I AM Burnsteen Sharrieff Mohammed, Reformer and Secretary To MASTER W.D.F. MOHAMMED

[258] I AM Burnsteen Sharrieff Mohammed, Reformer and Secretary To MASTER W.D.F. MOHAMMED

[259] I AM Burnsteen Sharrieff Mohammed, Reformer and Secretary To MASTER W.D.F. MOHAMMED

[260] Master Fard Muhammad & Elijah Muhammad, *Lost-Found Muslim Lesson No. 2,* Questions 12-13, February 20, 1934.

[261] Poem by Shadad Ali (1934), document from NOI History exhibit.

[262] Benjamin Karim, with Peter Skutches and David Gallen, *Remembering Malcolm* (New York: Carroll & Graf, 1992) 71-72.

[263] Lincoln, *The Black Muslims in America,* 224.

[264] A note posted on Facebook via Sis. Burnsteen's son.

[265] Lincoln, *The Black Muslims in America* 225.

[266] Haley, *The Autobiography of Malcolm X,* 231-232.

[267] I AM Burnsteen Sharrieff Mohammed, Reformer and Secretary To MASTER W.D.F. MOHAMMED

[268] I AM Burnsteen Sharrieff Mohammed, Reformer and Secretary To MASTER W.D.F. MOHAMMED

[269] "Muslim Pioneers Remember the Early Years of Islam." Article Photo's & captions reprinted from the March 16, 1973 edition of Muhammad Speaks Newspaper

[270] "Muslim Pioneers Remember the Early Years of Islam." Article Photo's & captions reprinted from the March 16, 1973 edition of Muhammad Speaks Newspaper

[271] "Muslim Pioneers Remember the Early Years of Islam." Article Photo's & captions reprinted from the March 16, 1973 edition of Muhammad Speaks Newspaper

[272] By Nathaniel 10X, "Pioneers remember early years of Islam," Muhammad Speaks, April 20, 1973, pg. 10?

[273] NOI Temple #2, *"Elijah Muhammad: The Solution to the so-called Negro Problem,"* Video documentary. Continental Studios, Elk Grove Village, Illinois. February 20, 1975.

[274] Sister Mary Ali, "Islam Brought Me Into The Glory of a Great New Life," Muhammad Speaks, January 29, 1965. Pg. 21.

[275] The following is an excerpt from "Muhammad Speaks Continues" Vol. 2, No. 49, pg 16.

[276] Minister John Muhammad, Muhammad Speaks website, http://www.muhammadspeaks.com/smJohnMuhammadpasses.html

[277] The Early History of Master Fard Muhammad as told by Minister John Muhammad, (Blood Brother of Elijah) Part 3

[278] The Early History of Master Fard Muhammad as told by Minister John Muhammad, (Blood Brother of Elijah) Part 4

[279] The Early History of Master Fard Muhammad as told by Minister John Muhammad, (Blood Brother of Elijah) Part 4

[280] Karl Evanzz, "The Messenger: The Rise and Fall of Elijah Muhammad", Pantheon Books, 1999.

[281] Emanuel Muhammad, "Faith and Obedience in Allah and His Messenger," Muhammad Speaks, March 7, 1975. Pg 3, 13)

[282] Min. Nathaniel Muhammad, interview with Author, Sept 30, 2010.

[283] Sahib, "The Nation of Islam," 84-85

[284] Sahib, "The Nation of Islam," 7 1.

[285] Min. Nathaniel Muhammad, interview with Author, Sept 30, 2010.

[286] E. Muhammad, *Message to the Black Man,* 16-17.

[287] Min. Nathaniel Muhammad, interview with Author, Sept 30, 2010.

[288] NOI Temple #2, *"Elijah Muhammad: The Solution to the so-called Negro Problem,"* Video documentary. Continental Studios, Elk Grove Village, Illinois. February 20, 1975.

[289] "Muslim Pioneers Remember the Early Years of Islam." Article Photo's & captions reprinted from the March 16, 1973 edition of Muhammad Speaks Newspaper

[290] "Muslim Pioneers Remember the Early Years of Islam." Article Photo's & captions reprinted from the March 16, 1973 edition of Muhammad Speaks Newspaper

[291] "Muslim Pioneers Remember the Early Years of Islam." Article Photo's & captions reprinted from the March 16, 1973 edition of Muhammad Speaks Newspaper

[292] John Hassan, "Out of Small Georgia Town—Into the Light of Islam," Muhammad Speaks, January 3, 1964. Pg 7.

[293] John Hassan, "Out of Small Georgia Town—Into the Light of Islam," Muhammad Speaks, January 3, 1964. Pg. 7.

[294] James Pasha, "Became Muslim After the First Speech I Heard From Lips of the Messenger," Muhammad Speaks, September 11, 1965. Pg. 4

[295] James Pasha, "Became Muslim After the First Speech I Heard From Lips of the Messenger," Muhammad Speaks, September 11, 1965. Pg. 4

[296] Written and sent to Ministers and Muslims in general in the Wilderness of North America. Written and sent by General Instructor and Servant of Allah: Elijah Muhammad, undated.

[297] Written and sent to Ministers and Muslims in general in the Wilderness of North America. Written and sent by General Instructor and Servant of Allah: Elijah Muhammad, undated.

[298] Written and sent to Ministers and Muslims in general in the Wilderness of North America. Written and sent by General Instructor and Servant of Allah: Elijah Muhammad, undated.

[299] Written and sent to Ministers and Muslims in general in the Wilderness of North America. Written and sent by General Instructor and Servant of Allah: Elijah Muhammad, undated.

[300] Min. Nathaniel Muhammad, interview with Author, Sept 30, 2010.

[301] "A Brief History of the Messenger," by Samuel 17X, interview with Karriem Allah, Muhammad Speaks Newspaper, undated.

[302] "A Brief History of the Messenger," by Samuel 17X, interview with Karriem Allah, Muhammad Speaks Newspaper, undated.

[303] "A Brief History of the Messenger," by Samuel 17X, interview with Karriem Allah, Muhammad Speaks Newspaper, undated.

[304] "A Brief History of the Messenger," by Samuel 17X, interview with Karriem Allah, Muhammad Speaks Newspaper, undated.

[305] "A Brief History of the Messenger," by Samuel 17X, interview with Karriem Allah, Muhammad Speaks Newspaper, undated.

[306] "A Brief History of the Messenger," by Samuel 17X, interview with Karriem Allah, Muhammad Speaks Newspaper, undated.

[307] Karriem Allah, "The Early Days of the Messenger's Mission: 'The Glorious Past', Muhammad Speaks, August 10, 1973. Pg 15.

[308] Karriem Allah, "The Early Days of the Messenger's Mission: 'The Glorious Past', Muhammad Speaks, August 10, 1973. Pg 15.

[309] "Muslim Pioneers Remember the Early Years of Islam." Article Photo's & captions reprinted from the March 16, 1973 edition of Muhammad Speaks Newspaper

[310] "Muslim Pioneers Remember the Early Years of Islam." Article Photo's & captions reprinted from the March 16, 1973 edition of Muhammad Speaks Newspaper

[311] By Nathaniel 10X, "Pioneers remember early years of Islam," Muhammad Speaks, April 20, 1973, pg. 10?

[312] Karriem Allah, "The Early Days," Muhammad Speaks, May 24, 1974. Pg 3.

[313] Karriem Allah, "The Early Days Pt. 2," Muhammad Speaks, December 27, 1974. Pg 3.

[314] Karl Evanzz, "The Messenger: The Rise and Fall of Elijah Muhammad", Pantheon Books, 1999.

[315] E. Muhammad, Message to the Black Man, 16-17.

[316] Elijah Muhammad, "Islamic World", New Amsterdam News, Feb. 8, 1958

[317] Elijah Muhammad, Our Saviour Has Arrived, pg. 23.

[318] Master Fard Muhammad, Taken from the Supreme Wisdom Lesson called "The Problem Book", Question #13, Undated.

[319] Karriem Allah, "The Early Days of Islam Part III," Muhammad Speaks, August 17, 1973. Pg 18.

[320] Karriem Allah, "The Early Days of the Messenger's Mission: 'The Glorious Past Part II', Muhammad Speaks, July 27, 1973. Pg 18.

[321] Karriem Allah, "The Early Days," Muhammad Speaks, June 14, 1974. Pg 3.

[322] John Hassan, "Out of Small Georgia Town—Into the Light of Islam," Muhammad Speaks, January 3, 1964. Pg 7.

[323] Karriem Allah, "The Early Days Pt. 2," Muhammad Speaks, March 7, 1975. Pg 3.

[324] NOI Temple #2, "Elijah Muhammad: The Solution to the so-called Negro Problem," Video documentary. Continental Studios, Elk Grove Village, Illinois. February 20, 1975.

[325] Imam W. Deen Mohammed's Address at "Savior Day" - Feb. 26, 2002, in Charleston, SC.

[326] Supreme Minister John Muhammad, "Sup. Min. John Muhammad Interview with Munir", CROE TV, August 30, 1995.

[327] The Hon. Elijah Muhammad's Letter to Imam Wallace D. Mohammed.

[328] Min. Nathaniel Muhammad, interview with Author, Sept 30, 2010.

[329] The Nation of Islam In Milwaukee, A Brief History, http://mosque3.org/history.html Muhammad's mosque #3 website Milwaukee
[330] Letter from Master Fard Muhammad to the Hon. Elijah Muhammad, from the SouthWest Part of N. America, December 18, 1933, at 4 A.M.
[331] Letter from Master Fard Muhammad to the Hon. Elijah Muhammad, from the SouthWest Part of N. America, December 18, 1933, at 4 A.M.
[332] Letter from Master Fard Muhammad to the Hon. Elijah Muhammad, from the SouthWest Part of N. America, December 18, 1933, at 4 A.M.
[333] Letter from Master Fard Muhammad to the Hon. Elijah Muhammad, from the SouthWest Part of N. America, December 18, 1933, at 4 A.M.
[334] Nuruddin, "The Five Percenters" 1994.
[335] Karriem Allah, "The Early Days of the Messenger's Mission: 'The Glorious Past Part I', Muhammad Speaks, July 20, 1973. Pg 15.
[336] Karriem Allah, "The Early Days," Muhammad Speaks, June 21, 1974. Pg 3.
[337] Karriem Allah, "The Early Days," Muhammad Speaks, June 21, 1974. Pg 3.
[338] By Nathaniel 10X, "Pioneers remember early years of Islam," Muhammad Speaks, April 20, 1973, pg. 10?
[339] John X. Lawler, "Sees New Day Rise In Islam," Muhammad Speaks, September 27, 1963. Pg 5.
[340] John X. Lawler, "Sees New Day Rise In Islam," Muhammad Speaks, September 27, 1963. Pg 5.
[341] J. Muhammad, This is the One, 167.
[342] Steven Barboza, American Jihad: Islam After Malcolm X, "The Messenger's Kin" interview with Ayman Muhammad. (Image Book, DoubleDay Publishing, 1994) 269.
[343] This article was reprinted in the January 1994 issue of Muhammad Speaks Continues Newspaper. It originally appeared in the April-May 1990 issue of Muhammad Speaks Continues Newspaper, and is written by The Supreme Minister, John Muhammad and entitled: "THE COMING OF ALLAH (GOD) AND HIS FOUR GREAT JUDGMENTS." Part #1 follows.
[344] The Hon. Elijah Muhammad, "Table Talks of the Hon. Elijah Muhammad", Track 9 "The Thinking of God". Aug. 1973.
[345] Sahib, "The Nation of Islam," 7 1.
[346] Elijah Muhammad, The Theology of Time audio excerpt. Youtube, http://www.youtube.com/watch?v=QU_gX9J7OMM&feature=channel_video_title
[347] Sahib, "The Nation of Islam," 98.
[348] FOI class with the Hon. Min. Farrakhan, July 9, 2012
[349] Elijah Muhammad, "The Gods at War," Muhammad Speaks, January 13, 1967.
[350] Elijah Muhammad, "The Theology of Time," pg. 24
[351] Elijah Muhammad, "The Knowledge of God Himself", Saviour's Day Speech, Feb. 26, 1969.
[352] The Hon. Elijah Muhammad's Letter to Imam Wallace D. Mohammed.
[353] Elijah Muhammad, Our Saviour Has Arrived, Chapter 11 "The Knowledge of God Himself," taken from Saviour's Day speech Feb. 26, 1969. http://muhammadspeaks.com/dietrying.html
[354] Sahib, "The Nation of Islam," 93-95.
[355] J. Muhammad, This is the One, 167.
[356] Youtube audio of the Most Hon. Elijah Muhammad (statement made at 14:30 mark) http://youtu.be/jvZ6LfBCspQ
[357] FBI file on W.D. Fard, September, 30, 1942.
[358] Hans J. Massaquoi "Elijah Muhammad, prophet and architect of the separate Nation of Islam", Ebony Magazine,
[359] E.U. Essien-Udom, "Black Nationalism", The University of Chicago Press, (1962)
[360] NOI Temple #2, "Elijah Muhammad: The Solution to the so-called Negro Problem," Video documentary. Continental Studios, Elk Grove Village, Illinois. February 20, 1975.
[361] Sahib, "The Nation of Islam," 7 1.
[362] "Voodooist Cult Revived in City," The Detroit Free Press, Tuesday, March 27, 1934.
[363] "Voodooist Cult Revived in City," The Detroit Free Press, Tuesday, March 27, 1934.
[364] 'Islam' Faces Double Probe," The Detroit Free Press, Wednesday, March 28, 1934.

[365] *"Voodoo University Raided by Police; 13 Cultists Seized,"* The Detroit Free Press, Tuesday, April 17, 1934.

[366] *"Voodoo University Raided by Police; 13 Cultists Seized,"* The Detroit Free Press, Tuesday, April 17, 1934.

[367] *"Voodoo University Raided by Police; 13 Cultists Seized,"* The Detroit Free Press, Tuesday, April 17, 1934.

[368] *"Voodoo University Raided by Police; 13 Cultists Seized,"* The Detroit Free Press, Tuesday, April 17, 1934.

[369] *"Voodoo University Raided by Police; 13 Cultists Seized,"* The Detroit Free Press, Tuesday, April 17, 1934.

[370] *"'Islam' Cult Faces Court,"* The Detroit News, Tuesday, April 17, 1934.

[371] *"U.S. May Fight Voodoo in City,"* The Detroit Free Press, Wednesday, April 18, 1934.

[372] *"U.S. May Fight Voodoo in City,"* The Detroit Free Press, Wednesday, April 18, 1934.

[373] NOI Temple #2, *"Elijah Muhammad: The Solution to the so-called Negro Problem,"* Video documentary. Continental Studios, Elk Grove Village, Illinois. February 20, 1975.

[374] NOI Temple #2, *"Elijah Muhammad: The Solution to the so-called Negro Problem,"* Video documentary. Continental Studios, Elk Grove Village, Illinois. February 20, 1975.

[375] *"13 Policemen Hurt Battling Voodoo Band,"* The Detroit Free Press, Thursday, April 19, 1934.

[376] This article was reprinted in the January 1994 issue of Muhammad Speaks Continues Newspaper. It originally appeared in the April-May 1990 issue of Muhammad Speaks Continues Newspaper, and is written by The Supreme Minister, John Muhammad and entitled: "THE COMING OF ALLAH (GOD) AND HIS FOUR GREAT JUDGMENTS." Part #4 follows.

[377] *"Cultists Start Hunger Strike,"* The Detroit Free Press, Friday, April 20, 1934.

[378] *"A Hunger Strike Ends with a Bang,"* The Detroit Free Press, Saturday, April 21, 1934.

[379] *"29 Arraigned in Cult Riots,"* The Detroit Free Press, Sunday, April 22, 1934.

[380] *"Girl Recounts Lore of Islam,"* The Detroit Free Press, Thursday, April 26, 1934.

[381] *"Girl Recounts Lore of Islam,"* The Detroit Free Press, Thursday, April 26, 1934.

[382] *"Girl Recounts Lore of Islam,"* The Detroit Free Press, Thursday, April 26, 1934.

[383] *"Girl Recounts Lore of Islam,"* The Detroit Free Press, Thursday, April 26, 1934.

[384] *"Voodoo Catechism Says Heads of Four Devils Are Passport to Mecca,"* The Detroit Free Press, Sunday, April 29, 1934.

[385] Elijah Muhammad, The History of the Nation of Islam, M.E.M.P.S (Atlanta).

[386] *Muhammad University of Islam - No. 2 - 1973 Year Book, pg. 24*

[387] The Early History of Master Fard Muhammad as told by Minister John Muhammad, (Blood Brother of Elijah) Part 2

[388] Sahib, "The Nation of Islam," 77.

[389] Sahib, "The Nation of Islam," 81.

[390] NOI Temple #2, *"Elijah Muhammad: The Solution to the so-called Negro Problem,"* Video documentary. Continental Studios, Elk Grove Village, Illinois. February 20, 1975.

[391] Emanuel Muhammad, "Faith and Obedience to Allah and His Messenger," Muhammad Speaks, April 18, 1975. Pg 24.

[392] NOI Temple #2, *"Elijah Muhammad: The Solution to the so-called Negro Problem,"* Video documentary. Continental Studios, Elk Grove Village, Illinois. February 20, 1975.

[393] NOI Temple #2, *"Elijah Muhammad: The Solution to the so-called Negro Problem,"* Video documentary. Continental Studios, Elk Grove Village, Illinois. February 20, 1975.

[394] *To the Ministry Class of No. 1 Michigan by Elijah Muhammad, Servant of Allah. December 3, 1934*

[395] *To the Ministry Class of No. 1 Michigan by Elijah Muhammad, Servant of Allah. December 3, 1934*

[396] *To the Ministry Class of No. 1 Michigan by Elijah Muhammad, Servant of Allah. December 3, 1934*

[397] John Muhammad, *The Journal of Truth* (U.B. & U.S. Communication Systems, July 1996) 86-87.

[398] Sahib, "The Nation of Islam," 206.

[399] NOI Temple #2, *"Elijah Muhammad: The Solution to the so-called Negro Problem,"* Video documentary. Continental Studios, Elk Grove Village, Illinois. February 20, 1975.

[400] NOI Temple #2, *"Elijah Muhammad: The Solution to the so-called Negro Problem,"* Video documentary. Continental Studios, Elk Grove Village, Illinois. February 20, 1975.

[401] James Pasha, "Became Muslim After the First Speech I Heard From Lips of the Messenger," Muhammad Speaks, September 11, 1965. Pg. 4

[402] NOI Temple #2, *"Elijah Muhammad: The Solution to the so-called Negro Problem,"* Video documentary. Continental Studios, Elk Grove Village, Illinois. February 20, 1975.

[403] NOI Temple #2, *"Elijah Muhammad: The Solution to the so-called Negro Problem,"* Video documentary. Continental Studios, Elk Grove Village, Illinois. February 20, 1975.

[404] NOI Temple #2, *"Elijah Muhammad: The Solution to the so-called Negro Problem,"* Video documentary. Continental Studios, Elk Grove Village, Illinois. February 20, 1975.

[405] NOI Temple #2, *"Elijah Muhammad: The Solution to the so-called Negro Problem,"* Video documentary. Continental Studios, Elk Grove Village, Illinois. February 20, 1975.

[406] NOI Temple #2, *"Elijah Muhammad: The Solution to the so-called Negro Problem,"* Video documentary. Continental Studios, Elk Grove Village, Illinois. February 20, 1975.

[407] Karriem Allah, "The Early Days of Islam," Muhammad Speaks, February 1, 1974. Pg 3.

[408] Karriem Allah, "The Early Days of Islam," Muhammad Speaks, February 1, 1974. Pg 3.

[409] "Cultist Riot in Court: One Death, 41 Hurt", *Chicago Daily Tribune*, Wednesday, March 6, 1935.

[410] "Cause of Trouble Sought", *The Chicago Defender*, Saturday, March 9, 1935.

[411] "Cultist Riot in Court: One Death, 41 Hurt", *Chicago Daily Tribune*, Wednesday, March 6, 1935.

[412] "Cult Fights Police in Court; Captain Dies; Bailiff Shot", *The Herald Examiner*, Wednesday, March 6, 1935.

[413] "Cultist Riot in Court: One Death, 41 Hurt", *Chicago Daily Tribune*, Wednesday, March 6, 1935.

[414] Karriem Allah, "The Early Days of Islam: The Glorious Past Part IV," Muhammad Speaks, August 24, 1973. Pg 18.

[415] Karriem Allah, "The Early Days of Islam: The Glorious Past Part IV," Muhammad Speaks, August 24, 1973. Pg 18.

[416] "Cause of Trouble Sought", *The Chicago Defender*, Saturday, March 9, 1935.

[417] "Cultist Riot in Court: One Death, 41 Hurt", *Chicago Daily Tribune*, Wednesday, March 6, 1935.

[418] "Cultist Riot in Court: One Death, 41 Hurt", *Chicago Daily Tribune*, Wednesday, March 6, 1935.

[419] "Cultist Riot in Court: One Death, 41 Hurt", *Chicago Daily Tribune*, Wednesday, March 6, 1935.

[420] "Cultist Riot in Court: One Death, 41 Hurt", *Chicago Daily Tribune*, Wednesday, March 6, 1935.

[421] James Pasha, "Brother Pasha Recalls Famed Chicago Court Case," Muhammad Speaks, September 11, 1965. Pg. 11

[422] James Pasha, "Brother Pasha Recalls Famed Chicago Court Case," Muhammad Speaks, September 11, 1965. Pg. 11

[423] "Cultist Riot in Court: One Death, 41 Hurt", *Chicago Daily Tribune*, Wednesday, March 6, 1935.

[424] "Cultist Riot in Court: One Death, 41 Hurt", *Chicago Daily Tribune*, Wednesday, March 6, 1935.

[425] "Cause of Trouble Sought", *The Chicago Defender*, Saturday, March 9, 1935.

[426] James Pasha, "Brother Pasha Recalls Famed Chicago Court Case," Muhammad Speaks, September 11, 1965. Pg. 11

[427] Karriem Allah, "The Early Days of Islam," Muhammad Speaks, January 25, 1974. Pg 16.

[428] Karriem Allah, "The Early Days of Islam: The Glorious Past Part IV," Muhammad Speaks, August 24, 1973. Pg 18.

[429] "Cult Fights Police in Court; Captain Dies; Bailiff Shot", *The Herald Examiner*, Wednesday, March 6, 1935.

[430] "Cause of Trouble Sought", *The Chicago Defender*, Saturday, March 9, 1935.

[431] "Cultist Riot in Court: One Death, 41 Hurt", *Chicago Daily Tribune*, Wednesday, March 6, 1935.

[432] "Cultist Riot in Court: One Death, 41 Hurt", *Chicago Daily Tribune*, Wednesday, March 6, 1935

[433] "Cultist Riot in Court: One Death, 41 Hurt", *Chicago Daily Tribune*, Wednesday, March 6, 1935.

[434] "Cultist Riot in Court: One Death, 41 Hurt", *Chicago Daily Tribune*, Wednesday, March 6, 1935

[435] "Cult Fights Police in Court; Captain Dies; Bailiff Shot", *The Herald Examiner*, Wednesday, March 6, 1935.

[436] "Cult Fights Police in Court; Captain Dies; Bailiff Shot", *The Herald Examiner*, Wednesday, March 6, 1935.

[437] "Cult Fights Police in Court; Captain Dies; Bailiff Shot", *The Herald Examiner*, Wednesday, March 6, 1935.

[438] "Cult Fights Police in Court; Captain Dies; Bailiff Shot", *The Herald Examiner*, Wednesday, March 6, 1935.

[439] "Cult Fights Police in Court; Captain Dies; Bailiff Shot", *The Herald Examiner*, Wednesday, March 6, 1935.

[440] "Cause of Trouble Sought", *The Chicago Defender*, Saturday, March 9, 1935.

[441] "Captain Palczynski a Chicago Policeman for Fifty Years", *Chicago Daily Tribune*, Wednesday, March 6, 1935.

[442] "40 Cultists Sentenced to Jail for Court Riot", *The Chicago Daily News*, Wednesday, March 6, 1935.

[443] "Forty Allah Cult Rioters Sentenced to Prison for Contempt of Court", *Chicago Herald and Examiner*, Thursday, March 7, 1935.

[444] "Cause of Trouble Sought", *The Chicago Defender*, Saturday, March 9, 1935.

[445] 'Allahs,' 'Hassans' and 'Shahs' Crowd court as Cultists Answer Rioting Charges", *Chicago Daily News*, Wednesday, March 6, 1935.

[446] 'Allahs,' 'Hassans' and 'Shahs' Crowd court as Cultists Answer Rioting Charges", *Chicago Daily News*, Wednesday, March 6, 1935.

[447] "Forty Allah Cult Rioters Sentenced to Prison for Contempt of Court", *Chicago Herald and Examiner*, Thursday, March 7, 1935.

[448] "40 Cultists Sentenced to Jail for Court Riot", *The Chicago Daily News*, Wednesday, March 6, 1935.

[449] "40 Cultists Sentenced to Jail for Court Riot", *The Chicago Daily News*, Wednesday, March 6, 1935.

[450] "Courtroom Riot Cases Convict 40", *The Chicago Defender*, Saturday, March 16, 1935.

[451] "40 Cultists Sentenced to Jail for Court Riot", *The Chicago Daily News*, Wednesday, March 6, 1935.

[452] "Courtroom Riot Cases Convict 40", *The Chicago Defender*, Saturday, March 16, 1935.

[453] "Courtroom Riot Cases Convict 40", *The Chicago Defender*, Saturday, March 16, 1935.

[454] Larry 14X, "Fast stepping Muslim marched with Garvey," *Muhammad Speaks,* August 2, 1974. Pp. 1,7,16.

[455] "Courtroom Riot Cases Convict 40", *The Chicago Defender*, Saturday, March 16, 1935.

[456] NOI Temple #2, *"Elijah Muhammad: The Solution to the so-called Negro Problem,"* Video documentary. Continental Studios, Elk Grove Village, Illinois. February 20, 1975.

[457] Hans J. Massaquoi "Elijah Muhammad, prophet and architect of the separate Nation of Islam", Ebony Magazine,

[458] Elijah Muhammad, "1964 Laborers Meeting", transcript.

[459] John Muhammad, *The Journal of Truth* (U.B. & U.S. Communication Systems, July 1996) 116-121.

[460] Sahib, "The Nation of Islam," 81.

[461] Sahib, "The Nation of Islam," 82.

[462] Sahib, "The Nation of Islam," 81.

[463] Nathaniel Muhammad, The Lance Shabazz Show #159. Part 2. Interview conducted by Lance Shabazz.

[464] Steven Barboza, *American Jihad: Islam After Malcolm X, "The Messenger's Kin" interview with Ayman Muhammad.* (Image Book, DoubleDay Publishing, 1994) 269.

[465] Elijah Muhammad, "1964 Laborers Meeting", transcript.

[466] Sahib, "The Nation of Islam," 81.

[467] Min. Nathaniel Muhammad, interview with Author, Sept 30, 2010.

[468] Elijah Muhammad, "1964 Laborers Meeting", transcript.

[469] Min. Nathaniel Muhammad, interview with Author, Sept 30, 2010.

[470] Min. Nathaniel Muhammad, interview with Author, Sept 30, 2010.

[471] BELIEVERS MEETINGIN 1960???? I GOT IT FROM TROY BEYAH DVD, it's also on youtube http://www.youtube.com/watch?v=96wbvsikkFY&feature=player_embedded#! "Elijah Muhammad on Hypocrisy of Son, Grandson and Malcolm."

[472] Elijah Muhammad, "1964 Laborers Meeting", transcript.

[473] Sahib, "The Nation of Islam," 81.

[474] Min. Nathaniel Muhammad, interview with Author, Sept 30, 2010.

[475] Karl Evanzz, "The Messenger: The Rise and Fall of Elijah Muhammad", Pantheon Books, 1999. Pg 110

[476] Ibid, 176.

[477] Emanuel Muhammad, "Faith and Obedience to Allah and His Messenger," Muhammad Speaks, April 18, 1975. Pg 24.

[478] BELIEVERS MEETINGIN 1960???? I GOT IT FROM TROY BEYAH DVD, it's also on youtube http://www.youtube.com/watch?v=96wbvsikkFY&feature=player_embedded#! "Elijah Muhammad on Hypocrisy of Son, Grandson and Malcolm."

[479] BELIEVERS MEETINGIN 1960???? I GOT IT FROM TROY BEYAH DVD, it's also on youtube http://www.youtube.com/watch?v=96wbvsikkFY&feature=player_embedded#! "Elijah Muhammad on Hypocrisy of Son, Grandson and Malcolm."

[480] NOI Temple #2, "Elijah Muhammad: The Solution to the so-called Negro Problem," Video documentary. Continental Studios, Elk Grove Village, Illinois. February 20, 1975.

[481] Elijah Muhammad, "1964 Laborers Meeting", transcript.

[482] Sahib, "The Nation of Islam," 74-75.

[483] Letter From Messenger Elijah Muhammad To Laborers & Muslims at #2, November 5, 1936.

[484] Letter From Messenger Elijah Muhammad To Laborers & Muslims at #2, November 5, 1936.

[485] Letter From Messenger Elijah Muhammad To Laborers & Muslims at #2, November 5, 1936.

[486] Emmett X, "Peace Has Been His More Than 30 years," Muhammad Speaks, December 23, 1966. Pg. 25.

[487] Lester X (Anthony), "How Islam changed Nightmare Life To Years Of Serenity," Muhammad Speaks, October 11, 1963, pg. 5

[488] Lester X, "Muslim, Messenger Jailed in 1942 on Phony Charge," Muhammad Speaks, April 8, 1966, pg. 25.

[489] By Nathaniel 10X, "Pioneers remember early years of Islam," Muhammad Speaks, April 20, 1973, pg. 10?

[490] J. Muhammad, This is the One, 173.

[491] Al-Wakeel Benjamin Ilyas Muhammad (Benjamin X. Mitchell), "The Early Days of Al-Islam in Washington, D.C., as taught by The Hon. Elijah Muhammad (1935 to 1942)" (B.E. Mitchell, October 29, 1981).

[492] Al-Wakeel Benjamin Ilyas Muhammad (Benjamin X. Mitchell), "The Early Days of Al-Islam in Washington, D.C., as taught by The Hon. Elijah Muhammad (1935 to 1942)" (B.E. Mitchell, October 29, 1981).

[493] Al-Wakeel Benjamin Ilyas Muhammad (Benjamin X. Mitchell), "The Early Days of Al-Islam in Washington, D.C., as taught by The Hon. Elijah Muhammad (1935 to 1942)" (B.E. Mitchell, October 29, 1981).

[494] Benjamin X. Mitchell, "The Early Days of Al-Islam in Washington, D.C."

[495] J. Muhammad, This is the One, 173.

[496] J. Muhammad, This is the One, 176.

[497] Elijah Muhammad, The True History of Master Fard Muhammad (Atlanta: MEMPS, 1996) 39.

[498] Elijah Muhammad, The True History of Master Fard Muhammad (Atlanta: MEMPS, 1996) 42-43.

[499] Elijah Muhammad, The True History of Master Fard Muhammad (Atlanta: MEMPS, 1996) 41.

[500] Benjamin X. Mitchell, "The Early Days of Al-Islam in Washington, D.C."

[501] Benjamin X. Mitchell, "The Early Days of Al-Islam in Washington, D.C."

[502] Benjamin X. Mitchell, "The Early Days of Al-Islam in Washington, D.C."

[503] Benjamin X. Mitchell, "The Early Days of Al-Islam in Washington, D.C."

[504] The Hon. Minister Farrakhan, The Tsunami Prayer Line, Ramadan, August 20, 2011.

[505] Benjamin X. Mitchell, "The Early Days of Al-Islam in Washington, D.C."

[506] Elijah Muhammad, Letter to Ministers, April 2, 1936.
[507] Benjamin X. Mitchell, *"The Early Days of Al-Islam in Washington, D.C."*
[508] Benjamin X. Mitchell, *"The Early Days of Al-Islam in Washington, D.C."*
[509] Benjamin X. Mitchell, *"The Early Days of Al-Islam in Washington, D.C."*
[510] Benjamin X. Mitchell, *"The Early Days of Al-Islam in Washington, D.C."*
[511] Benjamin X. Mitchell, *"The Early Days of Al-Islam in Washington, D.C."*
[512] Benjamin X. Mitchell, *"The Early Days of Al-Islam in Washington, D.C."*
[513] Sister Lydia Hazziez, "A Grandmother Grateful for Islam," Muhammad Speaks, September 13, 1963. Pg. 7.
[514] Sister Beatrice X, "Stark Story of Dixie Terror: I Lived in Fear Near Lynch Tree—Until Islam," Muhammad Speaks, June 5, 1964. pg 7.
[515] Sister Beatrice X, "Why I Made Islam My Life," Muhammad Speaks, June 19, 1964. pg 7.
[516] Reflecting and Humor-Elijah Muhammad http://youtu.be/7LNBF-QjgxU
[517] Reflecting and Humor-Elijah Muhammad http://youtu.be/7LNBF-QjgxU
[518] Benjamin X. Mitchell, *"The Early Days of Al-Islam in Washington, D.C."*
[519] Benjamin X. Mitchell, *"The Early Days of Al-Islam in Washington, D.C."*
[520] Reflecting and Humor-Elijah Muhammad http://youtu.be/7LNBF-QjgxU
[521] Benjamin X. Mitchell, *"The Early Days of Al-Islam in Washington, D.C."*
[522] Benjamin X. Mitchell, *"The Early Days of Al-Islam in Washington, D.C."*
[523] Benjamin X. Mitchell, *"The Early Days of Al-Islam in Washington, D.C."*
[524] Benjamin X. Mitchell, *"The Early Days of Al-Islam in Washington, D.C."*
[525] Benjamin X. Mitchell, *"The Early Days of Al-Islam in Washington, D.C."*
[526] John X. Lawler, "Sees New Day Rise In Islam," Muhammad Speaks, September 27, 1963. Pg 5.
[527] Jabril Muhammad, *This is the One: The Most Honored Elijah Muhammad, We Need Not Look For Another, Volume 1.* (Arizona: Book Company, 1993) 178.
[528] Benjamin X. Mitchell, *"The Early Days of Al-Islam in Washington, D.C."*
[529] Benjamin X. Mitchell, *"The Early Days of Al-Islam in Washington, D.C."*
[530] E. Muhammad, *Message to the Black Man*, 179…
[531] Benjamin X. Mitchell, *"The Early Days of Al-Islam in Washington, D.C."*
[532] Benjamin X. Mitchell, *"The Early Days of Al-Islam in Washington, D.C."*
[533] 1967 Public address by Elijah Muhammad delivered in Phoenix, AZ. Reprinted from Muhammad Speaks (01/19/68). Reprinted also from Jabril Muhammad, *This is the One: The Most Honored Elijah Muhammad, We Need Not Look For Another, Volume 1.* (Arizona: Book Company, 1993) 176.
[534] Benjamin X. Mitchell, *"The Early Days of Al-Islam in Washington, D.C."*
[535] Karriem Allah, "The Nation's Early Days," Muhammad Speaks, April 26, 1974. Pg 3.
[536] Karriem Allah, "The Nation's Early Days," Muhammad Speaks, May 10, 1974. Pg 3.
[537] Karriem Allah, "The Nation's Early Days," Muhammad Speaks, May 10, 1974. Pg 3.
[538] Benjamin X. Mitchell, *"The Early Days of Al-Islam in Washington, D.C."*
[539] The Nation of Islam In Milwaukee, A Brief History, http://mosque3.org/history.html Muhammad's mosque #3 website Milwaukee
[540] The Nation of Islam In Milwaukee, A Brief History, http://mosque3.org/history.html Muhammad's mosque #3 website Milwaukee
[541] Benjamin X. Mitchell, *"The Early Days of Al-Islam in Washington, D.C."*
[542] E. Muhammad, *Message to the Black Man*, 177…
[543] Benjamin X. Mitchell, *"The Early Days of Al-Islam in Washington, D.C."*
[544] Benjamin X. Mitchell, *"The Early Days of Al-Islam in Washington, D.C."*
[545] Benjamin X. Mitchell, *"The Early Days of Al-Islam in Washington, D.C."*
[546] Benjamin X. Mitchell, *"The Early Days of Al-Islam in Washington, D.C."*
[547] Benjamin X. Mitchell, *"The Early Days of Al-Islam in Washington, D.C."*
[548] Benjamin X. Mitchell, *"The Early Days of Al-Islam in Washington, D.C."*

[549] Benjamin X. Mitchell, *"The Early Days of Al-Islam in Washington, D.C."*

[550] Isaiah Karriem, "Thanks Messenger of Allah For Guidance of 20 Years," Muhammad Speaks, January 17, 1964. Pg 7.

[551] Isaiah Karriem, "Minister Isaiah: With Muhammad's Teachings I Win Over My Foes," Muhammad Speaks, November 18, 1966. Pg 25, 27.

[552] E.U. Essien-Udom, "Black Nationalism: A Search for an Identity in America", The University of Chicago Press, 1962. Pg 98-99.

[553] E.U. Essien-Udom, "Black Nationalism: A Search for an Identity in America", The University of Chicago Press, 1962. Pg 98-99.

[554] Sahib, "The Nation of Islam," 198-199.

[555] Sahib, "The Nation of Islam," 198-199.

[556] Sahib, "The Nation of Islam," 198-199.

[557] Benjamin X. Mitchell, *"The Early Days of Al-Islam in Washington, D.C."*

[558] NOI Temple #2, *"Elijah Muhammad: The Solution to the so-called Negro Problem,"* Video documentary. Continental Studios, Elk Grove Village, Illinois. February 20, 1975.

[559] 1967 Public Address delivered in Phoenix, Ariz. Reprinted fromMuhammad Speaks (01-19-68

[560] By Nathaniel 10X, "Pioneers remember early years of Islam," Muhammad Speaks, April 20, 1973, pg. 10?

[561] NOI Temple #2, *"Elijah Muhammad: The Solution to the so-called Negro Problem,"* Video documentary. Continental Studios, Elk Grove Village, Illinois. February 20, 1975.

[562] NOI Temple #2, *"Elijah Muhammad: The Solution to the so-called Negro Problem,"* Video documentary. Continental Studios, Elk Grove Village, Illinois. February 20, 1975.

[563] Lester X (Anthony), "How Islam changed Nightmare Life To Years Of Serenity," Muhammad Speaks, October 11, 1963, pg. 5

[564] Lester X, "Muslim, Messenger Jailed in 1942 on Phony Charge," Muhammad Speaks, April 8, 1966, pg. 25.

[565] By Nathaniel 10X, "Pioneers remember early years of Islam," Muhammad Speaks, April 20, 1973, pg. 10?

[566] NOI Temple #2, *"Elijah Muhammad: The Solution to the so-called Negro Problem,"* Video documentary. Continental Studios, Elk Grove Village, Illinois. February 20, 1975.

[567] The Nation of Islam In Milwaukee, A Brief History, http://mosque3.org/history.html Muhammad's mosque #3 website Milwaukee

[568] Cultists 'Guilty'; 32 Given Jail Sentences"; 3 Others Face Federal Court For Sedition; Men Spurn Legal Aid Offered By Judge; Put Trust In Allah," The Chicago Defender, October 10, 1942. Pp. 1-2.

[569] Cultists 'Guilty'; 32 Given Jail Sentences"; 3 Others Face Federal Court For Sedition; Men Spurn Legal Aid Offered By Judge; Put Trust In Allah," The Chicago Defender, October 10, 1942. Pp. 1-2.

[570] Cultists 'Guilty'; 32 Given Jail Sentences"; 3 Others Face Federal Court For Sedition; Men Spurn Legal Aid Offered By Judge; Put Trust In Allah," The Chicago Defender, October 10, 1942. Pp. 1-2.

[571] Cultists 'Guilty'; 32 Given Jail Sentences"; 3 Others Face Federal Court For Sedition; Men Spurn Legal Aid Offered By Judge; Put Trust In Allah," The Chicago Defender, October 10, 1942. Pp. 1-2.

[572] E.U. Essien-Udom, "Black Nationalism: A Search for an Identity in America", The University of Chicago Press, 1962. Pg 67.

[573] E. Muhammad, *Message to the Black Man*, 179...

[574] 1967 Public Address delivered in Phoenix, Ariz. Reprinted fromMuhammad Speaks (01-19-68

[575] NOI Temple #2, *"Elijah Muhammad: The Solution to the so-called Negro Problem,"* Video documentary. Continental Studios, Elk Grove Village, Illinois. February 20, 1975.

[576] The Nation of Islam In Milwaukee, A Brief History, http://mosque3.org/history.html Muhammad's mosque #3 website Milwaukee

[577] Emanuel Muhammad, "Faith and Obedience to Allah and His Messenger," Muhammad Speaks, April 18, 1975. Pg 24.

[578] Benjamin X. Mitchell, *"The Early Days of Al-Islam in Washington, D.C."*

[579] Benjamin X. Mitchell, *"The Early Days of Al-Islam in Washington, D.C."*

[580] Steven Barboza, *American Jihad: Islam After Malcolm X, "The Messenger's Kin" interview with Ayman Muhammad.* (Image Book, DoubleDay Publishing, 1994) 269.

[581] Karl Evanzz, "The Messenger: The Rise and Fall of Elijah Muhammad", Pantheon Books, 1999. 151.

[582] Karl Evanzz, "The Messenger: The Rise and Fall of Elijah Muhammad", Pantheon Books, 1999. 151.

[583] Karl Evanzz, "The Messenger: The Rise and Fall of Elijah Muhammad", Pantheon Books, 1999. 151.

[584] John Muhammad, *The Journal of Truth* (U.B. & U.S. Communication Systems, July 1996) 71.

[585] Benjamin X. Mitchell, *"The Early Days of Al-Islam in Washington, D.C."*

[586] *Muhammad University of Islam - No. 2 - 1973 Year Book, pg. 24*

[587] Samuel 17X, interview of Emanuel Muhammad, "My Father's Message, Fearless and Forceful: A Son Looks at a Great Father," Muhammad Speaks.

[588] John Hassan, "How the Light of Truth Led To Life of Peace, Serenity," Muhammad Speaks, January 17, 1964. Pg 7.

[589] John Muhammad, *The Journal of Truth* (U.B. & U.S. Communication Systems, July 1996) 116-121.

[590] John Muhammad, *The Journal of Truth* (U.B. & U.S. Communication Systems, July 1996) 116-121.

[591] John Muhammad, *The Journal of Truth* (U.B. & U.S. Communication Systems, July 1996) 116-121.

[592] NOI Temple #2, *"Elijah Muhammad: The Solution to the so-called Negro Problem,"* Video documentary. Continental Studios, Elk Grove Village, Illinois. February 20, 1975.

[593] Samuel 17X, interview of Emanuel Muhammad, "My Father's Message, Fearless and Forceful: A Son Looks at a Great Father," Muhammad Speaks.

[594] Imam W. Deen Mohammed's Address at "Savior Day" - Feb. 26, 2002, in Charleston, SC.

[595] Lester X (Anthony), "How Islam changed Nightmare Life To Years Of Serenity," Muhammad Speaks, October 11, 1963, pg. 5

[596] Lester X, "Muslim, Messenger Jailed in 1942 on Phony Charge," Muhammad Speaks, April 8, 1966, pg. 25.

[597] NOI Temple #2, *"Elijah Muhammad: The Solution to the so-called Negro Problem,"* Video documentary. Continental Studios, Elk Grove Village, Illinois. February 20, 1975.

[598] Benjamin X. Mitchell, *"The Early Days of Al-Islam in Washington, D.C."*

[599] NOI Temple #2, *"Elijah Muhammad: The Solution to the so-called Negro Problem,"* Video documentary. Continental Studios, Elk Grove Village, Illinois. February 20, 1975.

[600] NOI Temple #2, *"Elijah Muhammad: The Solution to the so-called Negro Problem,"* Video documentary. Continental Studios, Elk Grove Village, Illinois. February 20, 1975.

[601] Benjamin X. Mitchell, *"The Early Days of Al-Islam in Washington, D.C."*

[602] Elijah Muhammad "How to Live Over 100,"*Muhammad Speaks*, June 18, 1965. Pg. 3.

[603] Benjamin X. Mitchell, *"The Early Days of Al-Islam in Washington, D.C."*

[604] Lester X (Anthony), "The Story of Lester X: How Faith Surmounted Trials of Prison," Muhammad Speaks, October 25, 1963, pg. 7.

[605] Samuel 17X, interview of Emanuel Muhammad, "My Father's Message, Fearless and Forceful: A Son Looks at a Great Father," Muhammad Speaks.

[606] NOI Temple #2, *"Elijah Muhammad: The Solution to the so-called Negro Problem,"* Video documentary. Continental Studios, Elk Grove Village, Illinois. February 20, 1975.

[607] Lester X, "Muslim, Messenger Jailed in 1942 on Phony Charge," Muhammad Speaks, April 8, 1966, pg. 25.

[608] Lester X (Anthony), "The Story of Lester X: How Faith Surmounted Trials of Prison," Muhammad Speaks, October 25, 1963, pg. 7.

[609] Emanuel Muhammad, "Faith and Obedience to Allah and His Messenger," Muhammad Speaks, April 18, 1975. Pg 24.

[610] *Muhammad University of Islam - No. 2 - 1973 Year Book, pg. 24*

611 Samuel 17X, interview of Emanuel Muhammad, "My Father's Message, Fearless and Forceful: A Son Looks at a Great Father," Muhammad Speaks.

612 Lester X (Anthony), "The Story of Lester X: Light of Islam During Dark Days of Imprisonment," Muhammad Speaks, November 8, 1963, pg. 2.

613 Sahib, "The Nation of Islam," 83.

614 The Hon. Elijah Muhammad's Letter to Imam Wallace D. Mohammed.

615 Benjamin X. Mitchell, *The Early Days of Al-Islam in Washington, D.C.*

616 Benjamin X. Mitchell, *The Early Days of Al-Islam in Washington, D.C.*

617 Sister Elvie X, "The Messenger of Allah Is The Door to Our Salvation," Muhammad Speaks, March 5, 1965. Pg. 11.

618 Isaiah Karriem, "Thanks Messenger of Allah For Guidance of 20 Years," Muhammad Speaks, January 17, 1964. Pg 7.

619 Isaiah Karriem, "Minister Isaiah: With Muhammad's Teachings I Win Over My Foes," Muhammad Speaks, November 18, 1966. Pg 25, 27.

620 Lester X (Anthony), "The Story of Lester X: Light of Islam During Dark Days of Imprisonment," Muhammad Speaks, November 8, 1963, pg. 2.

621 Lester X, "Muslim, Messenger Jailed in 1942 on Phony Charge," Muhammad Speaks, April 8, 1966, pg. 25.

622 E.U. Essien-Udom, "Black Nationalism: A Search for an Identity in America", The University of Chicago Press, 1962. Pg 67.

623 Sahib, "The Nation of Islam," 221.

624 NOI Temple #2, *Elijah Muhammad: The Solution to the so-called Negro Problem,* Video documentary. Continental Studios, Elk Grove Village, Illinois. February 20, 1975.

625 *Muhammad University of Islam - No. 2 - 1973 Year Book, pg. 24*

626 Sahib, "The Nation of Islam," 81.

627 E.U. Essien-Udom, "Black Nationalism: A Search for an Identity in America", The University of Chicago Press, 1962. Pg 69.

628 Benjamin X. Mitchell, *The Early Days of Al-Islam in Washington, D.C.*

629 Sahib, "The Nation of Islam," 81.

630 Claude Andrew Clegg III, "Rebuilding the Nation: The Life and Work of Elijah Muhammad, 1946-1954, The Black Scholar, Vol. 26, No. 34. Pg 154

631 E. Muhammad, *Message to the Black Man,* 179…

632 Claude Andrew Clegg III, "Rebuilding the Nation: The Life and Work of Elijah Muhammad, 1946-1954, The Black Scholar, Vol. 26, No. 34. Pg 49

633 John Muhammad, *The Journal of Truth* (U.B. & U.S. Communication Systems, July 1996) 116-121.

634 John Hassan, "How the Light of Truth Led To Life of Peace, Serenity," Muhammad Speaks, January 17, 1964. Pg 7.

635 Benjamin X. Mitchell, *The Early Days of Al-Islam in Washington, D.C.*

636 Sahib, "The Nation of Islam," 83.

637 Benjamin X. Mitchell, *The Early Days of Al-Islam in Washington, D.C.*

638 Hubert X, "Marcus Garvey Said: 'A Messenger Will Follow Me!'," Muhammad Speaks, June 5, 1964. pg 7.

639 Hubert X, "Marcus Garvey Said: 'A Messenger Will Follow Me!'," Muhammad Speaks, June 5, 1964. pg 7.

640 Hubert X, "Marcus Garvey Said: 'A Messenger Will Follow Me!'," Muhammad Speaks, June 5, 1964. pg 7.

641 "The Journey of Minister Henry Majied". http://henrymajied.weebly.com/

642 "Yusuf Shaheed Abdullah," Masjidul Taqwa Mosque of San Diego website. www.masjidultaqwasandiego.org/YSACenter/AboutYusuf.htm

643 "Yusuf Shaheed Abdullah," Masjidul Taqwa Mosque of San Diego website. www.masjidultaqwasandiego.org/YSACenter/AboutYusuf.htm

644 ""Nation of Islam" FBI files. Part 1. Pg. 38.

645 Interview conducted with Min. James Muhammad of Mosque #10 Atlantic City, NJ.

[646] Jeremiah Shabazz, "The Top of the Clock", published by Rubin Bashir and First Impressions Group.

[647] Minister Samuel, "'The Messenger's Teachings Made Me a Different Man Through a Better Life," Muhammad Speaks, December 23, 1966. Pg. 25.

[648] NOI Temple #2, *Elijah Muhammad: The Solution to the so-called Negro Problem,* Video documentary. Continental Studios, Elk Grove Village, Illinois. February 20, 1975.

[649] Sahib, "The Nation of Islam," 87.

[650] Elijah Muhammad "How to Live Over 100,"*Muhammad Speaks,* June 18, 1965. Pg. 3.

[651] Sahib, "The Nation of Islam," 84.

[652] NOI Temple #2, *Elijah Muhammad: The Solution to the so-called Negro Problem,* Video documentary. Continental Studios, Elk Grove Village, Illinois. February 20, 1975.

[653] Karriem Allah, "The Early Days," Muhammad Speaks, June 28, 1974. Pg 3, 19.

[654] Karriem Allah, "The Early Days," Muhammad Speaks, June 28, 1974. Pg 3, 19.

[655] Ethel Sharieff, daughter of Hon. Elijah Muhammad, http://www.finalcall.com/artman/publish/article_325.shtml

[656] Karriem Allah, "The Early Days," Muhammad Speaks, June 28, 1974. Pg 3, 19.

[657] Imam W. Deen Mohammed's Address at "Savior Day" - Feb. 26, 2002, in Charleston, SC.

[658] Karriem Allah, "The Early Days Pt. 2," Muhammad Speaks, July 5, 1974. Pg 3.

[659] *Muhammad University of Islam - No. 2 - 1973 Year Book, pg. 24*

[660] Min. Lucius Bey, "A Talk With Min. Lucius Bey," Interview conducted by Cedric Muhammad for BlackElectorate.com, October 7, 2004.

[661] Min. Lucius Bey, "A Talk With Min. Lucius Bey," Interview conducted by Cedric Muhammad for BlackElectorate.com, October 7, 2004.

[662] Min. Lucius Bey, "A Talk With Min. Lucius Bey," Interview conducted by Cedric Muhammad for BlackElectorate.com, October 7, 2004.

[663] Min. Lucius Bey, "A Talk With Min. Lucius Bey," Interview conducted by Cedric Muhammad for BlackElectorate.com, October 7, 2004.

[664] Min. Lucius Bey, "A Talk With Min. Lucius Bey," Interview conducted by Cedric Muhammad for BlackElectorate.com, October 7, 2004.

[665] Min. Lucius Bey, "A Talk With Min. Lucius Bey," Interview conducted by Cedric Muhammad for BlackElectorate.com, October 7, 2004.

[666] Min. Lucius Bey, "A Talk With Min. Lucius Bey," Interview conducted by Cedric Muhammad for BlackElectorate.com, October 7, 2004.

[667] Min. Lucius Bey, "A Talk With Min. Lucius Bey," Interview conducted by Cedric Muhammad for BlackElectorate.com, October 7, 2004.

[668] Min. Lucius Bey, "A Talk With Min. Lucius Bey," Interview conducted by Cedric Muhammad for BlackElectorate.com, October 7, 2004.

[669] Min. Lucius Bey, "A Talk With Min. Lucius Bey," Interview conducted by Cedric Muhammad for BlackElectorate.com, October 7, 2004.

[670] Min. Lucius Bey, "A Talk With Min. Lucius Bey," Interview conducted by Cedric Muhammad for BlackElectorate.com, October 7, 2004.

[671] Min. Lucius Bey, "A Talk With Min. Lucius Bey," Interview conducted by Cedric Muhammad for BlackElectorate.com, October 7, 2004.

[672] Min. Lucius Bey, "A Talk With Min. Lucius Bey," Interview conducted by Cedric Muhammad for BlackElectorate.com, October 7, 2004.

[673] Min. Lucius Bey, "A Talk With Min. Lucius Bey," Interview conducted by Cedric Muhammad for BlackElectorate.com, October 7, 2004.

[674] Min. Lucius Bey, "A Talk With Min. Lucius Bey," Interview conducted by Cedric Muhammad for BlackElectorate.com, October 7, 2004.

[675] Min. Lucius Bey, "A Talk With Min. Lucius Bey," Interview conducted by Cedric Muhammad for BlackElectorate.com, October 7, 2004.

[676] Min. Lucius Bey, "A Talk With Min. Lucius Bey," Interview conducted by Cedric Muhammad for BlackElectorate.com, October 7, 2004.

[677] Min. Lucius Bey, "A Talk With Min. Lucius Bey," Interview conducted by Cedric Muhammad for BlackElectorate.com, October 7, 2004.

[678] Sahib, "The Nation of Islam," 99.

[679] Sahib, "The Nation of Islam," 105.

[680] Sahib, "The Nation of Islam," 122.

[681] Sahib, "The Nation of Islam," 200.

[682] Sahib, "The Nation of Islam," 199.

[683] Sahib, "The Nation of Islam," 236.

[684] Sahib, "The Nation of Islam," 172-173.

[685] Sahib, "The Nation of Islam," 172-173.

[686] Sahib, "The Nation of Islam," 245.

[687] Sahib, "The Nation of Islam," 176.

[688] Sahib, "The Nation of Islam," 141.

[689] Imam W. Deen Mohammed's Address at "Savior Day" - Feb. 26, 2002, in Charleston, SC.

[690] Sahib, "The Nation of Islam," 178-179.

[691] Elijah Muhammad, "I'm Your First and Last Teacher!", lecture at Muhammad Temple No. 6, 514 Wilson St., Baltimore, MD. Date unknown.

[692] Sahib, "The Nation of Islam," 254-255.

[693] Sahib, "The Nation of Islam," 255-256.

Made in the USA
Middletown, DE
26 December 2020